FABIANISM AND CULTURE

A study in British socialism and the arts
c. 1884-1918

FABIANISM AND CULTURE

*A study in British socialism
and the arts
c. 1884-1918*

IAN BRITAIN

CAMBRIDGE UNIVERSITY PRESS

CAMBRIDGE
LONDON NEW YORK NEW ROCHELLE
MELBOURNE SYDNEY

Published by the Press Syndicate of the University of Cambridge
The Pitt Building, Trumpington Street, Cambridge CB2 IRP
32 East 57th Street, New York, NY 10022, USA
296 Beaconsfield Parade, Middle Park, Melbourne 3206, Australia

First published 1982

Printed in Great Britain at
the University Press, Cambridge

Library of Congress catalogue card number: 81-12273

British Library Cataloguing in Publication Data
Britain, Ian
Fabianism and culture.
1. Socialism and the arts — Great Britain
I. Title
700   HX521
ISBN 0 521 23563 4

FOR MY PARENTS

Contents

Preface

I am particularly indebted to Dr Brian Harrison, who was the chief supervisor of this work in its earlier form as a doctoral thesis, and who proved throughout to be a model of that put-upon breed. Patient and rigorous, challenging without being intimidating, always sympathetic and interested, even where disclaiming expertise, and attentive to personal and social, as well as academic, needs, he helped ease much of the pain involved in the birth of a book such as this and contributed positively to much of the pleasure.

I was fortunate to have the services, at earlier and later stages of the work's gestation, of others equally skilled in the arts of intellectual midwifery. To Professor Alan McBriar, who supervised previous work of mine on a rather different (though related) topic, I owe the inspiration to embark on a study of Fabianism. He has been kind enough to cast his uncanny editorial eye over all of the drafts for the present work and has thus saved me from a number of slips and solecisms. To Professor Norman MacKenzie and his wife, Jeanne, I am indebted for invaluable assistance with research materials at an early stage of the work, for some very stimulating comments on its completion as a thesis, and for the encouragement to revise and publish it in book-form. Their support and generosity have been a source of continual reassurance.

Further thanks for reading, and commenting fruitfully, on the work in its earlier forms are due to Dr Paul Thompson, Mr A.F. Thompson, and Professor Peter Stansky; and for unfailingly conscientious assistance with research materials at various stages, I must mention in particular Miss Angela Raspin at the British School of Political and Economic Science, as well as the staffs of the Bodleian Library, Nuffield College Library, the British Library Students' Room, the Sterling Library at Yale University and the University of Illinois Library.

For assistance with funds to collect research material in the United States, I am very grateful to the trustees of the Arnold Historical Essay Prize and to the Tutors and Fellows of Corpus Christi College, Oxford. My years of research at Oxford would not have been possible without the grant of a generous scholarship by the Australian National University. The award of a research fellowship by Monash University relieved me from teaching commitments at a crucial stage of revising my thesis for publication and gave me the time and facilities to incorporate two completely new chapters (7 and 8) as well as to revamp the whole work.

I have received constructive and stimulating advice on a whole range of matters connected with the book from my parents and from many friends — 'non-experts' all, but invaluable precisely for that reason. I must single out the following for their especial forbearance in looking over and commenting on the drafts of various chapters or of the whole work: Clive Burgess, Colin Johnston, Iain McCalman, Janet McCalman and Al Knight, and Malcolm Wild.

Finally, I must thank Mrs Audrey Allen, who typed the final draft of the book, for coping so efficiently with a manuscript that at times can only have seemed like a hopelessly jumbled jigsaw-puzzle. Peter Fullerton kindly typed a difficult and intricate index.

Acknowledgments for permission to use, or quote from, copyright material are due to the following institutions: the British Library of Political and Economic Science (Passfield Papers, Wallas Papers); the Fabian Society, London (Fabian Society Papers); the Public Record Office (MacDonald Papers); Society of Antiquaries of London (William Morris's writings and papers); the Society of Authors on behalf of the Bernard Shaw Estate © 1982 — the Trustees of the British Museum, the Governors and Guardians of the National Gallery of Ireland and the Royal Academy of Dramatic Art (Shaw's writings and papers); the State Historical Society of Wisconsin (Lloyd Papers); A.P. Watt, Ltd., on behalf of the H.G. Wells Estate (Wells Papers); Yale University Library (Thomas Davidson Papers).

Ian Britain,
Monash University,
March 1981.

List of abbreviations

All printed works cited in this list, and in the notes, were published in London, unless otherwise stated.

B.L.P.E.S.	British Library of Political and Economic Science
B.S.C.L.	*Bernard Shaw Collected Letters*, ed. Dan H. Laurence (2 vols., 1965 and 1972)
B.W.D.	Beatrice Webb's Diaries (typescript version), Passfield Papers, B.L.P.E.S.
C.C.M.	*The Consumers' Co-operative Movement*, by Sidney & Beatrice Webb (1921)
C.R.	*Church Reformer*, ed. Stewart Headlam
C.S.C.G.B.	*A Constitution for the Socialist Commonwealth of Great Britain*, by Sidney & Beatrice Webb (1920; new edition, Cambridge University Press, 1975)
C.W.W.M.	*The Collected Works of William Morris*, ed. May Morris (24 vols., 1910-15)
D.L.B.	*Dictionary of Labour Biography*, ed. Joyce M. Bellamy & John Saville (miscellaneous volumes, 1972-9)
D.P.	Thomas Davidson Papers, Yale University
E.B.H.	*Essays by Hubert*, ed. Edith Nesbit Bland (1914)
E.L.G.	*English Local Government from the Revolution to the Municipal Corporations Act*, by Sidney & Beatrice Webb (10 vols., 1906-29)
F.E.S.	*Fabian Essays in Socialism*, ed. G. Bernard Shaw (1889 edition, unless otherwise stated)
F.N.	*Fabian News*
F.S.C.	Fabian Society Collection, Nuffield College, Oxford
H.F.S.	*The History of the Fabian Society*, by Edward Pease (1916)
L.P.	Henry Demarest Lloyd Papers, State Historical Society of Wisconsin, Microfilm edition (Madison, 1970)

L.S.B.W.   *The Letters of Sidney and Beatrice Webb*, ed. Norman
                MacKenzie (3 vols., Cambridge, 1978)
M.A.   *My Apprenticeship*, by Beatrice Webb (1926; Penguin
                edn, Harmondsworth, 1971)
O.C.   *Our Corner*, ed. Annie Besant
O.P.   *Our Partnership*, by Beatrice Webb (1948; new edition,
                Cambridge, 1975)
P.P.   Passfield Papers, B.L.P.E.S.
S.A.   *Shaw An Autobiography*, ed. Stanley Weintraub (2 vols.,
                1969 and 1971)
S.O.L.W.   *Sydney Olivier Letters and Selected Writings*, ed.
                Margaret Olivier (1948)
S.P.   George Bernard Shaw Papers, British Library
S.S.L.H.   Society for the Study of Labour History: bulletins
S.S.S.   *Sixteen Self Sketches*, by G. Bernard Shaw (1949)
W.C.W.   *William Clarke: A Collection of his Writings*, ed.
                Herbert Burrows & J.A. Hobson (1908)
W.J.R.   *The Works of John Ruskin*, ed. E.T. Cook & Alexander
                Wedderburn (39 vols., 1903-12)
W.M.A.W.S.   *William Morris: Artist, Writer, Socialist*, ed. May
                Morris (2 vols., Oxford, 1936)
W.P.   H.G. Wells Papers, University of Illinois
W.W.   *The Webbs and their Work*, ed. Margaret Cole (1949;
                new edition, Brighton, 1974)

Introduction

... to everyone who wishes to study Socialism duly it is necessary to look on
it from the aesthetic point of view (William Morris)[1]

Except with regard to Morris himself, and a few other major socialist
artists, little consideration has been given to the aesthetic or broader
cultural aspects of the British socialist movement of the late nineteenth
and early twentieth centuries. The revival of that movement in the early
1880s, following the disillusionment in various radical quarters with the
domestic and foreign policies of the recently elected Liberal government,
was one of the most striking political developments of the day;[2] though
the extent of its long-term significance in various directions is not at all a
clear-cut matter. It is hardly surprising, therefore, that historians should
have devoted so much time to working out, and debating, how far the
new socialist organizations were related to other equally striking
developments of the period, such as the growth of 'new' and more overtly
political forms of trade unionism and the emergence of a mass-based
Labour Party.

It would be superficial to regard such developments as purely political
in their nature or origin; and the economic climate is often invoked as a
factor in explaining why disillusionment with the existing political parties
and methods should have become so acute by the early 1880s. That
climate had taken a distinct turn for the worse around 1873, with the
onset of a severe depression. This had first afflicted the agricultural sector
of the economy but had then spread to industry and commerce, with
adverse effects on employment and the trade cycle that were still being
felt in the early 1890s. There is statistical evidence to suggest that the
depression in this period was not as intense, as general, and as unrelieved
as some contemporary descriptions might lead us to believe;[3] but such
statistics would hardly have brought comfort to those who suffered from
its effects, however sporadically, or to those observers who did not suffer
directly themselves but were sufficiently sensitive to suffering to have
their sympathies engaged. At certain times, such sympathies may have

been out of all proportion to the measure of suffering; but it would be surprising if the degree of adherence to any causes in history has borne a very close or precise relationship to such 'objective' calculations, especially when the evidence for those calculations was so elusive at the time.

An intimation of some of the less objective forces behind the advent of socialism in the 1880s is given in the autobiography of a slightly later convert to that faith — Beatrice Webb. As one of the chief characters in this book, she is worth quoting at some length on the question. Trying to work out the origins of the 'demand for state intervention' among a generation 'disciplined in the school of philosophic radicalism and orthodox political economy', she traced back from her fellow-Fabians a tradition — or counter-tradition — of social feeling which she dubbed 'a new consciousness of sin'. It was not, she insisted, a consciousness of 'personal' sin, but rather a 'collective or class consciousness': 'a growing uneasiness' among 'men of intellect and men of property' that 'the industrial organization which had yielded rent, interest and profits on a stupendous scale, had failed to provide a decent livelihood and tolerable conditions for a majority of the inhabitants of Great Britain'. The counter-tradition in question incorporated a number of components or phases, dating back far beyond the so-called Great Depression of the 1870s and 1880s:

at first philanthropic and practical — Oastler, Shaftesbury, and Chadwick; then literary and artistic — Dickens, Carlyle, Ruskin and William Morris; and finally, analytic, historical and explanatory — in his latter days John Stuart Mill; Karl Marx and his English interpreters; Alfred Russell Wallace and Henry George; Arnold Toynbee and the Fabians. I might perhaps add a theological category — Charles Kingsley, General Booth and Cardinal Manning.[4]

Later chroniclers of the evolution of socialism in England have fleshed out this account in various ways, and the most recent scholars in the field[5] have given particular attention to the complex of religious and ethical motifs in socialist ideas and to their psychological underpinnings. Personal feelings of insecurity and dislocation are shown to have been a factor of increasing force behind the questioning of traditional institutions and values which culminated in socialism. The sorts of insecurity involved, it becomes clear, were not just economic in nature, but reflected deep spiritual dilemmas or uncertainties, born partly of the disruptive impact of Darwinian evolutionary theories on conventional patterns of religious thinking. For its exponents, at least, socialism evidently presented itself as a new faith or system of values, and promised a new kind of security, both personal and social. The whole drift of Beatrice Webb's autobiography tends to bear out this interpretation.

While the religious or quasi-religious elements in British socialism and its origins have received due attention, the 'literary and artistic' elements to which Beatrice alluded in charting the growth of the 'new consciousness of sin' have been largely obscured, where not altogether ignored. These elements are not unrelated to the religious ones, as is shown most clearly in the case of Charles Kingsley, whose particular brand of socialism, rather than discarding the Christian framework, built upon it, and was embodied most enduringly in the form of novels that attacked various aspects of social and industrial organization in nineteenth-century England. The example of Kingsley, in fact, shows the overlapping of the artistic, religious and philanthropic inspirations, and suggests that Beatrice Webb's categories may be rather too rigid in parts.

In combination with religious impulses and yearnings — whether overt or displaced, Christian or non-Christian — aesthetic instincts were important both in germinating discontent with traditional institutions and values and in helping to define new or considerably renovated systems of values, such as came to be represented by socialism. This is an implicit theme of an essay on 'The Historic Basis of Socialism', written by another of the major characters in this book — Beatrice Webb's husband, Sidney. Tracing, in rather similar fashion to his wife, the roots of the reaction against orthodox political economy and its individualist ideals, Webb stressed that 'the first revolt came from the artistic side'. This he connected with the fact, or the feeling, that the practitioners of the individualist creed were a very philistine bunch on the whole, whose approach to life and society represented an extremely mean, narrow and literal-minded form of utilitarianism, symbolized by two of the most unpleasant characters in the novels of Dickens: Murdstone and Gradgrind. Webb made clear that Dickens was not the first artist to highlight the deficiencies and excesses of the utilitarian outlook. That honour went to the romantic poets of the late eighteenth and early nineteenth centuries, and subsequent support came from various non-artistic quarters as well:

The 'nest of singing birds' at the Lakes would have none of it . . . Coleridge did his best to drown it in German Transcendentalism. Robert Owen and his following of enthusiastic communistic co-operators steadfastly held up a loftier ideal. The great mass of the wage-earners never bowed the knee to the principles upon which the current 'White Slavery' was maintained. But the first man who really made a dint in the individualist shield was Carlyle . . . Then came Maurice, Kingsley, Ruskin and others who dared to impeach the current middle class cult.[6]

Again, most of these social rebels or critics were active long before the economic crisis which overtook England's agriculture, industry and commerce in the 1870s. For all of the intensity of their reactions against the seemingly unbridled individualism of England's capitalist economy, few of them were, or claimed to be, socialists of any kind. (Maurice and

Kingsley, as leaders of the so-called Christian socialists, were exceptions here.) It might plausibly be argued, therefore, that it took the economic crisis of the 1870s to direct these streams of social consciousness into more forceful socialist channels. The original sources of these new channels were not the kind to dry up during any lulls in the economic crisis; on the contrary, aesthetic or religious instincts were deep enough to sustain, even reinforce, the new socialist faith when its immediate and 'objective' *raison d'être* became less pressing.

Neither of the Webbs said as much in their respective accounts of the sources of the British socialist revival. Sidney Webb's catalogue, quoted above, limited itself to the (largely non-socialist) precursors of his colleagues in the socialist movement. He did not indicate at all there whether the artistic revolt which he saw as initiating the whole reaction against individualism played any direct part in the latest, socialist phase of that reaction. Beatrice's catalogue, on the other hand, went beyond a list of mere precursors, and included the most famous socialist artist of her younger days, William Morris, as well as her fellow-Fabians. She saw Morris as continuing the 'literary and artistic' reaction against the excesses of industrial capitalism, but she placed the Fabians in a separate category ('analytic, historical and explanatory').

Subsequent chroniclers have tended to follow her lead. Indeed, most of them have gone further than Beatrice by expressly discounting the importance of a literary and artistic element in Fabian socialism, or even the existence of any such element. Where the aesthetic aspects of British socialism are considered at all, we are presented with the spectacle of a radically divided or disjointed movement. At one extreme is William Morris's brand, representing a deep, perhaps disproportionate,[7] concern with the role of art in society, and a clear indebtedness to the romantic tradition, even as it modifies or transcends that tradition in various ways.[8] The Fabian brand is seen at the other extreme — representing an indifference, even a hostility,[9] to the arts, and subjected to infection by just the sort of philistine and narrowly utilitarian influences which the romanticist forebears of socialism were so keen to exorcize from political thought and economic policy-making.[10]

Morris, for all the criticisms made of particular aspects of his approach to socialism, has never been short of defenders, passionate or dispassionate; whereas the Fabian approach to socialism has been exposed to a general, and increasingly heavy, criticism from all sides. Even some of its own adherents or partisans join in the chorus of criticism when it comes to aesthetic or cultural matters, measuring the alleged deficiencies of Fabian socialism in these matters by the counter-example of Morris.[11] This tendency began early, and its fairness to Fabianism has never been questioned, let alone examined.

It is not the aim of this book to defend Fabianism in general as a brand of socialism *vis-à-vis* other brands. Rather, the abiding intention is to show that in ways quite unconnected with the advocacy or support of its particular cause, Fabianism is worthy of more considered, if not more considerate, attention than most commentators have been prepared to give it. This is particularly so in the area of culture, by which is meant in this instance the relationship of the arts (broadly defined) with various aspects of society (work, leisure and education; morality and religion; politics and class). For too long, the question of Fabian cultural concerns has been treated as a non-question: it is simply taken for granted that such concerns were negligible or, if detectable in certain individual Fabians, extraneous to the group's overall socialist beliefs and schemes. The cultural concerns of other socialist — and labour — organizations which emerged in the wake of the so-called Great Depression of the last quarter of the nineteenth century have not been examined in any thoroughgoing manner either; but neither have they been discounted. In a sense, then, the Fabian Society has suffered most from the general failure by students of English socialism to look on that movement 'from the aesthetic point of view'. In attempting to remedy that failure, there is a case for starting out with a rigorous exploration of the Fabian terrain precisely because of its assumed aridity.

An exploration of this kind provides a new angle from which to view the ideological traditions behind British socialism in general and the ideological tensions within that movement. Setting up dichotomies — such as that between romanticism and utilitarianism, or the William Morris brand of socialism and the Fabian brand — is a neat and plausible way of describing certain 'dissociations of sensibility' in a particular period and of clarifying the rifts within various political, social, intellectual or artistic movements. But are these dichotomies too neat to be true?

However negative they may appear on the surface, Fabian cultural attitudes are worth exploring for yet broader reasons. They can add to our understanding of various issues and forces in society which have persisted up to the present day and which have a relevance beyond, as well as within, the context of socialism. Indeed, philistinism would need to be regarded as one of these forces. In its more or less virulent forms (antipathy to artists; complete indifference to all art forms; consistent defects or deficiencies in 'taste'; lack of any aesthetic sensitivity in perceiving the world in general) it should be as much a concern of cultural historians and diagnosticians as atheism, secularism, and religious apathy are a concern of historians and sociologists of religion. Philistinism and its practitioners should not just be censured and dismissed, especially if it is hoped to counteract any influence they might have in society. As Matthew Arnold appreciated,[12] in his dealings with various politicians and

educational administrators in mid-Victorian England, the workings of
philistinism need to be fully elaborated and explained if an effective
struggle against this force is to be sustained. And the example of those, like
Arnold, who consciously fought against the workings of philistinism in
society is also worthy of elucidation, partly for its inherent historical
interest and partly as an object lesson for the present and the future.

Given the philistine reputation of the Fabians, one is in for a surprise
when one embarks on a detailed exploration of their cultural attitudes, for
it becomes clearer and clearer that these were not as negative as one was
led to assume; nor, it emerges, were the positive aspects of these attitudes
merely incidental to the socialist beliefs and schemes of the Fabian Society.
Fabians themselves used the term 'philistine' in a pejorative sense, at
times specifically in order to criticize deficiencies in taste or culture
among the middle class. They stated or implied that a collectively
organized state or economy was one which would help defeat, rather than
encourage, the forces of philistinism;[13] and in one instance Beatrice Webb
used the terms 'philistinism' and 'socialism' as if they were antitheses.[14]
Certainly, in any struggle between the forces of 'culture' and the forces of
philistinism, Fabians would have been much more likely, whether as
individuals or in the group, to be closer to Matthew Arnold than to his
philistine antagonists.

This is to oversimplify the battle-lines, of course, for there would have
been several anti-philistines (including William Morris) who would have
questioned or rejected the ineffably élitist notions of culture, and its social
role, which permeated Arnold's strategies. Whether the Fabians, as
socialists, would have shared these reservations is another question which
needs to be explored, once it is demonstrated that they had any positive
cultural concerns at all.

All membership records and contemporary observations testify to the
almost exclusively middle-class origins of the Fabian Society's adherents,
from the time of its foundation in 1884 onwards.[15] (As we shall see,
several of its earliest members — or their families — were from sections
of the middle class which suffered directly from the effects of the
economic depression in the 1870s and 1880s.) Middle-class socialists are
not normally associated with philistinism, though they are often assumed
to be élitist in their very socialism — that is, seeking to extend to the
population at large their own values, tastes and privileges, without really
considering how appropriate or how desirable these things may actually
be to the majority they are intended to benefit. There was a strong
middle-class element in the other main socialist organizations which
sprang up in the 1880s — the Social Democratic Federation and its
splinter group, the Socialist League. (The former was led by H.M.
Hyndman, the son of a wealthy merchant; and William Morris, who was

likewise born into a very prosperous section of the commercial middle-class, became a dominant force in the League.) But these groups attracted a large working-class following, especially among self-educated artisans, and directed their appeal specifically to this class.[16] The Fabian Society, on the other hand, never had anything but a very small — merely token — working-class following, and it deliberately aimed most of its propaganda at securing further converts from the middle class. If any organization was ripe for élitism, it was the Fabian Society, or so it has been generally assumed. An exploration of the Fabians' cultural attitudes provides a fruitful opportunity for analysing the various meanings of élitism within a specific historical context.

But when is a Fabian a Fabian and when not? Or, to be more precise, how far can the views of an individual member of the Fabian Society be taken to represent Fabianism? The unflattering images of the Society partly result from the attempts of certain individual members to distance themselves, in various respects, from the general run of the Society's members. Bernard Shaw, for instance, always liked to think of himself as something of a special case in the group, and made quite explicit and sweeping claims about his fellow-members' aesthetic insensitivities. 'Talking of the Fabians', he recalled on one occasion (and the charge was repeated by him several other times in later years)[17] 'they were Philistines':

Ruskin's name was hardly mentioned. My colleagues did not seem conscious of Oscar Wilde's *The Soul of Man Under Socialism* or even Morris's *News from Nowhere* and seemed to suspect people associated with art ... The artist should keep out of these organizations unless he can, like myself, take music, art, philosophy, science and economics in his stride. For me, they were one and the same thing.[18]

The fact that several other artists, far from keeping out of the Fabian Society, as Shaw advised, became active members of it for at least a part of their careers, casts an immediate doubt on his characterization of its pervading atmosphere. The more prominent of these — H.G. Wells, Harley Granville Barker, Arnold Bennett, Jerome K. Jerome, Eric Gill, Rupert Brooke, Virginia Woolf — belonged to the second, rather than the first, generation of Fabians; and the connections of some of this group with the Society — most notably Wells's — were, admittedly, brief and stormy. But the first generation could also boast a number of artistic and literary celebrities. Shaw himself had joined the Society in the year of its birth, and though he was not to begin his dramatic writings until the 1890s, he was already an experienced novelist. Other noted artists who joined the Society in its first decade included the poet and children's novelist, Edith Nesbit; William Morris's daughter, May (famous for her cloth designs and embroidery); the handicrafts designer and book-illustrator, Walter Crane (one of Morris's closest disciples); and the actor and director, Charles Charrington. There were several other early Fabians who may not be classified primarily as artists[19] but who still produced various forms of artistic work on a spasmodic basis. The novels of Emma Brooke, the poems of Ernest Radford, and the plays of Sydney Olivier — performed but never published — are examples to bear in mind here. Details of these sorts of artistic activity were reported regularly in a column of the *Fabian News*, entitled 'What Members are Doing' — a token perhaps of the importance with which they were regarded.[20]

Some of the more specific allegations which Shaw made in accusing his fellow-Fabians of philistinism — their tendency to ignore the work of Ruskin and Morris, for example — were insecurely based. The influence of these writers in shaping the socialist thought of the founders and chief formulators of Fabianism provides a recurrent theme of the first four chapters of this book. In 1891 two of these Fabian leaders, Sidney Webb and Graham Wallas, encouraged the membership to study the work of Morris and Ruskin in order to gain some insight into the 'non-Material side of Collectivism' (by which was meant such things as 'The Conditions of Art', 'The Endowment of the Artist' and 'Public and Private Taste').[21] The names of Ruskin and Morris were commonly invoked in the Society's main organs of propaganda — the tract and the lecture. Most of these references were incidental; though in the Fabians' highly popular 'Biographical Series' a whole tract each was devoted to a consideration of the two men's lives and achievements.[22] In the span between his conversion to socialism in the early eighties and his death in 1896, Morris himself made a number of appearances as guest-lecturer at the Fabian Society's main London branch;[23] and his ideas later became the subject of various lectures offered by the Society's speakers to other organizations.[24] Ruskin (who died in 1900) never gave any lectures to the Society; but Fabian lecturers were offering his work as a subject as early as 1890 — and frequently thereafter.[25] In 1906 his work formed the subject of one of six lectures, given before the main branch of the Society, on 'Prophets of the Past Century'.[26] In the same year, several of the most prominent members of the main branch — gathered together in a Special Committee to report on a paper by Wells entitled 'The Faults of the Fabian' — expressly recommended a reprinting, under Fabian auspices, of another work which Shaw later maintained had been unappreciated by his colleagues: Wilde's 'The Soul of Man Under Socialism'.[27] True, this recommendation reflected the Committee's own anxiety that the Fabians had insufficiently stressed the aesthetic and literary sides of socialist propaganda; the Committee hoped that Wilde's essay — which dealt with the individual artist's position in society, and with the kinds of relationship that should exist between art and the general public [28] — would help remedy the deficiency. On the other hand, those very feelings on the part of the Committee reveal a concern for artistic matters — and especially for those with social and socialist implications — which serves to break down the totally philistine image of the Society fostered by Shaw.

This sort of concern was not confined to the upper echelons of the Society. In the same year in which the Special Committee to inquire into Wells's criticisms was set up, the critic and journalist, Holbrook Jackson — one of a crop of young littérateurs who joined the Fabians in the first decade of the new century — told the Secretary that he had always felt the Society had 'concentrated upon the scientific and political aspects of socialistic propaganda to the neglect of such fruitful fields as Art and Philosophy'. He defined art as 'all those methods of interpreting life known under the terms Music, Painting, Literature, Sculpture etc. as well as such applications of these to social affairs as is contained in the various Handicraft Guilds resulting from the energies of Morris and his followers'. (This, incidentally, serves well as a working definition of the term 'art' in this book, though the range of categories and of social applications instanced in Jackson's letter will be extended in various ways.) Jackson claimed that the Society's effectiveness and potential appeal had been limited by 'an altogether too narrow view of the Fabians' work, due probably to some powerful intellect within the Executive giving the Society a bias which should have been temporary but has become traditional'; and he asked why it should be that this organization, having 'created a definite socialist attitude in both politics and sociology', did 'not do the same for Art and Philosophy'.

Again, such claims and questions as these, while lending some support to the image of the Fabians as a body with little or no concern for the arts, serve in the final analysis to break down that image. To begin with, Jackson's letter provides evidence not only of his own, highly-developed interest in the arts and their relationship with socialism; it also implies that this interest was shared, albeit on a less conscious level, by an appreciable portion of his fellow-Fabians, and that it could be fruitfully tapped, if directed into proper institutional channels. He told the Secretary that he wished to see the Society 'forming itself into groups with reference to certain ideas: Art, Philosophy, Science & Politics seem the main ideas under which social endeavour falls and therefore the most worthy of Fabian exploitation for Socialism. No small advantage of the adoption of some such scheme would be the use we could make of the *artistic and philosophical element in the Society* which at present . . . must be running to weed.'[29] A year after penning this letter to Pease, Jackson actually proceeded to establish a 'Fabian Arts Group' in collaboration with the journalist and literary critic, Alfred Orage.

There are plausible grounds, however, for viewing the Fabian Arts Group as a dissident minority which, from the start, had only the most

tenuous connections with 'orthodox' Fabianism. Could not the doctrine
and policies with which the Society has been most commonly identified —
its 'resolute constitutionalism',[30] manifested in its rejection of
revolutionary approaches to socialism, and its encouragement to the
gradual introduction of collectivist measures by a bureaucratically-
organized state — still have been philistine, in spite of the presence of an
'artistic element' in the Fabian ranks? That impression is certainly
fostered by the pronouncements and actions of the Arts Group's own
initiators. The fact that such a group came into existence more than
twenty years after the Society was founded — and that, in spite of an
initial vogue, it seems to have petered out after about four years — can
only cast further doubt on its effectiveness as a counterweight to the
general philistine image of the Society.

From early on, there are signs that the Group and its leaders had close
ties with other late-flowering (and transient) 'heretical' movements within
the Society — movements which had also been nurtured, in part at least,
by the alleged indifference of orthodox Fabianism to the artistic and
cultural aspects of socialism. In February 1907, a month after the Group
had been officially set up, Holbrook Jackson wrote to H.G. Wells to offer
the novelist his personal support (and the services of the Group itself) in
furthering that 'revolution in the spirit of the Fabian brought about by
yourself'.[31] Wells's attempted 'revolution' was in the end defeated by the
'Old Gang' of Fabians, led by Shaw and Sidney Webb; and Wells resigned
from the Society in 1908. 'Revolution' is probably too portentous a word
to describe the nature of his attacks on the 'Old Gang'. It would seem to
have been at least as much a bid for personal power in the Society as an
attempt to effect any 'spiritual' transformations there;[32] and was
attributable more, perhaps, to quirks and excesses in Wells's disposition
— his egoism, his ambition, his penchant for grandiose schemes and
restless impatience with the pettier details of social reform —than to any
fundamental disagreement with the Old Gang's socialist principles. The
Webbs themselves had shown an early enthusiasm for Wells's ideas, as
enunciated in such books as *Anticipations* (1901), and they had been
influential in bringing him into the Fabian fold in the first place. Even
after they diverged, Beatrice found much to praise and to sympathize with
in the novelist's writings.[33] Moreover, at the start of his campaign to
reform and expand Fabian activities, other members of the Old Gang —
most notably, Sydney Olivier[34] — found it possible to give their support to
several of his recommendations. The leaders of the Arts Group, however,
supported not only Wells's mildly heretical schemes, but also those of a
more serious and persistent heretical movement within the ranks of the
Society: the Guild Socialist movement.

To some extent, the conflict between the Guild Socialists and the

Fabian Old Gang was also one of clashing personalities and styles; but, as Margaret Cole (the widow of one of the most prominent exponents of Guild Socialism) has observed, there was 'a clear difference of theoretical approach' separating the two sides which had not been evident in the Wells dispute.[35] Stated very badly — for there were several variants — Guild Socialism was an attempt to replace capitalist control of industry not by full State control, administered through schemes of municipal collectivism or nationalization, but, rather, by the control of the industrial workers themselves, organized into a network of communal associations based on the present trade unions.[36] The movement was only in its infancy at the time of the Wells dispute and of the formation of the Fabian Arts Group; but even at that stage we find A.R. Orage to have been a firm convert to its basic tenets, and an opponent of the sort of collectivism to which he felt the bulk of the Fabians had committed themselves. A.J. Penty, one of Orage's oldest colleagues — and a Fabian himself — had recently issued a book which proved to be the primer of Guild Socialism,[37] and had set up a 'Gilds Restoration League' in order to work for the realization of his ideas. As early as July 1906, some six months before Orage and Jackson set up the Arts Group, the former wrote to Wells about the League's activities and gave his own version of 'the faults of the Fabian'. The object of the League, he informed Wells, was

to bring about a union between the economic aims of the Trades Unionists and the aesthetic aims of the craftsman. *Hitherto, the collectivist proposals have been designed solely to make economic poverty impossible; it is necessary to design them not only to make economic but also aesthetic poverty impossible.* This, of course, would involve a considerable modification of the usual collectivist formulas. As a member of the Fabian Society, I should have been glad to see that Society take up the present propaganda; but I am afraid the *major part of the Fabians is too rigidly bound to the collectivist formulas* to make such a hope practicable.[38]

It is hardly surprising, in the light of Orage's sentiments here, that the Arts Group which he and Jackson founded came to provide a powerful sounding-board for Guild Socialist ideas.

These closely related Fabian 'heresies' — the Arts Group, the Wells campaign and the Guild Socialist faction — are the clearest pointer to the Fabians' concern with artistic questions relating to socialism. Of course, precisely because of their heretical (or at least schismatic) tendencies, they cannot be taken as representative examples of Fabianism. Yet, in their initial stages at least, there was support and sympathy for some of their views within the Fabian establishment, and it is important not to make a hard and fast division between the heretical and the orthodox elements. The heretics themselves failed to be cautious enough in this regard, and later commentators have tended to swallow their propaganda. This has resulted in a picture of orthodox Fabianism which unthinkingly equates its scientific pretensions, collectivist aims and bureaucratic procedures with an indifference to artistic considerations and a lack of imagination. Orage's letter to Wells, cited above, is the most patent example of that line of argument, though there have been more influential specimens.

For instance, there is an anecdote concerning Penty[39] which relates how this early mentor of the Guild Socialist movement decided to give up the Fabian Society on discovering the unaesthetic (purely 'statistical') criteria which were used in trying to decide between competing designs for the London School of Economics. Though an early recounting of this anecdote referred to 'Pease and a colleague' as the offenders in question,[40] more recent accounts have singled out the Webbs. Without any attempt to check the basis of the story, it has been taken as an automatic sign not only of the Webbs', but also of the Society's, 'prevailing lack of concern for anything aesthetic'.[41]

So has a stray remark made in an obituary of Orage by the sculptor, Eric Gill, who had been an early member of the Arts Group. His tribute began with a reference to Orage's efforts, through the medium of the Group, to 'deprive Fabianism of its webbed feet — vain efforts'.[42] This no doubt referred to the domination of the Society by Sidney and Beatrice; and it was probably to Sidney that Holbrook Jackson alluded when he complained to Pease in 1906, in the letter quoted above, of 'some powerful intellect within the Executive' afflicting the Society with a 'narrow bias'. The suggestions here of a close identity between the sensibilities of the Webbs, orthodox Fabianism, and the unimaginative philistinism of that brand of socialist belief are explicitly articulated in the view of a recent writer on Jackson and Orage who concludes that the Arts Group which they set up was 'intended as a rallying-ground for socialists who thought the arts of fundamental importance and who were consequently opposed to the bureaucratic Fabian socialism of Sidney and Beatrice Webb and their supporters'.[43]

Intentionally, or unintentionally, H.G. Wells probably did more than any of the other Fabian heretics to spread and perpetuate the philistine image of orthodox Fabianism, as represented by the views of the Webbs. One of his best-known novels, *The New Machiavelli*, contained two leading characters — Oscar and Altiora Bailey — who, while not exact replicas of Sidney and Beatrice, bore sufficiently obvious resemblances to them for an easy identification to be made in the minds of any alert contemporary reader. The image presented of them was encrusted with a number of unflattering details representing their asethetic insensitivity. At times, the narrator explicitly contrasted his own preoccupations with beauty ('With me', he claimed, it 'is quite primary in life') with the Baileys' attitudes:

They seemed at times to prefer things harsh and ugly ... The aesthetic quality of many of their proposals, the manner of their work ... were at times as dreadful as — well, War Office barrack architecture ... Theirs was a philosophy devoid of *finesse* ... If they had all the universe in hand, I know they would take down all the trees and put stamped tin green shades and sunlight accumulators. Altiora thought trees hopelessly irregular and sea cliffs a great mistake.[44]

Later accounts of Wells's contention with the Webbs have tended to emulate the sort of contrast made in this passage, and to depict the underlying issues involved partly in terms of a clash between 'imaginative' and 'bureaucratic' or 'utilitarian' sensibilities.[45]

Part of the reason why the conventional picture of the Webbs has gone unquestioned for so long may lie in their own lack of defensiveness about it, manifested by a self-effacement in areas where they felt they had no expertise, and compounded by a propensity for self-caricature.[46] There were several occasions, as we shall see, when they themselves sorrowfully proclaimed their particular inadequacies in the area of artistic creativity and appreciation; and Beatrice's response to Wells's satirical portrait of her and Sidney was almost blithely acquiescent.[47] Such facts, however, cannot automatically be taken to validate Wells's portrait. It will be one of the central aims of this book to question the validity of such images by examining the full record of the Webbs' attitude to the arts.

It is necessary to concentrate on the Webbs' views and sensibilities because, though these do not wholly embody Fabianism, they have been most commonly identified with that creed and frequently used to define the limitations of its general approach to socialism. At the same time, one cannot attempt to clear Fabianism of such charges simply by vindicating the Webbs, for this would still be to assume, albeit from an opposite viewpoint, that that brand of socialism was automatically identifiable with, or definable by, what the Webbs thought and did. On looking into the views of other members of the Fabian Society — on whatever issues[48] and at whatever period — one is struck more by their heterogeneity than by their homogeneity: by their ambiguity, flexibility, and inconsistency, rather than any single-minded dogmatic certainty. Sidney Webb claimed in a letter to Wells that 'the Society was never very homogeneous because it was deliberately kept heterogeneous'.[49] And Wells recalled the 'intricate cross purposes of that bunch of animated folk' — symptomatic of the way in which many groups fall 'into morasses of complication and self-contradiction'.[50] Even those in the Society who were married to each other (the Peases and the Shaws, for example, if not the Webbs themselves[51]) can be found at cross purposes over various matters of Fabian concern.

These considerations throw considerable doubt on the concept of

Fabian socialism as uniform in its approach; and the notion that any such approach involved a rigid conformity with the particular ideas and sensibilities of the Webbs is beset by further doubts and objections. To begin with, Sidney did not become a member till May 1885 (nearly two years after the Society had begun to evolve from a small discussion group of ethical reformers) and Beatrice did not join till 1891, when the Society's seminal textbook, the *Fabian Essays in Socialism*, had been in print for two years. Between 1887 and 1891 Sidney wrote the bulk of the Society's official tracts, though his contributions to its literature dwindled considerably thereafter.[52] Beatrice remained comparatively inactive in the day-to-day business of the Society and its various committees till as late as 1913, when she became *de facto* chairman;[53] and she contributed only one signed tract up to that time.[54] Sidney adapted his lecture on 'The Historical Aspect of the Basis of Socialism' for publication in the *Fabian Essays*, but there were six other contributors to that volume, with varying approaches.

Bernard Shaw, who (at least nominally) had more to do with the publication of the *Essays* than Webb — he contributed two of them and acted as editor — made clear in the Preface that there was no single 'line' in Fabian Socialism. Not one of the essays, he admitted, could be what it was if its author had been a 'stranger to his six colleagues and to the Society'. But that sense of community among the contributors entailed 'no sacrifice of individuality'. They were

all Social Democrats, with a common conviction of the necessity of vesting the organization of industry and the material of production in a State identified with the whole people by complete Democracy. But that conviction is peculiar to no individual bias . . . so that the reader need not fear oppression here, any more than in the socialized State of the future, by the ascendancy of one particular cast of mind. There are at present no authoritative teachers of Socialism. The essayists make no claims to be more than communicative learners.[55]

The 'Basis of the Fabian Society', which all members of the Society had to sign on joining, prescribed a commitment to certain broad socialist principles, along the lines which Shaw indicated in the passage just quoted.[56] Webb was among those who drew up the principles, but they were established not by his dictates alone, but by agreement and compromise among the whole Executive Committee, fifteen in number.[57] Neither was Webb responsible for actually initiating any of the most characteristic policies and tactics of the Fabian Society as it developed in the eighties and nineties: its gradualist or non-revolutionary approach to socialism; its 'permeation' of non-socialist parties; and its adaptation of Radical Collectivism. This last measure he was even inclined to dismiss, at an early stage of his Fabian career, as having no necessary connection with socialism.[58]

The Webbs eventually achieved dominance as leaders of the Old Gang, championing a conservative version of Fabianism and resisting any major institutional or ideological changes within the Society. But that dominance was not achieved without a fairly constant struggle. They had to contend not only with the overtly heretical and schismatic movements led by newer or younger elements in the Society, but also with eruptions of dissent in the senior ranks. Ramsay MacDonald, Graham Wallas, Stewart Headlam and Sydney Olivier were among the most prominent of these dissenters. Their differences with the Webbs centred on various issues: the effectiveness of indiscriminate permeation as a political tactic; the administration of education; the ethics and politics of imperialism and protectionism. Sometimes these disputes were serious enough to lead to resignations. For example, MacDonald, accompanied by seventeen other members, walked out of the Society in 1900 because of its majority decision not to take any official stance on the issue of the Boer War.

MacDonald, in his later career as Labour leader, never abandoned his evolutionary concept of socialism and his belief in attaining it through constitutional means;[59] and those tenets have come to be identified as the most distinct (if not distinctive) traits of Fabianism. A more recent Labour leader, C.R. Attlee, welcoming a series of Fabian essays written after the Second World War, claimed that the original series of 1889 'had marked the beginnings of a new approach to Socialism: It was... the first clear statement of the philosophy of gradualism as against the utopian or catastrophic ideas of the past. The British Labour and Socialist Movement has to a large extent lived on the thinking of the Fabian essayists and their successors.'[60] In 1923, Sidney Webb had reaffirmed — though not with specific reference to the Fabian Society[61] — 'the inevitable gradualness of our scheme of change'; this phrase was used in his presidential address to the annual conference of the Labour Party. Beatrice reaffirmed his dictum the following year and expressly associated it with Fabianism.[62] If gradualism, however, is seen as the cornerstone of 'orthodox' Fabianism, then there is a sense in which the Webbs themselves (and their most steadfast ally in the Old Gang, Bernard Shaw) may be said to have developed heretical tendencies in their last years. After visiting Russia in the early 1930s, they came back full of enthusiasm for what Soviet communism had achieved in the brief span of time since the Revolution. Beatrice stated that she and Sidney had 'fallen in love' with the post-revolutionary regime there; and this love may well have been quickened by their disillusionment with labour politics in England after the collapse of MacDonald's government in 1931. A contemporary of theirs recalls their saying at about this time that 'the inevitability of gradualness is dead'.[63]

Shaw, in his introduction to a new edition of the *Fabian Essays* published in 1931, remarked that events such as the Russian Revolution had come as a 'staggering shock to constitutionalism' and that it was 'not so certain today as it seemed in the eighties that Morris was not right' in proclaiming the necessity of revolution in attaining socialism.[64] He retreated from the full heretical implications of such a statement in his postscript to the subsequent edition of the *Essays*, where he claimed that the 'catastrophic' policy of the Russian revolutionaries had proved ruinous, and that the 'New Economic Policy' introduced by Lenin in the 1920s to placate rural hostility to the Bolshevik regime 'was in fact Fabian'[65] in its spirit of comparative moderation. He neglected to point out here that by the time he and the Webbs went to Russia the N.E.P. had been replaced by Stalin's much less placatory and far from 'gradualist' policies of rural collectivization. The Webbs, for all their admiration of what they observed of Russia's economic and social policies in the thirties, at least expressed a regret concerning the coercive 'manner' in which some of these were carried out and a concern for the victims of coercion and of the 'disease of orthodoxy' behind it.[66] Shaw had no such reservations; if, in the final analysis, he preferred gradualist policies, it was because he felt them to be more practically effective, but in his heart he had been a revolutionary from his earliest days as a socialist.[67] In the pages of the *Fabian Essays* themselves he had disavowed any admiration for the 'inevitable but sordid, slow, reluctant, cowardly path to justice' which had been mapped out by himself and his colleagues in the book; and even throws a doubt on the inevitability of that path by claiming that a more militant, 'insurrectionary' brand of socialism 'still remains the only finally possible alternative to the Social Democratic programme'.[68]

Dogmatic certainty, then, was absent even in the attitudes of the most conservative members of the Old Gang, and this serves to confirm doubts about the existence of any such phenomenon as orthodox Fabianism.[69] The Fabians' approaches to socialism, if they can be summed up at all, may be defined by their very lack of doctrinal rigidity and uniform principles. Sidney Webb's description of 'the work of the Fabian Society' as consisting in 'the work of individual Fabians'[70] may be applied to the thought of the Society as well. The editors of the most recent series of Fabian essays talk of the 'collective view of the Society' but suggest the elusive nature of this by acknowledging that even a publication released under the Society's name and auspices can be taken to represent 'only the view of the individual who prepared it'.[71] To take the views of one or two individual Fabians — however prominent — as the sole basis for generalizations about Fabianism and its ramifications is to distort its inherently protean and eclectic nature. This does not mean, of course, that some common themes and assumptions may not be found. The only fair way of identifying these, however, is by considering, respectively, the beliefs of a whole range of individual Fabians and by working out from that complex of thought the points of intersection as well as the points of divergence. This will be the procedure adopted here in exploring the Fabians' beliefs about art and its connections with socialism.

It is true, as Holbrook Jackson pointed out, that the Fabians lacked a 'definite socialist attitude' towards art, in the sense of a cohesive body of thought on the subject — of a consistent and uniform 'aesthetic'. But then definiteness of that kind went against the whole grain of Fabian socialism. With regard to art, Jackson's fundamental divergence from the Webbs and the Fabian Old Gang lay not in his wish to extend the range of the Society's concerns with the subject and with its social applications (there was no antipathy among any of the members to this enterprise) but in his accompanying wish to establish some firm programmatic line. It was his mistake (and that of commentators after him) to confuse the lack of a programmatic line on art with indifference or neglect. In fact, that lack was symptomatic of a generally non-prescriptive policy on the part of the Society's Executive in most areas of thought and human activity. It reflected not an indifference towards what the individual member thought about the arts or how he involved himself in them; but, rather, an awareness that to lay down any formulae for approaching what was evidently among the most highly individual of human activities would be both unrealistic and insensitive. The *Report on Fabian Policy* (drafted by Shaw and published in 1896 as one of the Society's official tracts) explicitly declared that the organization had 'no distinctive opinions on the Marriage Question, Religion, Art, abstract economics, historic Evolution, Currency or any other subject than its own special business of practical Democracy and Socialism'; and it recognized the 'freedom of individuals. . . to practise all arts, crafts and professions independently'.[72]

The latter phrase appeared in a section of the tract that was explicitly headed 'Fabian Individualism'. The relationship between individualism and socialism — as reflected particularly in the question of how the individual would maintain his freedom in a socialist state — was a recurrent theme in Fabian literature. The common notion[73] that the two principles were antithetical or mutually exclusive was vigorously denied, and the conduciveness of a socialist environment to the development of individual freedom for all was just as vigorously attested.[74] The lack of a 'definite socialist attitude' towards art — and the concomitant freedom and independence which, according to Shaw's tract, individuals were to be allowed in their approaches to art — can be seen as an integral part of certain Fabians' whole conception of socialism and its relation to the individual.

Other, more direct connections between the Fabians' socialist beliefs and their diverse attitudes to art may be found, though these connections were often articulated in an indirect or implicit manner. Their lack of obviousness, as well as their lack of definiteness, has contributed to the philistine image of Fabian socialism. Thus Shaw backed up the charge of philistinism which he levelled against his colleagues by noting that 'an essay on the Fine Arts under Socialism' was 'conspicuously absent' from the original series of *Fabian Essays*;[75] and other commentators have also taken that absence to suggest the Fabians' neglect of art or their lack of qualifications to write about it.[76] These deductions prove to be completely superficial on examining less 'conspicuous' evidence — the actual (as distinct from the nominal) content of the *Fabian Essays*, and the background influences which shaped the essayists' views and sensibilities. Such evidence is considered in detail in the first part of this book. It shows that while none of the essays attempted a full-scale investigation of the relationship between art and socialism, all of them touched on the question at least incidentally, and there were several which devoted substantial space to working out various facets of the relationship. The influences on the essayists — influences which are apparent from a close analysis of the *Essays* themselves as well as of the other writings which their authors published — betoken a strong and sensitive receptiveness to art, especially to romantic literature of the nineteenth century or the romanticist elements in that literature.

The publication of the *Fabian Essays* represented the first climax of that 'long and clarifying experience' out of which Fabian socialism emerged.[77] As a distillation of early Fabian ideas, the book requires our special attention — together with other writings by its contributors — because the earliest generation of Fabians is generally assumed to have been the most philistine. Ascribing different sets of attitudes to particular generations, phases or 'bloomings' in the Society's history[78] can easily lead to distortion by setting up categories which obscure the elements of continuity in Fabian thought. On the other hand, the blanket labelling of Fabian attitudes in such a way as to cover all the members of the Society at all times can be just as distorting, in that it tends to obscure the differences between members on specific issues and the ambiguities and tensions in the views of each individual member. The cursory accounts that are usually given of the Fabians' artistic attitudes exemplify both kinds of distortion. Closer examination of these attitudes — in the years leading up to, as well as in the years following, the publication of the *Fabian Essays* — testifies at once to a strong element of continuity in the general orientation of Fabian thought and to the complexity and confusion of its ramifications.

I hope to demonstrate these things by concentrating on the first and second generations of the Society's existence, when it was most in the limelight; though some evidence from later periods will also be considered. In its manner of organization, as well as in the orientation of its thought, there was a strong element of continuity in Fabianism, despite numerous and often bitter controversies over the particular functions and approaches of the Society as a socialist body. In fact, these controversies were symptomatic of — even essential to — the continuities we can trace from the time of the Society's birth in the early 1880s to the end of the First World War. For under its various guises during this period and beyond — extra-parliamentary pressure group for the socialist cause in general; surrogate powerhouse for those of its members with personal political ambitions; centre for research into burning social questions of the day — the Society remained, at bottom, an intellectual clearing-house or debating club. This was summed up by none other than H.G. Wells, in 1906, when he spoke of the Society's original value and continuing potential as 'a common meeting-ground, a field for frank discussion, and wherever practicable a means of reconciliation and concerted action for Socialists of every party and type, however diverse their ideas of the political methods necessary for the attainment of their common social and economic ideals'.[79]

Since the drafting of the Fabian 'Basis' in 1887, there was no questioning the fact that the Society was pre-eminently a political, as distinct from an ethical or religious or scientific or artistic, body. As the contributors to the *Fabian Essays* made clear, however, both in that volume and in their other writings, the socialist aims and visions of the Society's members were never as narrowly or categorically conceived. And even the political functions which the Society saw as its chief *raison d'être* were open to a broad and all-inclusive interpretation. In facilitating, through permeation and propaganda, the application of socialism 'to the whole field of current politics', such areas as 'theatre, art, religion' were considered to be as worthy of the Fabians' attention as parliamentary parties and municipal authorities.[80] Though the pre-eminence of the Society's political role was largely accepted, there were endless disputes over the question of how that role should be played out: should it become an actual party itself; should it actively assist one party in particular — the Labour Party; or should it continue in its efforts to influence and permeate all parties, as it did in the days before the Labour Party officially came into existence?[81] The perpetual attempts by various members to sort out such issues no doubt provided a source of controversy without which the Society may have become rather staid and stagnant; but at the same time as sharpening the members' wits and tongues, and thereby helping to cultivate whatever talents they had as individual politicians, these wrangles may also have diverted the energies of the Society as a whole from the wider political arena and thereby served to curtail its collective influence.

The Society's political failures are now well-documented, though little has been done to explain them. That is not the purpose of this book; and perhaps one can only speculate on the matter. Certainly, it would be difficult to prove with conclusive evidence that the conflicting aspirations of members on the Society's behalf were one of the reasons that its political achievements did not live up to all of its boasts. But there were substantial achievements in other directions which have been insufficiently noticed, or where noticed also left unexplained. One of these was simply the resilience of the Society, despite its political failures — its ability as an institution to survive a number of lean or particularly disruptive periods. None of the other socialist organizations set up in the 1880s has come anywhere near to their centenary. I shall not be attempting a full explanation of this feat of survival either, though hints as to the possible reasons will be given throughout. What I hope to draw attention to is what the Society had to offer which other socialist groups did not and which helped it to survive and, at times, flourish.

Its artistic interests in themselves were certainly not unique. The leaders of the Socialist League were so committed to the arts of various kinds as to make careers out of them, or to attempt to do so. Morris was the most notable and successful in this sphere; though there were other striking examples. Edward Belfort Bax studied, composed, and wrote about music. Eleanor Marx and her common-law husband, Edward Aveling, participated in and organized a number of theatrical productions, as well as undertaking translations of foreign dramatic works into English. Such interests were reflected in the activities of the League, which included plays or dramatic readings in which the Avelings took a leading part, and concerts, recitals, and sing-songs in which some of the items were composed by Morris and Bax.[82] The Fabians' artistic interests were reflected in very similar kinds of activity, and these will be examined in some detail, as their existence up to now has been obscured by the more overtly political activities of the Society. These artistic activities were an integral part of the Society's club-like organization, consolidating and extending this in various ways. Indeed, it was in their mode of organization and their social context that their uniqueness lay, rather than in their nature or content; for the Society, whether in its political activities or its artistic activities, took on the atmosphere not only of a debating club but also of a rather exclusive and unusual social club for those of a broadly similar class and educational background.

From the start, it made its greatest appeal to an alienated section of the middle class that had been brought up in the commercial sector of that class and had then achieved — or aspired to — various positions within the professional or salaried sector.[83] For all the heterogeneity of its individual members' sensibilities and attitudes, the Society boasted a strong social homogeneity. This enabled the members to thrash out their differences in terms they could all understand and in an atmosphere that gave some coherence to their debates and a sense of basic solidity beneath all their differences on particular issues. The social and institutional structure of the Society was sometimes too solid for the liking of certain members, but it was never as stolid as they — or later observers — tried to make out. The Socialist League and the S.D.F., on the other hand, had none of the same sense of social solidity; and, if not exactly stolid, offered rather fewer beguilements for any of the classes of men and women to which they directed their socialist message.

Evidence of artistic activities or organized entertainments on the part of the S.D.F. is relatively thin (though we only have its newspaper, *Justice*, to go on for any regular information about its meetings). There is more evidence of such things scattered through the extant archives of the Socialist League; though, apart from a series of 'weekly entertainments' organized in aid of a strike fund in 1888,[84] its artistic activities appear to have been rather sporadic, *ad hoc* affairs. Those of the Fabian Society were organized (or at least recorded) more regularly and systematically, as befitted the more formal and elaborate club-like structure which it contrived to build up for itself. As it approached maturity in the first decade of the twentieth century — a stage to which the League never got — the Fabian Society even encouraged the setting-up of various sub-groups, or clubs-within-a-club, that catered specifically, if not exclusively, for the artistic interest of members. The Fabian Arts Group was but one of these; there were others, such as the Stage Society and the Fabian Summer Schools, which were much less fractious and gave further solidity to the Society in a far from stolid way. They helped make it fun to be a Fabian.

The existence of such groups also meant that there was less dependence on a few leaders to keep things going. As the experience of the League showed, when the Avelings and Bax defected after a few years, leaving Morris to contend with the more unruly, anarchist elements which it had attracted, leaders could not always be depended upon to retain their enthusiasm or sustain sufficient dynamism. If the League eventually foundered for want of sufficiently strong leaders, the S.D.F. always suffered from having an excessively dominating one in Hyndman. The Fabian Society, with its various committees and groups, seems to have struck a fairly workable balance at most times, even if the situation was not always as stable as Shaw described it in 1892:

if you consider that we are all persons of strong individuality and very diverse temperaments, and take along with that the fact that no one of us is strong enough to impose his
will on the rest, or weak enough to allow himself to be overridden, you will . . . allow me
to claim our escape from the quarrels which have rent asunder both the Federation and
the League as a proof that our methods do stand the test of experience in the matter of
keeping our forces together.[85]

The Fabian Society, as we shall see, even had the physical ambience of a rather exclusive club — in London, at least, where its greatest strengths always lay. (Provincial branches, while numerous, were mainly ephemeral.) Its meetings were able to retain an attractiveness for members by their style at least as much as by their content. This was one of the keys to its fortitude.

Yet in spite of the comforts, refinement and sheer fun of so many of the Society's gatherings, it has acquired a reputation for asceticism as well as for philistinism — in its socialist schemes and visions, if not in its own social practices. Was there, in fact, any such disjunction between its principles and its practices? Again, a study of the Society's artistic attitudes and activities provides some particularly illuminating insights. It allows us to see how this group approached the whole question of pleasure (artistic and otherwise) in their own lives and in their conceptions of a future socialist society.

My hope is that such insights will make the Fabians themselves more pleasurable to read about and will invest their ideas and actions with a fresh significance.

PART I

---

*The literary and artistic origins
of Fabian socialism*

1

Thomas Davidson, the New Life Fellowship and the earliest Fabians

The origins of the Fabian Society, as an institution, are still a matter of dispute.[1] The dispute centres on the precise relationship of the Society to a closely allied London coterie — the Fellowship of the New Life. One of these organizations began its independent existence by splitting off from the other, but uncertainties over the date of the official foundation of the Fellowship have made it difficult to tell which of the two bodies was the 'parent' and which the progeny that formally broke away. To attempt a full re-examination of this question here would be irrelevant to our present purpose, which is to focus not on the precise origins of the Fabian Society as an institution but, rather, on some neglected aspects of the general origins of Fabianism as represented by the ideas and activities of its early members. The significant fact to be kept in mind here is that personal or 'family' links of some substance existed between the members of the Fabian Society and the Fellowship of the New Life, and that these were never completely severed.

Whichever organization may be regarded as the immediate parent body, it is clear that the progenitor of both was an informal group of earnest middle-class young men who arranged meetings in London in 1882 and 1883 to converse with, and discuss the ideas of, a 'wandering scholar' and sage, Thomas Davidson. Of Scottish birth, Davidson had long been a resident of America, but was currently visiting England in order to enlist support for his ideal of a secular brotherhood devoted to the attainment of ethical perfection in its members and ultimately throughout all society. Those earnest young Englishmen who were attracted by Davidson's personality and by his general vision of the regeneration of mankind were by no means uncritical of all his assumptions and specific schemes. The eventual emergence of two organizations from the informal group which clustered round him in 1882-3 only confirmed differences in approach and emphasis that had arisen in the group almost from the outset.

One of the main differences, and that which led directly to the division of the Fabian Society and the Fellowship of the New Life, was over the question of how Davidson's vision of human regeneration could be implemented. There were participants in some of the earliest discussions of his ideas in England who doubted the practicability of any scheme to foster ethical perfection in society through the example and agency of a few select individuals gathered together into a brotherhood. Those dissidents — who included a number of early members of the Fabian Society such as Frank Podmore, Edward Pease, H.H. Champion, Hubert Bland — seem to have felt that ethical deficiencies were not the first nor the only ones of their age which needed to be rectified. They attempted to bring to the forefront of the group's attention rather more mundane, but also more immediately pressing, economic problems, such as the 'prevailing modes of money-making', based on 'speculative trading', which they felt were responsible for serious inequities in the distribution of wealth.[2] Basic material deficiencies, and the economic evils they stemmed from, had to be tackled before the more exalted campaigns for regenerating humanity could be launched. An active crusade for material improvements throughout society would be a much more effective means of fulfilling these immediate tasks than a contemplative movement for the moral and spiritual uplift of the individual self.

The attempt by certain sections of Davidson's original following in England to modify the intensity of the group's ethical preoccupations did not escape vigorous counter-criticism from other, more orthodox quarters. Davidson himself had some doubts and reservations at this stage, but they did not reflect that extreme moral purism which he was later to develop. For the present he was able to accept, at least in theory, the need for preparatory social and economic measures.[3] The more purist members of his group, however, tried to alert him from early on to the limitations of those who wanted to concentrate on the practical business of effecting such measures. Thus Percival Chubb, a government clerk and the youngest of the group, confided in Davidson that he felt 'fellows like Pease and Podmore' were 'not of the right fibre for such a movement as ours'. He criticized Pease in particular for not carrying 'anything of the ideal about with him' and made out that the material nature of such men's strategies for solving the problems of society and mankind reflected the truth of a criticism by Emerson on the limitations of the routine reformer. It is worth requoting the criticism in question. Reformers, claimed the American philosopher, 'affirm the inward life...but use outward and vulgar means...The reforms...are quickly organized in some low, inadequate form, and present no more poetic image to the mind, than the evil tradition which they reprobated.'[4]

The materialist, prosaic image of the Fabians and their reform schemes can be traced back, it appears, to a time even before the official foundation of the Society. The criticisms, however, which Chubb bases on this image are rather diminished in force by the fact that he himself became an active, if initially sceptical, member of the Fabian Society[5] while at the same time remaining within the ranks of those who formed the Fellowship of the New Life. Chubb was not alone in his double allegiance: he mentioned that 'several' others had followed suit.[6] He gave no names and the bulk of those he was referring to probably remained fairly anonymous within both organizations. But there are more striking examples later on of men who belonged simultaneously to the Fabian Society and to the Fellowship, achieving prominence inside and outside these bodies by writing and lecturing on their behalf (William Clarke, J.F. Oakeshott, H.S. Salt and the young Ramsay MacDonald can be included in this category). These examples suggest a pattern of overlapping membership right up until the demise of the Fellowship in 1898.

The mere presence of 'New Lifers' in the Fabian Society makes it difficult to understand how the Society has acquired the reputation of being entirely materialist in its aims and schemes and of lacking any idealistic or 'poetic' side to its conception of how mankind and society might be improved. Unless it could be shown that these members contrived or were forced to suppress their poetic idealism when working for the Fabian Society, it is impossible to see how that aspect of their sensibility could have been kept from continually elevating Fabian thought and activity above the mundane.

There is no sign of any such contrivance or coercion. It is true that the factions in Davidson's original discussion group which grew into the Fabian Society and the Fellowship of the New Life became quite independent of each other as organizations, rarely coming into formal contact. But this never involved — and was never intended to involve[7] — any kind of mutual exclusiveness. In the assumptions and aspirations of the two groups, as well as in their respective membership, there were many signs of a continuing affinity; and these show clearly that the Fabian Society, for all its concentration on quite mundane economic and social problems, did not outgrow its idealistic roots or lose all 'poetic' vision. Distinctly aesthetic as well as ethical and spiritual roots can be seen beneath the surface of the Fabians' economic and social schemes; and their ideas in those fields were not divorced from high ideals, themselves partly aesthetic in nature.

In a letter written to Thomas Davidson nearly a year after the formation of the Fabian Society, we have a small but striking portent of the affinities which continued to exist between that organization and the Fellowship of the New Life. The writer was Frank Podmore, whom Percival Chubb had stigmatized, in an earlier letter to Davidson, as a most unsuitable member of the sage's circle in London. Podmore had been prominent among the dissidents in that circle, had then left it altogether, and not only joined the Fabian Society but actually gave that body its name.[8] Yet he could now be found confessing to Davidson, who had recently returned to America to found a branch of the New Life Fellowship there: 'England cannot afford to lose you altogether. Won't you...live out your more than four score years in London? Won't you write a letter to us at the Fabian? We look upon you as our founder and should be glad to hear from you. And we need your sober and wise counsel.'[9]

Davidson did not heed the plea to return to England, though Podmore's attempt at this stage to tap the sympathies of the old mentor was not just a vain, placatory gesture. At this stage, Davidson was not nearly so hostile to socialism as he later became.[10]

Eventually, his native aversion to the materialist aspects and economic concerns of socialism led him to denounce indiscriminately the 'low tone' of its current exponents and the 'disintegrating' impulse behind their policies, which, he claimed, 'point to nothing and lead to nothing'.[11] This aversion became so strong that even the efforts of the New Life Fellowship to give prominence to the 'ethical side of life, as paramount to the merely economic' did not entirely satisfy him. Commenting on the first number of their monthly journal, the *Sower* (later *Seed-time*), he said: 'I should have been glad to see even a stronger insistence on the nobler side, and a yet clearer expression of the fact that economic relations form but one and a subordinate department of ethical life.'[12] Those slight inadequacies, from Davidson's viewpoint, can be readily appreciated by examining the Editorial Preface to the journal and the column which gave a résumé of the Fellowship's aims. The editorial stated that 'political and social re-organization...to be satisfactory must be accompanied by a moral regeneration' — which was not the same as saying that such reorganization should only be the secondary aim. The actual résumé of aims, given on another page, made no explicit reference to morals or ethics at all; and, in prescribing general principles such as 'Freedom', 'Equality' and 'Brotherhood', seemed to indicate that the realization of these in everyday life was not simply an end in itself but also a way of assisting, 'in a very necessary manner', the 'wider political and social movement which seeks to replace the present competition [*sic*] society, with all its injustices, by a co-operative commonwealth'.[13] That the Fellowship should have betrayed this much concern with the political, social and economic aspects of human regeneration is a clear sign, on its own behalf, of continuing affinities with the Fabians, or at least of a partial coincidence of interests between the two bodies.

In spite of his ever-mounting distaste for these more mundane pursuits, Thomas Davidson himself claimed paternity of the Fabian Society in retrospect.[14] To accept this sort of claim literally would be to oversimplify the intricate processes by which the Society came into being, but, in an indirect sense, it is not entirely unjustified. Even if he was not regarded as a father-figure by all the early Fabians — in the way Frank Podmore tried to suggest — it is clear that some of them looked on him as one of the strongest formative influences on the development of their thought.

As early as 1882 — probably the first year of their acquaintance — Percival Chubb stressed the 'peace, comfort and inspiration' which Davidson had already brought him; and nine years later Chubb talked of his 'great indebtedness' to Davidson and the 'invaluable helpfulness' which the latter had provided 'both in material and spiritual ways'. This testimony was all the more remarkable in that it coincided with a period of considerable tension between the two men, owing in part to Davidson's irritation at Chubb's socialist activities while visiting America.[15] A much earlier testimony — that of William Clarke — had a similar ironical twist. He wrote to Davidson: 'I have derived much good from your suggestions on social reform, and shall try to elaborate them and work them out.'[16] This letter dates back to about a year before the official foundation of the Fabian Society when Clarke was a relatively unknown journalist who participated, at Davidson's invitation, in the discussion group which later spawned the Fabian Society and the New Life Fellowship.[17] After an initial resistance to any form of socialism — not untempered by a sympathy with and admiration for particular socialists[18] — he eventually joined the Fabians in 1886 and became prominent enough in their ranks to be asked to write the chapter on 'The Industrial Basis' for the Society's most illustrious publication, *Fabian Essays in Socialism*. He had always entertained reservations — as deep as Davidson's at times — concerning any movement in society which threatened to subvert or subordinate 'ethics and the spiritual side of things'.[19] These had not only inhibited him from committing himself wholeheartedly to socialism at the time of its 'rebirth' in England in the early eighties; they also constituted an important reason for his disenchantment with and abandonment of the cause in the mid-nineties.[20] It is singular, then, that he should have cited 'social reform', rather than concerns of a more overtly spiritual nature, as the area in which Davidson provided especial stimulation and guidance for him. The old philosopher may well have winced at this in later years, but it is a token of the breadth of his influence. Unwittingly, he may have helped prepare Clarke for the young man's eventual acceptance of Fabian socialism by providing him with a personal demonstration of the possibility of attending to 'social reform' issues without surrendering to materialism. With Davidson's reassuring example in view, the further leap into full-scale socialism might have appeared so much less risky.

Another contributor to the *Fabian Essays* who had once been part of Davidson's discussion group consciously recognized the latter's potent influence even on the dissident faction within that group which had founded the Fabian Society: 'the little knot of men', Hubert Bland recalled,

who in the winter of 1883 met in Mr. Pease's rooms and who, a few months later, founded this Society, came there . . . with minds fresh from contact with the mind of Thomas Davidson . . . Many of the qualities that are most traditionally characteristic of our society — its dislike of exaggeration, its contempt for the gaseous and the flatulent, its suspicion of the mawkishly sentimental, its impatience of pretentious formulas . . . the critical attitude of its corporate mind, are largely due to his impress.[21]

On the whole, Davidson's general influence on early Fabian socialism is likely to have been stronger in those less mundane areas where his own interests were really engaged. Art, specifically, constituted one of these areas of interest, intimately related as it was in his mind to ethics, religion and philosophy. Though at times[22] he explicitly subordinated art to these other concerns, it was so passionate and wide-ranging an interest in itself that it is difficult to see how anyone drawn into Davidson's intellectual circles could have escaped its impress.[23] In a lecture he gave on 'The Significance of Art', he admitted readily that he was 'not an artist' himself, 'knowing very little of the methods and technicalities of practical art'.[24] This was not to deny his theoretical knowledge or critical appreciation; and the comments of contemporaries show clearly how his pre-occupation with art, simply on this theoretical level, was sufficiently powerful to appear as an important component force of his world-view and as a determinant of his whole cast of mind. Thus William Knight, who edited some 'Memorials' of Davidson in 1907 written by English and American colleagues, claimed in his introduction to the collection that the late philosopher's basic aim had been 'to present to the world a new example of "plain living and high thinking" by the courageous pursuit and advocacy of truth . . . and by the realization of the beautiful in Art and of the good in life'.[25] In another memorial, a fellow-philosopher, William James, observed of Davidson that 'he never outgrew those habits of judging by purely aesthetic criteria, which men fed more upon the sciences of nature are so willing to dispense with'.[26]

Davidson's particular artistic interests seem to have been literature and sculpture; and the direct impact that his exploration of such topics could have on the artistic views of his disciples is reflected in comments on his book, *The Parthenon Frieze*, made by Percival Chubb. That work appeared in 1882 and presented a comprehensive and highly technical interpretation of various specimens of Greek sculpture and building (not just the eponymous item), as well as an essay on Sophocles' *Oedipus Rex*. Soon after the publication of Davidson's book, Chubb wrote to the author: 'I feel highly interested in the subjects of your essays, both in their bearing upon Art and in their bearing upon ancient Greece . . . I am only sorry that my total lack of scholarship will prevent me from doing justice to the book. . . I am anxious to learn all that it has to teach.'[27]

Some nine years later, Chubb had learned so much more from independent explorations of artistic works and subjects as to be able to challenge Davidson's authority, in a gentle fashion, on the question of art's relationship to morality and the role of society in determining this. Davidson had developed a strong bias against 'Romantic art',[28] most of which he hardly considered worthy of the name, and he now evidently sensed an actual 'enmity between art and morality'. Because he neglected, in Chubb's eyes at any rate, to relate this enmity to prevailing social conditions, he seemed to be in danger of diminishing the total weight of 'significance' that he had attached to art; and Chubb felt bound to protest against the implication that 'art, as such and in its pure idea' meant no more than ' "self-embellishment" ' or 'that it has actually meant this with a great number of artists'.[29]

If Davidson, in his later exchanges with Chubb, was really in danger of denigrating all art out of a mounting suspicion and dislike of its more recent specimens, other comments of his at the time (and in following years) were much less drastic in their implications. It must be remembered, moreover, that Chubb's very protest against any such denigration stemmed in part from the seeds of enthusiasm and understanding which Davidson himself had first implanted.

There are other ways, connected more specifically with the origins of Fabianism, in which Davidson's discussions of art and of various artists may have provided an initial guide and inspiration to his young followers. *The Parthenon Frieze*, in concentrating on classical Greek sculpture and drama, typified Davidson's especial love for this period, which he characterized elsewhere[30] as the stage of 'highest development' in the history of art. This was a very broad generalization, however, as his view of art history following this peak in the fifth and fourth centuries B.C. was not one of simple decline into the trough of modern romanticism. In the same year that Chubb challenged Davidson on his apparent denigration of art and artists, Davidson was writing that in certain fields — painting, poetry and music — 'we moderns. . . far excel the ancients as they excel us in the other arts'. He cited Raphael, Dante and Beethoven as three outstanding examples of artists who had 'no rivals' among the ancients.[31] Davidson's reverence for Dante in particular was well known through his many writings and lectures on the Italian poet; and his ability to transmit that reverence to his disciples is hinted at in the very name — 'The New Life' — by which some of them chose to call their brotherhood. This was an English rendering of 'La Vita Nuova', the title of Dante's first major work, and an allusion to the experience of youthful human love and the visions and spiritual insights opened up by that love.

In Davidson's eyes, 'love', together with 'holiness', served to define the basis of the great contributions to art in the modern, as distinct from the ancient, period; while spiritual insight, in the sense of an awareness of 'man's inner nature', formed the basis of all art, which was the expression of that nature 'imprinted upon matter' so as to appeal to the senses. Material imprints of 'outward nature' *per se* — of the merely 'physical forces, whether in nature or man' — were not sufficient to constitute true art. The authority Davidson invoked to support his conception of true and false art was another artist of the 'modern' period whom he particularly revered: Goethe. He clinched his argument on the distinction between art and nature with the words: 'Art, as Goethe says, is called Art just because it is not nature.'[32]

This is a quotation from Goethe's novel, *Wilhelm Meister, Wanderjahre*;[33] and it is interesting that the same maxim should be quoted to clinch a similar argument by one of the most prominent artists ever to become active within the Fabian Society: the painter, handicrafts designer and book-illustrator, Walter Crane.[34] He had doubtless happened upon the quotation independently. Certainly, any connections through the Fabian Society were far too tenuous to account for the parallel. Crane became a Fabian towards the end of 1885, and there is no evidence that he had any prior associations with Davidson or his discussion group. The parallel, however, cannot be dismissed as pure coincidence, with no bearing on Fabianism. There is evidence to suggest that an engagement with such questions, and the use of such sources, were common among the early Fabians, and that for those members who had formed a part of his original discussion group, Davidson may have acted as the transmitter of Goethe's works, sparking off or at least consolidating[35] an interest in them as he had in the case of Dante's and those of classical Greek artists. Percival Chubb's early correspondence with Davidson contained several scattered references to the German poet and his concepts of culture and education. Chubb had reservations about certain aspects of Goethe's thought; but his general tone was admiring, and the criticisms he made were usually based on what he perceived to be limitations, rather than intrinsic fallacies, in that thought.[36] Whether criticizing or praising Goethe, Chubb was always aware of the possible application of the artist's notions and procedures to purposes and ends beyond the purely artistic.

There was a striking instance of this in a letter he wrote to Davidson a year after the Fabian Society was formed. Referring to a programme of study which he proposed to set himself, he claimed: 'My first German and *Sociological* task combined will be reading in the original Goethe's "Wilhelm Meister" — & giving careful study to the "Wanderjahre" — this having so particular a bearing upon our V.[ita] N.[uova] scheme.'[37] Chubb probably meant here that some direct practical guidance in setting up the sort of community to which the New Life Fellowship aspired might be gained from Goethe's novel. It contained various models of communities or 'unions' (social and economic, pedagogical and artistic) either observed in operation by the title character on his wanderings or worked out as plans and projects by him and his friends in their attempts to renounce a purely individualist basis for living. The novel was sub-titled (in the well-known version by Carlyle) 'The Renunciants'. Chubb might also have been alluding to this renunciation theme, which is touched on variously in several of Goethe's earlier works, but is here developed fully and explicitly with quite distinct 'sociological' overtones. The sum of what Wilhelm learns from his wanderings is given in the words of his friend, Leonardo: 'a man . . . is not, as an individual, sufficient for himself, and to an honest mind, society remains the highest want. All serviceable persons ought to be related with each other.' The society envisaged is a world brotherhood of countrymen and townsmen, based on co-operative and collective effort in useful occupations and handicrafts, and entailing the sacrifice of private concerns for the sake of the community, and ultimately of the individual himself. While in no way a specifically 'socialist' brotherhood, it has definite political dimensions which distinguish it clearly from any anarchist schemes: 'all forms of government' are to be respected, 'since every one of them induces and promotes a calculated activity, to labour according to the wish and will of constituted authorities'.[38]

If the sociological implications of Goethe's work had, in Chubb's words, a 'particular bearing' upon the practices of the New Life Fellowship, the closely related political implications had at least a general bearing on the principles of the Fabian Society, of which Chubb was also a member when he wrote these words. His letter to Davidson can be taken, in fact, as an implicit reaffirmation of the overlapping and complementary concerns of the 'New Lifers' and the Fabians. Sidney Webb explicitly echoed Goethe's theme of the need for individuals to renounce their own preoccupations and pleasures in serving the larger requirements of the social and political units to which they belonged.[39] He took this theme not from *Wilhelm Meister*, but from *Faust*, where in fact it was treated much more equivocally,[40] and without the overt sociological and political applications to be found in his later treatments of it. It is significant that Webb chose to publish his own elaboration of Goethe's theme in the pages of *Our Corner*, which was effectively a Fabian magazine at that time, edited by a prominent member of the Society, Annie Besant, and carrying articles by several other members as well as a regular column entitled 'Fabian Society and Socialist Notes'. The impact of the ideal of renunciation on the thought and the personal lives of Webb and his Fabian colleagues will be examined more fully in other chapters, with particular relation to the artistic attitudes and activities of that group.

No doubt Webb, like Walter Crane, came across Goethe's work without any assistance from Thomas Davidson. The acquaintance with the German's writings may even have dated back to Webb's schooldays, part of which were spent under a Lutheran pastor in Germany. Webb met Davidson briefly in America in 1888 and was impressed by him,[41] but there is no record of any earlier acquaintance. It is quite likely, on the other hand, that Davidson served as an important channel of Goethean ideas for Chubb, who had been one of the sage's earliest, youngest and closest disciples in England and who was evidently without a mastery of German until the mid-1880s. Perhaps under Davidson's influence, he had begun to learn German, as well as Italian and Greek, in 1882 or thereabouts.[42] He may, of course, have read Goethe's works in translation earlier on, including the Carlyle version of *Wilhelm Meister*, but the personal inspiration and example provided by Davidson — who, incidentally, derided Carlyle's translation[43] — would still have been a potent stimulus. William Clarke, another early disciple who went on to become an active Fabian, recalled his mentor as the living embodiment of Goethe's wandering scholar: 'Thomas Davidson would have delighted Goethe; the *Wanderjahre* of Wilhelm Meister was Davidson's own life.'[44]

In view of his own strongly avowed, if only vaguely explained, contempt for romantic art, Davidson's deep attachment to Goethe seems puzzling. It is true that Goethe's own attitude to romanticism was ambivalent, and that he would certainly have disowned the 'arch-romantic' label which some (mainly hostile) critics tried to pin on him.[45] Davidson at one stage went close to denying that Goethe had any romanticist inclinations at all, claiming that the German poet's vision (unlike his translator, Carlyle's) was 'undimmed' by such heresies, and that his thinking rested 'upon a basis of eternal reason'.[46] It was no doubt difficult to maintain such a thesis when dealing in detail with the philosophy of Goethe's *Faust*, which was the subject of six lectures given by Davidson in Boston in 1896. In that play, one of the central principles and procedures of romanticism had formed the basis of the whole action: the attainment of knowledge and the search for the highest truths of existence through direct and continual emotional experience on the part of the individual, rather than through a detached rationality. 'Feeling is all', the title character went so far as to proclaim on one occasion — a slogan which, especially out of context, has done much in itself to account for the play's reputation as a 'bible of Romanticism',[47] and which certainly highlights and encapsulates those elements in Goethe that Davidson had elsewhere ignored. Davidson could not ignore them when dealing specifically with *Faust*. In fact, in one of his lectures on the play, he conceded that the 'romantic tendency was always strong in Goethe'. He argued that while this put several of the German's works into the 'second', rather than the first, class of literature and that while it was responsible for particular excesses and flaws in *Faust*, this play remained a serious and powerful philosophic work, with many passages of 'great poetic value and beauty'.[48]

This represented something of a retreat from his position that 'Romanticism has no Art'; though even at the height of his attack on that doctrine he had admitted to a weakness at one stage in his life for 'Swinburne, and Keats, and Byron and Shelley', for fruit-pictures and landscapes and genre-paintings. He had now 'left off' such indulgences — 'all those fake works of Art which do not represent the divine in the world' — and devoted himself instead to a study of Greek sculpture and a 'thorough re-perusal of the Greek tragedians, of Dante, Shakespeare and Goethe'. In this way, Art had come 'daily' to have 'a deeper and greater significance' for him. It is ironical, however, that the change in his reading should have accorded in part with the prescriptions of one whom he himself had stigmatized as 'the embodiment of the romantic spirit'.[49] 'Close thy *Byron*; open thy *Goethe* ... Love not pleasure; love God': these twin pleas had appeared within a paragraph of each other in Carlyle's *Sartor Resartus*, and were both explicitly related there to the ideal of 'Renunciation' which Goethe's work was to impress on Sidney Webb in a slightly different form over fifty years later.[50]

It is uncertain, then, whether Davidson by repudiating the elements of hedonism and profanity in romantic art completely exorcised within himself the romantic spirit he saw in Carlyle. The imperatives that can be found in the latter's own work to repudiate such elements is an indication of the complexities and inherent ambiguities of romanticism.[51] While asserting the claims of the individual's emotions and feelings in attaining a knowledge of the universe — as distinct from the powers of 'reason' celebrated by the *philosophes* of the Enlightenment[52] — the romanticists did not always or necessarily countenance the free rein of those emotions, but could urge that the individual voluntarily contain some of them in his own ultimate interests, spiritual as well as material. Reason itself was a useful check; and was by no means completely derided by the romanticists.[53] Davidson's rejection of what he saw as the hedonistic excesses and spiritual deficiencies of certain exponents of romanticism could be seen as a self-corrective that was part of the romanticist tradition itself. The question of Davidson's vestigial romanticism is obviously important to any examination of his role as a source or filter of ideas, artistic and otherwise, for the early Fabians.

A vivid testimony to the pervasiveness of romanticism in the nineteenth century, to its irresistible intrusiveness, was its appearance in the works of a writer like Goethe, who had been reared on the ideals and forms of eighteenth-century neo-classicism, with its basis in what

Davidson termed 'eternal reason' and its dependence on strict rules of decorum and generic hierarchies in the arts.[54] Davidson, as we have seen, having himself formed a deep attachment to classicist ideals and forms, both in their original and more recent variants, tended to exaggerate the extent of their continuing hold over Goethe, until in confronting *Faust* he was eventually forced to recognize the strength of the competing romanticist stream. That he could still view the play with a large measure of sympathy, and certain parts of it with great admiration, adds doubts as to whether he ever fully succeeded in cutting himself off from the pervasive force of that stream.

The doubts are confirmed when we consider the admiration he showed at various stages of his career for artists and philosophers whose immersion in romanticism was more complete and wholehearted than Goethe's — Wordsworth, Tennyson, Browning, Emerson, Ruskin and Morris among them.[55] It is true that Davidson's conscious anti-romanticist bias never deserted him: he proclaimed it again, only two years before his death, in a book he published on Rousseau's educational ideas. At the outset of this, he made clear his preference for the 'ancient, classical and social education', epitomized in Aristotle's system, to the 'modern, romantic and unsocial Education' originating with Rousseau. He argued that the latter was based upon 'the private tastes and preferences of an exceptionally capricious and self-centred nature': it was a system which encouraged the mere 'animal spontaneity' of its deviser by training men to 'enjoy the maximum of feeling with as little reflection and restraint as may be' and to aim only at 'sensuous well-being without moral regard' or any 'rational organization of the feelings'.[56] In advocating restraint or renunciation, he countered Rousseau by citing Goethe, just as Carlyle (and Davidson himself) had countered Byron. Again, it does not seem to have occurred to Davidson that the course he advocated and the authority he cited in support of that course might have represented Romanticism in a self-critical mood as much as mere anti-romanticism.[57]

Davidson's reproof of Byron, Carlyle and Rousseau, explicitly in connection with their romanticist doctrines, should not be allowed to drown out his praise of other exponents whose association with the movement he usually failed to acknowledge or to see. That very failure can be taken as a measure of his own involuntary or unconscious attachment to certain romanticist traditions. Implicitly, at least, he shared some of the characteristic, if not peculiar, preoccupations of the movement.

The renunciation theme was but one of these. Its injunctions to refrain from hedonistic excess and merely self-directed pleasure found a positive side in the praises of the 'simple life', sung in various moods and modes by Ruskin and Morris and their disciples in England, as well as by

Emerson and his compatriots, Thoreau and Whitman, on the other side of the Atlantic.[58] Davidson spent long periods of his life studying in America as well as in England; and his aim, as described in his Memorials, to set an example of 'plain living and high thinking' was no doubt a partial reflection of his exposure in both countries to the pronouncements of these fervent champions of renunciation and simplification.

As noted above, the example in life he tried to set specifically involved the 'realization of the beautiful in Art'. Though he singled out the art produced by the contemporary romantic movement for some of his most clamorous denunciations against that movement, there remained points of sympathy and agreement between Davidson and various romanticist conceptions of art which were no less substantial for being unstated. Perhaps the most important of these concerned the question of the relationship between art and nature. There were many differences among romantic artists in their conceptions of nature, but all of them seem to have shared a reaction against the eighteenth-century notion of a 'mechanistic universe'. They saw nature as an 'organic whole' rather than as a 'concourse of atoms', the whole incorporating and reflecting not only 'abstractions of science' but also 'aesthetic values', linked to the creative powers and perceptual faculties of individual men. These values in nature were not readily appreciable behind the surface workings of nature, and it was the justification of art that it served to body them forth through the use of symbol and metaphor.[59] Davidson's own conception of the significance of art *vis-à-vis* nature accords largely with this view.

We have seen that he followed Goethe in making clear that true art was not the same as nature, or a mere image of nature's outward aspects. This distinction in no way implied a divorce between the two phenomena, but was a token rather of the depths and intricacies of their interdependence. The great function of art, according to Davidson, was to reveal 'the soul within nature' — that is, the powers 'whose action and reaction weave the sensible universe with all its wonder and all its mystery'.[60] If art largely depended on nature for its subject-matter, nature depended on art for the revelation of its most basic designs.

At times, Davidson's views on the relationship between art and nature led him into arguing against classicism, in at least quasi-romanticist terms. In a paper on education — of uncertain date, but adapted for publication in a volume of his writings which appeared posthumously in 1904 — he claimed: 'Only those works of art and literature which are directly dictated by nature appeal to us directly. Shakspeare and Burns are forever fresh, Milton and Pope who drew their inspiration from classical literature, are already consigned to the museum of literary history. Human experience is the great art school.' Though he did not make his meaning clear, Davidson would no doubt have drawn back from any

exclusive association of 'human experience' with emotional 'feeling' and
its impact; but his conception of the role and limitations of such non-
rational forces would still fit in fairly easily with all but the most extreme
romanticist position on these questions. Summing up the nature of 'the
will' at one point, he argued that it was 'little more than the combined
expression of the rational and irrational elements in the soul . . . the sum of
the irrational impulses directed by rational insight'. And at another point
he went so far as to state that 'Intellectual convictions are feeble motives
to action, compared with affections.'[61]

Davidson's very confusion on such issues probably encouraged his
disciples to wrestle with them in their own minds. Percival Chubb, for
one, in his correspondence with Davidson, was able to arrive at a more
clear-headed view of romanticism. While he was sceptical of any primacy
ascribed to the role of feeling in human behaviour, this did not lead him
into a prejudice against romanticism as such. He appreciated the distinction between the basic current of the movement and its wilder excesses —
its 'overdone' manifestations in certain works of art, for example; and he
objected only to these excesses.[62] In general, as we shall see, he perceived
the great debt which his own ideas, and those of his fellow-Fabians, owed
to the impact of various romanticist (as well as post-romanticist and
avowedly anti-romanticist) writers and artists.

Such influences have seldom figured largely in discussions of the
Fabians. Debates on the sources of their thought have centred on the
question of the relative impact of John Stuart Mill, T.H. Green, Auguste
Comte and Karl Marx — men who were primarily political economists or
political philosophers, albeit ones who showed considerable concern with
cultural questions as an integral part of their major preoccupations. It is
undoubtedly important to assess how far the Fabian Society's ideas and
policies accorded with or reacted against the utilitarian, idealist, positivist
and revolutionary-socialist traditions of political and economic thought.
From the outset, this organization had made politics and economics, in
relation to the present condition of society, its dominant concern, and had
consciously distinguished itself in this way from its progenitor — the
discussion group which gathered round Thomas Davidson in the early
1880s. Historians however, have concentrated on this concern to such a
degree that they have given insufficient attention to what the Society may
have shared with its progenitor, in terms of sources and traditions which
were not purely or directly political and economic. This neglect has led to
the impression that literary and artistic sources of the kind which
Davidson drew upon had no real bearing on Fabian thought, and that
Fabian sensibilities were somehow alien to, or at least untouched by, the
romanticist tradition.[63]

The origins — if not the nature — of Fabian political and economic thought have thereby been distorted or partly obscured. The influences which Fabians themselves looked back on as facilitating the spread of socialism in England and the texts which we know them to have read in their formative years included a large array of literary or artistic works in the romanticist tradition, as well as works of political economy and political philosophy reflecting different or opposing traditions. In fact, Fabian thought can be seen to reflect at least the possibilities of *rapproche- ment* between these various traditions. Its development and nature should alert us to the oversimplifications involved in depicting the relationship between romanticist and utilitarian ideas as completely antithetical, just as the development of William Morris's thought should prevent us from making too sharp a division between romanticism and Marxism. The Fabians cannot be said to have achieved as complete an integration of the traditions they drew upon as Morris is said to have achieved;[64] it is hard to see how a true and full blending could ever be effected between utilitarianism and the romanticist critique of utilitarian philosophy. Yet the admixture of the two which can be discerned in the Fabians' thought, particularly in that of the early members of the Society, was obviously not unfruitful in developing socialist ideas. As we shall see, they derived much inspiration from Morris himself, and though the romanticist element in their thought never acquired the same revolutionary impetus or colouring as it did in his, their type of romanticism cannot be dismissed as conserva- tive, regressive or escapist either.

Chubb, in an article contributed in 1887 to a periodical edited by his fellow-Fabian, Hubert Bland, claimed that certain recent literary and artistic sources were of more fundamental importance in the development of the socialist movement in England than any other kind. That movement, he stated,

draws its vital force, not from its economists, its Marx and his coadjutors; these are its enlighteners, but not its inspirers and instigators. These latter we find in names such as Wordsworth, Shelley, Byron, Carlyle, Emerson, Dickens, Ruskin, George Eliot, Thoreau, Whitman and the younger Swinburne who have quickened and nourished in us a deeper sense of human dignity, a more exacting demand for freedom, a keener susceptibility to beauty and recoil from ugliness, a wider sympathy, and more uniting spirit of comrade- ship. Out of the influences of these men it has grown; and such a kindred influence must continue to sustain or impel it.[65]

The importance of certain literary and artistic sources to other groups within the socialist and labour movement of the late nineteenth and early twentieth centuries — especially working-class groups — has at least been recognized, if not adequately discussed, by contemporary observers and historians alike.[66] Chubb's statement of the importance of such sources is clearly meant to apply as much to his own, predominantly middle-class socialist group as to any other, and is the earliest affirmation of this kind that we have. Yet it has gone unremarked by historians of that group, some of whom have simply accepted the retrospective claims of other Fabians (Shaw, Pease[67]) that the Society never had any time for artistic sources of this kind and that its members remained oblivious of the work of writers like Ruskin.[68] Chubb's emphasis on the relative importance of such sources was unusually strong and open to the charge of over-generalization, but he was certainly not alone among the Fabians in attributing a formative influence to creative writers of this kind.

In 1911, Ramsay MacDonald, who had been a colleague of Chubb's in the early New Life Fellowship and Fabian Society, observed that 'some of the best literary and artistic work' of the previous century has served as 'drum taps to which the steps of Socialism kept time'. The works he had in mind were not produced by socialists themselves (a socialist artist, like William Morris, was something of an 'exception', he pointed out); but in their 'protest against commercialism' these works and their creators had represented a 'powerful tendency in the direction of Socialism'. It was the role of socialism to give that protest a more 'definite and constructive' shape. The examples he gave of artists who had exercised an especially powerful inspiration on the development of socialism included some which Chubb had singled out: Wordsworth, Dickens, Carlyle, Ruskin. MacDonald also added more recent examples — Meredith, Hardy, Tolstoy, Ibsen, Turgenev, Anatole France — and included artists from outside the field of literature, such as Burne-Jones, Watts, and the founders of the arts and crafts movement. Representatives in various ways of the forces of 'romanticism, culture, humanism', all of these artists had 'declined to accept the companionship of commercialism'. Those 'other types of mind' who had been inspired by them 'brought down from the empyrean into the fogs and dust of the day, their thoughts and prophecies, their criticisms and their dreams and Socialism was the result'.[69]

A memoir written by Hubert Bland, a few years earlier, of his own journey towards Fabian socialism, could have served as a specific illustration of MacDonald's account. Bland recalled how from early youth he had been disgusted with the 'insistent sordidness and blatant ugliness of our surroundings' and had rebelled against the prevailing 'philistine' complacency towards these surroundings by harking back to the simple and beautiful ideals of the mediaeval past as evoked in Pre-Raphaelite painting and the poetry of William Morris. This pessimistic retreat from the present received 'philosophical justification' from the works of Schopenhauer. Bland sensed, however, that pessimism only bred paralysis; and his recovery from this condition was precipitated by the news that his 'laureate', Morris, had hit upon an alternative (and much more positive) way out of the sordidness of the present. In his maturity, Morris not only harked back to an idealized mediaeval past but also looked forward to a socialist future, surrendering none of his ideals of beauty in the process. Bland followed the example of his old idol: 'I knew,' he claimed, 'that if William Morris was a Socialist, whatever else Socialism might be it would not be ugly, and so I turned to the Socialists.'[70]

Bland mentioned three other individuals who had a powerful impact on the development of his socialist faith: Thomas Davidson (also, as we have seen, an admirer of Morris, sharing at least some of his aesthetic concerns and ideals); Henry George (whose writings on land nationalization were eagerly absorbed by many of the socialist converts of the early 1880s, including Morris himself[71]); and H.M. Hyndman (who originally collaborated with Morris on a book summarizing the 'Principles of Socialism' but later fell out with him over questions of political practice). On reflection, Bland concluded that Hyndman's influence had been the 'predominant factor' in his actual 'conversion to the Socialist faith'.[72] This might be seen as demonstrating the exaggerations in Chubb's view that artistic and literary sources were more influential than overtly political or economic ones, though it is clear that Bland referred to Hyndman here as the immediate catalyst rather than as the original inspiration: his previous acknowledgement of Morris's importance to him in the latter capacity went uncontradicted therefore.

Non-artistic sources of a more fundamental kind were given due emphasis in an article on the Fabian Society, written by William Clarke in 1894. Attempting to sum up the 'general intellectual forces' which had helped 'bring about' the growth of Fabian socialism among 'active young men' in England, Clarke listed six related points, three of which were plainly political or economic in orientation: the exhaustion of the 'older Liberalism', the effective extinction of '*Laissez-faire* individualist political philosophy' or 'philosophic Radicalism', and the death in all but the most 'hidebound' and 'orthodox' quarters in England, of the 'old political economy'. Clarke viewed the third factor specifically as a symptom of 'serious interest in advanced economics', based on 'the influence of German thought'. This was probably an allusion to Marx's *Capital* above all; though whatever the particular sources were, Clarke viewed them as directly influencing the many 'Socialistic' critiques of capitalism produced in England in the eighties and nineties, including the *Fabian Essays in Socialism* and 'half' of the 'Social Science Series' issued by the famous left-wing publishing house, Swann Sonnenschein and Co. He clearly distinguished these factual or quasi-scientific critiques from works such as Edward Bellamy's *Looking Backwards* and Morris's *News from Nowhere*, which he classified as 'romances that might have achieved their popularity simply on the basis of artistic qualities such as their ingenious narrative or charming style'.

It is strange that in discussing here the works which facilitated or signi-

fied the demise of traditional theories of political economy, Clarke should
have made no mention of Ruskin's writings. Elsewhere both he and other
leading Fabians paid ready tribute to the art critic's analysis of the
intimate relationship between beauty, usefulness and human labour, and
to the way in which that analysis had helped overturn orthodox views —
stemming from Adam Smith and David Ricardo — on the sources and
components of national wealth. Three months earlier, for example, Clarke
described explicitly how 'Ruskin's "political economy of art"' had, 'not
only led William Morris and many of the younger English artists to
Socialism' but had also 'undoubtedly affected economic thought among
all but the straitest sect of Ricardian pharisees'.[73]

Certain points, then, in Clarke's summary of the forces behind the
growth of Fabianism appear to have played down, or even ignored, the
role of sources which had any literary bent or artistic ramifications. There
were other points, however, which clearly acknowledged the Fabians'
debt to specific literary and artistic works or which openly asserted the
general influence of these sources. In discussing, for example, the ethical
impulses which made converts to the Fabian faith — impulses that were
now secular, and a faith that centred itself on the world here and now —
Clarke drew attention to the powerful impact of the idea embodied in a
key slogan from Morris's story, *A Dream of John Ball*: 'Fellowship is
heaven, and the lack of fellowship is hell.'[74]

Clarke attributed to Morris an even more direct role in engendering the
'new art feeling' which he felt to be another of the chief forces impelling
earnest young people of the 'cultivated classes' to seek outlets for their
conscience in Fabianism. That feeling he defined as 'a love to be
surrounded by attractive objects' combined with 'an intense hatred of the
smug and respectable'. The influence here of Morris, together with that
of his mentor, Ruskin, and his disciple and colleague, Walter Crane, was
very important because all three men had demonstrated how the
commercialism and profit instinct dominating economic relationships in
contemporary society was quite incompatible with true art. From that
demonstration had grown the conception that 'no person has any right to
inflict an ugly object of any sort on the world, especially for the sake of
making gain out of it'.

Closely associated with the 'new art feeling' as a factor in the growth of
Fabian socialism was what Clarke designated as 'a new spirit in literature'.
This, too, involved a reaction against smugness and respectability in its
urges 'to sound the plummet in the sea of social misery' and to have done
with the genteel make-believe of the 'thinner kind of romantic literature'.
Its products represented a much tougher, more powerfully realistic
school, and included the Russian authors, full of 'intense Socialistic
feeling', as well as a range of American, English and European writers

who had 'powerfully aided the growth . . . not . . . of Socialism, but of the feeling in the soil in which Socialism is easily developed'. Tolstoy, Whitman, Dickens, Carlyle, Ruskin, Arnold, Hugo and Zola were the particular examples cited; and all of them, according to Clarke, were united by an intense 'social feeling' which had 'contributed a distinct element to the expansion and liberation of the minds that have been formed, say during the last twenty years'.[75]

In discussing the revolt of these so-called realists against the 'thinner' kind of romanticism, Clarke did not make the mistake of seeing them, or those whom they influenced, as anti-romantic pure and simple. These mentors, as he indicated, make up 'a curious and medley list', and they defy the rigid categorization used by some critics, who have tended to exaggerate the reaction against romanticism among realist writers or to underestimate the persistent romanticist strains in later nineteenth-century art, not least in its social criticism.[76]

If it is to be held as a fundamental force behind the birth and development of Fabianism, or as a reflection of integral aesthetic elements in the socialist creed adopted by the Fabians, the inspiration of the writers and artists mentioned by Clarke and his colleagues needs to be documented, and accounted for, as fully as the extant evidence allows. Any attempt to show the roots of a particular creed must also examine how its exponents came into contact with those roots. Reading habits and tastes, and the stimuli by which these were engendered and developed, provide an essential guide here. Yet accounts of the Fabians' reading — even by commentators who supplement the usual list of political and economic sources with certain literary and artistic ones — have been superficial and selective. It remains now to make up for some of the deficiencies in these accounts by indicating how and why the early Fabians came under the influence of literary and artistic sources, and how that influence affected the evolution of their beliefs.

One of the chief agencies of influence has been discussed, in part, above: Thomas Davidson. In the letters he elicited from his young disciples in the discussion group which spawned the Fellowship of the New Life and the Fabian Society there were very few references to political philosophers and economists — and any to be found were usually rather unflattering.[77] Nor were there many references to straightforward political, economic and social issues of the day. The topics discussed might sometimes have had an indirect bearing on these issues, but they were predominantly ethical and aesthetic in orientation, and were concerned more with ideals than realities. They included such questions as the nature of beauty and duty and the relative allegiance demanded by each in life;[78] the components, procedures and values of 'Culture', and its intimate relations with nature;[79] the constituents of feeling;[80] and the value of utopian schemes for society as a corrective to the materialist concerns of 'ordinary life in most of its forms'.[81]

These were all topics very close to Davidson's personal preoccupations; and the authorities most commonly quoted in exploring them included many creative writers and artists who were part of the romanticist tradition and whose ideas Davidson instinctively admired and echoed in spite of his principled contempt for romanticism as a movement in literature and art. Goethe, Wordsworth, Carlyle, Tennyson, Browning, Matthew Arnold, Ruskin, Morris, D.G. Rossetti, Edward Carpenter, Emerson, Thoreau, Whitman were all discussed or quoted in the letters, not always uncritically but never less than respectfully.[82] Several of these writers also figured largely in the group discussions that were organized in the houses of Davidson's followers in London. Various members launched meetings with readings from Emerson in particular, but also from Goethe, Ruskin and Carpenter on occasions;[83] and, appropriately, there was an 'insistence' at the outset 'upon a prime aim to return to greater simplicity' which seemed to unite the different factions of the group.[84]

Davidson was not of course solely responsible for introducing the works and ideas of all these writers to his English disciples. Indeed, a two-way process seems to have been at work. We find Percival Chubb, for example, alerting Davidson's attention in 1883 to a new work 'by Morris the poet called "Hopes and Fears for Art"'. He went on to assert that the author was 'animated by a fine reformatory zeal, and... would be quite with us. He has all the saner ideas of Ruskin.'[85] A few years later, Chubb contributed an article to Morris's journal, the *Commonweal*, on the grave limitations of a 'commercial' (as distinct from a socialist) education in nurturing 'the leisurely and natural development of our capacities, and the culture of mind and heart to rejoice in the beauty and wonder of the world'.[86] Havelock Ellis claims in his memoirs — how accurately it is difficult to tell — that in the earliest days of his acquaintance with Chubb the latter was not 'keenly interested in art except to some extent in literature', though he had 'a wider and more eager receptivity than mine for the new philosophical, ethical and social movements of the day'.[87] It may have been Davidson who showed the possibility and profitability of combining philosophical with artistic interests. Certainly, in forming a circle of disciples around him, he was at least responsible for encouraging the sense of group identity based on a definable tradition of moral and artistic ideas — a set of implicit standards by which newer ideas (perhaps unfamiliar to the master himself) could be tested, and then assimilated into the tradition or rejected. Such ideas may have been picked up from the general intellectual atmosphere by the disciples' independent reading, but dialogues with the master on the subjects and sources in question, and discussions in the group that he inspired, must have facilitated the essential processes of clarification and assimilation.[88]

This all begs a number of more basic questions: why Davidson should have attracted the particular disciples he did, why they should have sought group identity or 'fellowship' in working out their own ideas, and why they should have found inspiration or support for these ideas in the works of particular writers and artists in the romanticist tradition. These are intimately related questions, the full answers to which no doubt involve a complex of sociological and psychological, as well as intellectual, factors. Unfortunately we do not really have enough detailed evidence to give full answers. From what scraps of evidence exist in letters to Davidson, and later memoirs, it would seem that the sort of men attracted to his circle in the first instance — whether they went on to become members of the Fabian Society or the New Life Fellowship or both — came generally from the same social grouping that the Fabians contrived to attract throughout the years covered by this book: the self-made professional middle class;[89] or, to be more exact with regard to the earliest part of this period, professionals still in the making. Thus Percival Chubb, in later years a highly successful teacher responsible for the organization of 'ethical culture' schools in America, was born into the family of a Newcastle tradesman, of 'good position', whose business started failing in the 1870s and never quite recovered. The young Chubb's formal education had to be cut short; in 1875, at the age of fifteen, he entered a merchant's office, and worked there for three years. Entertaining ambitions of a literary career, he joined the Local Government Board of the Civil Service as a clerk in the early 1880s, because it afforded him more spare time.[90]

William Clarke, born in Norwich in 1852, was also the son of a small, struggling businessman, and also aspired to a career in the literary (and journalistic) world. Scorning 'mere money-making' of the kind his father engaged in and tried to encourage in him, he resolved to escape the business world by entering university. After graduating from Cambridge in 1876, he worked as a free-lance lecturer and writer, and built up a sufficient reputation as a specialist in contemporary political and cultural affairs (especially American affairs) to secure him various kinds of journalistic work in London. Having given up the chance, however, of a more 'worldly position', financial problems continued to afflict him, and he informed Davidson in his first letter to the master that he often literally lived on 'bread and scarcely anything else' and could afford very few amusements and luxuries.[91]

Hubert Bland had been reduced to bankruptcy only two years or so before being drawn into Davidson's circle. The son of a businessman, he was born in Woolwich in 1856 and trained for a military career, but was then pressured by his family to enter the business world. Unlike Clarke, he gave in to these pressures, and joined a foreign banking company. A short time before his marriage to Edith Nesbit in 1880, he was persuaded to invest his capital in a small brushmaking business; this was his downfall, as a few months after the business got off the ground he fell ill with smallpox and his partner took the opportunity of his absence to embezzle all the funds. After this experience, Bland chose to make a profession of literature and political journalism, partly in combination with his wife, a budding poet, novelist and writer of children's stories. (The pseudonym for their joint literary efforts was 'Fabian Bland', and they co-edited the socialist magazine *To-Day*, while it was under Fabian auspices in 1887-9.)[92]

Edward Pease, who eventually made his profession inside the Fabian Society itself, as its full-time secretary, had also followed a business career in his youth, though evidently with greater success than Bland. Born in 1857, near Bristol, into a prosperous Quaker family connected with the railway industry, he was educated by tutors at home until he was seventeen. Then he moved to London, where he worked as a clerk for a firm of silk-merchants and finally, through a family connection, gained a partnership in a firm of stockbrokers. Imbued with the moral principles of his religious upbringing — though these had shed their specifically religious connotations — he baulked at the idea of continuing to make his living in the ruthlessly competitive world of high finance in London. He therefore gave up stockbroking in the mid-eighties and, before taking up his full-time position in the Fabian Society in the early nineties, he went to Newcastle to train as a cabinet maker — directly inspired by the craft ideals of William Morris and the desire for 'a simplification of life'.[93]

In his *History of the Fabian Society*, written twenty years or so afterwards, Pease alluded to his early aesthetic concerns, and those of his colleagues, though in the same breath he helped to foster the Society's philistine reputation by suggesting that these were a kind of youthful indulgence. His condescending attitude here seems all the more perverse — though also, perhaps, all the more understandable — when it is considered that he had once 'indulged' himself in art in a more practical and committed way than any of his early colleagues. Any kind of reaction, for whatever reason, was bound to be deeper than usual. As he acknowledged, there were still 'many who are no longer young' who felt 'anxiously concerned' about art.[94]

A rough pattern can be discerned in the early lives of all these founding Fabians: a link of some kind (past or current, personal or family) with certain sections (large scale or small scale) of the Victorian commercial world; but one that was clearly severed through revulsion or disillusionment or failure. Granted, it was not a completely uniform pattern among Davidson's disciples. Frank Podmore's family background, for example, was academic; his father was an Oxford don and public-school headmaster, and he himself went straight from a public school to Oxford and then into the Civil Service.[95] H.H. Champion's background was military: his father was a major-general, and he began following in these footsteps by taking up a commission in the Royal Artillery, but he retired early to become a publisher in London.[96] The pattern traced above, however, seems sufficiently persistent to suggest a link between adherence to Davidson's circle and a sense of social dislocation, financial insecurity or occupational anxiety based on forms of alienation from the prevailing economic structure. It is not hard to see why the group identity or fellowship offered by the circle should have proved attractive to those affected by such feelings, especially when its very concerns were with attacking the materialist values of *laissez-faire* capitalism and with seeking an alternative code of living based on spiritual, ethical and aesthetic values. The teachings of its mentor, encapsulating as they did some of the main ideas of writers and artists in the romanticist tradition, must have seemed particularly helpful and reassuring. For in various ways and degrees these writers themselves had suffered a revulsion from the materialist values of the capitalist system. Several had directly attacked the basis or the outward manifestations of these values: the cut-throat competition in all forms of trade and industry, which caused the competitors to disregard the personal welfare and environment of the workers they employed or the quality of the goods they produced; the resultant poverty, urban ugliness, destruction of natural beauty in the countryside, and general shoddiness in manufactured commodities. The same or other works in the romanticist tradition represented or explicitly advocated a code of values that was based not on mercenary considerations at all but on the pursuit of 'truth, and goodness, and beauty' in nature and art.[97] Moreover, these works often suggested or dramatized actual ways of subordinating materialist values and fostering spiritual, ethical and aesthetic values: for example, renunciation of individual pleasures and pursuits in the service of society at large; simplification of life, based on the avoidance of luxuries and of the use of any but the most basic machinery; and the spread of 'Culture' (in the sense of education) based on a 'knowledge of nature and the world of men' and acquired through practical experience as well as through a purposeful and systematic programme of reading.[98]

This is a very broad summary of those ideas and 'programmes' in the romanticist tradition most congenial to the kind of men who clustered round Davidson in the early eighties. Of course, there were many variations or differing emphases in these programmes, and individual writers in the tradition would no doubt have quibbled with the particular uses and applications of their ideas made by others. The less radical, or more equivocal, representatives of the tradition — Tennyson, for example, or Arnold[99] — would probably have been very disturbed at the way in which their criticisms of particular shortcomings in the social and economic structure, and in the sensibilities of the classes composing this structure, provided fuel and inspiration for those who wished to undermine it. Yet it is difficult to resist the conclusion that this was the special significance of artistic and literary sources in the romanticist tradition for those Fabians who emerged from Davidson's original circle. Such sources, perhaps because they were not simply or predominantly political and economic in their orientation, helped to crystallize discontents with the *status quo* that transcended materialist or pragmatic considerations.

The budding Fabians, of course, by no means dismissed these considerations: the dissident faction in Davidson's group which went on to found the Society had felt from early on that the economic and political problems of contemporary society must be tackled before the deeper spiritual deficiencies could be rectified. And when the Society was formed, a great deal of time was devoted to studying texts and themes which were more directly related to these problems. The protracted debates of the Fabian-dominated Hampstead Historic Club concerning the various theories of determining 'value' in a commodity (Ricardo's, J.S. Mill's, Marx's, W.S. Jevons') were an important example of these interests, crucial as they proved to be in the evolution of Fabian thought.[100] But such texts did not figure nearly as largely as certain literary and artistic works in the reading and discussions that the early Fabians carried out in their formative years. This is shown strikingly in a letter which William Clarke wrote to Davidson in December 1884 acknowledging the latter's services in providing him with guidelines for overcoming the 'huge barrier of materialism . . . in this country'. The sources he had been consulting included some non-literary ones (the writings of Herbert Spencer and Frederic Harrison, for example). But towards the end of the letter, Clarke stated that he had also 'been pondering over some of the great poets, notably, Wordsworth, Tennyson, Browning' and that these had given him 'greater faith and insight' than any other source apart perhaps from the Bible. He agreed with Emerson that these writers were 'the true spiritual teachers'.[101]

Given the power of such works (intended or not) to shape and reinforce incipient dissatisfaction with the condition of society, they were perhaps more important in initiating the development of future Fabians' thought in the direction of socialism than any other kind of written source. In clarifying the basic issues at stake by presenting them in a readily accessible and attractive form, they might even have prepared the ground or eased the way for confronting the more 'technical' works which served, in later discussion, to consolidate Fabian socialism. This in itself raises a central 'aesthetic' question: how far the impact of a written source depends on its generic form (poem, novel, play, essay, sermon, tract, exegesis) as distinct from, or in interaction with, its content (the ideas and implications it offers regarding all kinds of issues, including aesthetic ones in themselves, as well as political, economic, social, ethical, religious and scientific ones). The content of the sources, artistic or otherwise, is what the early Fabians drew upon consciously and explicitly; but the surface reflections of an influence tell us little about how it contrives to implant itself in the first place and how it works itself out thereafter — processes that are by no means completely clear or conscious even to those directly subjected to them. Unfortunately, because of the elusiveness of these processes, there is not enough tangible evidence to make any firm generalizations about the relative roles of form and content in determining the impact of various kinds of written sources upon the evolution of Fabian beliefs and schemes.

The part played by aesthetic sensitivities in fostering the socialism of the Fabians can be traced more definitely by going beyond a consideration of their written sources and examining broader aspects of their personal interests and backgrounds. Their conceptions of beauty (natural and artistic), and of the threat to beauty from the worst excesses of industrialization and urbanization under a capitalist regime, were never just ideas, picked up from an immersion in romantic art. Their responsiveness to the romantics' themes and motifs was, rather, a symptom of an intrinsic feeling for beauty — rooted partly in a shared love for the countryside[102] — and of a genuine concern for the fate of beauty at the hands of what they saw as the forces of ugliness in contemporary society. Bland's recollections, quoted above, of the impulses which led him to the socialist faith, vividly evoke that feeling and concern, albeit from a distance in time. There are various traces, nearer the time in question, in other founders of the Fabian Society or early recruits. The daily programme which Percival Chubb devised for himself early in 1884 is rather self-consciously romanticist in its resolution to explore and apprehend nature through direct experience as well as appreciating that force — and her interactions with man — through works of art.[103] His native capacity to appreciate beauty both in nature and art emerges, nonetheless, quite unselfconsciously: 'I must not forget,' he wrote to Davidson,

the time to be spent...out of doors in converse with Nature. I look forward to having many good walks and saunterings in the leafy Suffolk lanes or on the breezy downs. I have had one fine walk already...deepening the desire for more. I begin, too, to finger my Chaucer & Wordsworth & to revel in a recently acquired life of François Millet containing reproductions of many of his inimitable pictures of rural and peasant life.[104]

A later description of one of his country walks had the qualities almost of a lyrical reverie: he lovingly recounted his route, with two friends from the New Life Fellowship, 'along the lanes, in the woods, over the heaths,

and along the hillsides' of Surrey, remarking in particular the 'birds that
sang in hedgerows and copses', the trees 'bursting into leaf', the gorse
that 'had blossomed into full glory of gold', and the profusion of
wildflowers gracing the path.[105] The connections between these feelings
for beauty, on the one hand, and the impulse to regenerate society, on the
other, can be traced back to a time before he came into contact with the
New Life Fellowship or the Fabian Society. One of the earliest letters he
wrote to Davidson (May 1882) described how, some two years before, he
had taken his holidays in the Lake District, 'roaming about in the land of
Wordsworth, Coleridge, North and De Quincey', and had there conceived
the hope of establishing amongst those 'ragged hills and smiling lakes' a
'revolutionary organization' which should become the centre of a
'general regenerating movement'.[106] His rural nostalgia was not entirely
self-indulgent or escapist, therefore. He was conscious of the 'extravagance and one-sidedness' of a total commitment to nature, such as
Thoreau had attempted on his retreat to the woods at Walden; though it
was 'easy enough to understand', Chubb confessed, the American philosopher's overriding fascination with nature, 'whose plenitude, force and
plain dealing stand in such splendid contrast with the poverty, flatness and
uncertainty of Man as one ordinarily finds him'. He himself often felt the
urge to quit the 'smoky limits' of 'sordid city life', his 'ruling inclination'
being towards 'something rural and pastoral'.[107]

William Clarke's native inclination was also very much in this direction. Despite his appreciation of the opportunities for social, cultural and
intellectual life offered by cities,[108] he exhibited a persistent distaste for
London, that 'monstrous, over-grown centre of so-called civilization';[109]
and he yearned for the quietness and charm of the rural areas, and smaller
towns, in southern England. His love of these parts was based not on mere
idealization, but on an intimate acquaintance with them.[110] They formed a
striking contrast with the manufacturing towns of the Midlands and the
North which were, in his opinion, the 'most hideous places' that the
'perverted ingenuity of man has ever contrived to rear'. He invoked
various writers (William Blake, Emerson, Arnold among them) in support
of his observations on the English countryside and the remorseless
incursions of industrialization; and he went as far as to attribute to
Wordsworth the power of impressing on Englishmen for all future time
the idea of the sublimity of Nature, the idea of her interaction with the
mind of man, of her healing power, of her 'revelation of the divine'.[111]
Clarke's own enthusiasm for both natural and artistic beauty undoubtedly
had rather more personal roots as well, connected with his early
surroundings. These are described in a biographical sketch of his 'early
years' provided in the posthumous collection of his essays: a childhood
spent in 'the beautiful old city Norwich', and a young manhood in

Cambridge, awakening and fostering that 'passion for architecture which...rivalled William Clarke's love of Nature, and which...sowed the seeds of revolt in him against...commercialism'. This represented a true 'aesthetic education' which 'may well...have led up to a mental review of whether modern industrialism has given us any compensation for the loss of beauty in our cities which it has involved'.[112]

In reviewing such questions, Clarke consciously echoed Ruskin in stigmatizing the products of industrialization, in their vulgarity and hideousness, as representing mere riches, not true wealth: 'for it is not well that any man should have them, and the men who made them are not themselves morally or aesthetically well'.[113] Clarke was not, however, totally dependent on Ruskin's ideas either in forming or articulating his observations on the threat presented by industrialization to beauty. He specifically exposed what he felt to be 'a weak side in Ruskin's art teaching': the fact that, in 'seeing the unsatisfactory character of modern commercialism', he was 'for going back to methods of production that we have outgrown' — that is, 'simple hand industry'. Clarke himself perhaps over-simplified Ruskin's reactions against machinery, but it is important to stress that his criticism of these reactions did not signify an undiscriminating pragmatism or any crude utilitarian bias. True, Clarke's criticism was partly based on a conviction that widespread mechanization was now a *fait accompli*, and that it was simply not realistic to think in terms of abolishing or dismantling what had become so entrenched a part of the English scene: 'we shall certainly not pull up our rails as Ruskin would like, or destroy our machinery as William Morris would be glad to do'.[114] But there was a less fatalistic, more positive aspect of his criticism which answered Ruskin on indirectly aesthetic grounds. Clarke intimated that the art-critic had overlooked the potential advantages to artists and their work which accrued from machine-power. With appropriate controls on its use, that power could actually help in reducing 'man's more mechanical toil' and in giving him more time and opportunity for pursuing 'the higher creative efforts': 'every man should thus become, what every man is in germ from the savage who carves men on trees, to a Titian or a Beethoven, a genuine artist, a lover of true art'. It was on the basis of this belief, in particular, that Clarke's yearnings for beauty in the world came to provide an impelling motive for his adoption of socialism; for he felt that the controls which were needed to ensure the discriminating application of machine-power would have to be exercised 'by the people themselves instead of by landlords and capitalists'. Collective regulation of what had become the chief instruments of production and distribution constituted for Clarke the essential definition and 'foundation' of modern socialism, leaving aside 'all the difficult questions of value, of economic rent, &c.'[115]

A yearning for beauty, and a revulsion from the uglinesses manifest in contemporary forms of commercial and industrial organization, were common impulses in all of Thomas Davidson's immediate disciples. Some of these disciples became the founder members of the Fabian Society, and two — Bland and Clarke — contributed to the Society's seminal textbook, the *Fabian Essays in Socialism*. But there were five other contributors to that book who were not members of Davidson's original circle and who came into the Society via other routes. One of these was Sidney Webb, whose ideas — together with those of his wife — are sometimes depicted as embodying the essence of Fabian socialism. The legendary dominance of the Webbs in the Society, however questionable it may be in fact, necessitates a particularly close look at the impulses and influences behind their own socialist beliefs. Were the routes to Fabianism which they followed prompted by any of the yearnings or revulsions evinced by the earliest exponents of that brand of socialism?

2

The young Webbs: towards a socialist partnership

Sidney Webb once rather scornfully caricatured certain Ruskinian ideals held by early Fabians. This might seem to support the popular image of him as one who 'sought to eliminate or radically play down ethical or aesthetic motives' in socialism.[1] At the Fabian Society Conference of June 1886, he advocated the use of more, not fewer, machines in England, and then gave an account of the customary objections to this kind of scheme: 'Mr. Ruskin thinks it unpoetical. And in this very conference we have already had the charming idyll sung of every man living on his own garden, sitting by the shade of his own figtree, sweetly contemptuous of the Philistine millhand. Whether this be a good ideal or not, it is obviously a hopeless dream.' Webb's defence of machines, however, as with William Clarke's, was based partly on their 'labour-saving' capacity and the opportunities they offered — in combination with a greater supply of 'Personal' or 'Consumer's Capital' — for the population as a whole to have more leisure and to gain greater enjoyment from life, including artistic enjoyment. As well as wanting every house to have hydraulic lifts, the electric light, the telephone and a new 'hot & cold' water supply, he wished for all families to have comfortable clothes and furniture, pictures and music and for 'every man and woman to have the opportunity of being thoroughly taught, not only as now the mere elements of learning, but also one or two skilled handicrafts & the studies which are the pleasures of life'. He went on to ask: 'Are not these things that reformers all desire and work for?'[2] In a lecture to the Fabian Society a month earlier, he had already answered this question on behalf of socialists in particular. Their faith, he asserted involved neither 'contempt for machinery' nor 'dislike of education or culture...It is, in fact, because we want more of these things that we are Socialists.'[3] A press report of an Arts and Crafts exhibition held in 1889, at which a number of socialist luminaries were in attendance, noted the presence of Sidney Webb among those who were 'full of congratulation on the union of the progressive economic movement with the diffusion of the arts'.[4]

The association between Sidney's interests in socialism and art reflected

in these comments by or about himself throw doubt on the image of
Webb as a completely philistine socialist, indifferent (or indeed opposed to)
the aesthetic ramifications of his economic and political faith. But what
evidence is there, in Webb's particular case, of any aesthetic sensitivities
or concerns for culture actively fostering the development of his socialist
beliefs? We can, in fact, find traces of these things in a lecture he delivered
in February 1885, about a year before his actual conversion to socialism.
The subject of the lecture was the economic functions of the middle class,
and one of its themes was the diminution of those functions owing to the
increasing parasitism and declining abilities of this group as it grew larger
and more prosperous under the capitalist system. He claimed that one of
the extenuating features of that parasitism in the past had been 'the
function performed by the richer classes in developing taste, a sense of
Beauty, & a love for Culture, & the Fine Arts'. A certain ease in 'circumstances', he acknowledged, had 'hitherto been requisite' for the cultivation of such things; but 'wealth sometimes extinguishes and perverts
them'. He went on to suggest that this is precisely what had happened in
modern capitalist society. The middle class in particular had become an
'overgrown' and 'inflated' mass, which had appropriated to itself 'the
lion's share of the world's produce', but was unable any longer to boast
the skill which had produced its wealth or 'the taste with which to enjoy
it'. It could no longer exalt itself, therefore, as 'the most important and
indispensable element in the industrial kingdom'.

These remarks were made in the same lecture in which Webb stated 'I
am, I am sorry to say no believer in State Socialism', and 'I am not at
present aware of a better system of wealth-production and distribution
than the institution of private property.'[5] His resistance to socialism —
noticeably reluctant here — broke down within the next few months, and
his half-hearted acceptance of the economic *status quo* turned into
positive rejection.[6] These crucial developments in his attitudes were
possibly facilitated by the already profound lack of faith which he
exhibited here in the leadership capacities of the middle class — including
their capacities in artistic and cultural matters.

On being converted to socialism, Webb could contemplate an even
greater application of the machine-power which the dominant classes in
the capitalist system had used to fuel their financial ventures. As already
indicated, the applications he envisaged were for the social and cultural
benefit of the whole industrial community. What he criticized in the
Ruskinian attitude to machines was an over-reaction which denied these
wider benefits; he was every bit as aware as Ruskin of the abuses and
iniquities of machinery as it was applied, under the present commercial
system, to the mere purpose of mounting up personal profits for a few
individuals. In an article published in 1891, and later issued as a Fabian

tract, he saw the commodities of this system as being produced 'in the wrong way and for the wrong ends', reflecting 'the apotheosis, not of social service, but of successful financial speculation'. He intimated that this kind of production adversely affected the moral and aesthetic sensibilities of consumers as well as producers: 'With it,' he asserted, 'comes inevitably a demoralization of personal character, a loosening of moral fibre, and a hideous lack of taste.'[7]

The adverse effect of commercial pressures and undiscriminating mechanization on the artistic quality of various commodities was a theme which Webb and his wife developed in one of the earliest books of their partnership. They contrived to show how the 'introduction of a new machine' could 'annihilate the utility of a workman's skill as completely as the photograph has annihilated the miniature'. In a desperate attempt to compete with the machine, the handicraftsman lowered the rate for his labour; his former earnings could only be made up, therefore, by 'hurry' and 'overwork', which soon had injurious effects on standards of craftsmanship:

The work insidiously drops its artistic quality and individual character. In the losing race with the steam engine, the handiwork becomes itself mechanical, without acquiring either that uniform excellence or artistic finish which is the outcome of the perfected machine... The degradation of the handworker's craft...deprives the nation of the charm given to the old country stuffs and furniture by their artistic individuality.

The Webbs' tendency to take a more sympathetic view of machinery than Ruskin or Morris, and their recognition of its artistic potential, still comes out in this passage. 'Even the machine-made product,' they went on to argue, 'is the worse for the deterioration of the handicraft. It gradually loses the ideal of perfect workmanship, to which the inventor and operative were perpetually striving to approximate.'[8]

In the Webbs' view, the destruction of beauty in the natural environment was as much a matter for concern as the destruction of beauty in an individual commodity.[9] One of their later works suggested a close relationship between these two phenomena in describing the unfavourable climate which industrialization had created both for production and for the development of 'taste in consumption'. 'Who can measure,' the Webbs asked, 'the diminution in health, in happiness, in morality and in intelligence — all factors in human productivity — caused through the profit-maker by a defilement of air, water and land, and the destruction of all amenity and beauty in the surroundings of countless millions...?'[10] In a letter he wrote to Beatrice, before their marriage, Sidney Webb had stressed the great value to the workers of an appreciation of 'natural beauty', and confessed that his thoughts on these lines had become 'almost a monomania'.[11]

It is true that (in contrast to William Clarke) Webb also retained a great love for cities, especially his native London, and tended even to deride provincial towns and hamlets.[12] It is also true, as a recent historian has put it, that he was 'wholly lacking in the nostalgia for rural or simpler forms of community which pervaded the Socialist movement'[13] — and of which there were strong traces in fellow-Fabians such as Percival Chubb. Webb even warned his future wife that she would 'find "love for the country" a little incompatible' with what he conceived as the 'ideal life' for her.[14] On the other hand, in a lecture on London delivered just after his marriage, he showed some sympathy with the desire of many of the city's inhabitants to be 'in the country', seeing it as 'possibly...the last spark of poetry in our natures'.[15] He himself had courted Beatrice in Epping Forest, reading to her aloud from Rossetti and Keats; and he continued to find pleasure and solace in rural retreats.[16]

Neither Sidney nor Beatrice, then, were devoid of the earlier Fabians' feelings for beauty and of the anxieties concerning its fate under the present commercial system. Such feelings and anxieties had been nurtured in different ways of course. Sidney and Beatrice's respective backgrounds differed considerably in themselves; and both came into the Fabian Society too late to have gained from contact with Thomas Davidson or the discussion group he set on foot. These differences complicate any pattern which might be discerned in the roots of Fabianism; but there were certain broad similarities as well which serve to consolidate the pattern.

In a sense, Sidney Webb was the archetype of the self-made professional that figured so significantly in the Fabian ranks. He was born in 1859 into a lower middle-class family engaged in small, and precarious, business concerns. His father was a hairdresser-turned-accountant, and his mother managed a modest dressmaking establishment. Their limited means made it necessary for them to put an end to Sidney's formal schooling when he was sixteen and to send him out to work as a clerk in a firm of colonial brokers. Developing a distaste (similar to William Clarke's) for working from motives of personal gain, rather than those of social good, he declined the offer of a share in the firm and chose instead to join the Civil Service. By dint of extreme diligence and an extraordinary flair for competitive examinations, he rose very rapidly, attaining the rank of first-division clerk in the Colonial Service by the time he was twenty-two. He then went on to read for the bar, qualifying as an LL.B. from London University in the mid-eighties — about the same time that he joined the Fabian Society.[17]

Beatrice, on the other hand, came from a much higher stratum of the middle class. She was born in 1858 into the family of a large industrial and commercial magnate. As shown above, however, one of the founding Fabians, Edward Pease, shared a similar social background, so that Beatrice's position was not completely atypical. Moreover, her upbringing was not entirely without experiences or memories of financial insecurity. There had been risks and uncertainties associated with the speculative investments on which the Potter fortune was based;[18] and there was the example of perpetually reduced circumstances presented by Beatrice's relations on her mother's side, several of whom worked as mill-hands in Lancashire. Beatrice's visit to this poorer side of her family gave her a direct insight into conditions of life and work in the industrial North, and prompted her decision to become 'an investigator of social institutions'.[19] A girl of her class and means did not need a career for any financial reasons at all; she appears to have taken it up precisely because of a heightened conscience about her privileged social and economic position. She became sceptical of 'the ethics of capitalist enterprise' as represented by her father's 'acts and axioms' — not because these were intentionally vicious in any way, but because they were based purely on considerations of 'personal relationship' rather than of 'public good'.[20] We have seen that disenchantment with the prevailing commercial system, arising from direct experience of it through personal or family connections, was a common background factor in the making of Fabians. Beatrice's disenchantment can only have been increased by her work as a social investigator, which was centred on some of the worst victims of this system: the London dockers and the workers in the 'sweated' trades of the East End (such as tailoring).[21] She could not countenance the 'catastrophic overturning of the existing order' envisaged by members of the Social Democratic Federation whom she met in this area; and, by her own account, she seems to have considered socialism as a practical alternative only after coming across the non-revolutionary version of it presented in the *Fabian Essays* of 1889.[22] Soon afterwards, in the course of her research on the working-class 'Co-operative Movement' in Great Britain, she was introduced to the author of the essay she had most admired in the Fabian volume — her future husband. Her conversion to his political creed seems to have followed within a matter of weeks; though she continued to waver about actually becoming a member of the Fabian Society for a few more months, afraid as she was of the hold which her 'individualist antecedents' still had on her.[23]

During the period immediately leading up to her conversion there are no direct traces, such as can be found in Sidney's case, of dissatisfaction with the artistic shortcomings of the prevailing economic system. These were feelings she voiced later, in partnership with Sidney, and on full consideration of the evidence which he and she had been collecting on production techniques and habits of consumption in industrial (and pre-industrial) England. Some of this evidence, however, she had started collecting herself, before her introduction to Sidney, in connection with her study of the Co-operative Movement. And from her book on that subject, which came out between the time of her meeting Sidney and her marriage to him, it emerges that one of the things which attracted her about the movement was the 'unmistakeable rise in the standard of taste' displayed in the commodities that were produced and consumed in the co-operative communities. She claimed that the general run of manufacturers, even in the eighteenth century, was 'ignorant, unversed in the arts of civilized life, with few interests beyond the routine of daily work'. The co-operative communities, based partly on the 'socialist' principles and procedures of Robert Owen, had managed to eliminate some of these shortcomings and areas of apathy by ensuring a 'close and constant tie between the *entrepreneur* and the customer'; and the movement in general could be seen either 'as an alternative to State Socialism or a stepping-stone to socialist organization in all its forms'.[24]

Beatrice's notion of taste — in principle at least — was a broad and flexible one. In all of its dimensions, aesthetic and otherwise, she recognized and approved of considerable diversity, and on this score she expressly distinguished her views (and Sidney's too) from the Benthamite utilitarians. In a diary entry of 1901, for example, she summed up her end in life as being 'the increase in the community of certain faculties and desires that I happen to like — love, truth, beauty and humour'. But she went on to claim that

we differ from the Benthamites in thinking that it is necessary that we should all agree as to ends, or that these can be determined by any science. We believe that ends, ideals, are all what may be called in a large way 'questions of taste' and we like a society in which there is a considerable variety in these tastes.[25]

General concern with questions of taste or artistic faculty relating to the industrial workforce and its employers could hardly have been expected to play a conspicuous part at the time of Beatrice's actual conversion to socialism. For that period, particularly in London, was one of 'new ferment'[26] in the workforce, manifested by a series of domestic strikes and trade unionist agitations to which the Fabians lent their support; and the urgency of the particular economic and social issues involved naturally served to overwhelm the significance of wider concerns. Such concerns, however, were not totally absent from Beatrice's mind at the time, and not totally unconnected with her growing responsiveness to socialism, as her work on the Co-operative Movement, then in embryo, subsequently hinted.

There is a great deal in her own social and cultural background — much more than is apparent in Sidney's — to explain her concerns for natural and artistic beauty. Though her father was an industrialist, he owned a house in the Gloucestershire countryside in which all his children were born and brought up. The early effect of such an environment on Beatrice can be traced perhaps in her compulsive scene-sketching as an adolescent and young woman. On occasions, this pursuit became such a passion for her that she even thought of taking it up as a career and of trying to become a 'great artist'.[27] Her subjects were taken mainly from nature, and, though none of her sketches has survived, the verbal descriptions of scenery in her diaries and letters — scenery observed on her trips to America in 1873 and to the Continent in later years as well as on her walks and excursions at home[28] — convey by their very profusion her extraordinary love of natural beauty. That love, and the inspiration it provided to attempt her own renderings of natural beauty in artistic terms, were heightened by her reading of Ruskin in the late seventies and early eighties. In her first reference to his multi-volumed work, *Modern Painters*, she makes the claim that the book had opened a 'new world' to her 'in nature' and had also afforded her some 'very incomplete and half understood glimpses into the world of art'; a little later she referred to the active encouragement that it was giving her to carry on practising her own sketching and drawing.[29] In characteristic fashion, she continued to disown any genuine knowledge or comprehension of the visual arts, though her native interest in the work of the great or established practitioners in this field proves, on examination, to have been at least as passionate as her wish to further her own modest efforts. Her early letters and diary entries contain several reports of visits to art galleries, museums and exhibitions in England, Germany, Holland and Italy.[30] These include notes on a multitude of painters, representing various 'schools' and periods from Renaissance Italian to contemporary Pre-Raphaelite. Family means were obviously ample enough to permit several such visits; though the sheer detail of Beatrice's notes, and the strong discriminations she made (on moral as well as aesthetic grounds) reflected a critical engagement with what she saw that transcended the interests of the casual tourist or mere dilettante.

Some of these impressions were recorded in letters to her family; and there is evidence that her father in particular provided her not only with the necessary funds to develop her interests in the arts but also with the example and stimulus of his own personal interests. While his professional concerns were solely with commerce and manufacturing, and while any friends he made outside his work tended to come more from the political and scientific than from the literary and artistic worlds,[31] he in no way fitted the stereotype of the philistine businessman. Beatrice spoke of his 'love for poetry, of drama, of history and of idealistic philosophy', and recalled how he taught his children to appreciate from early on various novelists and humanists of the eighteenth and early nineteenth centuries.[32] Parental inculcation must have been an important part of Beatrice's early education, in the absence of any formal schooling; though her enormously wide reading in history and philosophy and science, as well as literature, became largely self-directed as she grew older. Certainly, none of her sisters seems to have shared the breadth or intensity of her interests, even though (according to Beatrice) their artistic abilities and talents were innately superior to hers. She recalled how one sister in particular looked on a pursuit like reading as mere 'relaxation' midst the business of getting married, whereas she herself 'reversed the relation, looking on culturing my mind as my business and flirting as my relaxation'.[33]

Having been brought up on the early English novelists so beloved of her father, she went on to sample the classics of later nineteenth-century English fiction — reading novels by Charlotte Brontë, Dickens, Robert Louis Stevenson, James Barrie and Thomas Hardy,[34] and immersing herself in the works of George Eliot. She also turned to Continental (particularly French) fiction, studying the works of Hugo, Flaubert, Balzac, de Maupassant and Zola.[35] The last of these novelists she acclaimed a 'true genius' on the basis of his uniquely powerful and comprehensive ' "social" diagnosis'. It is interesting in this respect that Zola was the one novelist whom Thomas Davidson is on record as prescribing to his early disciples in England. He recommended a joint study of the works of Antonio Rosmini — his favourite modern philosopher — and that of Zola: 'one for his ideal philosophy, the other for his hard realities'.[36]

In the field of poetry, there are more striking correspondences between what we know of Beatrice's reading tastes and those of the Davidson circle. She had no little acquaintance with classical, mediaeval and Renaissance poets, and reserved a particular enthusiasm in her youth for Shakespeare and Milton.[37] She later disowned, however, any particular admiration for the former and claimed that: 'Of all the great authors I tried to read only Goethe dominated my mind.'[38] At the age of fifteen, she was already making her own translation of *Faust*, a play that she found 'wonderfully clever and often very beautiful'.[39] And in her memoirs she claimed that she felt towards the German poet 'as if he were an intimate friend, sharing out his wealth of experience and knowledge, and revealing to me an entirely new ideal of personal morality, of the relation of art to science, and of art and science to the conduct of love'.[40] Her lifelong reverence for Goethe was almost unqualified, perhaps even exceeding that of Davidson and his followers, who were inclined to be more critical at times. On the other hand, she never seems to have had any time at all for another of Davidson's idols, Tennyson, whose work she dismissed as a collection of 'sentimental imageries'.[41] That she was nonetheless prey to certain species of romanticism is made clear by her especial admiration for *Faust* among Goethe's works; and by the inspiration she confessed to finding in Emerson, Browning and Arnold,[42] all of whom, as we have seen, had made a deep impress on members of the Davidson circle as well. She claimed that Arnold's summing-up of the chief 'lesson' which nature provided for man — 'toil unsevered from tranquillity' — had crystallized 'the ideal life' towards which she 'constantly' strove. Her reflections on the value of quiet work as a 'slow stepping' towards 'truth' and 'the ennobling of human life' were made in August 1889 — the month when the ferment in labour relations which accompanied her personal conversion to socialism came to a head in the great London dock strike. That such tranquillity was impossible in the circumstances may well have induced her to give voice to these reflections. It is important to note the persistence of this ideal for herself and its recent connection in her mind with a broader ideal for humanity as a whole at the very time when her socialist creed was on the verge of consolidating itself. Her personal 'search after truth by the careful measurement of facts' had 'of late', she said, been combined with and enriched by 'the consciousness of the supreme unity of science, art, morality; the eternal trinity of the good, the beautiful and the true; knit together in the ideal towards which humanity is consciously striving'.[43] This ideal, in its sources, scope and formulation, was not far removed from that of the small group of men who clustered round Thomas Davidson in the early 1880s and who went on to found the Fabian Society. It was an ideal she never lost; there are signs of its persistence throughout all the more mundane concerns of her partnership with Sidney, and she evidently saw it as the guiding impetus to those concerns, if not as their whole *raison d'être*.[44]

The *Fabian Essays in Socialism* — especially the contribution submitted by her future husband — appears to have given particular shape to the social, political and economic aspects of her creed, by drawing on the ideas of a number of nineteenth-century social philosophers, scientists, political theorists and economists with whom she had familiarized herself over the past decade or so, and presenting them in a light which suited her mood of deep, though not violent, discontent with the *status quo*. Thus she recollected how Webb's essay had come to attract her because it was an early testimony to the 'inevitability of gradualness' in social change, calling on a range of impressive witnesses (Comte, Darwin, Spencer) to back up that testimony, yet going beyond — even against — these in using the evidence of other witnesses (such as J.S. Mill) to indicate the course of change in a specifically socialist direction.[45] The influence of such writers in determining the final mould of her beliefs seems quite characteristic. Her recourse to an artist like Arnold in attempting to explain the underlying basis of these beliefs might seem less characteristic, but only because her general responsiveness to art as an adolescent and young woman has so often been ignored or underrated.

Recent acknowledgements of her youthful enthusiasm for the arts have tended to suggest that this was curbed, suppressed even, on her marriage to Webb and her acceptance of socialism. Such claims will be examined in detail below. The assumption on which they are partly based — Webb's own basic lack of taste for art — needs to be dealt with here. It might seem quite a plausible assumption in view of his social background, which was hardly as conducive to artistic cultivation as Beatrice's. Brought up in a lower middle-class family inhabiting an unfashionable area of London, and forced through financial need to seek routine employment at the age of sixteen, he had neither the opportunities nor the time to indulge in the cultural activities that were an integral part of his future wife's upbringing midst the leisured affluence of upper middle-class 'country life'. His early education, however, was a little unusual for someone of his social position, and it apparently provided some fertile ground for the ripening of cultural, as well as political, interests. There was a distinct intellectual atmosphere in the home, bred by the nature of his father's political beliefs. These represented a fervent commitment to Radicalism, involving not only practical participation on behalf of that cause in various (unpaid) local government activities, but also a close personal discipleship of one of the most powerful contemporary thinkers in the Radical tradition, J.S. Mill.[46] The precise nature and extent of Mill's influence over the young Sidney Webb is a matter of debate,[47] but he probably made his initial acquaintance with Millite ideas (and possibly with related doctrines in the writings of Spencer, Comte and various other political philosophers and economists who influenced his development) through his father's pronouncements.

The family also seems to have made some conscious efforts at self-cultivation in the field of art through the use of whatever public facilities were available for this in London. Sidney rarely talked about his childhood at all, but one of the things he recalled when pressed for some reminiscences were visits to national museums and picture galleries.[48] The special interest which his parents took in his education is highlighted by the fact that they had him tutored in Switzerland and Germany for a while to supplement the tuition he had been receiving at the Birkbeck Institute and the City of London School. This involved a 'considerable sacrifice' of income for the family.[49] The impact of his confrontation with German culture in particular — he was personally instructed in the language by a Lutheran pastor at Wismar — is reflected perhaps in the subsequent attention he gave to the works of German writers, and in his comparative neglect of other Continental literature, including the great French novels which Beatrice read so voraciously.

In a letter to Beatrice a few months after their first meeting in 1890, he stated that he had 'long been familiar' with certain works of Goethe (including *Faust*) and that he had just finished a 'plunge' into some other generally less well-known works. He was not as enthusiastic about Goethe's writings as Beatrice had been, instinctively reacting against what he saw as their strong apolitical element, symptomatic of the egoism and 'real selfish anarchism' in the poet's personality and approach to life. Against this recklessly individualistic approach, Webb pitted his view of the world as an organism in which all the constituent parts had duties towards one another that must be fulfilled for the general well-being, even if their own particular development was thereby limited. He referred expressly to the element of beauty, as well as of duty, inherent in the idea of the social organism.[50]

This idea came to provide one of the main forces behind Sidney's acceptance of socialism as a solution to society's problems and ills;[51] though it was not a new, nor an exclusively socialist, concept, as Sidney (and other Fabians) showed in discussing its origins. It had been expounded and developed by various nineteenth-century giants in the fields of science, sociology and philosophy — including Darwin, Comte, Mill and Herbert Spencer (the last of whom was a particularly vocal anti-socialist).[52] It had also found its way, Sidney suggested, into the writings of a whole range of romanticist writers and critics.[53] About the same time as Sidney's explication of this concept, his fellow-Fabian, William Clarke, succinctly and sympathetically alluded to its place in the romanticist tradition, and also indicated the departure it represented from the older and cruder forms of utilitarianism which Webb has sometimes been accused of championing within the Fabian Society. 'The literature of our time,' Clarke noted,

is permeated with this idea just as truly as our politics. Carlyle, Ruskin, Matthew Arnold, Dickens, Tennyson, William Morris, and (in his later years, when his father's spiritual poison had been eliminated from his system) John Stuart Mill, are all penetrated with the new organic conception of society, with the thought that 'we are all members one of another'. 'Benthamism' seems more old-fashioned and defunct than an Egyptian mummy.[54]

Goethe, himself, as we have seen, had presented a distinctly 'political' version of this organic conception of society in the last part of *Wilhelm Meister*, elaborating there the ideal of a firmly-governed co-operative brotherhood. It is significant in this regard perhaps that Webb found some merit in this work; it was, he commented, 'so mixed, good and evil'. The 'good' elements he may well have located in the last part, as this also contained a development of the 'renunciation' theme which he had picked out, approvingly, in *Faust*.[55]

Webb confessed that G.H. Lewes's biography of Goethe increased his tolerance of the German poet and novelist by supplying some extenuations for the latter's 'want of patriotism, & of interest in politics'. He nevertheless reserved greater admiration for other German writers —

Lessing, in particular, whom he felt to be 'a more important "spiritual father" of Modern Europe'. Lessing has been seen as a typical exponent of 'eighteenth century romanticism or pre-romanticism',[56] and Sidney's judgment of him is a tacit endorsement of this view, articulated as it is in the course of urging Beatrice to 'recognise instinct and feeling as of some claim to motives: as being, indeed, the organically registered expression of the past experience of the race, notifying to us the "general line" of human nature and the world'.[57]

Sidney was susceptible not only to the force of romanticist ideas but also to the charm of romanticist art forms. In another letter he wrote to Beatrice prior to their marriage, he spoke of the fundamental power of feeling *vis-à-vis* reason, and referred her to 'Burne-Jones' charming little picture of "Love in the guise of Reason"'. Admittedly, his pronouncements in these letters were rather tendentious, as his courtship of her was still at a very delicate, if not desperate, stage.[58] More significant perhaps were his slightly earlier comments on the poetry of Heinrich Heine. Heine had been at once more deeply involved in the romantic movement than Goethe and more expressly critical of certain aspects of it. His political commitments as an artist were also more intense and explicit than Goethe's.[59] Webb, in talking about Heine, made no reference to these criticisms or commitments, but described the impact of the German's poems purely in terms of their haunting emotional qualities, especially as rendered by Schubert in musical form.[60]

Webb's musical interests, indicated here, are also evident from references in his letters to attendances, and planned attendances, at concerts and the opera in Germany during return trips he made there in 1885 and 1890. On those trips he visited a number of art galleries as well. His recollections of such visits are not nearly as detailed as Beatrice's. There is enough evidence to suggest, however, that he had an informed and independent eye for the visual arts, developed early on perhaps during his family's visits to London galleries. Bernard Shaw accompanied Webb on his trip to Germany in 1890, one of their main objects being to see the Oberammergau passion play. Any suspicion that Webb's outlook on artistic matters during this trip was determined by the views of his travelling companion founders on the fact of their conflicting reactions to the passion play itself. Webb had a few misgivings about the acting and about 'the play's lack of connection with a vigorous popular "life" around it', such as its prototype would have had in the Middle Ages. But he was most impressed with the 'musical effect' which he found 'supremely beautiful', and with the spectacle of 'bright colours without the least tawdriness or bad taste'. The 'whole thing', he concluded, had been 'a great and vivid experience' for him, and he refused to endorse Shaw's 'deprecatory criticism of the play from the professional Art critic's point of view'. The experience of Oberammergau, he claimed, had helped to further his own understanding of mediaeval painting, especially the works of the 'early Germans' which he and Shaw had 'studied at Munich and Augsburg' directly after seeing the passion play. The very terms in which he voiced his criticisms of the play showed a prior knowledge of the painting of several other periods and schools, including late German Gothic, Renaissance Italian, seventeenth-century Dutch realist, nine-teenth-century French salon and English Pre-Raphaelite.[61]

While much of Sidney's knowledge about art and many of his artistic interests were German-centred, this was not exclusively the case, as those comments on other schools of painting suggest. As far as literature was concerned, he had gained some grounding in the classics, and also showed at least a nodding acquaintance with mediaeval Italian writers.[62] Though he was much less immersed than Beatrice in French literature, he shared much of her enthusiasm for the novels of Zola, especially *Germinal*: its horrific description of living and working conditions in an imaginary mining community in France seems to have struck him as a faithful representation of the conditions actually existing both in European and English collieries. 'We realised some of Germinal' was his comment to Graham Wallas on visiting the Walker colliery in Northumberland in, August 1886.[63] This casual allusion, assuming a ready knowledge of Zola's book on Wallas's part,[64] suggests the significance which the French novelist had for the Fabians in dramatizing the social misery around them, and it thereby lends some plausibility to William Clarke's account of how the recent purveyors of social realism in literary form had helped provide a fertile 'soil' for the growth of specifically socialist beliefs. At the time of Webb's comment on the Northumberland collieries, both he and Wallas were only very recent converts to socialism. Some ten years later, Zola's graphic images were still providing Webb with a potent symbol of the 'unrestrained competitive horrors' to be found in modern industrial organization.[65]

From his references to the work of Hawthorne, Emerson, Thoreau, Whitman, Twain, James and Bellamy,[66] it would seem that the young Sidney was more widely read in American literature than the young Beatrice. Emerson and Bellamy were evidently the only American authors she perused up to the time of her marriage; though her confessed love for the former possibly outweighed in intensity any of Sidney's responses to these authors, which were often admiring or affectionate, but never unreservedly enthusiastic. (His most enduring fascination seems to have been with a minor work of psychological fiction by Bellamy, entitled *Dr. Heidenhoff's Process*, though he indicated that its literary qualities were not great.[67])

Sidney was not incapable of deep emotional involvement in literature.

His response to Heine suggests this; and it emerges quite clearly from his detailed account of one of the most celebrated writers produced by his own country in his own day — George Eliot. Webb's knowledge of English literature in general was very wide-ranging, especially in the field of nineteenth-century fiction and poetry; and the precision of some of his references to particular works and characters bespeaks a more than passing acquaintance.[68] But George Eliot was the only creative writer to whom he devoted an entire lecture. The exact date of the lecture is uncertain, though it would seem to have been drafted about 1881. While it can be seen as part of his growing interest at the time in the social and ethical thought of the English (and French) Positivists,[69] it is important to emphasize that the lecture did not concentrate exclusively on these elements in Eliot's works, but dealt with them in close relation to her capacities as an artist. In the opening sentence he announced his theme as the 'merits of a great artist'. He then went on to give a definition of art, or, rather, to make a distinction between art and science, on the basis of the former's appeal to 'our emotional faculties' and the latter's appeal to reason. He acknowledged that the individual lines of demarcation were not fixed absolutely but were 'personal and individual', varying according to the sensibility of each beholder. Despite the subjective nature of this emotional 'test' of art, there needed to be a consensus of 'many hearts' responding enthusiastically to a painting or a piece of music or a novel before the creators of such works could be considered 'great artists'. The writings of George Eliot, Webb made out, could command just such a consensus: her readers rose from perusing them with 'full hearts', stirred on the one hand by their extremely life-like pictures of human vice and weakness, and on the other by the noble ideals they represented. This effect, he asserted, constituted the 'chief excellence' of her books, 'not only in our estimation of their ethical value but also as works of art'.[70]

In later lectures he reaffirmed the differences in the bases and mani-festations of art and science; at the same time, he made clearer his position that they were not opposing or rigidly divided categories. His views on the relationship between art and science are important for their bearing on his evolution as a socialist. In the months preceding his own conversion to socialism he gave a lecture on that creed and its relation to economics. He distinguished between them precisely on the ground that economics was 'a branch of science' whose only object was 'knowledge of the laws of nature', whereas socialism, if not an actual branch of art, drew mainly on artistic 'rules' in constructing its theory 'as to the social structure most likely to conduce to happiness'.[71] Judging from his earlier distinction between art and science, the implication here would seem to have been that the gauging of social happiness was largely an emotional or intuitive process, rather than one of precise rational calculation — another clearly romanticist dilution of Benthamite utilitarianism.

Webb was still critical of socialism at this stage — especially its Marxian variety, which he continued to attack after he came to accept the socialist label for his own beliefs a few months later. His acceptance of this label did not betoken any sudden conversion, but was the culmination of an early attraction to socialism that was based in part on the very connections he saw between that creed and the 'rules of art'. It was in no tone of criticism, but with approval and respect, that he referred to the adherents of socialism, before joining their number, as 'exponents of a new experiment in the great art of living'. What initially repelled him about socialism was not the artistic basis of its recommendations for social happiness but, on the contrary, its scientific pretensions, which he saw reflected in the claims of certain adherents to have discovered new economic truths. Marxists were the particular butt of his criticism here. The claims of such adherents, he indicated, were not only invalid but also quite unnecessary in establishing the legitimacy of their cause. 'Socialists have discovered no new scientific truth...in Economics...and it does not appear that their case needs any.' Their distinctive contribution, he implied, lay in the new truths they had discovered in their own domain of the 'art of living'. The real economist could not provide such truths because, as a scientist, he was 'neutral between competing systems of life'. That neutrality, in turn, nullified or made irrelevant any socialist opposition to the 'approved truths' of economic science for in these approved truths (embodied, for example, in the 'still triumphant method of Ricardo, Mill and Cairnes') socialists could find 'all the foundation they...need to have for their maxims'.[72] Socialism and economics, like art and science, should not be and could not be in opposition to one another, because they were 'not on the same plane'. They were complementary, rather than antithetical, in Webb's view, and he did not disdain the intrinsic nature of either. When he began identifying himself with the socialist cause, he explicitly affirmed his belief that its economic tenets simply followed 'the teachings of the orthodox economists'. 'Our contention as socialists...that the rent of land...the interest on capital and the reward of exceptional ability are national products...due to the co-operating efforts of the whole community' could be found, he maintained, in 'Mill, Cairnes and Marshall'.[73] Webb came to socialism, then, on the conscious understanding that its distinctive value lay not in its specific economic teachings but in its general theory of social life based on intuitive feelings concerning the greater happiness which would result from communal co-operation through the entire social structure.

He himself did not concentrate on expounding the essentially 'artistic' rules and recommendations of this theory — partly, as we shall see, because he felt unqualified to do so. But he never lost sight of them in dwelling on the more prosaic administrative tasks connected with the practical realization of socialism. The recent claim that he sought to 'eliminate the emphasis on ethical or aesthetic motives found in Morris, Carpenter and others'[74] would have upset him as much as the review of his book, *Socialism in England*, which maintained that he had shown conclusively that 'real Socialism' was 'not of the William Morris type, with its faith in "moral suasion" as a substitute for law and its treatment of human nature as if we were all simpletons'. Webb railed against this distortion of Morris's — and of his own — position, scorning the National Press Agency as an 'unfair house' for allowing such a statement to be issued.[75]

If we look at his actual comments on Morris in *Socialism in England* and in later writings, we find that their tone is usually deferential and sympathetic, and that although they may complain of limitations in Morris's approach to socialism they never suggest that it is intrinsically or essentially false. He could even present that approach as an emblem for socialism in general as when he invoked Morris's name as proof that a socialist regime would not involve a 'rigidly centralized national administration of all the details of life'.[76] Webb might claim that Morris's preoccupation with socialist principles or ideals entailed a lack of engagement with the practical political and administrative problems of bringing socialism about;[77] but this in no sense and at no time implied a criticism of these principles *per se*. Webb endorsed — sometimes explicitly — the recurrent exhortations to brotherhood and fellowship in Morris, and saw in these general recommendations for social happiness the whole meaning and ultimate end of the political and administrative activities in which he himself had chosen to specialize. As late as 1923, he could be found reminding the Labour Party, on the threshold of office for the first time, that there was an even 'higher need' than practical government, and that this was to be located in those very doctrines of brotherhood and fellowship preached by Robert Owen and 'that other great British socialist — William Morris — in *The Dream of John Ball*'.[78]

Admittedly, such statements may have reflected a degree of political opportunism on Webb's part — an attempt to exploit a famous name so as to lend authority, even respectability, to the socialist cause; and Morris would no doubt have recoiled from the tactic. More seriously, there was a degree of sentimental idealizing in Webb's representation of Morris. In drawing attention to Morris's ideals of fellowship and brotherhood, he ignored or evaded the very strong emphasis which Morris also laid on the class struggle as a prerequisite for destroying the competitive basis of society. Criticizing that emphasis in Marx, Webb was capable even of pitting the ideals of fellowship and brotherhood against it, as if these presented a preferable alternative to class struggle. This in itself involved a serious distortion of Morris's approach, which in fact had derived much from Marx himself on the particular issue of class struggle.[79] This caricature, however, betokened not a wholesale dismissal or condemnation of that approach but an underlying reverence for its ultimate ends and a deep, personal admiration for their proponent. *A Dream of John Ball* had been one of the works which Webb — remote for once from any political arena — had chosen to read to Beatrice during their courtship;[80] and towards the end of his life — when he had retired altogether from the arena and had no further use for tendentious rhetoric — he looked back on Morris as 'the greatest socialist he had known'.[81]

In a review of the *Fabian Essays* in 1890, Morris criticized Webb and his followers for tending to 'over-estimate the importance of the *mechanism* of a system of society apart from the *end* to which it may be used'.[82] His barely-disguised scorn for 'Sidney Webbian permeation' and his disavowal of faith in the municipalization of public facilities as in any way reflecting or facilitating socialism, highlighted crucial divergences from the Fabians; but these never amounted to an actual dichotomy in socialist principles and ends.[83] Webb, for one, did see beyond the mechanistic side of socialism which Morris berated him for endorsing: in a paper he had produced only a couple of years or so before his contribution to the *Fabian Essays*, he could be found insisting that socialism was not just a scheme of social reform but much more: 'a faith, a scientific theory, and a judgment of morality on the facts of life'.[84] For all its criticisms, Morris's review of the *Fabian Essays* suggests that he fully appreciated the existence of this less mechanistic side to the Fabians' approach: its predominant tone was one of regret that the authors of a book, 'honestly devoted to the regeneration of society', should be so distracted along the way by compromises and half-measures which he felt could only damage or hold up the realization of their common ends. He did not suggest that even Webb — whose essay came nearest to provoking real anger in Morris — failed completely to share or recognize such ends. And he openly acknowledged that another of the essayists, Hubert Bland, had himself spoken of the need to attend 'not so much to the thing which the state does, as to the end for which it does it'. Morris stressed that there was a good deal in Bland's whole essay to the same purport, 'making it rather a curiosity in the book'.[85] These comments testify to the strong bond of sympathy between Morris and Bland which the latter was to put forward many years later as one of the main factors in his conversion to socialism.

Bernard Shaw's suggestions that Morris eventually came to accept the non-revolutionary 'Fabian way' to socialism is patently a distortion.[86] On the other hand, in demonstrating the strength and fidelity of Morris's adherence to a Marxist way, it is possible to exaggerate the width of the gap between Morris's and the Fabians' conceptions of socialism, and to suggest too great a degree of hostility towards the Fabians on Morris's part, or vice versa.[87] The next two chapters will aim among other things to point up some of the affinities — personal and ideological — underlying the obvious differences.

Three Fabian essayists and William Morris

Clear signs of sympathy with William Morris, or with the socialist principles he represented, may be found in the ideas which Graham Wallas, Sydney Olivier and Annie Besant expounded in their formative years and in their contributions to the *Fabian Essays*. These ideas provide further pointers to the aesthetic and literary origins of Fabian socialism, and, more particularly, to the strength of the romanticist ingredient in the ideological mixture represented by the Fabians' concerns. There were other important ingredients, of course, in the thought of these three Fabian essayists — including (once again) utilitarian and positivist ideas, as well as the moral force of evangelicalism, left over from a reaction against evangelical theology. That reaction was consistent, in fact, both with a susceptibility to romanticisim[1] and the rationalist streak in utilitarianism. In the very tension it reflected between these dominant philosophies of the age, Fabian socialism points up the dangers involved in drawing any rigid distinctions or clear-cut boundaries between them.

Morris's own criticisms of the *Fabian Essays* serve to convey the underlying sympathies between him and its authors. This is particularly the case with his treatment of the essay by Graham Wallas on 'Property under Socialism'. Part of this, he claimed, represented 'a net statement of the exaggeration of the value of a mechanical system'. Wallas 'allows himself to speak of Socialism as the "system of property-holding which we call Socialism" and goes on to say that this is not necessarily the wished-for new life "any more than a good system of drainage is health, or the invention of printing, knowledge"'. Morris countered this narrow and mechanical definition of socialism with a much broader, more exalted view: 'Socialism,' he asserted, 'is emphatically not merely "a system of property-holding", but a complete theory of human life... including a distinct system of religion, ethics and conduct, which, if put into practice, will not indeed enable us to get rid of the tragedy of life, as Mr. Wallas hints, but will enable us to meet it without fear and without shame.' The words 'allows himself' and 'emphatically' are important here: they suggest that Morris did not think Wallas had an intrinsically narrow and mechanical view of socialism, but one that seemed that-way because of the limited and imprecise definition which he had come to use. This was a lapse or concession which Morris himself could not allow to pass, though he raised the issue as a 'friendly objection'.[2] Only a year and a half before, he had asked Wallas to contribute 'from time to time' to the *Commonweal*, adding that 'the points of difference between us are not very great'.[3]

There are aspects of Wallas's background and earlier writings which bring out and explain the points of proximity to Morris. He was born in 1858 in the north-east of England where his father was an Anglican clergyman of a strong Evangelical persuasion. He was brought up, however, in an area far removed from this heavily industrialized section of the country. In 1860 or thereabouts the family moved to the south on Wallas *père*'s appointment to a vicarage in Barnstaple. It was in that small market town, set in the Devonshire countryside and almost completely isolated at the time from the effects of the Industrial Revolution, that Wallas spent the remainder of his childhood.[4] In 1871 he was sent away to school at Shrewsbury where he received a fairly orthodox classical education which six years later qualified him for entry as a scholar to Corpus Christi College, Oxford. Here he came under a range of diverse intellectual influences, including the teachings of Ruskin, who was a resident lecturer at the college. Wallas later recalled how he attended Ruskin's lectures and 'for a short time saw him almost every day'.[5]

Ruskin's lectures focussed on subjects in art but made a point of examining these in close relation to social and moral questions. J.H. Muirhead, who also attended them, recalled their 'frequent tirades against the destruction of English landscapes by the spread of industrialism'.[6] Personal exposure to such teachings may well have helped to stimulate Wallas's interest in Morris when he began to mix in socialist circles in the early and mid-1880s. In an introductory essay he wrote in 1907 for an edition of some of Ruskin's lectures, Wallas claimed that Morris had been 'Ruskin's noblest and most fruitful disciple' and quoted from Morris himself on how Ruskin's chapter on 'The Nature of Gothic' in his book, *The Stones of Venice*, had 'seemed to point out a new road on which the world should travel' by teaching that 'art is the expression of man's pleasure in labour; that it is possible for man to rejoice in his work...and...that unless man's work again becomes a pleasure to him, the token of which will be that beauty is once again a natural and necessary accompaniment of productive labour, all but the worthless must toil in pain'. Wallas added his own testimony to the impact of Ruskin's pronouncements on art in relation to contemporary society: these, he claimed, had represented

the first effective protest against the ugliness, the monotony, and the grime which accompanied the expansion of manufacturing industry during the nineteenth century.

Art, for Ruskin . . . meant the life and purpose and surroundings which make possible the creation of undying beauty . . . He could look right through the paper returns of leaping and bounding trade which hid from most men of that time the sight of blackened valleys and wasted childhood . . . He had learnt to loathe the easy social arithmetic which made the 'pain' of the week's toil exactly balance the pleasure of the weeks' wages. Perhaps, indeed, one can best sum up the purpose which underlay all Ruskin's best teachings on art by saying that he recalled to men's minds the possible worth and happiness of the ordinary working day.[7]

Wallas, of course, was not a disciple exclusively of Ruskin (any more than Morris was) and he explicitly stated in his essay of 1907 that Ruskin's 'artistic teaching' and 'social teaching' were to be approached in a spirit of 'historic sympathy' rather than of discipleship, as 'the social-science of our own time, in its slow task of subdivided labour, has to seek and form many allies for whom Ruskin had small regard'. He cited Darwin as an example here, and spoke of the necessary and valuable ideals of scientists 'to which no use of the word ''beauty'' corresponds'.[8] He might well have cited the positivist philosopher, Auguste Comte, in whom Ruskin affected to take no interest at all, despite the numerous parallels which contemporaries saw between their ideas and assumptions.[9] Even more pertinently, Wallas could have cited J.S. Mill and the 'utilitarian' economists, whom Ruskin had severely censured in his book, *Unto This Last*, for subscribing to theories of value which had no moral basis. While at Oxford, Wallas had begun to immerse himself in the ideas both of Darwin and Mill — entirely on his own initiative in the case of the former; but with some external guidance and encouragement in the case of the latter. Wallas's tutor during his last two years at Corpus Christi, Thomas Case, had made Mill's *System of Logic* the foundation of his teaching, and had directed any student interested in economic questions to *Principles of Political Economy* — the work of Mill's which Ruskin had singled out for particular criticism in *Unto This Last*.[10]

Millite and Ruskinian ideas were not completely opposed, however, as the last chapter of *Unto This Last* itself showed. There Ruskin claimed that Mill 'deserves honour among economists by inadvertently disclaiming the principles which he states, and tacitly introducing the moral considerations with which he declares his science has no connection. Many of his chapters are therefore true and valuable.'[11] At least a superficial link is discernible between Ruskin's conclusion that 'that country is richest which nourishes the greatest number of noble and happy human beings',[12] and the utilitarian commonplace that the aim of any state should be the achievement of 'the greatest happiness of the greatest number';[13] though, of course, Ruskin approved of Mill only insofar as he believed him to have departed from or to have seriously modified this commonplace by introducing the notion of qualities of happiness. Wallas signified his awareness of a link between Ruskin's views and the Millite version of utilitarianism in the last two sentences of the passage quoted above, where he alluded to the art critic's rejection of the cruder applications of the Benthamite 'hedonic calculus'[14] but went on to show that a definite form of human happiness, manifested in men's everyday occupations, represented a basic ideal for Ruskin. In the same essay, as we have seen, Wallas had quoted Morris's pronouncements on the necessity of 'pleasure in labour' and his acknowledgement to Ruskin for spreading the doctrine.

Wallas's own writings from the mid-eighties on bore the traces both of the Benthamite—Millite utilitarian tradition[15] and of the Ruskin—Morris tradition, without any real sense of contradiction. By that stage he had left Oxford and had worked as a schoolmaster both in Maidenhead and in London. He had kept up contacts, however, with a close friend from his Oxford days, Sydney Olivier, who on leaving university himself had moved directly to London to join the Colonial Office and had started to mix in various humanitarian, positivist, land-reform and socialist organizations which were then cropping up in the capital.[16] Both Olivier and Wallas shared much the same kind of social and educational background and had experienced a similar spiritual, as well as intellectual, development. Olivier's background will be discussed in greater detail below; but because of the cross-fertilization in their thought, it seems pertinent to examine some of its common sources straightaway.

Olivier's father, like Wallas's, was an Anglican clergyman with Evangelical leanings, and there had been an intense (though not completely unenlightened) religious atmosphere in both their homes.[17] Olivier had also been sent away to public school — Tonbridge — where some of that intensity was dissipated by the influence of a headmaster who embodied, in Olivier's words, a 'fearless rationalism'.[18] At Shrewsbury, Wallas had come under the influence of a master who, if not quite so advanced in his actual views, was uncommonly flexible and challenging in his teaching methods and served to encourage, rather than suppress, any inquiring or sceptical turn of mind in his pupils.[19] Both Wallas and Olivier managed to retain the essence of their faith at school. The atmosphere of their college at Oxford, however (Olivier came up to Corpus Christi as a classical scholar the year after Wallas), proved more dissipating still in this respect. The leanings of the teachers with whom they came into contact there were anything but Evangelical: Ruskin, for example, had already long repudiated the 'rabid Protestantism' of his early beliefs;[20] and Case, as noted above, was an avid disciple of Mill's, encouraging a utilitarian rationalism in all his students. In view of their exposure to this type of atmosphere, and their own voluntary explorations of Darwinian evolutionary theory at about the same time,[21] it is hardly surprising that Wallas and Olivier should have undergone at this stage a definite reaction against their Evangelical backgrounds. This had culminated, by the time they graduated, in a total rejection of Christianity.

As in Ruskin's own case, and that of several other lapsed Evangelicals in Victorian England,[22] the intense moral fervour underlying the faith in which they grew up still remained with them after they had discarded its theological trappings. Olivier and Wallas proceeded to re-direct all their fervour into working for social salvation in the world here and now: their activities and writings in the 1880s exemplified vividly that secularized ethical impulse which a fellow-contributor to the *Fabian Essays*, William Clarke, later identified as one of the main forces attracting young men to the socialist movement.[23] In Wallas and Olivier, as well as in various other Fabians, that impulse was so highly developed as to give their socialism a distinctly religious tone, which was reminiscent of (if not specifically derived from) Comte's 'religion of humanity'. Mixed in with this religious aspect — and elevating their socialism still further — were various aesthetic concerns and impulses, which revealed the extent of their susceptibility to romanticist notions, as articulated by Ruskin and Morris in particular.

Olivier attached himself to the socialist movement first: working in London after coming down from Oxford in 1882, he had greater opportunities for contact with the early proponents of socialism than Wallas, who remained in his teaching-post at Maidenhead till the end of 1884. The predilections of the two men were so similar, however, that Olivier was able to convince his friend of the validity of his new-found creed simply by 'sending him books, &c', so that Wallas came to accept socialism before settling in London himself early in 1885.[24] There is no record of what these books, let alone the '&c', comprised; though if Olivier enclosed any recommendations for other reading with his parcels, they might well have contained the advice to look at that work of Mill's which their college tutor had prescribed as the authoritative work on economics — *Principles of Political Economy*. In an article he published in 1884 in the socialist periodical, *To-Day*, Olivier intimated that the overall 'social' feeling of Mill's work and its almost 'uniformly progressive' position on questions of 'social economy' had helped to 'put men on the track of Socialism' in a more effective way than any overtly socialist writings.[25] (Some ten years later, William Morris himself recalled that while it was through Ruskin that he had 'learned to give form' to his discontent with modern civilization, it was through Mill that he had become finally convinced of the necessity of socialism, even though Mill had been arguing against that doctrine in the particular writings Morris consulted: in provoking his disagreement, the latter claimed, 'those papers put the finishing touch on my conversion to Socialism'.)[26]

On coming to London to take up a post at a school in Highgate, Wallas joined Olivier, Webb and Shaw in the debates at the Hampstead Historic Club on the various principles of political economy formulated by Ricardo, Mill, Marx and Jevons. It was through these debates that the early Fabians sorted out their own ideas on economic questions such as the criteria of 'value' and came to define the Society's non- (or anti-) Marxist position on such issues. Wallas did not become a member of the Fabian Society itself until the spring of 1886; the delay may be explained partly by the fact that he went away to Germany for a few months towards the end of 1885 after a wrangle with his school 'on a question of religious conformity' which culminated in his resignation.[27] On returning to England, however, he soon became an active Fabian, lecturing on the Society's behalf and contributing to its journal, the *Practical Socialist* (a forerunner of the *Fabian News*). He treated a wide range of themes in connection with socialism, including economic subjects such as rent and interest, but his emphasis was always on the moral aspects and implications involved. This was indicated in the very titles he chose: 'The Morals of Interest', for example, or 'Personal Duty under the Present System'. His emphasis on 'personal duty' or 'self-sacrifice' reflected the evangelical mould of his ideas; though the substance of these ideas was no longer theological in any sense. Service to society, not to God, was what he meant in exhorting his readers and listeners to such practices. In his article on 'Personal Duty', he claimed that a man was obliged to give up 'anything beyond what would come to him if capital were fairly distributed, except. . .where such expenditure is necessary for the most efficient carrying out of his social work'; and he enjoined men from his own middle-class background in particular — preaching 'self-sacrifice to the working-classes would be. . .a heavy task' — to 'seek for comfort by simplifying, not by complicating your surroundings'.[28] At other times he was more positive about these procedures, suggesting that what they involved, in effect, was not so much self-sacrifice as 'self-realisation'. This way of looking at man's duty to his fellows, in the interests of 'the common good', took its inspiration from 'Robert Owen's sunny confidence' and 'William Morris's jolly laugh' — 'the best and healthiest state of mind for a man to aim at whilst he is in the midst of the fight.'[29]

In a lecture he delivered before a socialist gathering arranged by Morris at Kelmscott House in the spring of 1886, he referred to the basic 'social idea' shared by himself and the assembled audience as 'a new religion' which 'alone' would be able to 'reintroduce order and happiness' into a world where the 'old social organism' had disappeared; but it was a religion which could be preached 'without hostility or compromise alike to believers and disbelievers in any theological system. . .your religion will find its noblest sphere not in Churches and on deathbeds but in the workshop the cornfield the assembly and wherever associated human life is most strong and most delightful'.[30]

Morris's definition of socialism, which he propounded in opposition to the one given by Wallas in the *Fabian Essays*, simply encapsulated Wallas's own views as presented in earlier lectures and articles. The capsule, as proffered on this occasion, was not quite so sweet perhaps: Morris's 'theory of human life' embracing 'a distinct system of religion, ethics and conduct' did not promise to eliminate the 'tragedy of life' if put into practice. On other occasions, however, Morris had been readier to assert in a more positive way the degree of general 'happiness' which socialism would facilitate. In a lecture he delivered in 1887, for example, he claimed:

I am bound to suppose that the realization of Socialism will tend to make men happy. What is it then makes people happy? Free and full life and consciousness of life. Or . . . the pleasurable exercise of our energies, and the enjoyment of the rest which that exercise or expenditure of energy makes necessary to us. I think that is happiness for all.[31]

Links between Wallas's outlook as a socialist and the Ruskin — Morris tradition are particularly evident in his views on the condition of art in contemporary society. Among his papers, there is a draft of a lecture on this subject — merely dated 'early'. Its assumptions and statements about the interconnections between art, morality and society reflect a clear sympathy with both Ruskin and Morris. Whether it was prepared before he joined the Fabian Society or just afterwards,[32] it suggests that this sympathy (or 'art feeling', as William Clarke later called it) was a potent force in turning Wallas against the prevailing economic structure and in directing him towards socialism. Rejecting any ideal of 'art for art's sake' as 'idiotic', Wallas insisted on the importance of the artist's message and of an audience ready to receive his message. Because of the present distribution of wealth, that audience was restricted to the very small class that could afford the money to buy up works of art and give the necessary financial support to the artist. 'The vast majority of the English nation was thereby deprived of the whole legacy of great thoughts and feelings greatly expressed which makes civilization valuable'; and art itself had become paralysed as a 'moral force'. It was of no use, ultimately, for artists to seek a moral restorative in the 'old religion': that was now as 'worn out' as the social system. There was little hope for art as long as its practitioners remained financially dependent on the upholders of that system — a position which turned them effectively into 'slaves'. For 'service not of the general good, but of the caprice of the unworthy few *is* slavery'. This enslavement of the artist in turn had further grave implications for the whole of society, as 'human progress and human happiness' needed 'many forms of service' for the general good; and, Wallas made

out, the services of artists were among the most important, as 'the cause
of freedom and brotherhood is also the cause of beauty and clear-
sightedness'. This equation was manifested in Wallas's eyes by the
existence of a few 'noble works' — the paintings of Millet, for example,
or the poems of Whitman — which seemed to show 'the beginnings of an
art which may deal without patronage and without prettiness, with that
great human life which it is possible for all to live'.[33] The casual but
knowing allusions to such artists — there are also appreciative references
to or quotations from Browning, Arnold, George Eliot and Turgenev —
provide hints as to Wallas's early tastes in art and reinforce William
Clarke's suggestion about the particular impact on the early Fabians of
the less 'genteel', more socially realistic forms of contemporary art.

In his contribution to the *Fabian Essays*, Wallas alluded to the
deficiencies of private patronage again, and in explaining the improved
conditions for the artist which would exist under a state-run system in a
non-plutocratic society, he made a general connection between the
services of art to the public and the attainment of happiness that was
explicitly utilitarian in its formulation. 'It is certain,' he asserted, 'that
any government which aimed at the greatest happiness of the greatest
number could afford to pay a capable author or artist possibly even more
than he gets from the rich men who are his present patrons, and certainly
more than he could get by himself selling or exhibiting his productions in
a society where few possessed wealth for which they had not worked.'
Clearly this utilitarian element in Wallas's socialist outlook was not
incongruous with his concerns for art but served to bring that outlook and
those concerns into closer identity with each other. In stressing elsewhere
in this essay the superiority of public to private means in the 'production
of happiness', he gave as examples the delights which would be afforded
workingmen by the provision of such things as 'public galleries and
theatres' and 'public opera'.[34]

In fact, while Wallas's contribution to the *Fabian Essays* defines
socialism simply as an alternative 'system of property-holding' to the one
prevailing under capitalism, his discussion of this 'mechanical' change
from private to public property did not ignore the wider implications of
change — moral as well as artistic — which he had dealt with earlier. His
spelling-out of the implications of that 'system of property-holding we call
socialism' reaffirmed a personal conception of what socialism could offer
the world which far transcended the limits of the received definition he
used. It is significant that Morris's criticism of the essay was most forcibly
directed against this definition and Wallas's acquiescence in it. For
Wallas's broader conception here of the hopes — and limitations — of
socialism resembled Morris's own conceptions in a number of general
respects and in spite of the difference in their definitions. Wallas, in fact,

ascribed the growth of these conceptions in himself to Morris's direct influence: 'The rest of us are merely inventing methods of getting what we desire. William Morris taught us what to desire.'[35]

Admittedly, there were differences of emphasis and detail in mapping out these conceptions which his tribute to Morris did not mention. For instance, in the *Fabian Essays*, Wallas paid little attention to the particular kinds of popular art in which Morris was interested, though the latter did not pick him up on this in his criticisms. Wallas, characteristically, laid the weight of his emphasis on the happiness which socialism could bring, but he showed a full awareness that it would by no means get rid of all the 'tragedy of life': 'Under the justest possible social system we might still have to face all those vices and diseases which are not the result of poverty and overwork.'

As we have seen, on earlier occasions, Morris had not been so reticent as he was in his criticism of Wallas about stressing the happiness which would result; and even if he had meant by it only what he acknowledged on this occasion — the ability of socialism to ease men's 'fear' and 'shame' in meeting life's tragedies — that was what Wallas himself partly implied by happiness. Elsewhere Morris had explicitly associated socialism with happiness on the grounds of the 'free and full life', the 'pleasurable exercise of energies' and the 'enjoyment of rest' which socialism would bring. Wallas also acknowledged this more positive side to happiness under a socialist regime. After elaborating the 'vices and diseases' which could still persist, he stated:

But in the households of the five out of six men in England who live by weekly wage, Socialism would indeed be a new birth of happiness. The long hours of work . . . without interest and without hope, the dreary squalor of their homes, above all that grievous uncertainty, that constant apprehension of undeserved misfortune, which is the peculiar result of capitalist production: all this would be gone, and Education, Refinement, Leisure, the very thought of which now maddens them, would be part of their daily life.

Furthermore, Wallas associated happiness under socialism with the growth of true fellowship, achieved through a shared simplicity of life and the personal sacrifices this involved on the part of those who had escaped or profited by the 'misery of our century'. Even to this latter class, he asserted,

Socialism offers a new and nobler life, when full sympathy with those about them, springing from full knowledge of their condition, shall be a source of happiness and not, as now, of constant sorrow — when it shall no longer seem either folly or hypocrisy for a man to work for his highest ideal. To them belongs the privilege that for each one of them the revolution may begin as soon as he is ready to pay the price. They can live as simply as the equal rights of their fellows require: they can justify their lives by work in the noblest of all causes.[36]

This clearly echoed Morris's hope — articulated most succinctly in his lecture on 'Art and Socialism' six years before — that 'we now living may see the beginning of that end which shall extinguish luxury and poverty...when the upper, middle and lower classes shall have melted into one class, living contentedly a simple and happy life'. Morris had indicated on the same occasion that the sacrifices and tasks thereby involved for 'we of the middle classes, we the capitalists and our hangers-on' would include 'renouncing our class' by 'supporting a socialist propaganda' and 'casting in our lot with the victim: with those who are condemned at the best to lack of education, refinement, leisure, pleasure and renown'.[37]

That Wallas, in the face of his broader conception of socialism, allowed himself to define his creed simply in terms of a system of property-holding, may be partly explained by the nature of his assignment in the *Fabian Essays*, which was to focus precisely on the topic of 'Property Under Socialism'. Sydney Olivier — though his own assignment was to write on 'The Moral Aspect of the Basis of Socialism' — conceded at the outset of his contribution that the volume was concentrating on socialism in a 'restricted sense', dealing with it 'not...as a religion' but 'as primarily a property-form, as the scheme for the supply of the material requisites of human social existence'. He gave a philosophical justification for this approach by claiming that since 'any metaphysic of ethics' was 'necessarily universal', there was 'in this sense no special ethic or morality of Socialism'.[38] In view of these claims, it is puzzling that Morris's review of the *Fabian Essays*, which criticized Wallas for neglecting to emphasize socialism's 'distinct system of religion, ethics and conduct', should not have taken Olivier to task for questioning the existence of such a system. Morris even commended Olivier's essay as 'worth taking the trouble of reading' and as 'less obvious to the objections against the Fabian opportunism, partly no doubt because of the subject but also partly, I think, (judging from the paper), because of the turn of the mind of the author himself'.[39] It would seem to have appeased Morris that Olivier had at least acknowledged a moral basis of some kind for socialism. Olivier had sought to define that basis by 'canons of moral judgment' which were already 'accepted generally' in the community. He had insisted at the same time that the ordering of national life by the public facilities and forms of property which he associated with socialism was the 'indispensable process...for the realization, in individuals and the State, of the highest morality as yet imagined by us'. Socialism derived its morality from 'the common contemporary sense of humanity'; but it offered a far more 'effectual' guarantee than contemporary society of the viability of that moral sense in the everyday lives of the 'mass of mankind'.[40]

Olivier's appreciation of the moral dimensions of socialism revealed (as in Wallas's case) a conception of its ultimate implications for the world which was far broader than the actual definition he gave. In an article he had written three years earlier, he had expressed his own dissatisfaction with the tendency for connotations of this 'grand and comprehensive' term to be limited to economic and material aspects; though he had maintained that 'to avoid confusion in the interchange of ideas, it is, perhaps, necessary in general so to limit it'. He had completely repudiated, however, any suggestion that socialist plans for the reconstruction of society began or ended with the mere 'provision of material necessaries and conveniences'. In the concluding part of the article, he had explicitly associated socialism (as Wallas had done, in the same year) with a 'new social religion' — a 'perfect human religion', which found its 'secret' in 'love', its 'true spirit' in 'co-operation', and its 'method' in 'Education' and 'the study and following of duties'. Only by this religion, he had claimed, could the 'individualist motives for exertion' in a competition-based society be supplanted: 'competitive individualism' of all kinds — not just its manifestations under capitalism — was for him the object of any 'complete socialist criticism', so that something more positive and inspiring than anti-capitalist polemics was required.[41]

In another article, published only a year before his contribution to the *Fabian Essays*, he had spelled out some of the non-material aspects of human life which the present individualist system prevented 'the majority' from enjoying to any substantial degree: 'the moral elements of human existence, the healthy family life, the love of married companions, the dignified leisure of old age . . . access to literature and music . . . facilities of travel to scenes of natural beauty and centres of artistic or historical interest'. The access to the arts and to nature, he maintained, comprised 'the chief of the advantages' given by 'economic emancipation'. In a socialist community these advantages would be extended to all. 'The great surplus now consumed in rent and interest' would be redistributed in such a way as to ensure 'a relaxation of labour' sufficient for the 'wholesome leisure' of everyone and to provide a range of communal facilities sufficient for the fulfilment of 'all those conditions that are really desired by human beings when they are thinking not of their stomachs and their clothes, as the gauge of their prosperity, but of their freedom and their culture as the satisfaction of their human capabilities'.[42]

The 'turn of the mind' revealed by Olivier in these articles clearly tended in a similar direction to Morris's, reflecting basic sympathies on artistic as well as moral grounds. Morris may well have read them, as they were published in a prominent socialist journal (*To-Day*); and he was certainly acquainted with their author who used to attend his socialist gatherings at Kelmscott House.[43] Significantly, however, in the approving reference he made to Olivier when reviewing the *Fabian Essays*, Morris

indicated that he was 'judging' the young Fabian's turn of mind specifically on the basis of his contribution to that volume. On examining this
contribution closely, we find the same broad grounds of sympathy underlying the more overt utilitarian rationalism. Olivier made clear that the
particular forms of property and socio-economic schemes by which
socialism could be defined, in a 'restricted sense', were not important just
in themselves; their capacity for satisfying every man's basic 'material
requisites' created conditions of general stability and health in society
which were indispensable for 'the common birth and satisfaction of the
secondary desires, the desires which have created *all that is most valuable*
in civilization and which find their satisfaction in art, in culture, in human
intercourse, in love'.[44] Advances in the 'refinements of social morality'
and in the conception and fulfilment of these 'secondary and more
distinctly human desires' would be a matter of education, which capitalist
society had denied the bulk of its members by depriving them of any
'leisure to learn'. Under socialism, children would be released from all
'non-educational labour', and there would be no compulsion on the adult
'to work for more than the socially necessary stint'. Actual public
expenditure on education would also be 'considerably increased'. Most
of this would be used to finance schools for children. The 'remainder of
education,' Olivier stated, 'would be a comparatively inexpensive matter';
and there may yet come a time when parents were 'more generally in a
position to instruct their own children'. It is worth noting here that the
bases of Olivier's conception of education under socialism — be it of an
institutional or non-institutional kind; for children or for adults — were
almost entirely aesthetic and literary in nature. He saw the role of public
education for the young as being one of training the mind 'to appreciate
the inexhaustible interest and beauty of the world and to distinguish good
literature from bad'. For those whose mind had been trained in this way,
the process of schooling would continue through the provision of
literature 'dirt-cheap' and the communal enjoyment of 'all the other
educational arts'. The 'schools of the adult', he claimed, were 'the journal
and the library, social intercourse, fresh air, clean and beautiful cities, the
joy of the fields, the museums, the art-gallery, the lecture-hall, the drama
and the opera': such schools must become 'free and accessible to all'.[45]

The yoking together of Olivier's concerns with nature and art and his
concerns with socialism may have been consolidated under Morris's own
influence. By the middle of the 1880s, his wife recalled, Olivier had
already developed 'a great admiration' for Morris, evinced by his regular
attendance at the socialist gatherings at Kelmscott House and (on a more
personal level) by his reading aloud to her from Morris's works, rather as
Sidney Webb was to do while courting Beatrice. (Webb, as noted above,
chose to read *A Dream of John Ball*; Olivier's particular favourite was

Sigurd the Volsung, the epic poem based on an Icelandic saga.[46]) Olivier himself recalled the meetings which Morris held at Kelmscott House in an article he published in the *Spectator* in 1934 on the centenary of Morris's birth. He gave some impression here of the particular impact which Morris's synthesis of ideas on art, nature and society had on his young mind:

Morris, having received his most stimulating clue from Ruskin's chapter on 'The Nature of Gothic', and having improved on Ruskin's formulation of it — broadening it from the insistence that Art must copy Nature to the perception that art is actually the expression of Nature through the temperament of a human producer — was able to amplify and give profounder significance than even Ruskin did to the relevance of this clue to the ghastly scene of modern commercial and industrial society. It became obvious why it was that capitalist civilization should have been making the whole world hideous. First, the mechanization of industry...simply gutted the production of all vital ingredients whatever...and, secondly, the capitalist purpose of profit-making superseding the purpose of production for use...had converted the workers into undifferentiated batches of 'labour force', making they know not what for they know not whom, and...'working'... for their employer's rent, interest and profits.[47]

It needs to be stressed, however, that Morris's teachings, as summarized in this memoir, were important to Olivier not in forming but in helping to crystallize his dominant concerns. Their impact on him can be explained by the fact that they appealed to various instincts which were already ingrained in him and that they helped fulfil the need for clarification and synthesis which that complex of instincts had created. Darwinian evolutionary theory had left him dissatisfied because of its failure to explain the growth of spiritual values or art, particularly music.[48] In February 1884 (probably before he had come into contact with the Morris circle) Olivier had confided in his future wife that it was not enough for him that men should find 'perfect satisfaction for their nature in one line and religion, say Christianity, the Salvation Army, Socialism, Art': what he wanted to know was 'the common element in all these'. He described himself as 'full of desire to investigate all forms of religion and feeling'.[49] His sense of the existence of 'a common element' perhaps proceeded from the convergence or intersection of some of these 'lines' within his own sensibility. We have already seen how his very rejection of Christianity was closely linked with his immersion in socialism through the intense moral fervour he transferred from the one form of commitment to the other. The general feelings for 'Art', evident in his later socialist writings, can be traced back to a period long before his links with socialism began; but the particular way in which his feelings for art developed helped create those links.

Feelings for natural beauty had been engendered in him by the environment in which he spent his early childhood. He was born at Colchester in Essex in 1859, though his father succeeded to a series of curacies elsewhere in the south, and the young Olivier spent part of his childhood in areas that offered him easy access to the Sussex downs and opportunities for idyllic escapes 'into fields of spring-flowers and hay grass'. He was to remain an enthusiastic country walker and observer of natural scenery throughout all his travels in later life both in England and abroad. Never just a casual sightseer, he claimed in his memoirs to have had a special relationship with nature from about the age of four or five. A day spent alone on the downs at that age had resulted in the first stirrings of 'a distinct order of consciousness': an 'assured awareness of a private, privileged and exceedingly spacious world' of his own against which he set 'the established and orthodox and comfortably provided world' of his upbringing. It was 'not a critical consciousness' as such, though it induced in him a sense of dissatisfaction which put him at a distance not only from his family but also from his schoolfellows, who were more or less conventional products of 'that well-provided society of the period'. His discovery of a private world in nature, with 'no recognisable place in the established scheme of education, theology or religion', may well have sown the seeds of revolt against that scheme in later years. For to him 'the living and growing things in the fields and woods' offered a far greater sense of 'reality'.[50] Olivier's recollections of his responses to nature as a child cannot automatically be taken as a completely accurate record, subject as they might be to nostalgic oversimplification. Even as an adult gloss on childhood experience, however, they are significant in revealing a continuing strain in his make-up that has been generally overlooked: the romanticist strain. Its particular manifestation here — a reverence for nature as a repository of spiritual enlightenment and truth and as a stimulus in itself to a special consciousness of that truth — suggests that in one important area at least his sensibility and outlook can be associated more with the so-called 'Romantic—Naturalist' tradition of Goethe, Wordsworth and Thoreau than with the views of J.S. Mill, who attempted to counter the force of that tradition.[51] Wallas later recalled Olivier's susceptibility to the sort of bucolic romanticism which had influenced the earliest Fabians in Thomas Davidson's circle and which had been enshrined in the writings of Edward Carpenter. It seems that Olivier had even entertained plans at one stage of becoming an agricultural labourer.[52] Wallas's own romanticism certainly never went as far as this.

Olivier's contacts with art and literature served to heighten the sense of unreality he found in the values and conventions — social as well as religious — that were subscribed to by his family and class. There were connections from the start between his love of nature and his artistic impulses and sensitivities. He recalled coming back from his childhood excursions into the countryside 'shouting verses of inspiration to original melody'. The inspiration from nature, manifested in his own poetic efforts,[53] was more important than inspiration from the works of established artists until, at his first boarding school, he came across some novels by George Meredith. These, he maintained, were the first books which effectively contributed to his 'spiritual education'. For him they evinced a clear understanding of the truths and realities he had hitherto found only in private communion with nature. He did not go into detail about the sympathies he felt between himself and Meredith; though the latter's recurrent conception of nature as 'both a context and a contributing source to the awakening of spiritual energy in a human being'[54] had discernible links with the Romantic—Naturalist tradition and clearly accorded with Olivier's own discoveries. There were some apparently 'anti-romantic' tendencies in Meredith as well — further reflections perhaps of the ambiguities and self-critical elements in romanticism noted above. For example, in *The Adventures of Harry Richmond* (1871), which Olivier specifically mentioned as one of the works which had influenced him, Meredith had dramatized the triumph of 'trained reason'[55] over passion in the conduct of personal relationships and suggested the benefits for society which that triumph could provide — a theme which might have prepared Olivier for the rationalist teachings of his Millite tutor at Oxford, Thomas Case.[56] But it was the social criticism in Meredith's novels — the exposure of bourgeois snobbery, for example, and of the shams and illusions of the gentlemanly ideal[57] — which possibly proved the most arresting feature for a young boy accustomed to the 'comfortably-provided genteel life' of provincial vicarages.

Olivier's family was not highly prosperous, and certainly lacked the ample resources from large-scale industrial and commercial ventures which had supported Edward Pease's and Beatrice Webb's. Neither, however, was it prey to the financial insecurities besetting those families of other early Fabians which had engaged in rather smaller, more precarious businesses and trades (Clarke's, Chubb's, Sidney Webb's, for example). There were 'comfortable endowments' from ancestors who had dabbled in commerce and manufacture; and these helped to fill out Olivier's father's earnings. But both his father and mother looked down on money-making professions as 'not suitable for a gentleman'; and brought up their children to do likewise. The young Sydney's disapproval of 'buying cheap and selling dear', therefore, derived from an initial acceptance of his parents' values — and not a rejection, as in the case of so many other Fabians. What he did come to reject was the self-complacent philosophy and insulation from economic and social realities on which his parents' values were based. This was revealed not only in their rather snobbish attitudes to trade but also in their conception of poverty as either God-given or the fault of the poor themselves.[58] Olivier's own first direct contact with poverty came when he moved to London after leaving university and carried out voluntary work under the direction of Gertrude Toynbee's 'Sanitary Aid Committee' as a health-inspector in the East End slums. But his social conscience (or 'class con-sciousness of sin' as Beatrice Webb was to call it[59]), had already been raised by this stage, and he was on the verge of conversion to socialism.

One of the earliest factors in raising that conscience was the work of another novelist whose 'period of popularization' coincided with Olivier's last years at school: Emile Zola. His books, as we have seen, made a great impact on the young Beatrice and Sidney, and also on Graham Wallas, who claimed that 'he who takes up one of Zola's stories. . . puts it down with a picture of injustice, and brutality, and disease burnt into his brain'.[60] For Olivier, Zola's dissections of French urban and industrial life, revealing the squalor and poverty underlying the surface elegance and glamour, afforded him his first substantial (albeit vicarious) insight into milieux far removed from his own secure and comfortable middle-class existence. He talked of how the Frenchman's work had filled 'large gaps in the legible record of the known and visible world. It made that record a little less artificial and insincere'.[61] It certainly presented — as did Meredith's work — a sharp contrast with the art and literature that Olivier had been fed at home and at school.

The strong Evangelical basis of his parents' religious beliefs had not, in their case, entailed an excessive puritanism which frowned on all artistic activities. On the contrary, Olivier related how he had been 'reared among painters and musical amateurs'; his mother, for example, was a talented water-colourist, who taught her son to draw. He was also encouraged to read poetry and fiction: though most of this (even pages of Dickens that he was given to learn by heart) was of the 'orthodoxly accepted' variety. Any appreciation of the arts that he gained during childhood was limited, therefore, by their unchallenging conventions, or by the unchallenging way in which they were presented to him: 'they belonged for me,' he recalled, 'to that unquestioned, nutritive world' which provided his comfortable means of existence: 'I had no notions of what literature, or poetry, or music, or art, really were.'[62] His perusal of Meredith and Zola, away from the confines of his home, served to convey for him the realities of art and its potential connections with the realities of nature and life at large.[63] It was but a short step from here to a full awareness of the artificialities of the orthodox religious beliefs in which he had been brought up and of the limitations of their relevance to society. The capacity of art itself to heighten that awareness in him was reflected in some observations he made on visiting a church in the East End at just about the time of his acceptance of socialism. A service was in progress, and he heard a woman singing 'a very lovely setting of words' which struck him as one of the most perfect pieces of simple poetry, 'equal to Blake or Wordsworth'. The service as a whole, however, distressed him because

> here was the universal language, music, beautifully rendered, to a scanty congregation, in a district of London to all appearances utterly dead and hopeless in most respects and giving itself in all earnestness to forms which never-more . . . can supply what is wanted for these people.
>
> It seems like some madness, the eternal 'truth' of music, and the strength which simple bare expression in adequate language of conviction really felt gives to poetry, chained to this corpse.[64]

The teachings of William Morris soon demonstrated for Olivier how art could be related to the new social religion of which they were both adherents for the greater health of art itself and for the greater happiness and vitality of society as a whole.

It was by attending the Kelmscott House gatherings in the mid-1880s that Olivier and Wallas — as well as other early Fabians, including Sidney Webb[65] — were first exposed to Morris's personal influence. The Fabian Society as a whole had the opportunity of hearing him when he took up an invitation to deliver a lecture to the group in July 1886. His subject was 'The Aims of Art'; and the lecture was chaired by his close disciple in artistic principles and practices, Walter Crane (now a Fabian himself). Crane's presence was not the only mark of sympathy between speaker and audience. A report in 'The Fabian Society and Socialist Notes', published in the journal, *Our Corner*, said that Morris's paper had proved to be 'most interesting';[66] and another report, in the Fabian periodical, *Practical Socialist*, showed that the discussion which followed had been mainly taken up, not with criticism of the paper, but with a re-affirmation and elaboration of Morris's ideas. One of the contributors to that discussion was Annie Besant, who edited *Our Corner* and who was to write the chapter on 'Industry Under Socialism' in the *Fabian Essays*. She emphasized the point that 'the hard struggle for bread — in which the wronged classes are so constantly engaged — crushes out all desire for the beautiful, and indeed, blunts the aesthetic sense'.[67] This was but a summing-up of a theme which Morris had presented in his earliest socialist lectures, and which was clearly echoed in the current lecture under discussion.[68] Mrs Besant's point, however, did not represent a stray observation, made out of perfunctory respect for a celebrated guest speaker. She herself was firmly convinced that this point was important, reiterating it in various ways throughout her own socialist writings, and continually emphasizing its chief corollary, as Morris had expressed it in his Fabian lecture: that once men had shaken off that 'compulsion of the gambling-market to waste their lives in hopeless toil', their instincts for beauty and their imagination would be set free and result in the production of 'such art as they need'. Under socialism, Mrs Besant reaffirmed, 'all the treasures of knowledge and of beauty...all the delights of scenery and of art...all that only the wealthy enjoy today' would come 'flowing back to enrich the worker's life'.[69] This argument was not missing from her chapter in the *Fabian Essays*. She asserted towards the end of this chapter:

> The daily bread being certain, the tyranny of pecuniary gain will be broken; and life will be used for living and not in struggling for the chance to live. Then will come to the front all those multifarious motives which are at work in the complex human organism even now, and which will assume their proper importance when the basis of physical life is assured. The desire to excel, the joy in creative work, the instinct of benevolence; all these will start into full life, and will serve at once as the stimulus to labour and the reward of excellence.[70]

Morris disregarded this passage in his review of the *Fabian Essays*. Admittedly, the rest of Mrs Besant's contribution was mainly taken up with trying to work out the practical administrative and bureaucratic details of all the activities and institutions of a socialist state, or of a state 'during the transition period' to socialism. (These included suggestions concerning various artistic activities and institutions, such as the provision of communal concerts and entertainments, and the operation of a state patronage scheme.[71]) Morris, characteristically, failed to be impressed by any such 'mechanical' approach, dismissing the essay as an unsatisfactory sketch of 'State Socialism in practice in its crudest form'.

It is significant, however, that he exempted the author of this essay, claiming that her contribution was unsatisfactory because of 'the difficulty of the subject', and not through 'any shortcoming on her part'.[72] Having achieved a considerable reputation as an orator and publicist in several advanced causes in the 1870s — mainly associated with the Secularist movement led by Charles Bradlaugh — Mrs Besant was almost as celebrated a convert to socialism as Morris himself; and had proceeded to enlarge the scope of her activities within the new movement by various means.[73] As well as lecturing and writing articles, she could be found helping to organize conferences and committees among socialist groups, championing working-class causes and agitations (she effectively led the match-girls' strike of 1888), and running periodicals, such as *Our Corner*, which became a forum for socialists' views on a wide range of subjects (including the arts, on which subject she commissioned two other socialists of the day, Edward Aveling and Bernard Shaw, to contribute a regular column. This magazine also published, in serialized form, two of Shaw's novels, and several other items of imaginative literature by socialists). The breadth of interests and activities through which Mrs Besant established her prominence within the socialist movement no doubt obliged Morris to acknowledge that the limitations he discerned in her contribution to the *Fabian Essays* were not truly representative of her. If he had any direct acquaintance with her other writings, he must have known that she was actively sympathetic to his abiding concerns with the provision of beauty in the lives, surroundings and work of all, and that she abhorred as much as he the way in which the highly competitive, heavily mechanized system of trade and industry in England effectively deprived the bulk of the population of any such provision. He and she had been personally acquainted with each other from before the time of his Fabian lecture on 'The Aims of Art'. She recalled that, in the spring of 1886, she had helped organize a conference precisely on the topic of 'The Present Commercial System and the Better Utilisation of Natural Wealth for the Benefit of the Community', and that Morris had spoken at it along with various other socialist luminaries including Aveling, Edward Carpenter, Bland, Webb and herself.[74] At about the same time, she sent Morris her collection of articles on 'Modern Socialism' for comment, and he seems to have been sufficiently impressed to recommend the usefulness of republishing them, with certain revisions.[75] The basic sympathies between Morris and Mrs Besant, suggested by their appraisal of the various costs to the working class incurred by the current commercial system, were possibly a significant factor in the continuing cordiality of their personal relationships, enabling these to survive the increasing bitterness of his disputes with the Fabians (including Mrs Besant herself) over their recourse to 'parliamentarism' and similarly moderate political tactics.[76]

In her autobiography, published in 1893, Annie Besant drew specific attention to the 'devotion of that noble and generous genius, William Morris' in the cause of working-class socialism.[77] As in the case of other Fabians, her reverence for Morris, and her re-echoing of some of his basic ideas, did not mean that these ideas were actually formed for her by personal exposure to Morris's influence in the socialist movement. Their development and particular formulation may have been encouraged or assisted by Morris's teachings; but one still has to account for her receptiveness to such teachings in the first place. The roots of her ideas as expressed in the 1880s can in fact be traced back to instincts and sensitivities which were with her from childhood and their interaction with a range of other personal and environmental influences. It is not necessary to examine these in full here. There are already adequate accounts of the religious and even the suppressed sexual impulses which lay behind her various intellectual and political commitments.[78] Biographers and historians, however, have generally ignored the strong aesthetic impulses involved in her commitment to socialism in the later 1880s, even while acknowledging her aesthetic interests and tastes. The evolution of the relationship between those interests and tastes, on the one hand, and her political commitments, on the other, needs to be traced.

Her own early environment and education particularly favoured the development of those instincts for artistic and natural beauty which she came to see as part of a common inheritance denied to most of mankind by the present commercial system. Her father, a doctor by training, had benefited from that system by exploiting a family link with the City and gaining a lucrative position there in business completely unconnected with his professional qualifications. He died when his daughter was five (1852) but he made a lasting impression on her as a 'keenly intellectual and splendidly educated man' who found his 'daily household delight' in the 'treasures of ancient and modern literature'. On his death, the family suffered some financial hardship as he had left only a 'trifle of ready money'. It would accord with a pattern among certain of the early Fabians if Annie Besant's distaste for the world of Victorian capitalism was first occasioned by her family's own misfortunes at its hands. There is, however, no direct evidence of this.

The 'struggle and anxiety' which followed this sudden removal of financial security did not entail complete impoverishment. The family was still able to live in reasonably comfortable and congenial surroundings, repairing as it did to a charmingly old and rambling house in Harrow-on-the-Hill with a large garden and an impressive view of wooded countryside. This same view, Annie Besant pointed out in some early recollections, had once proved a great inspiration for Byron. Her own appreciation of this idyllic setting did not, however, reflect the specifically romanticist view of nature which can be discerned in the young Sydney Olivier. As a child, she even entertained a positive dislike of Wordsworth, though she read him 'conscientiously enough'. Shelley had been one of her father's favourites — perhaps appealing to his 'deeply and steadily sceptical' attitude to religion — but her own early enthusiasms in literature were for pre-romantic Christian allegory. Dante, Milton and Bunyan were all great favourites, and she recalled in particular the thrill she received from *Paradise Lost*, which she used to recite aloud while sitting in a tree in her garden, gazing into the 'unfathomable blue of the sky' and losing herself 'in an ecstasy of sound and colour'.[79] The combination of great art with intense religious feeling, in an idyllic natural setting, was an irresistible one for her. For if there was an important religious side to her artistic interests, there was also an 'artistic side of religion' which strongly appealed to her. This had formed an important element in her mother's attachments to higher Anglicanism; and its impact registered itself fully on the young Annie after she had visited some churches in Paris on a school trip and discovered in the rituals of the Catholic mass a real 'sensuous enjoyment' — a 'gratification of the aesthetic emotions. . .dignified with the garb of piety'.[80]

Her own religious development up to that stage had been in the hands of a strictly Evangelical schoolmistress. While imbuing her pupils with much more austere and puritanical forms of piety, she had by no means tried to stultify all 'aesthetic emotions' within them, but on the contrary had provided several outlets for these. For example, she had organized scenic walks and excursions in the English countryside and on the Continent, and encouraged her charges to write up their impressions of these. She also had them taught music by a special master, thereby consolidating in Annie an interest which was nurtured at home by her mother's musical activities and which proved to be a life-long passion for her.[81]

The religious confusions of her adolescence, reflected in the tension between her Evangelical upbringing and her attractions to Catholicism, turned to religious doubts, after a disastrous marriage to an Anglican curate (the Reverend Frank Besant) and the near-fatal illness of a beloved child of that marriage. The 'fearful agony caused by doubt' led her to consult various works of theological criticism — from Broad Church, Christian Socialist, theistic and agnostic viewpoints. These works conveyed elements of the 'poetry, beauty, enthusiasm, devotion' still to be found in Christianity; but Annie Besant was already appreciative of such elements from her own experiences and perceptions. What she sought, at the height of her crisis of faith, was a solid 'rock' of reassurance as to the basic validity of that faith on which she might build her own anew. This rock her reading failed to provide; and some of it made the former foundations of her faith shakier than ever. Matthew Arnold's *Literature and Dogma*, for example — one of the works to which she referred — rejected all notion of God as a person; tended to dismiss the miraculous and supernatural aspects of Christianity, or the conventional interpretation of these; and indicated that the spiritual truths which Scripture had to offer were to be apprehended by treating the Bible as a literary work, not as a literal guide. It was hardly surprising that on perusing this work (published in the early 1870s) she found a return to the fundamentalist notions of her old evangelical beliefs 'more and more impossible'.[82]

During her spiritual struggles she had come into contact with some influential members of the free-thought movement in London and had been introduced to its leading exponent, Charles Bradlaugh. It was not long before she came to accept his doctrine of atheism (defined as 'without God' rather than 'no God'[83]) and began to channel all her energy and zeal into writing and lecturing on behalf of his organization, the National Secular Society. In changing the focus of commitment from God to man, from spiritual to 'Materialist' or mundane concerns, Secularism lacked

none of the opportunities for 'enthusiasm' and 'devotion' with which
Christianity had provided her. In essence it represented a popular species
of the positivist religion of humanity, defining the object of life as the
'ultimate building up of a physically, mentally, morally perfect man'; and
it based itself on a firm ethical doctrine — derived directly from
utilitarianism — which 'judged all actions by their effect on human
happiness, in this world now and in future generations'.[84] Total loss of
faith in a righteous God, she explained — and she could have been
speaking for several of those who ended up taking the Fabian route —
only made her 'more strenuously assertive of the binding nature of duty,
and the overwhelming importance of conduct'.[85]

Elements of beauty — aesthetic as well as moral — which had exercised
such a strong appeal for her in Christianity were not missing from
Secularism either. God was removed; but she wondered how anyone could
maintain that that automatically removed all beauty: 'Is there . . .,' she
asked, 'no beauty in the idea of forming part of the great life of the
universe, no beauty in conscious harmony with nature, no beauty in
faithful service, no beauty in ideals of every virtue?' At least some of
these elements were actually enriched and compounded by Secularism.
She explained in her *Autobiography* that the 'Atheistic Philosophy'
underpinning that movement, having outgrown any 'anthropomorphic
deities', left one 'face to face with Nature, open to all her purifying,
strengthening inspirations', and she supplemented this claim with a
quotation from a tract she wrote in the mid-1870s: ' "There is only one
kind of prayer which is reasonable, and that is the deep, silent adoration of
the greatness and beauty and order around us, as revealed in the realms of
non-rational life and in Humanity." '[86] The peculiar inspirations and
revelations which she now confessed to finding in nature indicate that she
had grown closer to the 'Romantic–Naturalist' tradition described above
since arriving at a utilitarian–rationalist position. These two strains were
quite capable of co-existing, as we have seen also in Sydney Olivier's case.

In a later tract on Atheism, she explained how that creed would take
over the specifically 'artistic side' of the Christian religion and give it a
much wider and much more fruitful application:

Atheism will utilise, not destroy, the beautiful edifices which, once wasted on God, shall
hereafter be consecrated for man. Destroy Westminster Abbey, with its exquisite arches,
its glorious tower of soft, rich colour, its stonework light as if of cloud . . .? Nay, but re-
consecrate it to humanity . . . The glorious building, wherein now barbaric psalms are
chanted . . . shall hereafter echo the majestic music of Wagner and Beethoven, and the
teachers of the future shall there unveil to thronging multitudes the beauties and the
wonders of the world.[87]

This was written in 1885, the year of her conversion to socialism. It
suggests itself how her concerns as a socialist for the 'aesthetic sense'

and cultural welfare of the working classes grew naturally out of the
passion for art (and beauty generally) which was always associated with
her religious impulses, whether Christian or Secularist—Humanitarian.
Part of that passion, as it developed during her Secularist—Humanitarian
phase, consisted precisely in the desire to make 'the beauties of the world'
available to all mankind. She came to observe, however, that it was not
simply a God-centred religion which prevented the 'multitudes' from
attaining to a proper and fruitful appreciation of those beauties. The
poverty which the 'present method of wealth-production and wealth-
distribution' inflicted on them was a more basic cause. In an article she
wrote in 1886 on 'Why I Am A Socialist', she made clear that one of the
reasons was directly related to the 'failure of our present civilisation' to
solve the problems of poverty and thereby eliminate a situation in which a
section of society had access to 'art, beauty, refinement — all that makes
life fair and gracious' whereas the rest were condemned to 'drudgery,
misery, degradation'. Given the nature of modern civilization, those life-
enriching qualities had actually come to depend for their existence among
the higher classes on the continuing degradation of the lower and this
only accentuated class divisions:

The culture of their [the workers'] superiors is paid for with their ignorance; the graceful
leisure of the aristocrat is purchased by the rough toil of the plebeian...Such is modern
civilisation. Brilliant and beautiful where it rises into the sunlight, its foundation is of
human lives made rotten with suffering...Education, training, culture, these make class
distinctions, and nothing can efface them save common education and equally refined
life-surroundings.

Such facilities could not be made truly common until land and capital
themselves, now so ill-distributed, became 'common property', thereby
eliminating the basis of the present exploitation or 'enslavement' of the
non-propertied by the propertied. This was precisely what socialism
promised to bring about. 'My socialism,' she claimed, 'is based on the
recognition of economic facts, on the study of the results which flow
inevitably from the present economic system.'[88]

As she implied throughout this article — and indicated explicitly
elsewhere — it was not just the 'economic soundness of its basis' which
appealed to her in socialism but the combination of that with a 'splendid'
and 'beautiful' ideal which looked forward to a true 'social brotherhood'
and the 'rendering possible to all of a freer life' by the provision of
'health, comfort, leisure, culture, plenty for every individual'. That ideal
— or that interpretation of the basic socialist ideal — corresponded to a
deeply-felt and long-rooted sense of mission within herself. 'All my life,'
she rather vaguely recollected, 'was turned toward the progress of the
people and the helping of man.'[89] A specific clue to the impulses behind
that altruistic mission was contained in a letter she wrote to an Anglican

clergyman, J.W. Ashman, in 1889, the year that the *Fabian Essays* appeared. Alluding here to her 'love' for the poor — 'those rough, coarse people who have paid their lives for our culture and refinement' — she maintained that the devotion of her abilities to their interests represented the 'mere bare debt that I owe, for my class to them'; for those abilities had been 'cultivated at their cost'.[90] Here is a clear example of how the 'class consciousness of sin', which Beatrice Webb perceived as one of the chief motivating impulses of the Fabians, could be roused by specifically cultural considerations. In Annie Besant's case, its main focus seems to have been the causal relationship she came to see between the wealth of opportunities provided by her middle-class upbringing for the development of cultured tastes and sensitivities and the dearth of similar opportunities available to the working class.

She relates how she was brought up to regard the poor as 'folk to be educated, looked after, charitably dealt with'. A rather unorthodox family friend, who had been closely associated with the Chartists and had set himself up as a working-man's lawyer, attempted to wean her from this 'decorous Whiggism', impressing on her at every opportunity that the poor were the real 'wealth producers', with a right 'to self-rule, not to looking after . . . to justice, not to charity'.[91] The lessons she received from this 'tutor in Radicalism' must have helped prepare her for the progressive political views subscribed to by the leaders of the Secularist movement with whom she became acquainted on losing her faith. Her attachments to Radicalism (especially as personified in Bradlaugh) remained strong throughout the early eighties; though by the middle of the decade the socialist movement in England had been revived, and its texts and teachings (including Marx's critique of the current economic system in *Capital*) gave her an insight into the 'deeper economic causes of poverty' that had not been provided by any of the 'older English economists' she had read earlier.[92] She was gradually led by that insight into proposing more thoroughgoing changes in the economic system than Radicalism had envisaged, even to the point where Bradlaugh became unable to distinguish her more extreme collectivist alternatives (or her definition of these) from 'communism'.[93] This did not signify a complete break with her old mentor, however. She did not abandon the secularist cause until she became a convert to theosophy at the very end of the 1880s. And in joining the Fabians — rather than any of the other organizations — she chose the group which was the least hostile to the Radicals and was even willing to form an alliance with them. Perhaps the main attraction of the socialist movement was that it provided her with more direct opportunities than the secularist or atheist platform — a more relevant context — for devoting herself to attacking the ramifications of poverty, cultural as well as material, which she saw as the major obstacle to the attainment of her 'ideal' society.

Her election to the Fabian Society in the middle of 1885, which marked her official initiation into the socialist movement, was sponsored by Bernard Shaw, with whom she had been personally acquainted for about a year.[94] The intertwining of his own cultural and socialist concerns, even at this early stage of his career before he emerged as a major playwright, has been dealt with in countless biographical, critical and historical studies, and scarcely requires detailed re-examination here. It needs to be stressed, however, that his cultural concerns in no way represented a departure from general Fabian trends but rather a consummation of these trends. The influences acting upon him in his formative years resembled those which impelled Besant, Olivier and Wallas along the road to Fabian socialism, and they found an especially close focus in Shaw's case in his relationship with William Morris.

4

Bernard Shaw

As editor of the *Fabian Essays*, and the author of two out of the seven contributions included, Shaw might have been expected to bear the brunt of William Morris's criticisms of that book; in fact, Morris was hardly critical of Shaw at all, and proclaimed his sympathies with the latter at least as loudly, and almost as unequivocally, as he did in dealing with Hubert Bland's essay. Shaw, Morris claimed, had 'one of the clearest heads and best pens that Socialism has got', using both of these assets to produce a devastating criticism of the 'modern capitalistic muddle'. The only thing which Morris singled out as detracting from Shaw's items in the *Fabian Essays* was their attachment to the 'Sidney Webbian permeation tactic'. If Shaw could only rid himself of that remnant of 'opportunism', to which he clung reluctantly enough as it was, his trenchant style and 'reserves of indignation and righteous scorn' could not only play a great destructive role, but also a more positive, inspirational one for all of his colleagues in the socialist movement.[1]

Besides the appealing style and tone, there was much in the substance of Shaw's arguments — especially with respect to artistic and cultural questions — to command Morris's sympathy. These questions were related to social and economic matters in a way that recalled some of Morris's own basic arguments. One of the criticisms Shaw levelled at capitalist modes of production and wealth-distribution was their effective denial to the bulk of the workforce of any opportunities for 'artistic enjoyment': implicitly associating cultural with material deprivation, he viewed that form of denial as one of the chief symptoms — if not an actual cause — of human degradation in contemporary society. He went on to maintain that, with the elimination of privately-owned land and capital, the working masses would be rid of the thraldom of employers who regarded them as 'mere beasts of burden' and of the agonies and anxieties of struggling to survive in that capacity. The settlement of the 'bread and butter question', through a more equable distribution of property, would leave mankind free to develop and use its 'higher faculties', a process which would be facilitated by the natural tendency of social democracy to extend 'education and culture' to the masses, and thereby 'make men of them' rather than keeping them in a state of animal-like dependence.

Shaw also suggested that art itself was degraded by a social and economic system which allowed only a privileged few to enjoy it. It became 'tainted' by the narrow class bias of its chief patrons and owners and identified with items of vanity and luxury which in no way represented, or contributed to, genuine 'social wealth' but were merely part of an accumulation of personal riches. There were clear echoes here not only of Morris but also of his chief mentor, Ruskin.[2]

One of Shaw's contributions to the *Fabian Essays* was actually written at Morris's house,[3] and in a lecture he delivered a few years earlier, which focussed more directly on the relationship between art and socialism, he specifically cited the precedents of Ruskin, Morris and Walter Crane in mixing the two subjects up in this way. Much of the spirit of these men's pronouncements was evident in Shaw's lecture, though he did not just reiterate what they had taught, but elaborated freely on their themes and qualified or modified them at various points. He spoke with concern of the decline in artistic skill on the part of handicraftsmen, attributing this to the pressures of the profit motive behind capitalist enterprise; and he singled out the introduction of machinery in particular as responsible for reducing the initiatives and incentives of this group of workers to an extent where they became 'mere unskilled labourers'. In arguing in this way, he was not condemning machines *per se*, but rather the indiscriminate and insensitive ways in which they had been used purely in order to pile up profits for those who owned them.[4]

Ruskin and Morris had not completely condemned all forms of machinery either. The former had conceded on one occasion that there were 'conceivable uses of machinery on a colossal scale in accomplishing mighty and useful works', such as making the more inhospitable areas of the earth (mountains, deserts and so on) fit for human habitation.[5] The latter had stressed how, in a state of society where they were not being used for profit-making purposes but only as a way of relieving human labour from the burden of the most onerous and unpleasant tasks, certain machines could even be valuable in affording the community greater leisure for artistic and other pleasurable pursuits.[6] Both William Clarke and Sidney Webb, as seen above, had echoed similar sentiments. Shaw went beyond all these writers, however, in asserting the great artistic potential inherent in machines themselves which remained unrealized only because the working classes were 'too brutalised by excessive work and squalid surroundings to be able to use them'. He claimed that there were many 'masterpieces of machinery' and that the 'ideal workman of the future' was not 'the old handicraftsman revived and working with the old tasks' but rather an 'intelligent and artistic guider of complex machine tools'. Such workers, he concluded, 'would certainly breed first rate artists'.[7] This view was a definite departure from Ruskin, at least, who refused to accept as art any machine-made object, however admirable its ingenuity, and who regarded any attempts to use machines for ornament or other artistic purposes as inimical to good design.[8] Shaw's attitude stamps him as a remarkably early herald of 'a machine, as opposed to a craft, aesthetic'[9] in England.

The bulk of Shaw's lecture was devoted to the 'fine arts' — especially painting — rather than to the arts of manufacture. His treatment of the fine arts and of their social and moral implications was more firmly in accord with the Ruskinian tradition, though mixed in with a strain of hedonism which could have derived in part from utilitarian ethics. This admixture was not an unlikely nor an uncharacteristic one for a Fabian. Shaw later turned against certain aspects of utilitarianism (including its hedonistic philosophy),[10] though he declared on one occasion that he had been 'saturated with its traditions'.[11] Some evidence for this claim may be found in his early lecture on Art. Completely rejecting any notion of 'Art for Art's Sake', he insisted that the arts 'are certain methods of seeking happiness; and they are mischievous or beneficial, moral or immoral, just as the other methods of seeking happiness are. A work of art is good or bad according to the side on which the balance appears when its total effect on human welfare for good and evil are set against one another.' He admitted that in many instances the calculations of this balance were 'beyond our arithmetic'; though in referring to one particular genre — the painting of the human face — he claimed that the paramount criterion in discriminating the value of one work from another was 'the number of ideas' it contained with relation to the subject's 'character', as expressed by facial signs.[12] Even this frankly 'quantitative' means of moral judgment in art recalled Ruskin's dictum that 'the picture which has the nobler and more numerous ideas, however awkwardly expressed, is a greater and better picture than that which has the less noble and less numerous ideas, however beautifully expressed'.[13]

Shaw concluded his lecture by reasserting, in more general terms, the close relationship between the quality of the arts and the conditions of society, as judged by the welfare of all contributing to the operation of that society. In a statement which crystallized common elements in the recent teachings of both Ruskin and Morris, he warned: 'we need look for no improvement in the beauty of our lives, and therefore for no valuable advance in Art unless we redistribute our immense Wealth and our immense leisure so as to secure to every honest man his due share of both in return for his due share of the national labour'.[14]

Shaw, more than any other Fabian, had close personal ties with Morris, which dated back to the earliest years of the socialist revival in England.

They first became acquainted in 1884 at a meeting of the Democratic Federation, the proto-socialist organization of H.M. Hyndman which was to become known, towards the end of that year, as the Social Democratic Federation. Morris was already making arrangements in the summer months for Shaw to speak before various socialist gatherings.[15] Neither of the two men retained connections with the S.D.F.: Morris fell out with Hyndman and formed his own organization, the Socialist League; and Shaw joined the Fabian Society in the autumn of 1884, becoming one of its earliest recruits from outside the original Davidson circle. The two men remained friends till Morris's death in 1896. The details of their relationship over this twelve-year span, and of the various ways in which they influenced each other's outlook, have been documented to an extent by Shaw himself in retrospective accounts and filled out by various historians.[16]

Shaw never knew Ruskin personally, and it may have been partly through his contact with Morris that he imbibed Ruskinian ideas; though his diary reveals that he was acquainting himself with them at least as early as 1880 when he spent an afternoon in a South Kensington library reading *The Stones of Venice*.[17] As noted above, the chapter in this book on 'The Nature of Gothic', which incorporated an attack on modern capitalism for effectively removing any beauty or pleasure from the lives and work of industrial operatives, had been a formative influence in the development of Morris's own thought in the direction of socialism; and it might well have facilitated Shaw's development in that direction.[18] Shaw was also familiar with Morris's work before entering socialist circles and coming into personal contact with the latter; he recalled a prior acquaintance both with Morris's poetry and with his contributions to the arts and crafts movement.[19]

The actual catalyst in Shaw's conversion to socialism seems to have been a lecture he heard in 1882 by the visiting American land-nationalizer, Henry George. Shaw recalled how, on hearing that lecture and subsequently consulting George's most popular work, *Progress and Poverty*, he was 'plunged into a course of economic reading, and at a very early stage of it became a Socialist'. (His reading included a French translation of Marx's *Capital*.) Until that stage, he claimed,

I was a young man . . . of a very revolutionary and contradictory temperament, full of Darwin and Tyndall, of Shelley and De Quincey, of Michel Angelo and Beethoven, and never having in my life studied social questions from the economic point of view, except that I had once, in my boyhood, read a pamphlet by John Stuart Mill on the land question.[20]

One who was so steeped in artistic works and sources — as we shall see, there were many others, besides the writings of Ruskin and Morris, that could be added to his list here — was unlikely to relinquish his passion for them on discovering a new field of interest. Shaw managed to conjoin the new and the old interests immediately, as was shown most strikingly in his habit of reading the translation of Marx's *Capital* available to him in the British Museum side by side with the score of Wagner's opera, *Tristan und Isolde*.[21] He began to insinuate socialist economic ideas into the art-form which he himself was then practising — the novel. Sidney Trefusis, the leading character in *An Unsocial Socialist*, which Shaw wrote in 1883, is in revolt against the commercial system which has made a rich man of his father, a Manchester cotton manufacturer. He stigmatizes all capitalists as those who 'could only secure profit by obtaining from their workmen more products than they paid them for, and could only tempt customers by offering a share of the unpaid-for part of the products as a reduction in price'. This attack on the modes of social and economic exploitation under capitalism is extended to include artists themselves, whom the hero regards more as 'parasites' on the current commercial system than as victims of it. Most of them, he maintains, are simply 'the favoured slaves of the moneyed classes', contriving to escape the drudgery and destitution which is the lot of their 'fellow-slaves' in field and factory by trading their special gifts for special privileges in terms of greater financial remuneration and shorter working hours. There are exceptions to this general rule, represented in the novel by the socialist painter, Donovan Brown, who rejects all opportunities for making a profit out of his work.

It would be misguided to equate Trefusis's views on art and artists (or on any other subject) entirely with Shaw's; though some of them anticipate, or are in accord with, later Shavian pronouncements on iniquities in the system of artistic patronage under capitalism and on the general degradation of art in the kind of society that lends support to such a system. 'Art rises when men rise, and grovels when men grovel', Trefusis declares. He makes this remark in support of his argument that 'the sole refiner of art is human nature' and in reply to the proposition of the poet, Erskine, that the 'sole refiner of human nature is fine art'. It is not that Trefusis, or his creator, is denying that art has any refining qualities — Shaw's insistence elsewhere on the potential moral value of art, as judged by its effect on human welfare, is an implicit affirmation of these qualities. Trefusis's retort to Erskine should be seen, rather, as countering an aesthetic reductionism which effectively exempts its exponents from having to concern themselves with more prosaic social or political issues and activities.[22]

The economic ideas which Shaw and his chief mouthpiece in the novel came to preach as socialists gave precise shape and definition to their own social and political concerns, providing a framework for their reactions against contemporary values and institutions. But in Shaw's case the origins and basis of those concerns seem to have lain partly in aesthetic feelings themselves. By his own account, his interest in the arts predated his interest in economics; and both before and after his conversion to socialism he displayed a much more active and passionate engagement with art than his socialist hero, Trefusis, ever showed. For all of the scepticism about the artistic profession and its practitioners which he voiced through Trefusis, Shaw remained a practising artist himself, and he could be as vehement in his defence of what he conceived to be socially and morally valuable forms of art as he was in his denunciation of those forms which he felt reflected the interests of an irresponsible cult.[23] In some autobiographical sketches, he recalled how, from early childhood, his intrinsic 'artist nature, to which beauty and refinement were necessities' had fed his repugnance for poverty. He claimed that his visits with his nursemaid to her friends in the slums of Dublin provoked in him an 'esthetic hatred of poverty and squalor, and of the species of human animal they produce' which formed the basis of his notion, articulated in later years, that such conditions represented 'not the natural and proper punishment of vice' but a grave 'social crime'.[24]

Assuming that his recollections here can be trusted, Shaw appears to have exhibited, at a remarkably young age, symptoms of that class consciousness of sin which can be identified in several of his later colleagues within the Fabian Society; and those symptoms appear to have been associated, remarkably closely, with aesthetic instincts and sensitivities. There are further details concerning his early background which suggest just how conducive this was to the development of a strong social conscience, related to his own class position, and of an intense yearning for beauty in art and in the natural and social environment.

He was born in 1856 in Dublin, where his father was a partner in a firm of corn merchants. The business was not a flourishing one, however; and the financial troubles which came to plague the Shaws took its toll on the head of the family by compounding various other insecurities (social and emotional) to which he was subject and by driving him increasingly to seek his consolation in drink. The pathetic spectacle of his downfall remained a haunting one for his son,[25] and it is not surprising that the latter should have reacted against the Victorian business world at least as strongly as his fictional hero, Trefusis, whose father had actually managed to succeed in that world. As we have seen, a revulsion from the values and procedures of the Victorian commercial system, stemming in part from personal or family misfortune at its hands, was a common factor in the making of several early Fabians.

The Shaw family was not reduced to the depths of abject poverty which the young Bernard had witnessed on his visits to Dublin's working-class suburbs with his nurse; theirs was more the 'Shabby Genteel' variety, which managed to maintain a facade of respectability by sporting the remnants of a more distinguished past. Shaw's father retained a snobbish pride about his gentlemanly origins, based on some tenuous aristocratic connections — one of his cousins was a baronet — and reflected in an outward observance of the Evangelical faith, designed to emphasize his social superiority to his Catholic neighbours.[26] He had at one stage held a comfortable sinecure in the government; and it was his pension from this which enabled him to set up in business. He attempted to dissociate himself from the general run of the commercial middle class by dealing wholesale; 'the family dignity', his son noted, 'made retail business impossible'.[27]

Bernard Shaw inherited a strong consciousness of social rank from his family, but he also gained an insight, from their example, into the shams and pretensions on which rank could be based, and into the desperate snobberies which it involved. This insight provoked a reaction in him against all the trappings of the 'Shabby Genteel' class, including its religion. His repugnance, again, was partly aesthetic in nature. As in Annie Besant's case, the artistic aspects of religion constituted a major part of its appeal for Shaw, sustaining his interest in churchgoing long after he had lost his faith. But the 'genteel, suburban Irish protestant church', to which his father insisted on sending him as a child, provided him with no opportunity for the 'essentially artistic and luxurious' devotional pursuits which tempted him; the insipid music and uninspiring architecture he was confronted with there only served to crush his faith out of him.[28]

Shaw's contempt for the hypocritical values and shabby trappings of genteel impoverishment represented by his family was as intense in its way as his hatred of the far more squalid conditions he had witnessed in the slums. Yet the 'artist nature' in him which helped foster such reactions was itself partly cultivated by his family or, more precisely, by some rather incongruous elements in the atmosphere of his home. Beneath the genteel surfaces was a bohemian streak. Shaw's mother was the daughter of an Irish country gentleman; while a suitable social 'catch' for her snobbish husband, she was no languishing debutante and became eager to pursue a career as a mezzo-soprano. The family's concerns for social respectability did not prevent her from inviting into the Shaw household a man who could help further her professional ambitions: George Vanderleur Lee, 'mesmeric conductor and daringly original teacher of singing', as her son later called him. There is no evidence of a sexual relationship between Lee and Mrs Shaw, though he became the effective head of the household, as her husband slipped further and further into alcoholism, and when he went to London in 1872 she had no hesitation in quitting Dublin to join him. The young Bernard followed the pair to London some four years later, making that city his base for the rest of his life. His formal education in Ireland had been so deficient and disorganized — a series of inferior church and 'commercial' schools was the only form of tuition his family could afford — that he looked back on Lee's influence in the home as the crucial stimulus to his self-education, especially as regards his appreciation of art and the beauties of nature. Lee actually purchased a cottage for his adopted family on Dalkey Hill, which afforded some spectacular views of Dublin Bay and the Wicklow Mountains and which gave Shaw his first sustained opportunity for indulging his love of natural scenery. In his recollections of his education he gave the impression that if he had had to remain confined to the depressingly 'unpicturesque' area of Dublin in which the main family home was situated, his aesthetic sensitivities and understanding might have been rather less acute than they became.[29] He regarded Lee as a saviour and perhaps even exaggerated the latter's influence at times. He recalled that when his schooldays came to a close at the age of fifteen, he 'knew nothing of what the school professed to teach' but was 'highly educated' all the same:

I could sing and whistle ... leading works by Handel, Haydn, Mozart, Beethoven, Rossini, Bellini, Donizetti and Verdi. I was saturated with English Literature, from Shakespeare and Bunyan to Byron and Dickens. And I was so susceptible to natural beauty that, having had some glimpse of the Dalkey scenery on an excursion, I still remember the moment when my mother told me that we were going to live there as the happiest of my life.

And all this I owed to the meteoric impact of Lee, with his music, his method, his impetuous enterprise and his magnetism ...

Shaw qualified this last sentence a little further on by intimating that there were large 'holes' in Lee's culture. The latter had no real literary bent, it appears; and he tended to ignore the visual arts — a gap which Shaw filled in for himself by diligent study of the collections of sculpture and old masters at the National Gallery in Dublin.[30] Even in the field of music, Shaw had probably gained an initial grounding or had his interest roused before Lee appeared on the scene: 'the Shaws', he recalled elsewhere,[31] were 'naturally a musical family': his mother's singing abilities represented their most accomplished achievement in this field, but many of his relations (including his father) were competent and sensitive players of one kind of musical instrument or another. During his childhood, he was treated to displays of their talents at musical evenings held in the country house of his second cousin, Sir Robert Shaw. Admittedly, such occasions were a fashionable convention among upper middle or aristocratic families at the time, as Shaw himself intimated. It may well have been Mrs Shaw's singing teacher, then — with his completely unconventional methods of instruction and a 'startlingly eccentric' personal demeanour, hypnotic to behold — who gave the young Bernard his first glimpse into music as something other than a genteel diversion, and thereby evoked in the boy what was to prove a lifelong passion. Lee's own passion for music was in fact limited only to the vocal side; and Shaw recalls having to investigate instrumental forms such as the symphony and the string quartet for himself.[32]

In accounts of his education, written in his old age, he laid great stress on the role played by 'personal experience' as distinct from formal academic study, concluding that 'without living experiences no person is educated'. Experience of 'contemporary developments in art' was particularly instructive in his opinion.[33] 'Listening to music, looking at pictures and roaming over Dalkey Hill', he claimed, were 'the things that really educated me and made me loathe my school prison, where art and beauty had no place'.[34] Shaw's view that the basis of true education lay in direct personal experience of such things as art and the beauties of nature — not to mention his own course of self-education — clearly accorded with certain romanticist precepts and programmes of the late eighteenth and nineteenth centuries.[35]

In an article he wrote in 1897, he disavowed any precise knowledge of what 'the Romantic movement' was, but confessed to being 'under its spell' in his youth.[36] He intimated that the spell had now been broken. Reared on 'romantic opera' and 'romantic fiction', he had come to discover that on the whole such genres represented 'a freak of the human imagination, which created an imaginary past, an imaginary heroism, an imaginary poetry' as a way of 'escape' from a 'condition in which real life appears empty, prosaic, boresome'. They were 'therefore essentially a gentlemanly product'. He did not condemn them, their makers or their audiences completely: some of the 'mirages' which they created 'were once dear and beautiful' and the 'land of dreams' was still a 'wonderful place'. But he had lost much of his patience with them — as he had with the social and religious aspects of gentility fed him during his youth. The artistic genius (a Mozart or a Goethe) at least had the power to contain the phantasmal excesses of these genres; but the 'journeyman artist' who tried his hand at them tended to be blinded to 'nature and reality from which alone his talent could gain nourishment and originality . . . with the result that Romanticism became, at second hand, the blight and dry rot of art'.[37]

It is important to note that what he was criticizing here was not romanticism in the sense of the particular cultural and philosophical movement which had developed out of, and in reaction to, the values and ideals of the Enlightenment of the eighteenth century. Rather, he was presenting a critique of 'romance' as a general art form and of the tendency to romantic escapism in the sensibility of certain individuals or classes in all ages.[38] 'All its beginners were anticipated', Shaw said of the phenomenon he was describing; and the examples he gave — going back to 'the tales of the knights errant beloved of Don Quixote' — make clear that his application here of such terms as 'Romantic Movement' and 'romanticism' was broad and ahistorical. There was no real contradiction, therefore, between his disenchantment with this general romantic tendency and the persistence in his own thought of ideas and assumptions which reflected romanticism in its more specific historical sense.[39]

Those whom he cited as his predecessors in the reaction against romantic forms included a number of writers and artists — Carlyle, Ruskin, Wagner, Ibsen, for example — who have usually been accepted as among the chief exponents or adherents of romanticist ideas in the nineteenth century. This, again, does not really amount to a contradiction, when it is recognized that Shaw's target of criticism was the escapist and genteel element of romance. As noted above, one of his colleagues in the Fabian Society, William Clarke, spoke of the reaction against the 'make believe' of 'the genteel, the conventional, the thinner kind of romantic literature', and the turning to a more powerful 'realistic school' as one of the main forces associated with the growth of Fabian socialism in England. It was precisely as 'realists' that Shaw categorized Carlyle and Ruskin, Wagner and Ibsen in his article of 1897.

In his book on Ibsen, published six years before, Shaw included one of the earliest and most important exponents of romanticism (in its more specific sense) in the 'realist' category, explicitly linking him with the Norwegian dramatist on this basis.[40] This was Shelley, with whom Shaw had firmly linked himself for many years, on the basis of three main beliefs. At a meeting of the Shelley Society in March 1886, he had announced that, 'as a good Shelleyan' he was a 'Socialist, an Atheist, and a Vegetarian'.[41] Elsewhere he recalled how he had been converted to vegetarianism in 1880 or 1881, having had his attention first drawn to the subject by Shelley ('I am an out and out Shelleyan', he reaffirmed on this occasion[42]). There is no evidence that the poet played any such role in Shaw's actual conversion to socialism a few years later; though his belief that his great idol had been a socialist may well have helped facilitate his acceptance of that creed. We have already seen how another of Shaw's colleagues in the Fabian Society, Percival Chubb, specifically included Shelley (among other prominent romanticists) in his list of those writers and artists whom he felt to have been the prime 'inspirers' of socialism in England. Shaw's direct identification of Shelley with socialist doctrines — however valid — and his own identification with the poet on this basis, constitute a particularly striking illustration of Chubb's hypothesis.

Shaw, in giving his reasons for joining the Fabian Society rather than the Social Democratic Federation, to which he had been initially attracted, stated that he was 'guided by no discoverable difference in program or principles, but solely by an instinctive feeling that the Fabians and not the Federation would attract the men of my own bias and intellectual habits'. Alert as ever to considerations of social rank, ingrained in him from childhood, he went on to claim that 'the significant thing about the particular Socialist society which I joined was that the members all belonged to the middle class' and 'addressed itself to its own class' in order that it might set about doing 'the necessary brainwork of planning Socialist organization for all classes'. It thereby distinguished itself in his eyes from the S.D.F. or from the Socialist League which were led by middle-class men but professed to be 'working-class societies'.[43] As we have seen, several of the earliest members of the Fabian Society had been alienated from the conventions and values of their middle-class homes in broadly similar ways to Shaw and they had developed a concern for the misfortunes and deprivations suffered by the working class which stemmed in part from their experience of the misfortunes to which even members of their own class were subjected by the current economic organization of society. Some of them had started out their adult lives impecunious and adrift. They nonetheless bore the traces of their class background, one of the most conspicuous of these being a sophisticated literacy with which their educational opportunities as children, at home or at school, had served to endow them. Their very advantages in this respect over the bulk of the working class, as well as the financial disabilities and social insecurities which several of them came to suffer through impoverishment, fed their antagonism towards the *status quo*. As Shaw himself put it, by being 'liberally educated', they had been 'brought up to think about how things are done, instead of merely drudging at the manual labour of doing them', and were therefore among the first to perceive that 'Capitalism was reducing their own class to the condition of a proletariat'.[44]

The Fabian Society appears to have offered Shaw the same sense of security and sense of identity as it did to those young men who had formed the organization out of the informal group which gathered round the Scottish sage, Thomas Davidson, in the early 1880s. It provided not only an institutional base for working out particular grievances against prevailing economic assumptions and structures; it also offered the attractions of a club for men and women of like social and educational backgrounds. The common image of the Fabian Society as a group of philistine utilitarians — an image which Shaw himself, in later years, was not above fostering — has always made it something of a puzzle as to how a dramatist of his stature, with such a wide range of interests in the other arts, could have remained such an active and enthusiastic member of the group. When it is realized that, in fact, an immersion in the arts —

especially romanticist literature of the nineteenth century — formed a crucial part of the educational background of most of the early Fabians and that a strong feeling for the fate of beauty in art and nature supplied a powerful motive for their more precise economic and social preoccupations, Shaw's choice of the Fabian Society as the main venue for preaching his socialist beliefs becomes all the more explicable. To a large extent his fellow-Fabians shared not only his 'intellectual habits' but his cultural views and assumptions as well.[45]

The 'bias' of members was itself strongly, though not exclusively, aesthetic. An exclusive aesthetic bias would have been bound to alienate Shaw. At the height of the London dock strike in 1889, he claimed: 'If the dockhands came to me tomorrow and said that they were going to start burning and demolishing, but could not make up their minds what to start on, I should recommend them to go for the works of art first as for their most dangerous rivals in the attention of the thoughtful.'[46] Shaw's own involvement in art was never so intense as to make him neglect more immediately pressing social and political commitments. His abiding artistic passion at the time was Ibsen, but when confronted with the choice of spending a spare guinea on a 'de luxe' edition of *A Doll's House* or in helping out the embattled dock-strikers, he had no hesitations about forgoing the personal pleasure which the book would have brought him and contributing his money to the strike fund instead.[47]

This small token of his priorities during a period of political upheaval hardly reflects the remorseless iconoclasm with regard to art suggested in the passage just quoted. There was doubtless an element of rhetorical exaggeration in that passage anyway; and it needs to be emphasized that such iconoclastic statements were directed not so much against art itself as against an all-consuming worship of art. The full context of the passage bears this out. Avowing that he was 'no critic of art', Shaw went on to say that what he hated about it was 'the whole confounded cultus, which is only a huge sponge to sop up the energies of men who are divinely discontented'.[48] In his own novels he had already expressed his distaste for the excessive and indiscriminate reverence accorded art and artists by members of the middle and upper classes, some of whom betrayed an 'entire practical ignorance of the subject'. He reserved his sympathies for those who had a keen knowledge and appreciation of the arts but who resolutely seceded from any worship of them.[49] He was to reiterate these distastes and sympathies in even stronger terms after he abandoned the novel-form and took up playwriting as his principal artistic activity. For example, in the preface to his *Three Plays for Puritans*, written in the 1890s, he explained that he himself had 'always been a Puritan' in his attitude towards art: he was as 'fond of fine music and handsome building' as some of the earliest and most prominent Puritans (Milton,

Cromwell, Bunyan), but if he found such arts 'becoming the instruments of a systematic idolatry of sensuousness', he would account it 'good statesmanship to blow every cathedral in the world to pieces with dynamite, organ and all, without the least heed to the screams of the art critics and cultured voluptuaries'.[50]

Shaw's apparent readiness to destroy art — should it involve any measure of idolatrous worship — and to sacrifice his own artistic pleasures in the interests of other, more urgent commitments reflected a complex of impulses and considerations that were partly aesthetic in nature as well as social, political and religious. A visit to Venice in 1891 provoked a typical resurgence of his 'old iconoclastic idea of destroying the whole show' of art and architecture which he saw before him. Recounting his visit to William Morris, he referred to the 'wonderfully spontaneous and happy' nature of Italian architecture in general — its 'handsome, distinguished ... joyous effect' — but said that he felt it was inferior to northern architecture because it was 'not organic' and was 'flagrantly architecture for the sake of ornamentality'. Venice, in his eyes, exemplified these limitations in particularly vivid form:

It is a show and nothing else. Neither the Italians nor the trippers ... have any part or lot in the fine things they see. They didn't make them; couldn't make them; consequently can't appreciate them ... The people here who are chock full of Ruskin are just as bad as the authorities who cut out illuminated capitals from the old MSS ... for exhibition. And they are much worse than the Philistines, who show a healthy preference for the penny steamers, the sunsets and the Lido.

Again, the obeisance paid to art, without any practical knowledge of it, was the main target of Shaw's criticism. The reference to Ruskin in this context was meant as a slight not on the author of *The Stones of Venice* — whose appreciation of the city's architecture could hardly be reproached with being uncritical or ill-informed — but rather on those who tried to dress up their basic ignorance and insensitivity by spouting him. Shaw, in the heat of reaction against the attitudes of the more pretentious tourists, did tend to go beyond Ruskin in criticizing Italian — especially Venetian — architecture, making few discriminations between the Gothic style, which Ruskin had seen as symbolizing the high point of Venetian art and civilization, and the Renaissance style which he had regarded as the symptom of the city's corruption and decay. 'I do not believe,' Shaw told Morris, 'that a permanent, living art can ever come out of the conditions of Venetian splendour, even at its greatest time. The best art of all will come when we are rid of splendour and everything in the glorious line.'[51] Nonetheless, the assumption behind his rather sweeping criticism of Italian architecture — that the quality of art was debased by its associations with opulence and luxury — was firmly in accord with Ruskin's ideas and with the teachings of the correspondent to whom Shaw addressed his remarks.[52]

Shaw's distaste for splendid display can be seen as another aspect of his so-called 'puritanical' attitude to art. Traces of the austerity which characterized the evangelical faith inculcated in him as a child would seem to have remained with him in adulthood for all his resolute reactions against that faith. Ruskin, too, we have seen, was brought up in the evangelical faith; and it appears to have been practised rather more conscientiously in his childhood home than in Shaw's. Vestiges of it may be discerned not only in the passionate attacks that Ruskin waged against luxury and opulence in art; but also in the moral fervour with which he invested his closely related teachings on social and economic questions. Shaw recounted in later life how the evolution of his own artistic and socio-economic concerns and of the priority which he came to place on the latter, precisely followed the Ruskinian path: 'Ruskin, beginning as an artist with an interest in art — exactly as I did myself, by the way — was inevitably driven back to economics, and to the conviction that your art would never come right whilst your economics were wrong . . . You may aim at making a man cultured; but you must feed him first.'[53] It is important to note how the initial concern for art still comes through here, and far from being submerged by wider social and economic considerations is indissolubly wedded to them. Even at his most austere, or most iconoclastic, Shaw never contemplated the destruction of art in all forms. He indicated in fact that the death of traditional forms of art, as of traditional forms of economic organization, may be a part of the process by which art would find wider audiences and new practitioners throughout society. He clearly entertains this possibility in an early statement of his 'food before art' theme. In 1889 a young composer had written a letter to the *Star* on 'The Music of the People'; commenting on this in his regular music column in the same newspaper, Shaw asserted: 'What we want is not music for the people, but bread for the people . . . equal respect and consideration, life and aspiration, instead of drudgery and despair. When we get that I imagine that the people will make tolerable music for themselves, even if all Beethoven's scores perish in the interim.'[54] Even earlier, just after his conversion to socialism, he had his socialist hero, Sidney Trefusis, looking forward to a time when all the familiar artistic activities and genres, would be replaced or transformed and every artist would be an 'amateur', with a 'consequent return to the healthy old disposition to look on every man who makes art a means of money-making as a vagabond not to be entertained as an equal by honest men'.[55]

While adhering on the whole to the commonplace Victorian belief in art's humanizing and refining powers, the Fabians did not let that belief divert them — as happened with so many of their contemporaries[56] — from directly considering the most urgent social problems facing the working classes under industrial capitalism. Their general assumption was that an appreciation of art represented only a part of the humanizing process; and that the effectiveness of this process in rescuing the labouring masses from degradation and squalor was dependent on several other factors. It was a process which involved no less than a total change in the way in which current society was organized and its benefits distributed — from an economic as well as a cultural viewpoint. In his lecture of 1908 on the introductory statement in the Fabian 'Basis' — 'The Fabian Society consists of Socialists' — Shaw affirmed that a socialist by definition had to be convinced of the 'complete substitution of Public Property for Private Property' as the 'indispensable and fundamental condition for which alone civilization can be rescued from its present misery'. That substitution constituted the 'specific method' of Socialism, 'involving, fundamentally, public property in Land ... and Capital, Public Organization of Labour and Public control of Industry and derivatively Public control of Religion ... and Education, Public Enterprise in Art ... and Science.'[57]

While the roots and aims of Fabian socialism were strongly aesthetic in nature, its adherents were aware — and none more so than the Society's most famous artist, Shaw — that the arts could work no magic on their own in humanizing and refining the mass of mankind. This was especially the case when, as at present, art itself was liable to be corrupted by ignorant idolatry, or by its association with the luxury and opulence of the prosperous few. Generally, Fabians recognized that for art to be fully effective as a humanizing force, a radical reordering of society as a whole was required, and one which would entail considerable changes in the present conditions and organization of artistic production, if not in the nature of art itself.

PART II

Art, austerity and pleasure in Fabian socialism

5

The Webb partnership: the practice of renunciation

In laying the weight of their emphasis on the preparatory methods — largely economic in nature — by which the general reordering of society was to be brought about, the Fabians did not lose sight of their ultimate aesthetic and cultural aims. Nor did they completely relinquish the personal interest in art which they had developed in the days before they became socialists. This is undeniable in the case of Shaw. The case of the Webbs is rather more complicated. Their concerns with art have been explicitly denied by many commentators, or acknowledged only in the case of Beatrice before she met Sidney. Once the Fabian partnership began, it has been argued,[1] she turned her back on artistic interests or creative pursuits, partly out of deference to her husband's distaste for them. That distaste has been greatly exaggerated, as can be seen from the breadth of Sidney's own early interests in the arts. Misunderstandings concerning his attitudes to the arts have been compounded by a highly selective reading of the evidence relating to the years which followed his conversion to socialism. If this evidence is examined more thoroughly, it will be found that his attitudes did not differ substantially from Shaw's.

Webb acknowledged on various occasions the limitations of his aesthetic sensitivities and experience, but these claims should not be taken as pointing to an inherent narrowness of mind or a complacent indifference on his part.[2] He explained in an early letter to Beatrice that he was indeed capable of 'culture and enjoyment', but that his preoccupation with social and political work did not give him time to realize this capacity. His preoccupation was not, in fact, as exclusive as he suggested, and any tendency to a 'holier than thou' attitude here was outweighed by his rather pathetic disclaimer that his way of life should be regarded in any way as exemplary: 'it is . . . cramped and joyless . . . Heaven forbid that I should pretend that my life should be the type'.[3]

During his courtship of Beatrice in the early 1890s she once expressed the wish to take him away from 'current politics' for a couple of years so as to enable him to engage in 'a study of literature and history for its own sake': 'you and I are both of us lamentably ignorant of whole spheres of thought'.[4] Sidney would probably never have countenanced giving up politics even for a short while; but he agreed with her about their needing more 'cultivation' in their lives, feeling as he put it 'horribly incapable of anything but detail and current matters'. He insisted that in the fields of art and music at least 'I *am* humble . . . and sincerely anxious (in the intervals of business) to learn more appreciation of them'. He told Beatrice it would be an excellent idea for them to be taken around the National Gallery by someone more knowledgeable, and he actively encouraged her to go to concerts: 'we will try to save a little time for that, and you shall teach me to appreciate it'.[5]

Sidney's gifts to Beatrice while courting her consisted of volumes of Matthew Arnold and D.G. Rossetti (he chose these with some care, and even worried over such particulars as the binding). Though 'not a fanatic' about Rossetti, Webb found some of his sonnets to be 'perfect expressions of feeling' and was fond of quoting from the love poems in his early letters to Beatrice.[6] Such pleasure in art as something which crystallized profound human emotions — his response here echoes his appreciation of George Eliot, or the songs of Schubert and Heine — should help dispel any impression that Sidney was merely moved by what the arts could offer him in the way of self-improvement. And whatever his basic 'motives' in pursuing culture — pleasure or self-improvement or both — the fact that he should want to share such experiences with Beatrice scarcely conforms with the image of someone who, from the start of their relationship, effectively suppressed her artistic and literary interests.

Though born into very different social milieux, both Sidney and Beatrice had been subjected to strongly puritanical influences in their early years. Their mothers were models of frugality and austerity in their domestic habits, mainly through severe religious scruples; though in the case of Sidney's mother, financial insecurity, as well as a strongly developed evangelical conscience, may have led to her insistence in the house on 'open windows', 'cold baths' and 'good habits'.[7] The family simply could not afford to permit any laziness or indulgence in its members. Beatrice's family was much more prosperous, and she recalls how she was tempted as a young girl by the giddy whirl of entertainments and frivolities provided for and by her class: balls, the races, and amateur theatricals. Her mother's manifest disapproval of these frivolities, however, and the stirrings in Beatrice herself of a strong religious — if not specifically Christian — conscience, gave rise to periods of intense guilt during adolescence concerning her hedonistic tendencies. These tendencies she tried to check by denying herself pleasures she had enjoyed before and by prescribing herself strict regimens of food, reading and study.[8]

Her reading programme, as we have seen, by no means excluded the work of creative writers; though it was in a moment of disenchantment with one of her favourite novelists, George Eliot, that Beatrice articulated the austere principle by which she attempted to guide her own personal life and which she strongly urged on society as a whole: 'Renunciation, that is the great fact we all — individuals and classes, have to learn.' This statement was made in 1885, some five years before her conversion to socialism, and was provoked by reading some of George Eliot's letters. Discovering in these a rather complacent and self-indulgent attitude towards questions of morality, she now wondered whether some of the 'grand passages' in the novels which she had admired so much were not, after all, 'rubbish'.[9] The degree to which George Eliot fell short, in her life and personality, of Beatrice's ideal of renunciation thereby came to affect the latter's judgment of the novelist's work.

It is interesting that in his lecture on George Eliot, a few years earlier, Sidney had depicted her works as an outstanding embodiment of that ideal. (There is no evidence that he had read any of her letters.) The same 'great lesson of Work, Renunciation and Submission' which he himself would have learned as a child from personal experience of his mother's rigorous discipline he found perfectly summed up in the pages of *Silas Marner*, *The Mill on the Floss*, *Felix Holt* and *Middlemarch*.[10] Behind Sidney and Beatrice's divergent opinions of George Eliot lay a shared assumption: the undesirability of any form of self-indulgence in life and art.

The ideal of self-sacrifice was as much a part of the positivist creed (of which George Eliot was one of England's chief exponents) as of evangelicalism.[11] Despite his reputation, it was not in fact uncharacteristic of Sidney that he should have sought support for his version of that ideal in works of creative literature rather than in more formal expositions of political, social and religious thought. He found support not only in George Eliot's novels but also in that 'bible of romanticism', Goethe's *Faust*. Albeit through a possible misreading, Sidney saw the 'emphatic motto' of that play in the words: 'Thou shalt renounce, renounce, renounce.'[12] As noted above, Goethe had been one of Beatrice's favourite authors, and this motto would have appealed to her too, and may even have provided a source for the formulation of her own motto along similar lines. Sidney, in fact, had far more reservations about Goethe's works than Beatrice; though these stemmed in part from similar sorts of considerations to those which led to Beatrice's disenchantment with George Eliot. In singling out for censure the selfishness and egoism which he discerned in Goethe's personality, Webb suggested that the German poet failed to live up to his own motto of renunciation.

Rigorously moral criteria had formed the basis of many of Sidney and Beatrice's judgments on art and artists long before they took up the socialist cause. As we have seen, these moral considerations did not prevent them from finding genuine pleasure and enjoyment in the arts. In Sidney's eyes as much as Beatrice's, however, that very enjoyment was closely associated in contemporary capitalist society with the leisure of the more economically privileged classes: it was a luxury which the unprivileged classes could not afford, in terms of time or money.

Though not born into the 'idle rich' class, to which Beatrice was nearer, Sidney still accounted himself among the relatively privileged — by virtue no doubt of his unusually good education and the high position in the Civil Service which this had secured him. There are signs that because of these things he suffered a degree of social guilt which he attempted to assuage by embracing the socialist cause in the mid-1880s and throwing himself increasingly into the work it demanded in the fields of propaganda and municipal reform. This was crystallized in his letter to Beatrice explaining his neglect of artistic pursuits: there was a reluctant compulsiveness about his attitude to work there which suggests a real desperation to dissociate himself at any cost not only from the 'idle rich' but also from 'those people of ability who assume to work, but who really spend only an hour or two a day outside their own enjoyment'.[13] That such a dissociation could not be fully effective — that he was inextricably linked with these self-indulgent people by ties of social class and financial position — he had recognized several years before. As early as 1884, a year before his final acceptance of socialism, he spoke of how 'the poor' were being 'pressed to death by the weight of *our* luxury, sacrificed to the Moloch of *our* cultured comfort' (Emphasis mine). Already in this lecture the artistic pursuits and interests of the exploiting classes were seen as luxuries or indulgences in the present context of social misery, and had become an integral component of those feelings of social guilt in Webb arising from his inescapable identification with the exploiters. He implied strongly that he himself was by no means immune to the temptation held out by these luxuries:

Excess expenditure ... is ... equally robbery to the nation, whether devoted to champagne or to pictures, to beer or to books, to the most stupid self indulgences or to the highest culture. I preach therefore the doctrine of extreme social Asceticism as regards comforts which have a money value. But it is a hard saying ... It *is* hard to see around us carriages and music, pictures and books, luxurious seats at the theatre, and not only to forgo them now, but to know that we can never hope to enjoy them without guilt. It is a hard saying almost harder than we can bear ... And it is especially hard upon us of the middle class ... to find that as a class we have abstracted most from the poor[14] (Webb's emphasis).

It is important to note the stress on 'excess expenditure' as the iniquity to be eradicated. Webb never said that music, pictures, books and the theatre were in themselves iniquitous — but only what they represented in terms of the money and time lavished on them in capitalist society. Two years later, when his conversion to socialism had been completed, and he was seeking to convert others to the cause, he claimed that the 'one alternative' to taking the socialist path was to care only for one's own comfort, stifling one's conscience about the mass of misery around one by making a 'false idol' of such things as religion, literature or art. It was, however, a very destructive path. Devoting oneself to activities like these, at the expense of any effort to attend to the problems of eradicating poverty, was to take a part in creating or compounding the miseries of the poor in capitalist society, and would eventually be repaid by the merciless vengeance of the oppressed. We see Webb here developing a case similar to Shaw's: not against art and literature as such, but rather against the self-indulgent and all-consuming idolization of such activities.[15] In this same lecture he put forward his claim that, far from socialism's involving any dislike of culture, it was because its adherents wanted more of such things that they were socialists. The implication was that under the much more equitable system which socialism would ultimately provide, many of the really pressing material problems would be solved, and there would then be more time and more widespread opportunities for cultural activities.

For Sidney, the extravagance, waste and self-indulgence which he saw reflected in many of the cultural products of capitalist society were not only socially reprehensible but also damaging to art itself. It was partly out of a respect for art and a concern for its health and well-being that he counselled restraint and austerity. This becomes clear in his article, 'The Difficulties of Individualism', published in 1891 and reprinted as an official Fabian tract five years later. He launched a strong protest here against the 'preparation of senseless luxuries where there is need for more bread'. The 'inequality of income' inherent in an individualist system had resulted 'in a flagrant wrong production of commodities' which were urgently demanded by the affluent few without any consideration of 'genuine social needs'. One of the examples he gave of this process was the provision of Italian opera in London.[16] Characteristically, he nowhere showed himself to be against the art form as such. It was the present social and financial arrangement of this form which he thought was wrong, involving as it did the expenditure of grossly disproportionate amounts of money. The main measure of that disproportion was the infinitesimal number of people who had the means to enjoy opera in a world where the bulk of the population lacked even the means of subsistence; though Sidney hinted, in some earlier remarks on this subject, that another measure was the actual quality of the enjoyment experienced by those classes who did possess the requisite funds and leisure-time. In his eyes, what they demanded of opera was merely a diverting spectacle, and their enjoyment of it lacked any real vitality or intensity or sense of commitment. Here again he echoed Shaw, who as early as 1879 had railed against 'Italianized opera in England' as 'aristocratic in the worst sense' and 'effete because it never appealed to the people'.[17]

It was no sign of national prosperity, Webb argued, that 'a thousand pound prima donna' should be 'faintly amusing a languid audience' at the moment when 'forty thousand children may be without bread, and several persons dying of starvation'. There was now the possibility of yet more Italian opera being provided in London. In considering the question of whether the supply of this commodity should be increased or not, no attempts would be made by those responsible for the decision to assess either general social need or the 'intensity of desire' exhibited by particular groups within society. This question, Sidney felt, would be resolved merely by the momentary whim of a few hundred families with the money to invest in such ventures, the direction of their whim being determined by whether or not they thought the venture in question would add to their personal fortune. He showed concern that these mercenary motives and speculative procedures adversely affected the taste of the consumer and ultimately the quality of the commodity itself. Not only opera, among cultural commodities, was affected by the financial implications of the individualist system of production. It was 'not easy to compute,' Sidney stated, 'the loss to the world's progress, the degradation of the world's art and literature, caused by the demoralization of excessive wealth'.[18] There were clear echoes of Ruskin and Morris here as well as Shaw.[19]

Sidney Webb conceived of art as a luxury to be curtailed only when that activity and its products had become items of purely financial concern for their sponsors — where any consideration of social value or even aesthetic taste were completely subordinated or ignored. The degradation of art in this way was a process which he felt the capitalist system of wealth production in particular had encouraged. That process was symptomatic of the general destruction of beauty — in the natural environment and in the commodities of everyday use as well as in the fine arts — which both Sidney and Beatrice perceived in contemporary society. We have already seen how their comments on these various symptoms are scattered throughout their joint writings, forming a recurrent theme of their socialist critique of the *status quo*.

It was the actual process of bringing socialism about which came to involve for the Webbs the sacrifice or positive renunciation of many of the luxuries enjoyed by the members of their own class, including the luxury of immersing themselves in art. A few months after Beatrice's conversion to the socialist cause, she wrote to Sidney that they 'needed to show by works as well as words that socialism does not mean simply the grasping of good things by the Have nots, but a deliberate giving up of luxury and fashion by the ''Haves'' '.[20] And this is what they proceeded to show throughout their own careers as socialists, both their 'works' and their 'words' enshrining their notion of the necessity and desirability of simple economical living.[21] To fashionable colleagues of theirs, this simplicity might appear to be 'sordid' and to involve a distinct 'lack of culture'.[22] But the Webbs felt it much more important, for the sake of their own consciences and for the reputation and progress of socialism, to avoid the opposite appearance of a life of opulence and continual aesthetic diversions. In later life Beatrice castigated various luminaries connected with the Labour Party (including Lady Warwick, Philip Snowden and Ramsay MacDonald) for living or entertaining in magnificent houses and hotels surrounded by extravagant furniture and other treasures. ' ''The inevitability of gradualness'' in absolving poverty,' she wrote in 1924, 'should not be combined with living in luxury or the appearance of luxury.'[23] By all accounts the house in Grosvenor Road, Westminster, where the Webbs spent most of their lives, was without any pretence of magnificence in its fittings and furnishings. Beatrice herself spoke of the harsh interior redeemed only by the unique interest and beauty of the outlook over the Thames.[24] She was still capable of feeling guilty about the comfort, ease and prosperity of her existence, and that of other prominent Fabians, compared to the situation of other socialists in the world, such as Russian revolutionaries.[25]

The daily regimen of research and administrative work which the Webbs set themselves involved, as Beatrice acknowledged, cutting out 'many pleasant pursuits and pastimes'.[26] She, at least, did not really enjoy all this drudgery; it was a duty which became extremely tedious at times, but not to fulfil it would only lead to a more gnawing emotional discomfort or guilt concerning those less fortunate than herself. What Sidney had intimated in one of his earliest lectures about the difficulties of overcoming a fondness for a life of leisured artistic pursuits is borne out in Beatrice's case by the slight note of regret and the sense of deprivation evident in her summing-up of their career: 'alas! owing to our concentration on research, municipal administration and Fabian propaganda, we had neither the time nor the energy, nor yet the means, to listen to music and the drama, to brood over classical literature, ancient and modern, to visit picture galleries, or to view with an informed intelligence the wonders of architecture'.[27]

It was a studious policy of austerity on the Webbs' part, not an unthinking philistinism, which accounted for their relative lack of indulgence in artistic pursuits after their partnership had consolidated itself. Lest this be thought to confirm from another angle the dominant impression of Webbian socialism as a brand which effectively excluded art from its concerns, the following three points need to be clearly emphasized and considered in relation to one another. First, while their growing absorption in the particular kinds of socialist work they chose to do led to increases in the degree of their austerity, it by no means entailed the renunciation of all artistic enjoyments and interests. Second, the Webbs' policy of renunciation with regard to the arts was not intended to be a completely prescriptive one, applicable to all people of all times; in many respects, it was a purely personal policy, stemming in part from combined feelings of their own inadequacy in the field of art. Third, the Webbs nowhere questioned, and on many occasions affirmed, the fundamental importance of art in society — especially in the socialist society of the future.

To take up this last point first, it is clear the importance of the arts as a humanizing influence was the basic assumption behind the Webbs' attack on capitalism for effectively debasing artistic works by treating them as luxury items and thereby putting them out of easy reach of the bulk of the working population. The Webbs sometimes made this assumption explicit in the course of demonstrating the far-reaching effects of imbalances in the distribution of money and property. For example, in 1891, Sidney claimed that 'we' — thereby implicating all members of his class, even those in such modest circumstances as himself — have 'virtually denied' the working man 'the means of having any share in the higher feelings and larger sympathies of the cultured race'.[28] In another work, published in 1920, he and Beatrice elaborated on this point, explaining how the capitalist system of wages had robbed 'the "common lump of men" ' of all but the 'slightest' chance of 'surrounding themselves and their children with the refinements of beautiful furniture, books, pictures and music'.[29]

Associated with this financial deprivation was another kind: a lack of effective amenities provided by society for the elevation of working-class tastes. The municipalization of cultural facilities had, according to Sidney, made significant strides over the past century. In his contribution to the *Fabian Essays*, he pointed out how far the State — on the colonial and national level as well as the local municipal one — had already proceeded in making provision for various facilities both in the field of the 'high arts' and of the more popular variety connected with 'amusements' and 'entertainments'. Centres of cultural, educational and recreational activities, such as museums, parks, art-galleries, schools of design, libraries, concert-halls, theatres, music halls, dancing-rooms and pleasure-grounds, figured largely in his lists of the facilities now sponsored or controlled — at least in part — by the bodies representing the community as a whole.[30] William Morris, in his review of the *Fabian Essays*, made out that Webb was so preoccupied with the strides made in state regulation as to give the impression that these represented 'the first stages of socialistic life', whereas it was 'surely necessary never to cease saying: The test of the realization of Socialism will be the abolition of poverty.'[31] It cannot be denied that Webb — at least for propaganda purposes — tended to depict municipalization as manifesting the irresistible growth of socialism in England. At the same time, he did not neglect to apply the test on which Morris insisted. By that test, Webb adjudged the present organization of society — however much advanced along the road to socialism — still gravely wanting. The provision of cultural and recreational facilities was a case in point. In an unsigned tract which he wrote for the Fabian Society in 1891, advocating a bill for an eight-hour working day, Webb affirmed that 'new possibilities of enjoyment, physical, emotional, intellectual', were 'daily opening for the masses'; but he went on to point out that the 'power and opportunity' to exploit such possibilities were 'now denied the mass of the workers'.[32] The implication was that the excessively long hours which they were forced to work in order to make up for their excessively low wages prevented them from taking advantage of many of the new facilities which existed. In one of their joint works, written in the 1920s, Sidney and Beatrice pointed to a further — and less easily remedied — disability arising from conditions of poverty and overwork: a blunting of aesthetic sensitivities. Attempts to elevate working-class taste, 'degraded by generations of industrialism, and very imperfectly educated', were bound to be 'slow and gradual', they maintained.[33]

It may be seen as symptomatic of his so-called philistinism that Sidney in his contribution to the *Fabian Essays* referred to the public funding of certain cultural and recreational facilities as 'comparatively unimportant services' when looked at in the light of what local authorities were providing in the way of other facilities such as gas, water and transport. This should be taken, however, as a statement of administrative priorities in a transitional period to socialism, and not as a principled belief in the subordinate status of cultural activities in society. Webb still felt that institutions such as municipal galleries and design schools were 'worth mentioning' as indicators of the 'extent to which our unconscious Socialism has already proceeded'; and he viewed the widest possible extension of municipal administration in such fields as an intrinsic part of the socialist programme.[34] Even William Morris, in one of his earliest and most popular socialist lectures, was willing to accept the necessity of a 'passing phase of utilitarianism' as the 'foundation for the art which is to be'. And he went so far as to envisage that phase as 'wholly without art or literature', arguing that the 'past degradation and corruption of society may force this denial of pleasure upon the society which will arise from its ashes'.[35] In a letter he printed in the *Commonweal* a few years later, he took up this argument again, contending that while 'the realization of Socialism would give us an opportunity of escaping from that grievous flood of utilitarianism which the full development of the society of contract has cursed us with', this release would come about 'in the long run only'. He thought it probable that 'in the early days of Socialism the reflex of the terror of starvation would drive us into excesses of utilitarianism'; and to back up this prediction, he spoke of 'a school of Socialists now extant who worship utilitarianism with a fervour of fatuity which is perhaps a natural consequence of their assumption of practicality'.[36] This may well have been an allusion to the 'Sidney Webbian' brand of socialism he was to attack explicitly a few months later in his review of the *Fabian Essays*. If Morris did associate this brand or 'school' with the kind of utilitarianism which would altogether exclude activities such as art and literature, he was being as unfair to Sidney as later critics were to prove.

Beatrice claimed in an interview she gave in 1893 that the reason she and Sidney concentrated their efforts on collectivizing 'the kitchen of life' was to make such 'well-considered arrangements for the material side' that 'all may have freedom for the drawing-room of life — at least a little corner of it'. And Sidney, on the same occasion, insisted that 'what we are in pursuit of is not the better housing, feeding and clothing of the people except as a means to an end — the development of individual character'.[37] In later writings, where they attempted to define the non-material components of freedom under social democracy or to sum up those factors most conducive to the 'expansion of individual character', they continually emphasized the importance of public access to the arts and of the general provision of opportunities for the development of personal creative faculties.[38]

In some cases, there was a direct link between their schemes for administering the most basic and prosaic municipal services and their broader interests in developing educational, recreational and cultural facilities. With regard to municipal gas and electricity supplies, for example, they advocated the general introduction of a system whereby a definite charge per unit consumed be levied as a way of discouraging waste in use, and whereby any surplus accruing to the municipality from these rates 'be used to supply elementary education or parks or music gratuitously to all'. They were prepared to countenance the deliberate raising of a surplus for such purposes.[39] The spread of electric power services was seen to have definite aesthetic, as well as social advantages, in that it would serve to enhance the health and cleanliness of the community, and through these the 'beauty of our cities and our countryside'.[40]

Such schemes might not have impressed William Morris, had he been alive to see them articulated or put into operation; they could well have struck him as only confirming the 'mechanistic' approach of Webbian socialism. But the Webbs themselves recognized the limitations of bureaucratic systematization through municipal and state control, and they never lost sight of the ends of socialism as distinct from the mechanisms. In their prospective *Constitution* for a socialist commonwealth, fully drafted after the end of the First World War, though sketched out in a series of articles in the *New Statesman* before the War, they talked of 'Local Authorities' undertaking responsibility for 'the whole mental and physical environment' — in such things as town-planning, conservation and, 'above and beyond all', the 'provision of art, music and the drama'.[41] They made it clear, however, that their responsibility would not result in official interference with the actual nature of an artist's work or in the imposition of any uniform or inflexible cultural policy. 'The State or Municipality,' they affirmed, was

unlikely, otherwise than exceptionally, to organise the production of the individual artist in painting or sculpture or artistic handicraft, any more than that of the writer in prose or in verse... Generally speaking, the enlargement of individual freedom for the many, which the greater equalisation of income will produce, may be expected to result in all sorts of new individual enterprises, supplementary to or competing with those undertaken by the national or local government.[42]

Even the dissemination of culture in the community at large was not, it appears, to be placed exclusively in the hands of bureaucratic bodies. The Webbs saw the main responsibility of these bodies as consisting in the universal provision of the basic material conditions of life so that man's higher 'intellectual, artistic and spiritual aspirations' may have greater chances of being realized. In one of their earliest joint works, published in 1897, they laid characteristic emphasis on the importance of material prerequisites while at the same time articulating the values of beauty and fellowship underlying that emphasis:

So long as life is one long scramble for personal gain — still more, when it is one long struggle against destitution — there is no free time or strength for much development of the sympathetic, intellectual, artistic, or religious faculties. When the conditions of employment are deliberately regulated so as to secure adequate food, education, and leisure to every capable citizen, the great mass of the population will, for the first time, have any real chance of expanding in friendship and family affection, and of satisfying the instinct for knowledge or beauty. It is an even more unique attribute of democracy that it is always taking the mind of the individual off his narrow and immediate concerns, and forcing him to give his thought and leisure... to considering the needs and desires of his fellows.[43]

The Webbs' reservations about the capacities of bureaucracy were appreciated by R.H. Tawney, the socialist historian with whom they had many deep political disagreements. Some remarks he made in a memoir of the Webbs throw considerable doubt on any depiction of those disagreements as a simple conflict between 'bureaucratic' and more 'humane' approaches to socialism.[44] He maintained that portrayals of them as 'bureaucratic energumens, conspiring to submit every human acitivity to the centralized control of an omnicompetent State' were 'a caricature, which the subjects chosen for their researches should be sufficient to refute'.[45] Art was never, in itself, a subject of their researches; but their incidental comments on the role and organization of the arts in society testifies vividly to the truth of Tawney's observation. Their conception of art's humanizing power serves in fact to humanize them.

The same is true of their personal response to art and to artists. This shows clearly that their austerity was by no means unrelenting. To begin with, they nowhere demanded that others — even their colleagues in the socialist movement — renounce artistic pursuits and pleasures to the extent which they themselves did. They seem to have felt that it was more fitting for them, in their avowed ignorance of artistic matters, to devote their energies to the more mundane 'bread and butter' or 'gas and water' aspects of socialism. Even then, Beatrice was glad to find Sidney, in the early stages of her relationship with him, taking the time to study the works of an artist like Goethe, because 'one needs the high air of the mountain when one is fighting on the plain'.[46] Both of the Webbs continued to take a discerning interest in the works of several playwrights and novelists. These included a number of prominent literary figures who were attached to the Fabian Society itself at various times: Bernard Shaw, H.G. Wells, Harley Granville Barker, Arnold Bennett, Rupert Brooke, and Leonard and Virginia Woolf.

Beatrice is on record as actively endorsing and encouraging the literary activities of several of these writers, as well as of others (like E.M. Forster) who had no formal connections with the Society.[47] Both she and Sidney enjoyed the novels of Leonard Woolf as well as valuing his political and diplomatic writings. Some of his factual writings developed into official Fabian literature under the Webbs' influence, but Beatrice also saw to it that his fiction was included in the library of the Fabian club-room.[48] In the case of Bernard Shaw, Beatrice even preferred on occasion that he get on with his writing for the theatre — where she felt his intellect was centred — than with any socialist writing outside that medium.[49] On looking back on the Webbs' friendship with Shaw, Beatrice was fond of drawing a contrast between the pragmatism of herself and Sidney and the intellectual and literary brilliance of the dramatist.[50] This exemplifies her tendency to categorize people rather rigidly according to particular roles, capacities and temperaments — to construct, as Leonard Woolf put it, 'a kind of psychological and occupational card index of all her acquaintances'.[51] The possession of artistic gifts or sensibilities formed the basis of one such category in her eyes. She excluded herself and Sidney from this

category, not only because of their avowedly pragmatic, scientific procedures, but also because of the very restraints which they imposed on
their own social and emotional lives. 'Absence of restraint', as Beatrice
saw it, was one of the defining qualities of the artistic temperament. It
was, moreover, the key factor in an artist's conception of liberty, to be
distinguished from the Webbs' own emphasis on 'presence of opportunity'.[52] In principle and practice, it linked the artistic temperament with
the anarchistic and the aristocratic temperaments — the three 'A's in
Beatrice's mental filing-cabinet. The Webbs themselves, Beatrice is
reported to have said, fitted rather into the 'B' category: 'bourgeois',
'bureaucratic' and 'benevolent'. There was a rather absurd arbitrariness
about this process of classification which led to an over-simplification of
the Webbs' own sensibilities, it should be stressed, as well as those of the
artists they knew. The classifications themselves, however, were not so
arbitrary or so rigid as to posit a complete separation between them or to
imply mutual antagonism between the different sorts of temperaments
which formed their basis. Beatrice warned Sidney from early on about the
dangers of ignoring or dismissing as unworthy aspects of 'human life and
human effort' outside one's own sphere or range of interest: 'try not to
judge others always by your own standard and your own experience'.[53]

The value which a novelist like E.M. Forster (and other members of the
Bloomsbury Group) placed on the personal and aesthetic aspects of
human relationships — 'the presence of beauty of soul and body' —
seemed in direct opposition to her and Sidney's emphasis on the need for
perfecting the general social and ethical aspects. 'Perhaps men cannot be
at once aesthetic and ethical?' she mused.[54] Beatrice made clear
elsewhere, however, that the Webbs' differences with what they regarded
as a primarily aesthetic creed did not imply total opposition to all aspects
of that creed. With special reference to the views of Virginia Woolf,
Beatrice stressed the common goals and common areas of concern which
linked the novelist's set with the Webb partnership: 'We all aim at
maximizing human happiness, health, loving kindness, scientific curiosity,
and the spirit of adventure together with the appreciation of beauty in
sight and sound, in word and thought. Where we differ is how to bring
about this ideal here and now.'[55] There might be two distinct sides to
human sensibility, 'aesthetic', and 'ethical', unable to be synthesized
completely in one person, but, Beatrice implied, these two sides were not
intrinsically hostile to each other, nor mutually exclusive in every respect.

Neither was the scientific temperament, which the Webbs ascribed to
themselves, necessarily antagonistic to the artistic temperament. From the
time before he became a socialist, Sidney had implied that science and art
were complementary pursuits. Beatrice, looking back at the end of her life
over her and Sidney's good relations with Shaw, concluded that the

'political scientist wastes his time if he argues with a witty and dramatic genius. They must complement, not fight each other.'[56] With half a century's experience and self-restraint behind her, she was prepared to acknowledge that restraining regimens prescribed by institutions or other individuals would be quite inappropriate and undesirable for the artist. She went so far as to agree with the anarchist art critic, Herbert Read, that the artist should be 'free-lance' and that the 'absence of restraint when there is genius — especially artistic genius, is of great importance'. Far from wishing to impose any disabilities on those whom she included in her category 'artist', Beatrice seemed to be suggesting that they were entitled to special privileges.

The implicit élitism of this position — made explicit in her concern for the genius in particular — was tempered by her corresponding concern for a general availability of opportunity to all those who were capable of becoming artists. Beatrice felt that those who were already established in the art-world tended to show no such concern: she contended that Read himself, for instance, as the son of a well-to-do farmer, simply assumed the 'presence of opportunity' because he had always enjoyed it.[57] Beatrice, in placing greater weight on this factor as a basis for freedom, was not necessarily opposing the other basis — 'absence of restraint' — in all fields of human endeavour; rather she was attempting to see that this basis was extended to more people (at least more 'artistic' people) than it had been hitherto.

The Webbs' personal renunciation of many artistic pleasures while working for the achievement of socialism certainly involved no principled intolerance of artistic pleasure, whether from the artist's point of view or his audience's. Beatrice and Sidney, as we have seen, were particularly censorious of any symptoms they divined of over-indulgence in pleasure — artistic or otherwise — at the expense of social and political service. And Sidney's censoriousness — perhaps because he had never experienced any conscious artistic impulses himself — was unqualified by the sympathetic concessions which Beatrice was prepared to make in exceptional cases to the creed or practice of unrestraint in artistic matters. He tended to make in his own way as rigid a categorization as she between artistic and other pursuits, capacities and roles in society; and he clearly subordinated his own artistic interests to more direct and immediate socio-political concerns. In all this, however, he showed no intrinsic hostility to artists or the committed art-lover. Though he seems to have thought there could be a clear separation between politics and art as areas of human involvement and concern, and implied the primacy of the former, Sidney admitted, far more than Beatrice did, the possibility that the two areas might co-exist in one man's life and sensibility. He was anxious about the 'curious ignoring of the public duties (of citizenship, etc.) which literature joins with theology in encouraging'. He perceived a strong apolitical streak in various Victorian novelists and poets, reflected in the fact that none of them 'ever thinks of man as a citizen. He is a lover, husband, father, friend — but never a voter, town-councillor or vestry-man.'[58] This need not and should not be the case. A few years later, he gave examples from the past, which would serve as exemplars for the future, of writers who in themselves had successfully managed to combine their artistic capacities and impulses with political and social duties. Schiller, for instance, he pictured as 'a type of the socialistic poet, writing his poetry overtime, after his duties as a civil servant were ended for the day'.[59] Clearly, while believing there should be some obligation for artists, as for others, to carry out certain political and administrative work on a regular basis, he by no means expected them to devote nearly all their time, as he had done, to this work and to subordinate their artistic concerns completely. As we shall see, he even suggested ways in which an artist's political duties could be directly related to matters of aesthetic interest for the community at large. It should always be remembered, too, that his and Beatrice's own devotion to pragmatic and often quite mundane public work had certain cultural ends for the benefit of artists and non-artists alike.

Beatrice felt strongly that the artistic temperament, as she defined it, was much more intolerant of the pragmatic temperament than the other way round, and that it was inclined to be quite exclusionist in its concerns. On meeting Rabindranath Tagore in 1920, and sensing the Indian poet's disdain for all that the Webbs stood for, she concluded:

he is not content to be the seer and the poet...he must needs condemn the man of action, the lawyer, the administrator, and even the scientific worker. This quite unconscious and spiritual insolence...is...due to the atmosphere of adulation in which the mystic genius lives...The practical man is always being opposed and criticised...This tends to make him humble and tolerant...He seldom becomes insolently contemptuous of all other types of man. He may dislike the artist, the poet, and the mystic. But he does not condemn them.[60]

Sidney Webb showed more than just tolerance when the literary side of the *New Statesman* came under attack for its avant-gardism; he actively defended the paper's literary editor, J.C. Squire, and while admitting again to a limited personal taste in literature, he averred that the new generation of writers and artists had 'to be welcomed and encouraged, even if their elders don't appreciate them!'[61]

The fact that the Webbs saw themselves as pragmatic, scientific socialists who had little or no proper appreciation of art, may help explain why they could acquiesce so resignedly in the carica-tures of them presented by a socialist artist like H.G. Wells. Any element of condescension or complacency in their pose, *vis-à-vis* the artist, masked a more basic humility and self-effacement.

It is impossible, of course, to measure precisely changes in the intensity of their artistic appreciation before and after marriage. But the idea that their socialist austerity involved turning their backs on art completely founders on a number of objections. First, a close attention to literature formed an integral part of their work. Throughout their historical and social investigations, Sidney and Beatrice testified implicitly and explicitly to the great value of novels, plays and poems as sources of evidence. Their massive study of *English Local Government* was peppered with references to a wide variety of imaginative writers, especially from the eighteenth century. Though the Webbs consciously suppressed their responses to the aesthetic aspects of their source material,[62] they occasionally revealed their enjoyment of the more imaginative works. They commented in passing, for example, on the amusing qualities of a poem by Pope, on the liveliness of Smollet's novel, *Roderick Random*, and on the charms and delights to be found in Addison's portrayal of Sir Roger de Coverley and his milieu.[63]

Apart from various allusions in their history of local government, there is little testimony to the Webbs' interest in poetry in the years of their partnership, whether as source material or for their own stimulation and enjoyment. Evidence of their continuing interest in other branches of literature can be adduced from a wide variety of their published and private writings. This suggests that the Webbs felt more at home with prose forms. It does not, however, indicate an incapacity for appreciating poetry: their interest in the works of a number of poets in their more youthful days undermines any such charge. If Beatrice was 'poetry blind', writes F.R. Leavis, it is 'impossible to believe that she was congenitally so — indeed she hadn't supposed herself to be in the formative years'. Even in the days of the partnership, she would occasionally invoke the words of nineteenth-century poets to crystallize her innermost feelings.[64] In the early stages of his relationship with Beatrice, Sidney had turned to poetry in 'times of discouragement',[65] as well as using it to court her; and, on continuing into marriage this courtship ritual, he chose as his texts the two great poetic plays of Ibsen (*Brand* and *Peer Gynt*). Sidney's recitations from these two verse-dramas provided real enjoyment and solace for Beatrice herself — feelings which contrast with her marked irritation and impatience at a performance in 1901 of one of Ibsen's earliest (and admittedly crudest) 'social—didactic' plays, *Pillars of Society*.[66]

Beatrice's lack of attention to the work of twentieth-century poets may have sprung in part from a suspicion that the values (or lack of values) which repelled her in so many post-Victorian novels would only be found in intensified form in modern verse. One of the Webbs' most prominent friends in the world of letters, Arnold Bennett, claimed that reading novels was possibly the only 'distraction' that Sidney and Beatrice permitted themselves.[67] It is true that they read many novels which were not strictly relevant to the particular subjects of their historical and social research. Apart, however, from the years of their retirement, when Beatrice started borrowing copies of Trollope, Thackeray and the like to satisfy Sidney's increasingly voracious appetite for 'old-fashioned' novelists,[68] it is doubtful whether they approached even their extra-curricular reading as a completely pleasurable diversion which needed to bear no relation to day-to-day concerns. There are anecdotes — related, it should be noted, by a rather hostile witness — which picture Sidney reading, but detesting, the historical romances of Walter Scott, and craving a novel of 'business life'.[69] Beatrice acquired a taste in the inter-war years for solid 'sociological' novels, especially by modern American writers.[70] This contrasts with her neglect of American literature in the pre-war years. She discovered in many of its later products an un-shirkingly realistic emphasis on the degeneracy of the capitalist order, combined with some life-sustaining philosophy or vision which conveyed a real sense of how that order would be eradicated and what might supersede it. These qualities, she indicated, were partially or wholly lacking in nearly all the works of English fiction she had read from both the immediate pre-war and post-war generations.

There were novelists such as Aldous Huxley and Virginia Woolf who depicted the decay of contemporary civilization, but whose consciousness of it, in Beatrice's eyes, assumed the proportions of a cynical or morbid obsession that positively precluded any 'living philosophy' concerning 'man's relation to the universe, still less man's relation to man'.[71] There were a few English novelists of the present century whose works seemed to offer some kind of positive philosophy or vision; but in nearly all cases Beatrice found this to be deficient or completely alien to her sensibility. Both she and Sidney had taken a keen interest in H.G. Wells's work (fictional and non-fictional) from the early years of the century; though their attitude to it was ambivalent almost from the start, complicated as it was by their personal acquaintance with the author and their bitter conflicts with him over policy in the Fabian Society. Wells, however, was inclined to be much more embittered than the Webbs. After the Fabian storm had blown over, and he had resigned from the Society, Beatrice attempted at least to keep open the channels of communication. On the publication of *Tono-Bungay* (1909), his fictional exposé of the corruptness he saw at the heart of the Edwardian business world, Beatrice penned him a congratulatory letter. In this she said how she had 'thoroughly enjoyed' the novel, though had felt that it might not outlast his apocalyptic fantasy of the year before, *The War in the Air*. The few criticisms that she offered were much milder than those she recorded in her diary;[72] but, judging from his wounded response to them,[73] they served only to fan the fires of his fury, which blazed on for several more months, reaching its height in his searing caricatures of Beatrice and Sidney in *The New Machiavelli*.

Beatrice's assessment of D.H. Lawrence was not complicated by any direct personal association with him. Partly for that reason, perhaps, she felt free to criticize him in unequivocal terms. But there was a deeper reason: she had severe doubts about the basic humanity of Lawrence's vision of mankind. She designated his ideal as a cult of sex and primitivism, lacking any kind of 'ethical code' or 'fixed scale of values', divorced from 'personal affection' and 'social obligation', and antagonistic to 'intellect' and 'social purpose'; and if it was in any sense a life-sustaining philosophy, the life it appeared to prescribe was the purely instinctual one of 'the pre-human animal' or even the 'pre-ape animal'.[74]

For Beatrice, 'purpose' came before pleasure in literature as in life. In the mid-1920s she had claimed that one of the 'unforeseen pleasures' of old age had been the 'faint beginning of a liking for exquisite literature irrespective of its subject matter';[75] but all of her judgments on literature during the last two decades of her life show clearly that her main discriminating criteria continued to be based on the nature or degree of moral or social purpose which she divined in an author's works. Beatrice claimed that this 'insistence on a purpose' in twentieth-century literature might well be dismissed as the 'delusion' of an 'aged Victorian'. Her 'Victorianism' also revealed itself in her related insistence on the necessity for artists to emphasize those 'civilised' and ethical qualities in man that distinguished him from animals.[76] The early influence of Ruskin on her view of art clearly outlasted all of the attacks on his assumptions mounted by the late-Victorian and Edwardian champions of 'art for art's sake'. In the mid nineteenth century, he had reinforced the notion that 'good art' required a 'stout moral purpose' as well as the 'luminous attraction of pleasure'. Acknowledging that 'you must not follow Art without pleasure', he added: 'nor must you follow it for the sake of pleasure', and this admonition was repeated in various forms throughout his writings.[77]

It needs to be stressed, however, that just as Ruskin's insistence on 'purpose' in art by no means entailed a ban on pleasure, neither did Beatrice's; and that her own native prejudice against 'art for art's sake' never resulted in an indifference to artistic concerns or an insensitivity to aesthetic criteria. Even in the midst of attacking writers for their lack of moral or social purpose, she could acknowledge their stature as great artists and her own appreciation — as distinct from the world's — of their artistic capacities. She did this in the case of Lawrence, though without going into detail about what aspects of his artistry she particularly appreciated.[78] In the case of Virginia Woolf, she referred specifically in her diary to the 'great charm and finesse' of the novelist, to her excellent (if 'précieuse') craftsmanship, her 'sensitiveness', her 'subtle' observation and her 'symphonic style'. In a letter to Leonard Woolf some years earlier, Beatrice wrote that his wife had such 'an extraordinarily valuable instrument in her spiritual insight and literary gift' that 'it would be a sin against humanity' if it were lost to the world through Virginia's ill-health.[79]

Conversely, Beatrice could extend her usual line of attack on the moral deficiencies of contemporary English novelists to include aesthetic deficiencies. For example, she dismissed Aldous Huxley's novel, *After Many a Summer*, as an 'ugly book' on account of the fact that she could find in it neither 'thought of any value, nor beauty in expression'.[80]

For all her emphasis on the significance of moral and social purpose in fictional writing, Beatrice was well aware from her own experience that novelists were, at bottom, defined and distinguished by the nature of their artistic medium and faculties, not by their ideas. In the days before her partnership with Sidney Webb she herself had been strongly tempted to take up novel writing.[81] And, on at least two occasions following the consolidation of the Webb partnership, Beatrice expressed a positive desire and, moreover, a positive intention to devote some of her time to writing a novel. She revealed explicitly on these occasions her conception of novel-writing — in contradistinction to social and historical writing — as above all an artistic process requiring literary skills beyond the mechanical, and peculiarly rich imaginative resources. In February 1895 she wrote:

For the last three months an idea has haunted me that after we have ended our stiff work on Trade Unions I would try my hand at pure 'Fiction' in the form of a novel dated '60 years hence!' It should not be an attempt to picture a Utopia. It should attempt to foreshadow society as it should be . . . if we go on 'evoluting' in a humdrum way . . . The truth is, I want to have my 'fling'! I want to imagine anything I damn please without regard to facts as they are — I want to give full play to whatever faculty I have for descriptive and dramatic work — I want to try my hand at artistic work instead of mechanics. I am sick to death of trying to put hideous facts, multitudinous details, exasperating qualifications, into a readable form. Doubtless when I discover that I have no artistic faculties I shall turn back to my old love and write with equanimity, 'The History of Municipal Institutions'. But before I can have this debauch I have a grind before me that must be got through however little I like it.

Some fourteen months later she spoke of continuing 'broodings' of discontent. These were, she asserted, the 'special curse of a vivid and vigorous imagination', at present 'occupied' in her 'dry work of analysis and abstraction'. She felt she 'must some day write that novel' and work in all those 'brilliant scenes' she was 'constantly constructing'.[82]

These passages show clearly her view that the artistic process in itself could effectively combine constructive purpose with pleasure. Fiction might provide a realistic vision of the future of society without involving the sheer drudgery of so much factual writing. The extracts also reveal, however, a lingering guilt on Beatrice's part about engaging in the artistic process herself: even the pleasure of purposeful novel-writing she deems a 'debauch'; and she refers to the source of the artistic impulses within herself as a 'curse'. Associated with the guilt feelings are her old feelings of inferiority and personal inadequacy regarding any artistic faculties.

The novel she was so determined to write never in fact got off the ground: her feelings of guilt and inferiority, and her habit of austere dedication to more mundane concerns, were probably too ingrained even by the mid-1880s for them ever to be resisted sufficiently long. Her diary itself, however, provided a channel for her artistic resources and frustrations, both in the opportunities it provided for personal observation and the construction of 'brilliant scenes', and in the regular relief it offered from the grind of her research work. She continued to see the people she met as possible characters for novels.[83] Furthermore, she remained interested throughout her career in the artistic process as it manifested itself in others: if she denied herself the pleasure of participating directly in the process, she gained vicarious pleasure through the advice, criticism, and encouragement she offered various colleagues of hers in the artistic world. 'I am delighted,' she told H.G. Wells in 1909, '. . . that you are at work on a novel which is to combine all the great qualities of *Tono-Bungay* with a study of the more ideal elements of human character.'[84] The desire for novelists to produce the sorts of works she herself would probably have written had she felt she possessed the requisite artistic talent is even clearer from the remarks she made many years later on (and to) E.M. Forster. Though critical of his 'aestheticism' she tried to persuade him to write 'another great novel' (analogous to *Passage to India*) on the very theme of the conflict 'between those who aim at exquisite relationships within the closed circle of the "elect" and those who aim at hygienic and scientific improvement of the whole of the race'.[85] The fact that she considered an art-form like the novel a potentially fruitful medium for such an examination is very significant. It shows that her differences with 'aestheticism', and her own social and ethical preoccupations, never blunted her intrinsic interest in artistic methods and procedures, and could in fact extend her appreciation of the areas in which art had a particular or peculiar contribution to make to human understanding.

We know far more about Beatrice's opinions on art than about Sidney's. Most of this information comes from her diary; and Sidney did not keep any such record, apart from contributing the odd entry to Beatrice's when they were travelling abroad. But various sources —

including Beatrice's own recollections in her diary — show that Sidney shared several of her artistic experiences throughout the period of their partnership.

Travels abroad provided the only sustained break from the Webbs' usual routine of research, writing, lecturing and sitting on committees, so that records of these travels produce the largest concentration of evidence relating to their experiences and interests in the field of art. Not that art was a mere holiday indulgence for them. We have already seen in the case of literature how their research itself involved the use of artistic material; and to a lesser extent this was the case with painting (Hogarth's engravings and portraits by Raeburn and others were among the sources which the Webbs cited in their major historical works).[86] They simply had more leisure time when away from England, and the continual demands of their private and public work there, to go to theatres, concerts, galleries and so on; though they still managed to squeeze some of these activities into their routine at home.

Whether at any time Sidney and Beatrice approached such activities as mere diversions is questionable. Even as a form of relaxation, art was endorsed by the young and pious Sidney as 'necessary for the fullest efficiency of life'.[87] His travels abroad with Beatrice in later life were partly for purposes of efficiency-boosting relaxation; but they had a more direct curricular purpose as well. They provided the Webbs with first-hand lessons in the ways in which social institutions in foreign countries compared with those they were studying at home. Under the head 'social institutions' they included not only such things as the family, the educational system, the structure of government (local and national), but also the 'organizations of recreation and games, religion and science, poetry and art, and, indeed, every sort of cultural relations among men'.[88] The most comprehensive work to come out of their travels — their two-volume study of Soviet communism — devoted considerable attention to the cultural policies of the U.S.S.R. government and the recreational and artistic facilities provided for the Russian people. There was one specific section on 'Artistic Culture', with sub-sections on 'Museums and Picture Galleries', 'Theatre and Ballet', 'Music and Literature'.[89] In a sense, the Webbs' own visits to exhibitions, plays, operas, ballets, concerts and such like, in whatever country, reflect their conscientiousness as social observers. At the same time, it would be misguided to claim that they did not enjoy many of these artistic activities for their inherent qualities, or that they were incapable of discriminating between them on any kind of aesthetic grounds.

Of all artistic activities, theatre was the one which engaged most of their attention while they were at home. In the period before 1918 they went to performances of a number of Shaw's plays, as well as reading them in published form, or having them read out by the author himself.[90] They saw productions of plays written by another prominent member of the Fabian Society at the time, Harley Granville Barker; and they appear also to have taken some interest in his capacities and fortunes as an actor, director and theatrical manager.[91] That they did not attend to the work of these dramatists merely out of a sense of loyalty to fellow-Fabians, or purely for the sake of the ideas which could be mined out of the plays concerned, is clear from both Sidney and Beatrice's retrospective remarks. They approached the plays in a far from perfunctory manner, not hesitating to pick out and criticize faults or deficiencies which they found in the works themselves or in their production; and, in making these criticisms, they showed at least some desire for the plays to please or excite on an artistic level as well as on an intellectual level.

Beatrice's suspicions that Barker's faculties may be 'more analytic than artistic'[92] were apparently borne out for her when she attended a performance of his play, *The Madras House*, in 1910 and found it 'intellectual but dull'. The basic theme was not to her taste, in its preoccupation with 'the mere physical attractions of men to women'; though her accusation of dullness seems to refer rather to the playwright's treatment of the theme. By way of comparison and contrast, she branded Shaw's play, *Misalliance*, which shared the same theme in her view, as 'brilliant but disgusting'.[93] Without ever entirely separating such categories as theme and treatment, she could show more fascination at times with the way in which the playwright had embodied his ideas than with the ideas themselves. This is borne out explicitly in her response to Shaw's *Man and Superman*, which the author read to her and Sidney in 1903. The chosen subject was much more to her taste than that of *Misalliance*; but what particularly impressed her on this occasion was the 'form' of the play — not its dramatic form, admittedly, but one which she saw clearly in artistic terms (poetic and musical) as well as in intellectual terms. To her *Man and Superman* seemed to be Shaw's 'greatest work' to date: he had found 'his *form*: a play which is not a play; but only a combination of essay, treatise, interlude, lyric — all the different forms illustrating the central idea, as a sonata manifests a scheme of melody and harmony. I was all the more delighted with it as I had not been impressed with the bits I had heard before, and Sidney had reported unfavourably on the play itself.'[94]

Sidney had found very little to admire in earlier drafts of *Man and Superman* which he had been given to peruse; though he judged the preface, which he felt had little to do with the play, as 'brilliant'.[95] This did not represent a general prejudice against the literary or theatrical expressions of Shaw's ideas. His comments on a production of *The Devil's Disciple* which he and Beatrice saw in New York in 1898 evinced at once enthusiasm and critical discrimination, especially with regard to the central performance by the American actor, Richard Mansfield. Sidney enjoyed Shaw's work on the stage and he clearly wished the actors to do proper justice to that work.[96] The civilized delights which theatre could offer did not escape him, even though his personal routine did not allow him to partake of these very much himself. On visiting the capital of South Australia in 1898, he had noted its physical and social resemblances to the small German towns he had known as a schoolboy; but added the qualification that it lacked the 'charm of the German ''Residenzstadt'' in history, art (especially music and the theatre), and scholarship'.[97] The early impact of German culture had clearly not lost itself on him. When the Webbs went to Russia in 1932, they were very struck by the popular appreciation of drama which they witnessed first-hand.[98] Sidney managed to see a wider range of theatre than Beatrice by making a return visit to Russia without her in 1934; though he regularly reported back to her on the details of the various plays he had seen. Soviet theatre as a sociological phenomenon, as a manifestation of mass culture, was by no means the only aspect of that activity which impressed the Webbs. Observations on artistic and technical aspects — the quality of the acting and the staging — were always included in their reports, and were usually flattering to the productions concerned.[99] While they approved the notion of theatre as an ethical force or medium they had sufficient respect for the integrity of the form to be against its use for any crudely ideological purposes. Commenting on the plays specially produced for children, the Webbs observed that these were 'interestingly written about subjects and situations within the children's comprehension' and were 'free from didacticism, and of anything that can fairly be called propaganda, although...subtly penetrated with a ''healthy moral tone'' and a strong ''civic patriotism''. The packed child audiences are thrilled with excitement at every phase of the drama acted before them.'[100] The Webbs sought a healthy moral purpose in all art; but it was something which, in their eyes, did not necessarily detract from the excitement art could give. Neither was it to be confused with simple tendentiousness, which was really inimical: long before, Sidney had explicitly identified 'crude didacticism' in artistic form with 'philistinism'.[101]

It was what she saw as an unhealthy, life-denying morality, combined with an over-didactic stance in presenting that morality in the theatre, which made Beatrice critical of many of the Shaw plays which she saw in London in the 1920s and 1930s. Reviewing *Too True to be Good*, for instance, which Shaw wrote in 1931, Beatrice claimed that it was 'a farce spoiled by a sermon, and a sermon spoiled by a farce: the farce being far better than the sermon'. The first act, in being 'pure farce', was 'great fun', but the sermonizing which began in the second act had taken over by the third, and became so 'boresome' as to make Beatrice want to go to sleep.[102]

Beatrice's attitudes to Shaw in the inter-war years show how highly she had come to prize 'fun' and a genuine dramatic excitement in the situations which playwrights presented before their audiences. She opined that the 'only redeeming feature' of *The Apple Cart*, the 'savage burlesque of a Labour Government' which Shaw penned in 1928, was that it was 'very good fun'.[103] In commenting, over ten years later, on a play that Shaw had just started, Beatrice summed up many of her disappointments with his achievements over the past decade, on the dramatic as well as moral level. The play was *In Good King Charles's Golden Days*, and Beatrice acknowledged that in the first scene there was much 'brilliant dialogue'. If only he could bring in 'some sort of striking incident', she felt, and 'not limit himself to sparkling talk', the piece may 'turn out A. one'. She suggested to him that 'his greatest plays, St. Joan, Major Barbara, John Bull's Other Island, Man and Superman' had all gained from having truly 'dramatic events' as a basis of their situation. It was the loss of the excitement and vitality which these had provided, as much as the loss of 'any definite scale of values', which sapped her enthusiasm for much of Shaw's dramatic work in the 1930s.[104] This is brought out vividly if we consider her initial attitude to one of those plays which she later ranked among his 'greatest' — *Major Barbara*. She had attended the first performance of this in 1905 with Sidney and the Conservative leader, A.J. Balfour; and had come away shocked and dismayed:

G.B.S.'s play turned out to be a dance of devils — amazingly clever, grimly powerful in the second act — but ending as all his plays end...in an intellectual and moral morass...I doubt the popular success of the play: it is hell tossed on the stage — with no hope of heaven. G.B.S. is gambling with ideas and emotions in a way that distresses slow-minded prigs like Sidney and me.[105]

It is clear that Beatrice, long before the 1930s, had entertained grave suspicions about the solidity of Shaw's sense of moral values. It would seem, then, that the sheer dramatic power of some of his earlier plays impressed itself on her more and more, so as to become an important measure of their greatness in her eyes when compared with the merely garrulous or sermonizing spectacles which she took his thirties plays to be.

The 'firm placing judgment', which is how F.R. Leavis has described Beatrice's initial response to *Major Barbara*, and on which he partly bases his own claims for her as 'potentially a good literary critic', [106] did not remain firm. But the shift in her attitude demonstrates, if anything, an increasing sensitivity to the more overtly dramatic qualities in Shaw's work — those which determined the degree of its effectiveness as theatre. By the inter-war years, in fact, her increased exposure to the theatre seems to have brought her to a fairly rounded appreciation of its attractions; she became as appreciative or as demanding of its artistic and technical aspects as of its moral and intellectual ones. She could thus dismiss the 'metaphysics' of J.B. Priestley's time-fantasy, *We Have Been Here Before*, as 'absurd'; and yet still be receptive — in a discriminating way — to other attributes of the play and production. The characters, she said, were 'cleverly conceived and admirably acted'; though the leading lady was a 'washout, whether in charm or credibility'. The dialogue she found 'serious, dramatic and at times amusing'. Altogether 'the play excited us and never bored us'.[107]

Sidney didn't just tag along behind Beatrice to the plays they attended in the inter-war years. He shared at least some of her enjoyment in these breaks from their routine; and there is evidence that he proposed and arranged some of the outings himself. Concert-going was another activity he seems to have taken the initiative in arranging on occasion.[108] The Webbs' interest in music blossomed in the inter-war years, when the advent of radio made music much more readily accessible to them, bringing it into the confines of their home. Beatrice maintained in December 1925 that the B.B.C.'s programmes were teaching her to listen to music with a degree of appreciation that might even create a drug-like dependence upon it.[109] The craving for music which those programmes induced had already prompted her to seek out alternative sources in the traditional 'live' forms which she had long neglected. Sidney, she implied, shared in the musical pleasures which the wireless brought — 'to our little household it has been a source of delight' — but was not affected to nearly the same degree as she:

The curious result to me personally is that I have attended as many concerts these last six months as I have in the last twenty years. Music has become my main recreation; and if I can afford it, I shall make my future visits to London chiefly for the purpose of hearing more and more music. I am already contemplating a course of reading on music and musicians.[110]

The Webbs' own record collection suggests rather limited and orthodox tastes (nothing but Beethoven, Mozart and Brahms, apart from some French songs[111]). When she attended the Gloucester music festival with Shaw in 1931, Beatrice reported how she had been 'swept away' by some of Gustav Holst's music;[112] though on the whole she could never bring herself to appreciate much that was beyond the range of a standard Victorian concert repertoire. She couldn't understand the cult for folk music reflected in D.H. Lawrence's tastes. She inveighed against the B.B.C.'s tendency, in the late thirties, to play what she termed 'jazzy music'. And she was gravely disturbed by the 'subtle lowering of the sense of beauty', the idolizing of the 'superhuman' (for which Wagner, or

'Wagnerism', set a trend), and the 'prevalence of crude animalism' in 'much of the music of the twentieth century'. Her conservatism in these matters would appear to have sprung directly from the deeply religious impulses in her which lingered from adolescence. Prayer, albeit not of the specifically Christian variety, came to constitute an increasing preoccupation in her old age, together with music. She herself commented on the intimate association, 'whether as cause or effect', between prayer and the 'nobler and more enduring' forms of music as well as of architecture, poetry and painting. The ugly, crude qualities she found in twentieth-century music she also found in contemporary manifestations of other art forms, and explicitly attributed those qualities to the 'decline of the religious habit'.[113]

The modern movements in painting seem to have had little or nothing to offer her, from an 'ethical' or 'aesthetic' viewpoint. She seems in fact to have made little effort to cultivate a proper knowledge of the work of any major painters after the Pre-Raphaelites, which contrasts with her efforts to become acquainted with the works of modern novelists and playwrights, no matter how distasteful some of these might have been for her. Perhaps the noblest and most 'enduring' schools of painting in her eyes were those of late-mediaeval and Renaissance Italy: holidaying in Florence in 1909, she found herself 'revelling' once more in the pictures she had 'loved so well' on her previous visit to that city some thirty years before.[114] The walls of the Webbs' own houses in London and Liphook, Hampshire, were hung with reproductions of Botticelli, Lorenzo di Credi, Michelangelo and Titian, as well as major English painters of the nineteenth century (including Turner, Burne-Jones, Watts) and several original landscapes, portraits and etchings by lesser-known artists.[115]

With regard to the more overtly 'functional' arts, such as architecture and town-planning, the Webbs do not seem to have harboured any decided prejudice against the modern manifestations they saw around them in England and abroad; though they had decided tastes and distastes in specimens both of the past and present. These discriminations were not based wholly on functional criteria, and were more often cast in aesthetic than in purely practical or technical terms. Examples we have of Beatrice's responses to university architecture are pertinent, in that they hardly suggest someone who could have been infected by 'the statistical and sheerly utilitarian' standards imputed to her husband in judging the designs for the permanent buildings of the London School of Economics. In 1898, only four years before the official opening of the School's main buildings, the Webbs were inspecting another academic institution, Columbia University in New York; and Beatrice criticized the look of its buildings and fittings precisely on the grounds of their 'utilitarian' nature, which she found charmless and even squalid.[116]

Sidney's impressions of other buildings (including academic ones) show a tendency to respond more to their aesthetic appearance and overall 'feel' than to technical and functional details. Writing to Graham Wallas a year or so after joining the Fabian Society, Sidney expressed considerable contempt for the 'pedantic', 'red-tape' considerations which he saw behind the Romans' approach to architecture. Typical epithets of his in condemning or praising various buildings were: 'grossly materialist and industrial', 'splendid', 'magnificent', 'really beautiful', 'odd but attractive', 'ugly and squalid'.[117]

When directly confronted with the problem of how to go about erecting, from scratch, a permanent home for the London School of Economics, all those involved in the planning necessarily paid a great deal of attention to basic practical and technical considerations. The sheer physical (and financial) problems of providing space and facilities in the heart of a congested metropolis for whole generations of students, unable or unwilling to be accommodated by the traditional universities, no doubt led to compromises in the design whereby aesthetic considerations lost out to more functional ones. Webb himself cannot be entirely blamed for these. An account of the building of the L.S.E. provided by a former director, Sir Sydney Caine, indicates that the design competition for the Passmore Edwards Hall, the focal building of the School, was judged by a committee in which other voices — notably that of William Garnett, Secretary of the Technical Education Board of the London County Council — had at least as much say as Webb's. The question of the building's outward appearance was not ignored, as is shown, for instance, by the 'inclusion in the design of external decorations in the fashion of the time'. These adornments might appear to modern eyes as 'absurdly fussy and very remote in feeling';[118] and even in their day they could certainly not have appealed to all tastes. The Fabian Society's own tract on architecture and the 'arts of use', issued some thirteen years after the opening of the Passmore Edwards Hall, criticized architectural adornments which were not properly integrated with the general concept and framework of a building; and made out that, ideally, aesthetic considerations and functional considerations in a design should not and could not be separated. But the tract also made out that contemporary capitalist society — as distinct from mediaeval society or a future socialist state — hardly provided the social and economic conditions for these ideal standards to be applied.[119] And 'realism', in the face of adverse conditions, rather than philistine insensitivity, is precisely how Caine prefers to characterize the regard which the planners of the L.S.E. paid to 'utility and economy of space'.[120]

Writing to May Morris in 1910, Webb himself defended the London County Council against charges of philistinism in its architectural policies.

'The poor L.C.C.,' he wrote,

has no malign or Philistine intentions. It is deadly anxious to do the right thing in these
art matters, but is bewildered by the *diversity* of the artistic advice pressed upon it. And
no artist person will come forward to take his share in London government. . . I fancy the
artists of the 16th century would not have thought the L.C.C. work alien to or beneath
them. I speak feelingly, because the L.C.C. means well in art, necessarily exercises great
influence on art education and production, is always very adversely criticised by the art
world — but no art person comes forward to fight a seat.[121]

In other words, Sidney suggested, the cause of civic art suffered more
from the political irresponsibility of artists than from the aesthetic
deficiencies of politicians.

These were not just vain rationalizations. From the 1890s, Webb had
made active attempts to recruit artists to the L.C.C., at least in a
consultative capacity. During that decade, while serving as a member of
the Technical Education Board, he persuaded his colleagues to appoint
one of William Morris's best-known disciples, W.R. Lethaby, as 'art
adviser' to the board, together with the architect and designer, G.T.
Frampton. That appointment prepared the way for Lethaby's co-
principalship (with Frampton) of the Central School of Arts and Crafts,
founded under the aegis of the L.C.C. in 1896.[122]

This aesthetic permeation of a political body was not a completely
fruitless undertaking. Other architects, who had found their inspiration in
Morris and the arts and crafts movement, were employed by the L.C.C.
to design its housing estates, and these have won the admiration not only
of recent observers, for whom any contrast with the monotonous
bleakness of most modern estates could not help command respect, but
also of fastidious contemporaries. One of these was Eric Gill — not
normally an enthusiast for any enterprise with which Sidney Webb was
associated.[123]

Webb's special pride, as voiced in his letter to May Morris, was not the
new houses built by the L.C.C. so much as its preservation policy with
regard to houses of historical interest. In this matter at least, he claimed,
'we have done well from the artistic point of view'.[124] With respect to
places relatively free of London's congestion, Sidney was well able to
appreciate any harmony achieved between beauty and function in more
recent buildings. For instance, he enthused over the lay-out and
architecture of Adelaide, the South Australian capital, as 'charming,
attractive. . . wisely planned and full of amenity, unostentatious and
refined'.[125] Both the Webbs found a real magnificence, from the 'architectural standpoint', in some of the most functional buildings in the Soviet
Union; though they readily acknowledged that the execution did not
always match the quality of the architects' conceptions, and that a large
heritage of ugliness from 'previous centuries of Tsardom' still pervaded

the outward forms of Russian life.[126] For Beatrice, at least, an ideal of architecture seems to have presented itself in the 'mingled art and nature' which she saw immortalized in the building and setting of the ancient Greek monuments in Sicily. Visiting these in 1926, she observed:

> The peculiar charm is that these magnificent buildings stand away from human habitation, in the midst of rocky mountains with background of seacoast and surrounded with semi-tropical plants and shrubs and trees — a setting that is far more attractive than that of a modern city like Rome...I certainly had never realised the wonders of Greek art before I came here.[127]

This passage clearly demonstrates Beatrice's continuing enjoyment of natural beauty in the days of her partnership with Sidney, and numerous other instances can be cited.[128] H.G. Wells's depiction of the Beatrice-figure in *The New Machiavelli* as insensitive, even hostile, to the beauties of nature and the countryside is perhaps the grossest distortion of all in his caricature of the Webbs. There is evidence to suggest that Sidney shared much of her simple pleasure in the countryside.[129]

The Webbs renounced many pleasures (aesthetic and otherwise) out of a deliberate and conscientious policy of austerity; but this austerity did not amount to a completely joyless and comfortless asceticism. They lived simply and frugally and worked long and hard — but by Victorian middle-class standards and in middle-class terms.[130] The houses they inhabited did not boast any sumptuousness in fittings and furnishings; but as can be seen from the inventories of furniture and household goods which they compiled, there was a solidity and lack of tawdriness about these things which went beyond the bounds of serviceability or utilitarianism, leave alone bare necessity. We know that Beatrice went shopping for Morris wallpapers and furniture; and, testifying further to their fondness for the products of the arts and crafts movement, there was a firescreen by C.R. Ashbee in the Webbs' house which was photographed by the *Art Journal*.[131]

Beatrice even claimed that the nature of the work to which the Webbs had chosen to dedicate their lives, being of a quite different order from manual routines, made special working and living conditions imperative: 'I am, of course, disqualified,' she claimed, 'for the ordinary communal life by my need for privacy as an intellectual worker. For me a private sitting-room is not a luxury, but a necessity.'[132] She continued to feel guilty about the 'relative luxury' of her and Sidney's life, compared to the 'daily grind' of the majority, but she felt that from the point of view of efficiency, a resolute sacrifice of all physical comfort and amenity was pointless. Chastizing, on the one hand, those leaders of the left who surrounded themselves with luxuries, she stated, on the other, that those who 'have taken the extreme ascetic line — C.R. Buxton, Stephen Hobhouse, have not thereby increased their usefulness'. She and Sidney had 'tried to compromise — leaning heavily towards the simple life'. Forms of religious ascetism did not win her sympathy either.[133]

As noted above, in the year before his full conversion to socialism, Sidney had gone so far as to preach a doctrine of 'extreme social asceticism'. This, however, was soon modified, as his commitment to a definite faith forced him to work out the practical details and implications of living by it on a daily basis. While continuing to urge very strongly the need for simple living, Sidney maintained that this did not rule out being 'comfortable': 'we need not be ascetic', he told Beatrice.[134] It was not purely for the sake of efficiency that the Webbs, in following a path of simplicity and austerity, avoided the verges of asceticism. Summing up, in their prospective *Constitution* for a socialist state in Britain, their ideal of 'honest public service', they asserted: 'no socialist expects, or even desires, a race of self-sacrificing saints who deny to themselves that enjoyment of life which they seek to maximize in the life of other people'.[135] The record of their responses to the arts, during the years of their partnership, is significant for the evidence it provides of the Webbs' own capacity and desire for enjoyment within the restraints of their rigorous work-routines and their anti-hedonistic principles. Those routines and principles have usually been seen as prohibitive of enjoyment or pleasure, and symptomatic of a grimly ascetic approach to life, 'intended as much for others as for themselves'.[136] This is a misleading label as far as it applies to themselves; and as far as it applies to their policy for others, it does not square with their reference in the *Constitution* — nor with earlier and later references elsewhere[137] — to the general socialist aim of maximizing the enjoyment of life.

6

The Fabians as anti-ascetics

From a variety of motives, individual Fabians themselves have often voiced substantial criticisms of Fabian socialism. In attempting to redirect Fabianism along new paths as a way of dealing with the limitations of the old, some members of the Society have tended to overstate the extent of these limitations and to exaggerate the novelty of their own reforms. Overstatements of that kind may have a constructive intent and value in keeping the movement buoyant, but too much should not be read into them. If taken at face value as historical evidence, they can be damaging and distorting. Thus the criticisms of one of the most renowned of recent Fabians could very easily be used to corroborate the grim, ascetic image of the Society favoured by outside observers. Anthony Crosland has argued that an active concern with 'human happiness' can 'at least claim the sanction of one powerful stream of socialist thought — that stemming from William Morris'; but he then says that 'other, Non-conformist and Fabian, influences wear a bleaker and more forbidding air'. He associates this bleakness with 'the Webb tradition' in particular, and claims that 'for one brought up as a Fabian' the time has come for a 'reaction' against it, involving 'a greater emphasis' on such things as 'culture, beauty, leisure': 'Total abstinence and a good filing system are not now the right sign-posts to the socialist utopia.'[1]

Certainly, there were important differences of substance and style between Morris's conceptions of socialism and the Fabians' conceptions; but to suggest a clear-cut dichotomy between their general approaches to socialism, simply on the basis of the received picture of Webbian austerity, oversimplifies the historical facts with regard both to Morris and the Fabians. Broad parallels, as well as divergences, can be found between the two lines of approach, even if one associates Fabianism merely with the Webbs' views. We have seen in the last chapter that 'total abstinence' from life's pleasures — especially artistic pleasures — was never observed or prescribed by either member of the partnership. On the other hand, both Sidney and Beatrice censured any abandon to pleasures associated with mere self-indulgence or personal luxury. What self-indulgence or luxury may have constituted was a matter of individual interpretation; but to have countenanced any association between pleasure and these things would have meant breaking with a basic principle of all brands of socialism, including William Morris's.

Morris's ideal of future society envisaged 'the utter extinction of all asceticism' and he equated this with 'a free and unfettered animal life for man' in which there would no longer exist 'the least degradation in being amorous, or merry, or hungry, or sleepy'. The passionate extremity of Morris's stance against asceticism — which the Webbs never emulated, and may well have shrunk from — was nevertheless accompanied in his writings by pleas for 'renunciation' on the part of the middle class and by an acceptance of the 'inconveniences of martyrdom' thereby involved. Such hardships were to be expected in the struggle to achieve the future society. And Morris emphasized that once that society had been established, the 'exercise of the senses and passions' was to be free only up to the point where this 'did not injure the other individuals of the community and so offend against social unity'. The extinction of asceticism necessarily demanded the 'extinction of luxury', as luxury was a product of 'sickly discontent with the simple joys of the lovely earth'. A 'non-ascetic simplicity of life' was the phrase he chose to sum up his conception of the goal to which socialists should be aspiring,[2] and this somewhat tempered formulation of his views is one which could be used to sum up the personal habits and social goals of the Webbs as well. The fact that the austere measures taken by the Webbs to simplify their own lives exceeded those which they expected of their colleagues or of the citizens of any future socialist state highlights some of the difficulties involved in summing up and comparing attitudes in this way. The rule of simplicity was not only variously interpreted by different individuals but could also be variously applied by the same individuals, and there were corresponding variations in the degree to which they attempted to avoid the excesses of asceticism.

The phenomenon of asceticism itself is difficult to define precisely: there are so many possible forms of it. Understandably, neither Morris nor the Webbs explained their own conception of it in so many words. One Victorian writer, however, in whose works they all steeped themselves, offered in passing a convenient capsule definition. This was Ruskin, who in *Modern Painters* equated asceticism, in general, with 'the refusal of pleasure and knowledge'. He contended that there was 'much to be respected' in several of its forms ('religious', 'military', 'monetary') but. that on the whole it did not represent 'a healthy or central state of man' and was not advisable for 'large numbers'. He spoke of the 'due comforts of life' and of the 'refinements' allowable when 'connected with toil', and in presenting in a later work his model of an alternative form of society to the one existing under industrial capitalism — the so-called St George's Company — he assured prospective members that they need fear 'no monastic restrictions of enjoyment': 'we profess no severities of asceticism at home'.[3] The Webbs' conceptions of 'pleasure' or 'knowledge' may have differed considerably from Ruskin's — there is as much confusion over these terms as there is over 'simplicity'. Clearly, however, in their own terms, the partnership never 'refused' or rejected pleasure and knowledge *per se*. While urging the renunciation of any socially irresponsible form of these things, Sidney and Beatrice also conveyed the positive value to mankind which such phenomena could have, especially under socialism. And, in practice, they never aspired to live by the example of modern 'ascetics', such as Gandhi.[4]

While rejecting the severities of asceticism, they both acknowledged a streak of 'puritanism' running through certain attitudes of theirs, and this is perhaps a more appropriate label to describe their personal and social strictures. Stripped of its historical connotations, the word 'puritanism' has several varieties and levels of meaning too, and caution must still be taken, when applying it to the Webbs, to dissociate it quite clearly from any connotations of asceticism. Beatrice unhesitatingly ascribed a puritan view of life not only to herself but also to other 'leading Fabians', and the context of her remarks suggests that what she meant by puritanism was no more than a repugnance for sexual libertarianism and social glamour.[5] Sidney Webb, on the other hand, had some reservations about the suitability of the term puritan even as a label for himself, and contended that the strength of the puritan streak in him had been exaggerated by his colleagues — notably by a fellow-Fabian, Stewart Headlam.[6] As we shall see, the latter does seem to have identified puritanism with the 'refusal of pleasure', especially in the arts; and Webb's reservations were in response to this interpretation of the term.

Bernard Shaw, as noted above, described his own attitude to art as a 'puritan' one; though he made clear that this meant not a reaction against the 'pleasure of the senses' — which he could 'sympathise with and share' — but against the 'idolatry' of the arts and the 'substitution of sensuous ecstasy for intellectual activity and honesty' in apprehending them. 'I am no ascetic', he insisted in the Preface to one of his late plays. He went on to explain that he 'would and could live the life of the idle rich if I liked it', and that his sole reason for not living that sort of life sprang simply from dislike, and not from any positive inclinations to 'self-mortification'.[7] In a lecture to the Fabian Society a few years earlier on 'The Climate and Soil for Labour Culture' he openly criticized various forms of asceticism, claiming that if a Labour Government came to power, its continual task would be trying to decide 'where to draw the line between the extremes of a simple lifer who is really a beach-comber, a gipsy, or a savage, and the artificial voluptuary ... Also ... between the two sorts of ascetics, who desire, respectively, as much strenuous work, and as much pious meditation as the human frame can bear.' Shaw implied elsewhere in the lecture that his fellow-Fabians may not be very good at drawing this line; without specifically calling them ascetics of any sort, he maintained that 'the members of the Society had as a whole turned their backs on anything written from the point of view of the artist aiming at a rich, free, and joyous life', and had proceeded on the 'common British assumption' that 'art is immoral' and that 'painters and musicians are long-haired cranks and free lovers'.

This was not simply a reiteration of his view that the Fabians were philistines. Their resistance to the 'joyous life', rather than to art, was the focus of his criticism here; a few sentences later, he even conceded the existence of a Fabian 'art culture', but this itself, he contended, was of a 'melancholy' variety which could not be of much use to the 'Labour movement'. There is a half-truth in his observation that the 'special business' of the Society had been to 'work out the political and industrial environment of Socialism, and leave others to rhapsodize about the joys that would follow their application'; but the general impression he gave that most Fabians somehow reacted against joy and against art anticipates the serious oversimplifications in Crosland's criticisms forty years later.[8]

There was one member of the Society, Ramsay MacDonald, who, in a speech of 1898, expressly lamented the fact that the present 'scramble of living' under the rule of 'commercialism' made it 'impossible for us to be so simple as to lose art in asceticism or the love of the beautiful in the humility of our lives'. The next sentence, however, makes clear that he in no way entertained the prospect of art's demise under simpler or less competitive forms of social organization. Looking forward to a time when the blight of commercialism would be eradicated, he said: 'mere decoration and show will be gone, but the chastity and simplicity of all true representations of our sense of beauty can never be wanting from the art of a natural and free people'. What he advocated here was not the refusal of any kind of pleasure associated with art so much as the containment of those outward and gratuitous pleasures pursued at present by a commercialist world: 'the tinsel of the rich'.[9]

As in describing the Webbs' personal regimen of daily living, so in summing up MacDonald's social and cultural ideals, it is more accurate to speak in terms of 'austerity' than of 'asceticism'. The former term was used specifically by the writer of the official Fabian tract on the arts, Arthur Clutton Brock, to sum up the processes involved in attaining an ideal which was closely akin to MacDonald's. Delivering a lecture on 'Art' in a series organized by the Fabian Society in 1916 on the general subject 'The World in Chains', Clutton Brock stated:

We lack art . . . because we think of everything in terms of something else. That is the disease of our capitalist society which betrays itself most plainly in our art. But there is hope . . . We have a desire, half conscious, to recover the sense of absolute values. We know that we have lost the natural delight in art. We long for it, and through that longing we may find the way back to absolute values. But we must be austere if we are to succeed. The way to freedom is through an austerity.[10]

From early on in the Society's history, several prominent Fabians — including some of the most 'puritan' or 'austere' in their general principles or personal practices — took up an explicitly anti-ascetic position, especially in connection with art. We have already noted this in the case of the Webbs. An examination of its manifestations in other members of the Society — some of whom were opponents of the Webbs on various issues — suggests that that position was a general one in the Society.

In accordance with his avowed distaste for romantic art, the father-figure of the Fabians, Thomas Davidson, defined true art as 'the sum of those means and methods which intelligence, love and freedom employ to subordinate and regulate the sensual faculties — instinct, sensation, action'. But he made clear that the sensual faculties were not intrinsically bad or dangerous; and that if they were properly held in check, they actually served an invaluable function: 'the intellectual faculties are starved if the sensual faculties are not made to toil for them'. He concluded that for this reason 'sensuality and asceticism are both great drawbacks to high spiritual life'.[11] In some of his later utterances, Davidson appears to have developed a moral repugnance for all art which could be seen as a type of asceticism, but he was expressly criticized for this by one of his closest and earliest Fabian disciples, Percival Chubb.

While mapping out a programme of rigorous self-discipline in his educational pursuits, Chubb showed an anxiety to avoid any tendency to a 'mere narrow asceticism' in his personal behaviour. And though censorious of the 'contaminating influences of luxury', especially on the arts, he found himself having to defend art, in its more recent forms, against the increasingly severe strictures of his old mentor. In its 'pure idea', Chubb argued, art did not represent mere 'self-embellishment' on the part of its creators, as Davidson appears to have suggested in his later years. 'The trouble so far,' Chubb told Davidson, 'has been that art has never flourished under just and proper social conditions. It has naturally been the product of . . . societies verging on . . . rottenness.' Even under these conditions, some artists had managed to achieve a 'genuine self-forgetfulness', though not at the expense of pleasure. Chubb defined 'true art', in terms very reminiscent of Morris, as 'the natural and inevitable flowering of wise and noble and useful activity, the expression of a man's joy in his work . . . free, generous self-bestowal'.[12]

Another member of Davidson's discussion group in London in the early 1880s, William Clarke, could be found at the beginning of the next decade echoing the warnings of his former mentor against the extremes of asceticism and unbridled sensuality. 'Ascetic dogma', he states, was 'an obvious reaction against extreme licence, but the one is as false as the other'. These words appeared in his book on Walt Whitman, published in 1892. Though they referred specifically to sexual, rather than artistic, matters, it was in the art and philosophy of the American poet that Clarke saw embodied the ideal mean between the two extremes which he derided. 'It is in reasonable self-control that virtue resides, in the positive, healthy direction of all human actions by a good will and a clear intellect. This is exactly what happens in Whitman's "great individual, fluid as Nature".'[13]

Clarke showed a distaste for religious asceticism also, associating it with a retreat from social realities. It was on similar grounds that he tended to criticize even the great practitioner of the simple life, Henry David Thoreau. Clarke felt that 'much as we may admire Thoreau, much as we may esteem the message he had for a generation which is disposed to fritter away its energies in accumulation and adornment, we shall not save our souls alive by living in a wood and eating roots'. Simplification, as a guiding principle in life, was not in question here — only the more excessive, isolationist practices of some of its adherents. Elsewhere, Clarke made clear how fortunate it was for America — particularly for her literature — that so many of her writers, including Whitman, had been 'brought up in the country and in simple fashion'. Luxury distressed him as much as sexual and moral licence.[14]

It was partly over moral issues that he became alienated from the Fabian Society in the 1890s. He was particularly revolted by Shaw, who, in his famous Fabian lecture on Ibsenism in July 1890, had attacked all conventional ethical standards and ideals. That Shaw was not thereby endorsing complete moral licence but, rather, searching for a new 'relativist' base for morality, escaped Clarke in the heat of his reaction against the more destructive aspects of Shaw's case. Annie Besant, who had agreed to chair Shaw's lecture, was equally revolted by his attack on traditional values, and a few months afterwards she left the Fabian Society — though not solely because of Shaw's views.[15] She could be as critical as Shaw of shortcomings in the current moral practices of capitalist society, but she could not bring herself to question the principles on which such practices were supposed to be based. For all these traces in herself of a basic moral conservatism, she came out strongly against what she called the 'Puritan narrowness of English middle-class life' which had 'made healthy and natural art impossible' and 'stamped as evil brightness, gaiety and laughter'. This denunciation was published in the pages of her journal, *Our Corner*, a year after her adhesion to the Fabian Society.[16] Evidently, the sense she attached to the word 'puritan' was quite different from that given it either by Shaw or Beatrice Webb. Rather than redeeming it, as they tended to do, from any association with asceticism or the 'refusal of pleasure', she tended to emphasize that association, albeit implicitly, and attacked puritanism on that basis.

The association of puritanism and asceticism in Annie Besant's mind, and her joint reaction against both these phenomena, as she conceived them, may have originated through her connections with the anti-sabbatarian and free-thought movements in the decade before she took up socialism. One of the first occasions on which she gave vent to her celebrated oratorical powers was in a discussion of a paper dealing with the question of opening museums and art-galleries on Sundays.[17] Her interest in this question culminated in her taking over the leadership of the National Sunday League, an organization devoted to the task of lifting bans on cultural and recreational activities on the Sabbath. These bans, imposed by municipal administrations, were a symptom of the sort of puritan attitude she later stigmatized in her article in *Our Corner*. The Sunday League was closely linked with the Free-thought movement with which she had come into contact in the 1870s after losing her faith;[18] and, as she related in her autobiography, the tenets of scientific materialism to which she and other freethinkers subscribed had a strong anti-ascetic bias, particularly with regard to sexual matters. This did not imply, however, any tolerance of sexual libertarianism — something which would hardly have squared with her fundamental conservatism in moral matters. Regarding it as 'hopeless, as well as mischievous to preach asceticism', she claimed that the doctrines of scientific materialism sanctioned 'the exercise of the sexual instinct within the limits imposed by temperance, the highest physical and mental efficiency, the good order and dignity of society, and the self-respect of the individual ... In all this there is nothing which ... implies approval of licentiousness, profligacy, unbridled self-indulgence ...'[19]

In the practice and enjoyment of art, as well, she counselled restraint and castigated self-indulgence or over-indulgence. She criticized the early poetry of Swinburne, for example, for its 'unrestrained and unpruned luxuriance of fancy' and its 'wealth of musical language which replaced instead of expressing thought'.[20] And in accounting, in her socialist writings, for the cultural deprivation of the labouring masses, she tended to place even more blame on the tendency of the upper class to luxuriate in art and beauty without doing their share of daily work than on the repressive 'puritan' elements within the middle class.[21]

The kind and degree of restraint which she demanded in artistic matters could, in fact, qualify Annie Besant herself as a puritan in the modified

Shavian sense, just as the restraint she counselled in sexual matters, and her reasons in support of it, align her viewpoint to an extent with the sort of puritanism subscribed to by Beatrice Webb. This is not to suggest, of course, that there was a basic unanimity on all issues behind the semantic differences. The outrage of Annie Besant and William Clarke at Shaw's lecture on Ibsenism — Sidney Webb and Graham Wallas were not nearly so disturbed by it[22] — shows clearly that the Fabians' moral views at least, and the implications these had for their attitudes to art, cannot be reduced to any simple programmatic line. Nonetheless, a shared anti-ascetic tendency — often strongly avowed — threads its way throughout all such disagreements among the Fabians. While resistant, in itself, to any uniform definition, appearing as it does in various shades and grades, its general persistence needs to be emphasized strongly here, as a counter to the prevailing image of Fabian socialism as a grey and joyless creed.

The extent to which the Webbs, personally, renounced various artistic activities in the interests of more immediately pressing social concerns represents the furthest extreme of austerity practised by any of the Fabians. That deliberate austerity sprang not only from their sense of priorities, but also from their own lack of confidence and sophistication in artistic matters. Almost from the time the Society was born, however, there can be found representatives of an opposite 'extreme' who, if not actual practitioners of the arts in some way, were passionate connoisseurs and indefatigable advocates of the pleasures which art could afford all classes of men. Among their number may be included such long-standing Fabians as Hubert Bland and Stewart Headlam, both of whom joined the Society in the 1880s and remained active members throughout all those phases of anti-Webb feeling over the next two decades when several younger members felt compelled to resign. The extreme which Bland and Headlam represented did not, in fact, take the form of a cohesive faction (like the Guild Socialist Group) working in direct opposition to the Webbs. Apart from the contacts afforded them by their work for the Fabian Society itself — both Bland and Headlam were sufficiently prominent to be elected to its Executive Committee several times and to be asked to contribute every now and then to its lecture-programme and printed propaganda — the activities and writings of these two men were almost totally independent of each other, as were their specific ideas and enthusiasms. Their general concern for the proliferation of pleasure, especially in the arts, brought them closer together for a short while in the early years of the new century, when they became leading activists with various other Fabians in a body calling itself the Anti-Puritan League. The Manifesto of the League, which will be dealt with in more detail below, gave no indication that the so-called puritanism of the Webbs was among its targets. Its specific attack was directed against certain policies of the

London County Council. Though we know from other sources that Headlam at least did include Sidney among the Puritan bugbears despite the latter's protestations, it is clear that neither this issue, nor the much more fundamental dispute between the two men over the administration of London schools, threatened to alienate Headlam from the Fabian Society or poison his cordial personal relationships with Webb.[23] He initially supported H.G. Wells's attempts to renovate the Society, serving on the Special Committee of Fabians which in 1906 endorsed the novelist's criticisms of traditional methods of socialist propaganda; but he never followed Wells in turning the dispute over policies into a bid for dominance over the influence of the 'Old Gang' — after all, by virtue of his age, Headlam was really a member of the Old Gang himself — and he did not abandon the Society, as Wells abandoned it, after the attempt to reform it had failed.

Bland became actively opposed to Wells, though not purely out of deference to the feelings of his beleaguered colleagues of the Old Gang. There was a personal motive too, in that Wells, notorious for his philandering, began to turn his sexual attentions towards Bland's daughter, Rosamund. Before that, Bland found sufficient grounds of sympathy between their viewpoints to invite the novelist to support the Anti-Puritan League.[24] Though he was capable of affecting an extreme rectitude at times on matters of sexual morality, Bland's own private life showed him to be as active an amorous adventurer as Wells, and while his unconventional sexual practices were conducted with relative furtiveness,[25] they were not in contradiction of all his avowed principles. Passages in some of Bland's journalistic and literary works plainly endorsed a relativist, circumstantial and self-determined morality in preference to an absolute, universal and socially-imposed one.[26] Such sentiments suggest an affinity with Shaw's 'Ibsenist' views; though some of Bland's statements appear to go well beyond Shaw or Ibsen in the direction of libertarianism, and to disregard any kind of moral considerations. Take, for example, the concept of pleasure which he put forward in a volume of epistolary essays addressed to a fictional daughter, Alexa. 'The pleasures of life,' it was claimed here, 'consist in the gratification of instincts, either inherited or cultivated. To suppress an instinct ... is to shut oneself off from an opportunity, to narrow the range of one's emotions and one's intellect, to diminish the number of one's sensations; it is to be incomplete.'[27] If Bland had been talking of life as he envisaged it in a socialist state of the future, there might be some grounds for associating the pursuit of pleasure which he endorsed here, based on the uninhibited play of instincts, with Morris's vision of a 'free and unfettered animal life for man'. Morris and Bland themselves, we have seen, both testified to the bonds of sympathy which linked each other's outlooks; it was in the year following the publication of his *Letters to a Daughter* that Bland recalled Morris's potent influence in turning him to the socialist 'faith' in the first place. The remarkably 'advanced' Edwardian father, however, who was supposed to have penned the above passage, did not place it in any kind of socialist context, and was evidently proffering his views on pleasure as a guide to conduct in the present. Without any acknowledgment — such as Morris explicitly made in proffering his socialist vision — of the need for certain checks on personal freedom in the interests of the whole community, the views in this passage could even be interpreted as a form of amoral individualism. It would be wrong to identify any such views automatically with Bland's own position, because of the fictional framework in which he chose to expound them, and because of what we know from other sources of his adherence not only to the socialist faith but also to the Roman Catholic faith.[28] The fact, however, that he could even toy with extreme libertarian notions, and risk having his name associated with them, emphasizes his distance from the Webbs. His adherence to the socialist and Catholic faiths, with their implicit social and moral checks on the individual's behaviour, was by no means self-evident from all his writings (even non-fictional writings) and may have gone completely undetected by the casual reader of *Letters to a Daughter*.

Bland's position on questions relating to artistic pleasure in particular indicates further confusions and inconsistencies in his thought; though, again, these can be partly attributed to the fictional or semi-fictional mode of much of his writing, and to the variety of voices and *personae* he adopted. While on some occasions he explicitly acknowledged the association of art and beauty with wider moral and social considerations, on other occasions he ignored these associations altogether, or came close to denying their significance either for artistic creativity or for artistic appreciation. Whatever view he happened to be putting forward, whether in his own voice or that of a *persona*, his main concern was almost always with the qualities of artistic style and form which gave pleasure to the senses, and the particular weight of his emphasis on these qualities was the measure of his divergence from Shaw as well as the Webbs. It was not as radical a divergence as it appeared on the surface, but it was nonetheless an important token of the wide range of approaches to art and artistic questions in the Fabian Society.

Bland put into the mouth of his Edwardian father-figure a clear endorsement of the pursuit of 'Art for Art's sake' which he defined as the notion that 'Art should seek no end outside itself: that if you set about painting a picture, say, your aim should be just to paint a beautiful picture, not to inculcate moral habits in a Sunday school.'[29] In a collection of essays he published in 1905 there was one devoted specifically to the subject of Beauty, and in this he defined 'a beautiful picture' as one which gave the beholder 'a certain sensation' — which produced a distinct emotional or physical 'thrill' in him.[30] This was not a very precise definition, but it clearly placed Bland in the tradition of *fin de siècle* aestheticism[31] and reflected his adherence to its high priest in England, Walter Pater, who had identified the arts in general as 'powers or forces producing pleasurable sensations'.[32] Another essay of Bland's appearing in the same collection, concluded with a remarkable paean to Pater, in which the art-critic's own exhortation to pursue the 'love of art for its own sake' was quoted and richly commended: 'Never was a sounder philosophy given to man, by prophet, priest or sage', Bland contended.[33]

This statement might be thought to cut right across his allegiance to William Morris, whose artistic sensibility Bland claimed had confirmed the attractions of socialism for him. But it needs to be borne in mind that Pater had originally enunciated his doctrine of 'art for its own sake' in the coda to an enthusiastic review of one of Morris's own works (*The Earthly Paradise*), and had later dubbed that work an exemplar of 'Aesthetic Poetry'.[34] There may have been some distortions or evasions involved in categorizing Morris's work in this way[35] and in any case both the poem and the review were written before Morris became committed to socialism. Nonetheless, traces of the aesthetic tradition can be found in some of Morris's own comments on other artists long after he turned to socialism. Referring, for example, to various novelists in a lecture of 1887, he expressed a strong preference for those who, like Scott and Dickens, 'tell their tale to our senses, and leave them alone to moralize the tale so told'; and his continual stress, both on this occasion and in other lectures of his socialist years, was on the pleasures which art could or should afford the senses. At the same time, these kinds of pleasure had come to mean for him much more than a series of momentary 'thrills' or 'sensations' produced by individual works of art or by professional artists, and were supposed to be capable of realization, under the justest possible social conditions, in the processes and products of all forms of human work. Eschewing Ruskin's overt emphasis on the necessity of 'stout moral purpose' in an artist's work, Morris took the broader Ruskinian ideal of art as 'man's expression of joy in labour', and made it a central feature of his vision of the socialist world to come.[36] Bland could hardly have been unaware of that feature, but the wider boundaries of art and pleasure which it incorporated were ones which he himself did not explore.

Bland was careful, when speaking in his own voice, not to let his endorsement of aesthetic pleasure be identified with a selfish hedonism. In the essay where he equated beauty with 'sensation' and 'thrill', he told the reader that 'if you reply to me that things which produce the feeling of beauty make also for the good of society — well, I think I agree with you'.[37] This statement also modified the apparent exclusivism of Bland's notion of 'art for art's sake' and the rather crude literalness with which that notion was voiced by the *personae* he adopted in some of his writings. Such refinements, however, were presented in terms that were vague and tentative when compared to the refinements and qualifications which Pater himself made to his aesthetic doctrines. In conclusion to his essay on 'Style', the latter had asserted unhesitatingly that 'great art' as distinct from merely 'good art' was devoted not only to the perfection of its own form but also to 'the increase of men's happiness, to the redemption of the oppressed, or the enlargement of our sympathies with each other, or to such presentment of new and old truth about ourselves and our relation to the world as may ennoble and fortify us in our sojourn here'.[38] Bland, toward the end of his essay on 'Beauty', confessed to wondering 'sometimes' whether it was 'possible to have a sensation of Beauty all by itself, abstracted from all relations, associations, prejudices, and preconceptions', and he conceded that the 'Thrill of Beauty' depended in part on the 'moral implications' of the object apprehended. He did little, however, to elucidate what these implications might be, and in discussing the question of 'moral beauty' earlier in the essay, with reference to acts of human heroism, he insisted that it was the 'aesthetic side' of such 'moral actions' which made one call them beautiful and touched off that certain sensation or thrill which he identified with beauty. For him 'The Thrill' remained 'the final and ultimate word of beauty' whether applied to works of art or anything else.[39]

The aesthetic reductionism of Bland's position was certainly at odds with Shaw's general philosophy, and in another place Bland openly drew attention to their specific differences on artistic questions. In the 'Epistle Dedicatory' to *Man and Superman*, Shaw had made his famous declaration that ' "for art's sake" alone' he would not 'face the toil of writing a single sentence' and that 'a truly original style is never achieved for its own sake . . . He who has nothing to assert has no style.'[40] Bland published an imaginary critical dialogue about this play, in which one of the speakers (who was also the narrator) maintained that the delightfulness of Shaw's own style proved the folly of his 'scoff' at 'art for art's sake'. The playwright was 'inspired by a passion for conduct'; but that had nothing to do with his artistry or with the pleasure his artistry gave to his audiences: his style would have been every bit as enjoyable had he asserted 'exactly the opposite' views on conduct. 'It is always just so with art', the speaker concluded.[41]

There are loosenesses and evasions in this argument which suggested that, in fact, the divergences between Bland and Shaw were at most ones of emphasis and did not represent antithetical positions. Simply in challenging Shaw's theory of art by praising his artistic practice, the speaker implied that social or moral concerns in a work of art were not destructive of the pleasures which it could bring. His claim that he would have been able to appreciate the expression of 'exactly the opposite' views on conduct shows that he was quite willing to accept the treatment of moral and social questions in a work of art, even though he didn't think it important. Now Shaw's point was that the assertion of some such views was absolutely crucial both to artistic creativity and artistic appreciation; but he never made out that those views were the be-all and end-all of art. Their particular standpoint and validity were, in the final analysis, as irrelevant to his conception of art as to the conception voiced by Bland's *persona*. What mattered to Shaw was the fact of their assertion and the degree of conviction with which that assertion had been invested. Shaw scoffed at writing ' "for art's sake" *alone*'; the speaker in Bland's dialogue exaggerated his difference with the playwright in omitting the word 'alone'. Shaw's own concern and fascination with artistic style and form shone through his arguments about the necessity of 'assertion' and constituted an integral part of those arguments:

Effectiveness of assertion is the Alpha and Omega of style ... He who has something to assert will go as far in power of style as its momentousness and his conviction will carry him. Disprove his assertion after it is made, yet its style remains ... All the assertions get disproved sooner or later; and so we find the world full of a magnificent debris of artistic fossils, with the matter-of-fact credibility gone clean out of them, but the form still splendid.[42]

As far back as 1889, the year of the *Fabian Essays*, Shaw showed his dissatisfaction with the exclusiveness of the 'art for art's sake' school and the 'didactic art' school. He implied that the polarity set up by these two schools, in their conflicting critical prescriptions, was both false and debilitating. In an article (never published) tracing literary developments between Dickens and Ibsen, he stated:

A novel or a play has two aspects, the documentary and the artistic ... There are people who protest against the documentary element in works of literary art on the ground that art should not be didactic because it exists solely for its own sake. There are also people who declare that the value of such works is purely documentary, because the art is valuable solely for its efficiency in spreading documentary content more widely. These are deficient, one in the appetite for knowledge, the other in the appetite for beauty, and their wranglings are such as might arise between a blind musician and a deaf painter over the comparative merits of a beautifully designed musical instrument which could not be put in tune, and an ugly one with divine tone and perfect intonation.[43]

The popular image of Shaw as one concerned with artistic achievements purely for their political, social and ethical content, or for their propaganda value, must labour heavily to maintain itself in the light of such pronouncements. Shaw was never entirely antipathetic to the 'aesthetic movement' of the 1880s and 1890s, with its stress on the role of sensuous pleasure in the arts; nor was he divorced from it in practice, as is indicated by his cordial relationships with several of its representatives and by their influence on his own artistic creations.[44]

Conversely, Bland could be as insistent as Shaw on the importance, in an artist's work, of 'something to assert'. In 1903 he refused to go ahead with preparing a lecture for the Fabians on the subject of Maxim Gorky, because he could not 'find a philosophy' or 'new view of life' worth talking about. He told the secretary of the Society that 'mere literary criticism' was a 'mere waste of time'.[45] For all the vacillations and complications in his attitudes, the pleasures afforded by the beauties of style and form remained the most consistent and the most intense focus of interest for Bland in the arts.[46]

The same may be said of his colleague in the 'anti-Puritan' camp of the Fabians, Stewart Headlam, though there was a stronger, or at least more obvious, co-ordination in Headlam's case between his artistic concerns and his socio-political and religious commitments. Like Bland, and unlike many other leading Fabians, Headlam managed to retain his faith in Christianity, though it went through various phases. Whereas Bland was brought up and remained a Roman Catholic, Headlam was brought up an Evangelical, was attracted as an undergraduate to the Broad Church views of the early Christian Socialist, F.D. Maurice, and (as an ordained priest of the Church of England) drifted into Anglo-Catholicism. So strong was Maurice's influence on Headlam in his formative years that he became interested in socialism long before the formation of the Fabian Society,[47] and was a founder-member of one of the earliest socialist organizations in England, the Guild of St Matthew. This body was set up in London in 1877 and named after the parish church in Bethnal Green where Headlam was employed as curate. He was thirty years old at the time, and the curacy was his second ecclesiastical appointment. After completing his education at Eton and Cambridge, he had first taken up a position as curate in the parish of St John's, Drury Lane.[48] The problem of poverty was not as intense or as widespread in this district as in the East End parish to which he succeeded; though his active sympathies with the socially depressed classes found an early focus in the plight of the rank and file of the theatrical profession — chorus girls, dancers and the like — who eked out a meagre living on the stages of Drury Lane. They were the victims not only of low and irregular wages, but also of a social and moral prejudice which deemed their career disreputable. Headlam's parents, who adhered to the evangelical beliefs in which many of the early Fabians had been brought up, were a party to that prejudice; and while not frowning on all the arts — Headlam *père*, we are told, was a great lover of poetry[49]—prohibited their son from having anything to do with the theatre. This was plainly impossible in Drury Lane, where young Headlam's parishioners included a number of the local actors and dancers — albeit clandestine ones who feared ostracism by the Church should the nature of their profession be discovered. Headlam made friends of them, and mutual trust was established. Through his contacts with them, he came to see the general groundlessness of the slights on their personal character, and he also had the opportunity and incentive to witness at close quarters the actual nature of their work. His attendances at their performances planted the seeds of a lifelong passion for the theatre in all its forms — not only Shakespeare and the dramatic classics, but also the ballet and the music hall.

These enthusiasms, as well as the rather unorthodox social and theological beliefs which he derived from the teachings of F.D. Maurice, brought him into a conflict with the higher authorities in the Anglican Church, which culminated in his suspension as a clergyman from the mid-1880s to the end of the next decade. He was not happy that he should provoke such disputes, and devoted much of his energy to attempts at conciliation. As early as 1879, he had set up, in association with the Guild of St Matthew, a 'Church and Stage Guild' which defined itself as a 'society of members of the dramatic profession, clergymen and others, who feel it their duty ... to get rid of the prejudices widely felt by religious people against the Stage, and by theatrical people against the Church ... and to vindicate the right of religious people to take part in theatrical amusements whether as performers or spectators'.[50] This organization attracted 470 members in its first year, and won substantial support from outside its ranks. Among its most ardent sympathizers was Ruskin who, as Headlam recalled, 'had always rated dancing high ... and hated ... religious intolerance of the arts'. Ruskin was also an enthusiast of the Christian Socialist journal which Headlam edited from 1884-95 — the *Church Reformer*.[51] In the first number of that journal issued under Headlam's charge, the editorial had expressly praised Ruskin for demonstrating how the richer classes under the present social system not only robbed the poor in a material sense, but deprived them of the opportunities for achieving 'wisdom ... virtue ... salvation' — all those things which made for 'independence, self-respect, culture, and spiritual sustenance'.[52]

Headlam was not to join the Fabians until nearly three years after he penned this editorial, though the critique of contemporary society he offered here differed from theirs only in being set in a specifically Christian framework. As Sidney Webb recalled in later years, Headlam was soon to discover that of all the major socialist organizations, the Fabian Society was the most tolerant of his religious principles.[53] (The Webbs, indeed, appear to have used their influence to have Headlam's licence to preach restored to him.)[54] A more positive attraction of the Society might have been those elements in its atmosphere — at once congenial and bracing — which had drawn Shaw to its ranks: the opportunities for fellowship and discourse which it offered with other disaffected middle-class intellectuals. Headlam shared a number of enthusiasms with Shaw — including the theatre, of course, as well as the writings of Ruskin, and the land-tax proposals of Henry George, which remained the basis of Headlam's socialism long after Shaw moved on to Marx and other economic theorists. Biographers of Headlam have tended to make out that it was 'the sentimental, the emotional side of Socialism' which had the strongest appeal for him and that this made him a solitary and rather uncomfortable figure in the Fabian Society.[55] His resolute commitment to the campaign for land nationalization, however, indicates in itself how any high-flown idealism on his part was balanced by quite mundane and practical concerns. He criticized the Fabians for neglecting this particular concern in their preoccupation with 'municipal socialism', but that criticism did not imply a prejudice against municipal socialism, such as William Morris gave hints of harbouring at times. Their limitations notwithstanding, Headlam roundly defended the schemes with which Fabianism was identified; and for all his differences with Fabian leaders on certain issues, he was sufficiently active and popular in the Society to be 'always very near the top at elections for the Executive.'[56]

In 1907, at a time when the socialism of the 'Old Gang' had come in for a renewed battering at the hands of Wells, Headlam asserted:

What has contemptuously been termed Gas and Water Socialism — is genuine Socialism so far as it goes, and will probably still be necessary when the ideal of Socialism has been reached. Municipal Socialism, the collective ownership by a definite community of Gas, Water, Trams, Electricity, and indeed of all the industries which can conveniently be owned collectively — this is all to the good.

He was keen to see that institutions such as the theatre and the music hall also be brought under collective control;[57] and in rehearsing a year later his rather more far-reaching proposals for land-reform, he laid particular stress on the advantages — artistic as well as economic and social — which would accrue to those institutions, should his proposals be adopted. He presented an elaborate case to support the conclusion that 'it is English landlordism which is destroying and hindering the development of English drama'.[58]

Shaw later suggested that Headlam's artistic concerns were in themselves a sign of his isolated position in the Fabian Society, and that he (Shaw) was the only other member to have any real understanding of them.[59] This statement, however, accentuates the distortions in Shaw's general picture of Fabian sensibilities, and makes his own position in the Society look more incongruous than it was. On the other hand, it tends to obscure the actual nature of Headlam's differences with other Fabians — including Shaw himself — on artistic questions. As in Bland's case, the differences were ones of emphasis. Headlam was, in fact, much clearer than Bland in showing his awareness of the general social applications and moral implications of art. In acknowledging the role which the arts could play in refining and educating mankind, he was at one with Ruskin as well as with the leading Fabians. Where he diverged was in his repeated insistence that this role was a secondary or incidental one and that the chief and distinctive role of art lay in its capacity to give pleasure. In a lecture he gave in 1886, for example, on the function of applause in the performing arts, he said of those artists who worked on the stage that

They may by chance instruct, convey useful information to their audience; they must of necessity educate, draw out the faculties of their audience, purify their pity and their fear, make the great principles of morality current coin, but neither instruction nor education is the object of their art: the object of their art . . . is to please. And applause shows . . . that they have taken their audience out of themselves by giving them pleasure.

He quoted from Ruskin himself here on art's twin functions of 'pleasing' and 'teaching' but the whole weight of his emphasis was on the prime necessity of the former.[60] In a lecture he delivered a few years later he reaffirmed that 'instruction, education, edification may accrue from plays, but pleasure *must*: a work of art has failed of its object if it does not give pleasure'. Without going as far as Bland in expressing direct sympathy with Pater or with any notion of 'art for art's sake', Headlam made clear that his concept of pleasure was closely identified with the intrinsic beauties of style and form in various types of art. 'The contemplation of what is beautiful, and the enjoyment of what is pleasurable, is right and good in itself', he insisted. Drawing on the example of his favourite art, the ballet, he said: 'Suppose that the story goes for nothing . . . there is still the poetry of vital motion, there is still the beauty of form, music, and colour.' The main moral and social roles which he assigned to art grew out of its pleasure-giving capacity. 'The moral ministry of the stage,' he claimed, 'depends upon the fact, that we can be made better people by being made brighter and happier people . . . Overworked and worried, living too often in gloomy streets, surrounded with mud, dirt, grime, meagreness, can you overestimate the ennobling, healing, exhilarating influence [on them] of merely a bright, spectacular ballet, quite apart from any plot or story.'[61]

Headlam placed such a high value on the provision of opportunities for artistic pleasure in society that he was apt to react indiscriminately — and perhaps overreact — against any person or organization that he felt to be holding back the proliferation of such pleasures. In 1904 he delivered a lecture to the Fabian Society in which he directed an attack on the 'municipal puritanism' of the Progressive wing of the London County Council. Associating this doctrine with vestigial teetotalism and sabbatarianism, he discerned its influence behind a wide range of the

Council's policies relating to cultural and recreational facilities. For their failure to supply certain facilities (dancing-schools and theatres, for instance) as much as for the restrictions and prohibition they put on others, these policies were criticized by Headlam for endangering the 'splendid socialistic work of the L.C.C.' and for contriving to diminish 'the joy of living'. He characterized the typical modern puritan as looking on the human body as 'vile' and as regarding the 'delights of sight or taste or touch' as 'mere temptations'.[62] Sidney Webb — who (with Headlam himself) had been among the Fabians that served on the Council — defended its work against these charges; though, judging from the press reports, his defence was somewhat limp, amounting to little more than a recital of excuses and qualifications. Webb complained, for example, that Headlam neglected to mention 'the facilities that existed on Sundays for swimming, boating and listening to music'[63] — a valid enough point in itself but one that scarcely confronted the charge of puritanism head on or questioned the basic semantic assumptions behind the use of the term. In an article he wrote on the L.C.C. a few years before, Webb did much more to stress the positive enjoyments which its musical programmes and other such facilities provided London citizens.[64] The pride and relish with which he recounted there the scope and popularity of those facilities amply justified the protest he made, in writing an obituary of Headlam many years later, against the latter's tendency to lump him with the extreme 'puritan' faction of the L.C.C.

Webb, however, overstated Headlam's commitment to the opposite extreme when he claimed in this obituary that Headlam had 'disliked the idea of any restraints being placed on the people'. In fact, Headlam maintained that 'the people' themselves would welcome certain measures of restraint, and that these would enhance the pleasure he sought to spread among them. In a defence of the ballet, which he wrote in 1894, he claimed that in view of 'the dull dreary lives that many of our fellow citizens lead . . . any ballet is better than no ballet', but he also criticized the tendency of some recent productions to sink into 'mere spectacular display' by masking the simple beauty of the dance with extravagant accessories in the way of costume and properties. He therefore recommended that management be encouraged to cut down their expenditure on such items. Entertaining the hope that 'we are . . . for refining upon our pleasures; at any rate for preventing their degradation', he felt that the public would be better pleased with greater simplicity.[65]

The need for various restraints in the business of day-to-day living was implicitly acknowledged in the manifesto of the Anti-Puritan League. The echoes of Headlam's own phraseology in that manifesto, and the traces there of his particular preoccupations — the subject of dancing, for instance — suggest that he was largely responsible for drafting the document. Its main themes were the importance of pleasure, especially artistic pleasure, in cultivating the best and healthiest elements in the 'life of the senses'; and the iniquity of attempts to stamp out pleasure. By no means, however, did the manifesto's championship of pleasure involve an attack on all forms of regulation in personal or social behaviour:

> We want to get all those who believe in life to realize how much evil is being wrought by those who would cramp the joy of living, by those who are for putting all sorts of hindrances to the obtaining of life's smaller but most valuable pleasures, and who think it is the part of the serious man to mutilate instead of to regulate and to educate the senses and the appetites.

The author asserted that prohibitions of pleasure increased, rather than removed, the dangers to the healthy development of the senses: 'After the saints of the Commonwealth,' he pointed out, 'come the voluptuaries of the Restoration.' Like Annie Besant, he advocated 'temperance' as the only workable solution, defining that as

> the kind of virtue which consists in controlling our desires and living soberly and modestly ... Let Temperance prevail or to-morrow Puritanism loses its hold and licentiousness is rampant ... The life of the senses is to be frankly acknowledged and made the best of ... The Puritan tone and temper and view of life is as stunted and mutilated as it is aggressive and tyrannical ... It has to be undermined and attacked persistently. But the full, frank, refined, disciplined enjoyment of the whole life of the senses must take its place.[66]

It is difficult to imagine Sidney Webb writing that last sentence, which seems much closer in spirit and emphasis to one of William Morris's utterances.[67] To depict its writer as a champion of unrestrained pleasure, which Webb later did, was clearly misleading; though it was no more so than Headlam's tendency to interpret Webb's reticence in passionately espousing the cause of pleasure as a sign of hostility to that cause. The mutual misunderstanding shown by the representatives of these 'extremes' in the Fabian Society exaggerates the extent of their differences and masks their basic agreement on the importance of avoiding the real extremes of luxury and licence, on the one hand, and of asceticism on the other.

This tenet was held by several leading Fabians, and may be seen as an underlying assumption of their socialism. A recent literary critic, charting the general devaluation of pleasure as a life-principle in the works of various nineteenth- and twentieth-century writers, takes care to acknowledge where that principle has continued to be endorsed, if not celebrated; and one of those areas of survival, or potential areas of survival, he sees in the 'benign socialist society'. This sort of society, he claims, 'by modern definition, serves the principle of pleasure'.[68] The Fabians' schemes and hopes for a socialist society tended to be more in accord with that definition than they have been given credit for, notwithstanding divergences among members on the question of what pleasure itself constituted and variations in the tone and volume in which they sang its praises.

7

Powerhouse or club?: artistic activities of the Fabian Society

The Fabians' differences over the practice of pleasure in the socialist society of the future were echoed in disputes about their own practices as Fabian socialists. The following issues, stemming in part from those un-resolved tensions which led to the schism between the Fabian Society and the Fellowship of the New Life, continued to divide opinion among members — most conspicuously after the 'second flowering' of the Society in 1906. What was the chief role of the Fabians as a group, and which of their multifarious interests and activities should become the dominant one in their lives — or at least that part of their lives which they chose to devote specifically to the service of the Society? What weight should be attached to the subsidiary roles of the Society and to the extra-curricular activities of members, and what was the nature and extent of the relationship between these and the central concerns of Fabian socialism?

Artistic activities were never as prominent in the group life of the Fabian Society as they were in certain other famous coteries in Victorian and Edwardian England, such as the Pre-Raphaelite Brotherhood or the Bloomsbury Group. Attempts on the part of various Fabians (including several artists or professional critics of art) to give such activities a more overt place in the Society's agenda did not go unchallenged, as this chapter will show. The disputants, however, were at no stage rigidly divided between those members professionally involved in the arts and those who were not. There was nothing clear-cut about the divisions at all; the most intense ones — in the years following H.G. Wells's disruptive passage through the Society — were largely along the lines of age and of position within the Society's ranks: the 'Old Gang' of the Fabians with entrenched places in the Society's hierarchy of committees and conservative notions of the Society's role versus the newer or younger members with no direct administrative power and a restless urge to change the Society's traditional concerns so as to give them a more secure and forceful base within it.

Even these divisions were by no means rigid. The Fabians who joined the Society in the first decade of the twentieth century were as apt to exaggerate the complacent narrowness of their elders as some of their elders were apt to exaggerate the impulsive iconoclasm of the young Turks.

There was no more convinced exponent of the Society's political role than Sidney Webb; and, in his public statements at least, his notion of what politics involved was more austerely single-minded than that of any other of his colleagues, save perhaps his wife. ' "Politics", with us,' he told the up-and-coming young Fabian, R.C.K. Ensor, in 1903, 'always means such very practical politics, and thus is "insular" and temporary.'[1] Even he, however, took some pride in the variety of his colleagues' interests and activities within the Society. Introducing the 1920 edition of the *Fabian Essays*, he looked back to the days of the original publication when the Society had no other income than 'its meagre membership could contribute from their scanty earnings' and the members themselves spent what time they had after working for those earnings 'in reading and talking — in studying everything from bluebooks to art, from history and politics to novels and poetry; and perpetually discussing and lecturing, among ourselves and before anybody who could listen to us'.[2]

There are grounds for arguing that the Fabian Society continued to operate rather more effectively as a talking-shop for its own members — as a kind of club — than as a political powerhouse for the nation at large.[3] Symptomatic of this were the very disputes over the Society's role as a political body. These intense and never-resolved wrangles need not be regarded in an entirely negative light, as a source of the Society's failures and impotence, for they were also a token of continuing vitality, a guarantee against stagnation.[4] There were, however, several other sources of vitality, connected with the club-like functions and atmosphere of the Society, which had rather less of a destructive edge to them and, indeed, could have helped sustain the interests of many Fabians in their Society whenever political disputes seemed particularly fruitless.

Some of the most notable of these sources were directly concerned with the arts, though none was totally unconnected with the political functions or concerns of the Society, and few of them were devoid of the disputatiousness which seems endemic to any socialist organization. The relationship between the political and artistic concerns of members was a focus of dispute in itself. The inescapable links between the two are shown no more vividly than in the regular lecture-meetings of the Society — not only in their subject-matter but also in their general style. Because of the central importance of these lectures to the Society's activities throughout the period under consideration here, they deserve particularly close analysis. The relevant evidence is very comprehensive but also rather complicated, so it is best left to special treatment in a separate chapter.

The ground can be prepared by looking first at various other activities of the Fabian Society in which art was somehow involved. These range from the smallest committee meetings of the Society's elected officers to large (often informal) gatherings, involving a considerable proportion of the total membership and a sprinkling of invited guests as well. Special attention will be given to three enterprises in which the arts played a very important, if not dominant, role: first, and most obviously, the Fabian Arts Group, founded in 1907; second, the Stage Society, a somewhat older group whose artistic concerns were just as obvious and even more widely known, but whose Fabian origins and connections have been obscured; and, third, the Fabian Summer Schools, which started up in the same year as the Arts Group, yet survived much longer and provided rather greater scope for active artistic involvement in spite of many concerns outside the field of art.

As art, even in the eyes of the most austere Fabians, was regarded as a source of pleasure as well as a form of work and a subject of sociological interest, a study of its role in the everyday activities of the Society can provide some instructive sidelights on the nature of middle-class culture and recreation in late-Victorian and Edwardian England. Some of the tensions inherent in the general attitudes of the middle class towards its own forms of pleasure and recreation[5] are illuminated all the more vividly by a special study of this small group, as its members were in active and articulate revolt against the values and conventions of their class while at the same time inescapably imbued with so many of them.

Fabian Society gatherings were hardly the most appropriate or conducive place for the actual creation of works of art, and especially not for those kinds (novels, poetry, plays) which were among the most directly exploitable for political purposes. It took an inexhaustible genius like Shaw's not to find some sort of clash between these essentially private pursuits, demanding sustained if irregular bursts of intensive, individual labour, and the constant round of lectures, discussions and official committee meetings involved in being an active Fabian. The clash was never so debilitating for a budding artist as it was for Beatrice Webb (who was, however, debilitated more by an abiding guilt about her personal artistic impulses than by the burden of the group's official activities, in which she took comparatively little part in her earlier years as a member). But a definite, if reluctant, choice sometimes had to be made between such competing pursuits, even in Shaw's case.[6]

When H.G. Wells resigned from the Fabian Society in 1908, one of the reasons he gave to the Secretary, Edward Pease, was that he wanted 'very much to concentrate now upon the writing of novels for some years'.[7] The impression here of competing commitments may appear a little disingenuous, in view of the way in which Wells went on to use the novel form[8] to attack the Fabian 'Old Gang' from without, just as he had attempted earlier to usurp its power from within by making himself a very strong counter-influence on the Society's various committees.

An earlier and perhaps more genuine division of loyalties and commitments is to be found in the case of Walter Crane, whose particular artistic media were in some ways more suited to collaborative activity than novel-writing. Long before he resigned from the Fabian Society over its failure to condemn the Boer War, he told Sydney Olivier that he was sorry he could not attend Fabian meetings more regularly but they clashed with his duties at 'the Art-workers', a handicrafts guild, 'on two Fridays a month'.[9] The Arts and Crafts Movement, pioneered by Crane's most influential mentor, William Morris, operated through various organizations of this kind; and, in their early years at least, they offered considerably more scope than Fabian Society gatherings for combining anti-establishment activities in both politics and art.[10]

This, however, cannot be taken to imply that the Fabian Society offered no such scope. It is true that one of the few full-time officials employed by the Society suppressed, or came to lose, much of his own enthusiasm for Morris and the arts and crafts after embarking on his job with the Fabians. This was the Society's Secretary, Edward Pease. In his official history of the Society, published in 1916, he could barely conceal his condescension towards the artistic involvements of his colleagues or, indeed, towards his own youthful interest in art.[11] He had to acknowledge, however, the intensity of such enthusiasms. And he did not succeed in dampening them in others, if that was ever his intention. It may have been his peculiar dedication to the everyday administrative business of the Fabian Society which drained his interest in other things; but if he regarded these, in his dessicated older years, as mere indulgences, he never tried to use his position to cut them out, and was obviously aware of their uses, if only as garnishings. Indeed, his duties as Secretary had involved him from the start, and continued to involve him, in making arrangements for various artists to put their work at the service of the Society.

It was with Pease, for example, together with Shaw, that Walter Crane conferred over the details of his design for the cover of the *Fabian Essays in Socialism*.[12] And later we find Pease acting as the intermediary in the negotiations between Edith Nesbit and the Society's Executive Committee concerning the publication of her socialist 'ballads and lyrics' under Fabian auspices.[13] More generally, whenever advice was required about the suitability of projected lectures on artistic subjects, it was to Pease that the matter was first referred, though the Executive Committee had the final say.[14]

That Committee, and its various sub-committees, as well as dealing with the financial and organizational problems involved in keeping the Society afloat, spent no little time in conferring about literary matters, such as the style and structure of Fabian publications, particularly the Society's famous tracts. There was even a special 'Committee on Taste' set up in the early 1890s to consider such matters as the lay-out, typography and overall design of the tracts. Its members were co-opted from the Publishing Committee of the Executive, for whom it was a recurrent concern over the following decades to find ways of improving 'the look of the page' in Fabian literature.[15]

The bureaucratic formalities over such questions may appear faintly ludicrous to us now, and conjure up bleak images of committee-determined art and design in any Fabian state of the future. Nonetheless, these concerns on the part of the Society's administration betoken the seriousness, however heavy-handed, with which its members regarded aesthetic considerations in carrying out their political work and disseminating their propaganda. And the committees concerned were not necessarily insensitive, as is shown by their eagerness to recruit first-rate book-designers such as Crane, Emery Walker, Arthur Watts and Eric Gill, for the design tasks involved.

The Fabians' attention to such details was possibly an important factor in boosting the membership of their 'club' with the particular class of person they hoped to win over for socialism. Shaw intimated as much in his tract on the Fabians' early achievements, published in 1892. Those 'professional men' of 'polished manners', whom he predicted would keep on swelling the socialists' ranks, may have been first attracted to Fabian Society meetings not only by the reassuring lustre of their ambience — some of them were held in the 'most aristocratic' rooms in London — but by 'little smartnesses' such as 'our pretty little prospectus with the design by Crane' and 'our stylish-looking blood-red invitation cards'. Shaw wrote:

it was by no means the least of our merits that we always, as far as our means permitted, tried to make our printed documents as handsome as possible, and did our best to destroy the association between revolutionary literature and slovenly printing on paper that is nasty without being cheap. One effect of this was that we were supposed to be much richer than we really were, because we generally got better value and a finer show for our money than the other socialist societies.[16]

Sidney Webb was not insensitive to the importance of good design in Fabian literature; and Beatrice, too, albeit from a different vantage point, recognized that aesthetic form and style were as important as content and argument in securing audiences for Fabian propaganda and maximizing its impact. Her recognition of this is particularly evident in her attitude to lectures,[17] but it also influenced her approach to the kind of literature which she devoted herself to writing after the mid-1890s. It was mainly sociological in content; but this did not mean it should be any less literary in form. When drafting the Minority Report on the Poor Law, for instance, Beatrice aimed consciously at making it 'a work of art in the best sense' for 'every word must tell'.[18] Her private journals, it appears, were not the only outlet for the frustrated novel-writer within her.

The writing of sociological or political literature, such as Beatrice Webb's reports or the general run of Fabian tracts, remained at bottom a solitary activity, like any imaginative writing. A committee might often have decided on revisions or embellishments to these texts, have suggested their subject matter, and determined their outward format, but a single individual was still largely responsible for the substance, style and shape of the final product; and even the format reflected the sensibility of the individual designer, chosen by the committee concerned, more than any 'collective' sensibility. The committees themselves were elected bodies, containing only a small proportion of the Fabian Society's total membership, so that even if their own very limited, and largely vicarious, artistic activities satisfied any of their number's aesthetic instincts, these kinds of satisfaction would not have extended to the group at large.

Among the group activities of the Fabian Society, the best-known artistic enterprise was the Fabian Arts Group, set up in London in 1907. The late starting date is significant, for the Group's importance is usually talked about in terms of its fulfilling a long-neglected need among members of the Society for defining the relationship of the arts to socialism.

The Group's founders, Holbrook Jackson and A.R. Orage, certainly took this view, and the implication behind it — sometimes spelled out — is that the 'Old Gang' of the Fabians, under the influence of the Webbs, had effectively contrived to prevent members from exploring the wider dimensions of socialism beyond the bounds of economic collectivism.[19] Jackson and Orage, freshly arrived from Leeds, where they had founded an 'Arts Club' that provided the model for the Fabian Group,[20] clearly saw themselves as missionaries of light attempting to save Fabianism from the powers of greyness.

After a glorious start, acknowledged even by the dour Pease, the Group soon started fading away, and its decline can only have confirmed the two founders in their melodramatic view of Fabianism and its divisions. There was a good deal of delusion in this view, and in their 'corrective' actions, not because they were attempting to save Fabianism from itself — its adherents were far from being completely philistine or irredeemably dour — but because the leadership did not differ markedly from the rank and file in its sensibilities, and was neither as grey, nor indeed as powerful, as supposed. If it had been, would it have permitted the Arts Group to get off the ground?

It is significant that Orage and Jackson, on moving down from Leeds to London, should have lit on the Fabian Society in the first place as the new centre for their activities. It obviously provided a ready-made institutional base. Having, from its inception, operated along the lines of a discussion-club, it showed a willingness to extend these at just about the time Orage and Jackson migrated southwards. Perhaps in order to cater for the new, younger elements which had come into the Society after 1906, in the wake of H.G. Wells, special 'Subject Groups' were being set up to supplement the general meetings. These were empowered to elect their own members from amongst the members of the Society,[21] so as to form a corpus of clubs-within-a-club. A 'Local Government Group' and an 'Education Group' proved to be among the most enduring of the new societies; though it was not for want of early encouragement from the Society that the Arts Group failed to acquire the same staying power.

The condescension of Edward Pease towards the Arts Group, following its failure, was not typical of the Fabians; and his general implication that it was little more than a band of youthful idealists who had not yet ex-perienced the hard realities of the world seems a half-truth at best, borne out only by the self-delusions of the Group's own founders. No membership records survive, but it is clear from other evidence that several of the older members, including Pease himself, were among the Group's earliest sponsors and supporters. As he had to concede in the same breath as his put-down of the Group, it was still possible for 'many who are no longer young' to retain some concern for art midst all the other concerns they had acquired in their maturity.[22] Certainly, none of the Old Gang of Fabians put any obstacles in the way of the Group's being formed, and several of them were positively welcoming when Holbrook Jackson officially proposed the formation of such a body — in tandem with a Philosophy Group — at a meeting in January 1907.

Criticisms of the Fabian Society's traditional approach to the arts — or lack of approach — were more than implicit in Jackson's proposal, though they were expressed more moderately than in his (or Orage's) un-official pronouncements. For whatever reasons, the old-guard Fabians did not take offence at these criticisms: some may even have agreed with them as expressed in their muted fashion; others may not have noticed them at all, and others again, out of a spirit of good-will towards the general idea of an arts group, may have thought it more tactful, if not better tactics, simply to ignore the negative underside to the proposal. When Jackson had first requested the Executive Committee of the Society to assist in the formation of an 'Arts & Socialism' group, the Committee had immediately assured him (through Pease) of its 'cordial cooperation' in the matter. True to its word, it deputed Shaw to draft an invitation to younger members of the Society to come forward with further suggestions about such groups, and he was also entrusted with chairing the meeting at which Jackson's proposal for the Arts Group was officially moved.[23]

The gist of the proposal was that

a group called the Fabian Arts Group be formed . . . with the object of interpreting the relation of art and philosophy to Socialism . . . It would make *an appeal to minds that remained unmoved by the ordinary Fabian attitude* . . . [H]e hoped that the meeting would see the advisability of combining the study of art and philosophy in one group, so as to prevent their becoming merely academic contests . . . which usually happened upon their forced separation.[24]

Forty members were at the meeting where this proposal was moved, and it was eventually carried unanimously. There were several veteran Fabians who spoke fully in favour of the motion, including Shaw himself, Sydney Olivier, the poet Ernest Radford, and a former leader of the long-suppressed 'anarchist' faction in the Society, Charlotte M. Wilson.[25]

The only real issue was over the inclusion of philosophy within the Group's agenda; but the few who advocated its separation did not bother pushing their claims to the amendment stage. If they had done so, they might have helped clear up a confusion of aims which was evident even in the pronouncements of the two founders and which contributed in various ways to the Group's decline.

Jackson, in his motion, stressed the importance of concentrating on those 'more subtle relationships of man to society which had been brought to the front in the works of such modern philosopher-artists as Nietzsche, Ibsen, Tolstoy and Bernard Shaw'.[26] This aim, unexceptionable enough as stated here, foreshadowed the increasingly heavy emphasis in the Group's activities on philosophy in particular — an emphasis which might have alienated those whose artistic interests did not fit into such a groove.[27] Orage, in seconding Jackson's motion, began by echoing him on the 'importance of art and philosophy to the propaganda of socialism', and we know he himself had a particular interest in Nietzschean philosophy.[28] Yet he spent the rest of his speech in riding another hobby-horse of his — 'the relation of the handicrafts and craft guilds to Socialism' — and in stressing 'the necessity of the Society considering so vital a question'. In support of this, he claimed that 'The Arts and Crafts movement had entrusted its politics to socialists' and that 'the business of the group would be to give effect to the political ideals of the original founders of that movement'.[29]

Jackson, perhaps diplomatically, had not mentioned this aim at all; and the Fabians who attended the meeting passed over it as well — again, perhaps, for diplomatic reasons. They were certainly not unsympathetic to the Arts and Crafts movement as such. Only a few years before, one of its current representatives, Selwyn Image, was invited to the main branch of the Society to lecture on 'Some Aspects of Modern Art and Modern Life'.[30] And we know that there had always been strong affinities, as well as strong differences, between Fabians and the 'original founders' of the arts and crafts movement; Walter Crane had felt able to join the Society for a number of years even though Morris had not. The political differences, however, which had kept Morris away became yet wider, and took on a more defined, ideological form in the decade after his death; and it was rather disingenuous of Orage to suggest in public that Guild Socialist ideals could simply be hitched on to the Fabians' concerns when in private he was stressing the incompatibility of those ideals with Fabian collectivism, as currently formulated.[31]

Orage clearly held on to some hope, however slender it appeared at times, that Fabian collectivism could be modified so as to assimilate itself to Guild Socialist ideals and he no doubt aimed to use the Arts Group, among other agencies, to bring about that modification. His overriding ambitions on behalf of Guild Socialism only became quite clear in later years, and on being exposed probably contributed to the alienation of many stauncher Fabians from the Arts Group. At the time, however, of Jackson's original proposal for the formation of such a group, Orage's supporting speech, though heavily tendentious, was also sufficiently evasive to contain any grave suspicions regarding that Group's ulterior purposes.

Initial support among the old-guard Fabians for the new guard's ventures was expressed not only in their positive response to the idea of an Arts Group but also in their sponsorship of another of Jackson and Orage's enterprises — a weekly newspaper called the *New Age*, which the two men began editing in 1907. Its first number contained several welcoming letters from members of the Old Gang, including Edward Pease, Hubert Bland and Sidney Webb. Shaw did not send a letter, but he had already shown his support for the paper by donating half of the money required to purchase it from the former owners.[32] He also became a regular contributor — free of charge — to this 'Independent Socialist Review of Politics, Literature and Art' (the full sub-title chosen by the new editors for their paper). Webb, in his letter of welcome, stated that the project could 'not fail to be of use' as nothing was more 'urgently needed' than the 'scientific investigation of the various unsolved problems which confront the Collectivist'.[33] This hardly betokens any overt suspicion on his part of Jackson and Orage's interests in 'Literature and Art', or even of their particular brand of 'Politics'. Still, his apparently confident assumption that the editors' approach to such 'problems' would be a 'Collectivist' one may have hidden some foreboding to the contrary or even an element of guile. He was certainly putting incongruous words into the mouth of a paper which became known for its Guild Socialist sympathies; and if this was not naivete — hardly likely in Webb's case — it suggests a degree of disingenuousness to match Orage's own.

There is no reason, however, to question the basic sincerity of Webb's conviction about the applicability of Fabian collectivism to a range of problems beyond the merely economic or political; nor is there reason to attribute to him an intrinsic hostility to any Fabian involvement with artistic problems in particular. As he told H.G. Wells, a month after his letter in the *New Age* appeared — and some six months after the Arts Group was founded — he was not at all opposed to the development of an 'artistic side' to the Fabians' activities, so long as it did not interfere with, or replace, the Society's traditional political concerns and practices.[34] If there was an element of suspicion here, it was a suspicion not of art as such but of the uses to which artistic activities might be put to change the fundamental nature of the Society's role.

As it turned out, Webb was justified in entertaining such suspicions of Jackson and Orage's activities. For over a year, the *New Age* kept true to its claims to be an 'independent socialist' publication, and steered clear of any Guild Socialist propaganda which could be construed as expressly anti-Fabian.[35] By early 1909, however, leading Fabians were being criticized in its editorials (on the grounds of their failure to respond to pleas to dissociate the Society from the Labour Party[36]); and the paper began to identify itself more specifically and more ardently with the cause of Guild Socialism.[37]

It was by about this time, too, that the Arts Group was becoming less of a Fabian 'club' than a Guild Socialist one. In his *History of the Fabian Society*, Pease claims that in its early days the Group 'obtained ... audiences scarcely less numerous than the Society itself', but that 'after the summer of 1908' it 'disappears from the calendar'.[38] This is accurate up to a point: in the 'London Fabian Calendar', published in the *Fabian News*, details of the Arts Groups' lectures were not given after June 1908, though this should not be taken to mean that the Group disappeared altogether. Up until January 1911, it continued to be listed among the special 'Subject Groups' in the 'Fabian Directory', another part of the *Fabian News*; and it appears to have had a brief revival in the middle of 1911.[39] But it may have been as early as 1908-9 that the Group started to shed its Fabian membership and to take on the appearance of a front for Guild Socialist propaganda.[40]

There is, unfortunately, no way of validating this, as we lack not only membership lists but also any records of the Group's activities, apart from lecture and discussion programmes. The trend is suggested, however, by the subjects of some of these sessions ('The Limits of Collectivism' in February 1908, 'The Organization of Craft Industries' in March 1908, 'Trade Unions and Craft Guilds' in May 1908). It may have been that there were no activities of a propagandist nature or otherwise outside these sessions. Again, Pease's *History* isn't very helpful or reliable in the matter. All he says about the nature of the Group's activities is that they 'included philosophy' but 'almost excluded Socialism': 'in eighteen months "Art and Philosophy in Relation to Socialism" seems to have been exhausted'.[41] By 'Socialism' he no doubt meant the approved Fabian variety; and possibly any attempt to establish a *definite* relationship between art and Fabianism was bound to be self-defeating, in that that variety of socialism was inherently resistant to such prescriptive procedures. If Jackson and Orage did not know this from the start, they soon found out.

Whatever the founders' original hopes and intentions may have been, the Arts Group for various reasons did not prove satisfactory — or very satisfying — as an outlet for the artistic instincts of the Fabians. In theory a club-within-a-club, it assumed in practice the air of an alternative club, contriving to change (if not disrupt) traditional Fabian procedures. Fabians were always interested in the ways in which art was related to the Society's political concerns or the ways in which those concerns could be applied to the arts; and the Arts Group must have seemed a good way for those who were particularly interested in these matters to explore them more deeply and more regularly than the general schedule of meetings would allow. When the idea for such a group was first mooted, it might also have appeared as a rich opportunity for organizing some collaborative artistic activities among members. All these hopes would have met with disappointment. The Group's 'artistic' pursuits showed no sign of going beyond the academic; in fact, they became more and more abstrusely philosophical. And they were related to politics only in the sense of being used to impose a socialist creed on the Fabians which ran counter to the Society's studiously non-dogmatic approaches both to art and socialism. In view of the increasingly blatant connections of the Group's leaders with the cause of Guild Socialism, it is easy to understand how old-guard Fabians could have seen that Group not simply as an alternative club but as one which threatened to become an alternative powerhouse as well.

There was an earlier artistic group associated with the Fabians which presented no such threat and which offered rather greater stimulations for its members — in a more than academic way. This was the Stage Society, founded in 1899. It was never an official part of the Fabian Society in the way the Arts Group was; and it did not consist exclusively of Fabians. But it was, in effect, an affiliate organization, having been formed 'under Fabian influence' and depending for much of its support, in its early days at least, on a 'Fabian public'.[42] According to the *Fabian News*, it was 'largely officered by Fabians'[43] as well, though this statement is something of an exaggeration. Fabians were prominent on its various committees, though not dominant in numbers.[44] Nonetheless, close connections with the Fabian Society were reflected in its structure and its programmes as well as in its personnel.

Rather like the embryonic Fabian Society, the Stage Society first came together in a private house in London to which a select group of people known to be interested (about one hundred and fifty in this case) were personally invited. The house belonged to Frederick Whelen, a clerk at the Bank of England who served on the Fabian Executive Committee between 1896 and 1904. There were other members of the Fabian Executive among those who issued the original invitation, including Walter Crane, and the actor and director, Charles Charrington. Also included in the list was Charrington's wife, Janet Achurch, who had created the role of Nora in Ibsen's *A Doll's House* and became a life-long friend of Shaw's. The avowed aim of this group was the formation of a small private subscription society for 'the production of Plays' — particularly plays 'of obvious power and merit which lacked, under the conditions then prevalent on the stage, any opportunity for their presentation'.[45] Forty or fifty of those invited turned up to the meeting in Whelen's house, though the number of members grew so rapidly that very soon proper theatres had to be hired to accommodate everyone.[46] By 1907 the figure had reached fifteen hundred, which one old member, J.T. Grein, considered much too large for a 'club, which began so well . . . when the members were few and the efforts great'.[47]

Active participation in the productions concerned, whether on stage or backstage, was no doubt spread very unevenly when the numbers swelled to these proportions; the great majority of members would have attended only as spectators, though that is not to question their commitment to the club nor their enjoyment of its activities in this limited capacity. Moreover, when the Society became officially 'Incorporated' in 1904 — a testimony to its growing reputation — an amateur offshoot was formed by two Fabians (Millicent Murby and Louise Salom) for the purpose of providing fellow-members with more opportunities for 'performing in and witnessing interesting plays by British and foreign dramatists'. One of its first productions was Oscar Wilde's *Salomé*.[48]

Grein's anxiety that the professional wing of the Stage Society was 'in danger of losing caste artistically by having won it socially'[49] crystallizes the dilemma of all *avant-garde* groups, and remains a salutary warning against the perils of respectability. Whether his criticisms are entirely fair to the Stage Society as such is another matter. If it became a victim of success in any sense, that success was of the artistic kind at least as much as of the social kind. This is suggested by the career of one of its most brilliant protégés, Harley Granville Barker (1877-1946).

Barker was often to be seen as an actor in early Stage Society productions, and he made his debut as a director at one of its sessions in 1900. It also sponsored a production of his first major play, *The Marrying of Ann Leete*, in 1902.[50] The determinedly 'Experimental' policies of the Society clearly nurtured his youthful talents at a time when the commercial theatre could only have blighted them with its oppressive conventionality and its subjection to 'the crippling influence of the censor'.[51]

Barker was stimulated politically as well as artistically by his contacts with the Stage Society. Through these, he was attracted to the Fabian Society around 1903; and he followed both Whelen and Charrington on to its Executive Committee, serving between 1907 and 1912. After the first year or so, a fellow-Fabian recalls, his attendance became rather erratic; but he kept 'being re-elected on his theatrical reputation'.[53] By this period, too, his links with the Stage Society, though not completely severed, had naturally weakened as he had begun to achieve independent successes in the world of *avant-garde* theatre.

Between 1904 and 1907 he had mounted a triumphant series of productions at the Royal Court in association with the theatrical manager, J.F. Vedrenne.[54] The Stage Society could take some credit as the testing-ground, if not the breeding-ground, of this venture, but the very success of the Royal Court's seasons inevitably robbed its prototype of the lustre and urgent vitality of lone, pioneering enterprises. It also drew off much of the talent and energy which would normally have been channelled into Stage Society productions.

Several of Shaw's plays, for instance, had been given their first airing in the Society's productions. (*You Never Can Tell* was the Society's opening attraction in the first season, *Candida* the closing one, and there followed in other seasons *Captain Brassbound's Conversion, Mrs Warren's Profession, The Admirable Bashville* and *Man and Superman*.)[55] These were performed in whatever theatres happened to be available; it was ominous, however, when *Man and Superman* was produced at the Royal Court, for though the first performance (on 21 May 1905) was officially accredited to the Stage Society, the link which that suggested between the latter institution and the former was not acknowledged subsequently. Indeed, the Barker-Vedrenne management at the Court had already asserted its independence the year before in staging a new Shaw play (*John Bull's Other Island*) completely without the Stage Society's sponsorship. And Shaw, though he became a life-member of the Society in that year, never again wrote a play specifically for it, apart from some minor *jeux d'esprit* at a much later date.[56]

Barker himself never looked back after the success of the Royal Court seasons, or only begrudgingly. When asked in 1907 to take over the leading role in a Stage Society production of his own play, *Waste*, he did so, but confessed in a letter to Gilbert Murray: 'Waste has wasted me and

I am finding it difficult not to leave undone the things I ought to be doing.'[57] From 1904 on, one of his abiding preoccupations had been the formation of a fully-fledged National Theatre.[58]

The Stage Society could not have hoped, and would not have wished, to divert Barker from this more ambitious enterprise;[59] nor would it have wished to prevent Shaw from gaining wider exposure for his plays. Any such reluctance would have been quite at odds with the 'permeation' strategies of its Fabian members. Though the Stage Society might have become, in the process, just another arts club, stripped of its original (and unique) cutting edge, it is very difficult to gauge how far its continuing 'social' success — it survived until 1939 — served to encourage artistic complacency and mediocrity.

Grein's impressions of its declining standards are not those of an ignorant or insensitive critic; he was very much a man of the theatre himself, having provided the prototype for the Stage Society with his Independent Theatre Society of the 1890s, which had mounted similar programmes and was devoted to similar ends. For precisely that reason, however, his impressions can hardly be accounted dispassionate. The Secretary of the Stage Society referred to Grein's 'paternal pride in his spiritual children'.[60] There are hints, too, of a less pleasant side to paternalism in his attitude, including a desire to lay down the law about how things should be done; and this may well have given rise to disenchantment and resentment when those things were not done.

He was one of the early non-Fabian members of the Stage Society, and if he did not join it of his own accord he was probably asked to do so out of deference to his pioneering work at the Independent or because the Society thought it could make good use of him. And, indeed, he helped it secure permission for the production of various plays from the Continent, as well as serving on its 'Reading and Advising Committee'.[61] His name, however, never appeared on its Managing Committee; and perhaps this hurt his pride from the outset. As early as 1900, he started to criticize the Society's choice of individual plays,[62] and in 1905 he launched an attack, albeit a constructive one, on its whole structure:

No theatre is possible unless there be one dominating spirit. That spirit may make mistakes ... but ... if he be strong, his record will prove superior to the inevitable collection of blunders of syndicated 'dilettanti'. There are in the cabinet of the Society a few men quite capable of single-handed rule. Let the Society select one to be the *intendant* ... then there may be policy instead of drifting towards irresolution.[63]

Grein could only have become more frustrated with the Stage Society as the years went by, as there was little likelihood of changing its committee-dominated administration in favour of one-man rule. The former approach was a quintessential and time-honoured Fabian way of doing things; and, in the express interests of greater democracy, old-guard members continued to affirm its applicability to artistic organizations as much as to political ones.[64]

The artistic programmes of the Stage Society also bore the mark of its Fabian links. To begin with, there were productions of plays written by Fabians, both of the old guard and among the up-and-coming: by Shaw of course; by Sydney Olivier (whose 'domestic drama in four acts', *Mrs Maxwell's Marriage*, was never published but was mounted for production by the Stage Society in its first season[65]); by Granville Barker (who did not prove as steadfast a Fabian as either Shaw or Olivier, but whose experiences in Fabian circles were reflected in the themes of much of his writing for the stage[66]); and by Arnold Bennett.[67] Autobiographical references were not the only pointer to Fabian inspiration in these plays; their abiding concern with social problems (such as class divisions, poverty, prostitution) and their critical stance towards many established institutions (the business world, the church, marriage and so on) mirrored some major — though admittedly not distinctive — preoccupations of the Fabians, whether in the political work of the Society or in private. It was precisely the attempt to tackle such controversial or discomfiting themes in dramatic form which deterred the commercial theatre on the whole from producing these plays, and which made them such ripe fare for the Stage Society.

The same is true of the plays by non-Fabian authors which were given their first production in England by the Stage Society. Many of these were written by foreign dramatists (including Ibsen, Tolstoy, Sudermann, Hauptmann, Wedekind) and at first sight their presentation may appear to be far from characteristic of the Fabians, whose socialist concerns were notoriously insular. Even Sidney Webb, reflecting in 1930 on the Society's record, had to acknowledge its failure to 'think internationally' before the Great War.[68] It is clear, however, from the wide artistic interests shown by the earliest Fabians — including Webb himself — that the domestic preoccupations of the Society in its political and social work had never precluded an active engagement with foreign literature.

Any influence which writers such as Goethe, Heine and Zola had in shaping or consolidating the socialist beliefs of these early Fabians reflected in part a process of appropriating foreign material to domestic concerns and purposes;[69] and a similar process was at work behind the Fabians' continuing enthusiasm for European writers, as evinced not only in the Stage Society's repertoire but also in the Fabian lecture-programmes discussed in the next chapter.

The example of Ibsen's reception is particularly illuminating here. As we shall see, his work was very popular with the Fabians on the whole, both as a subject for lectures and as a vehicle for stage production. One of his earliest non-poetic plays, *The League of Youth*, was given its first

English production in the opening season of the Stage Society (Granville Barker was in the cast, playing the role of Erik Bratsberg, and Charles Charrington was the director).[70] As a biting political satire on the faddism of progressive liberal groups, this play was eminently transportable from its Norwegian setting in the late 1860s to turn-of-the-century England. It no doubt proved a timely weapon for the Fabians in their struggle against the competing attractions of the Liberal Party, which seems to have gained, rather than lost, vitality from its increasing fragmentation into 'faddist' sections after the death of Gladstone.[71]

The Fabians' appropriation of Ibsen was, however, a rather more complicated and sensitive business. For a start, there were complexities and ambiguities in his works which would not have allowed their easy adaptation to Fabian causes. Like many Fabians, Ibsen was a rebel against various institutions and values of the middle classes in which he was brought up, but he was far more an individualist than a socialist — a point Shaw hammered home in the lecture he gave on the Norwegian dramatist to the Fabian Society in 1890.[72]

There was, in fact, a strong anti-political streak in Ibsen's individualism, hinted at in the motto of Dr Stockmann, the leading character in another play to which Fabians were drawn, *An Enemy of the People*.[73] 'The strongest man is he who stands alone', Stockmann proclaimed; and his creator's own determination to 'stand alone' was shown in his refusal to commit himself to any group or party ideology, socialist or otherwise. *The League of Youth* could even have been interpreted as a barely-concealed attack on all progressive political movements, including the anti-liberal variety typified by the Fabian Society.[74] Only a year or two after it was completed, Ibsen was making openly anarchistic statements. 'The State must go', he told the Danish critic Georg Brandes in 1871: 'That revolution I shall join in . . . Changing the forms of government is nothing more than tinkering with degrees, a little more or a little less — rotten, all of it.' As Ibsen saw things at this time, 'Special reforms' were ultimately futile, and 'revolutions in externals' were 'merely trifling. What is all important is the revolution in the spirit of man.'[75] For the Fabians, on the other hand, achieving 'special reforms' in a piecemeal, gradual way became the basis of their strategy in facilitating the development of socialism.

They were neither so dogmatic nor so austere as to be incapable of enjoying a parody of their kind of approach to political change; but Ibsen's work amounted to rather more than this, and their responsiveness to it was on a deeper level. They rarely gave express reasons for his impact on them; but from the scraps of evidence which do exist, it would appear to have been based partly on feelings of affinity that transcended both nationality and political belief. The fact that Ibsen was not a socialist in the conventional Fabian mould, or perhaps in any mould, was clearly irrelevant, in the last analysis, to those Fabians who took him up in England; what mattered much more was the sense of sharing a similar social background to his, and of experiencing a comparable form of rebellion against that background. Shaw, for one, instinctively associated himself with the Norwegian dramatist and a long line of other 'middle-class revolutionists' — by no means all of them socialist in their beliefs.[76] Though Shaw may not have been a 'conventional' Fabian, one wonders who was amidst that 'Queer Heterogeneous Bundle of Humanity'.

This was a phrase applied to the Fabians in the same year as the Stage Society's production of *The League of Youth*,[77] and it suggests something about the nature of their ideas, too, which from the earliest days had constituted a rather queer, heterogeneous bundle of assumptions and aspirations. In the 1880s they were not immune to what Shaw termed the 'influenza of anarchism'; he had been susceptible himself, and even those Fabians who were not affected (Sydney Olivier, for example) could be found making passionate claims on behalf of 'the individualist ideal' and asserting that socialism was 'merely' a more rational form of individualism.[78] It is not so surprising, then, that lone rebels like Dr Stockmann should have struck a responsive chord in some Fabians at least; his denunciation of the 'solid liberal majority' in *An Enemy of the People*, and the attack on liberal groups in *The League of Youth*, may also have appealed to an authoritarian or élitist side in their make-up. As we shall see, there was a continual tension between élitist and egalitarian tendencies in their schemes and visions. Though Ibsen's plays did not mirror these tensions exactly, there was much in them for Fabians to identify with; they brought to the surface, indeed powerfully articulated, the inevitable dilemmas and self-conflicts faced by anyone rebelling against his own class.

Not all Fabians shared a taste for Ibsen; some, like Annie Besant and William Clarke, had found the themes and tensions in his plays far too discomfiting. It would be unwise, in any case, to suggest that his work was taken up by Fabians simply because they felt an emotional bond with him that acted as a kind of therapeutic support. Some of their number clearly found his work as ill-fitted to their own psychological needs as it was to the particular political purposes of the Fabian Society.

Their distaste for his themes, however, was as much a tribute to his impact as other Fabians' enthusiasm — to his impact as a dramatic artist with a genuine power to disturb. It was on the stage 'alone', Shaw had claimed in his Fabian Society lecture on Ibsen, that the true extent of the Norwegian dramatist's power could be conveyed.[79] And many Fabians, aside from Shaw, were in the van of those who put this claim to the test. They not only flocked in great numbers to see his plays performed by other groups,[80] but they also participated themselves in various Ibsen productions, amateur and professional. The Stage Society's presentation of *The League of Youth* was but one of these;[81] and interest was not just confined to the London Fabians. In the 1890s, the Liverpool branch of the Fabian Society had mounted a performance of *An Enemy of the People*; and, if we can credit the recollections of one of the participants, Ibsen himself had been so struck with the group's interest that he promised to write another play specially for its members.[82] Evidently nothing came of that promise.

In London, at least, the Stage Society came to provide a regular vent for the theatrical interests of Fabians. Numerous other dramatists, especially on the Continent, were now emulating Ibsen in writing plays calculated to disturb social and political, as well as religious, pieties; and it behoved the Stage Society, as part of its aim in filling the gaps left by commercial theatrical managements, to test the dramatic power of these newer plays as well as any untried or rarely-performed Ibsen pieces, such as *The League of Youth*. Their adaptability to the Fabians' domestic (and personal) preoccupations helps explain the frequent appearance of such plays in the Stage Society's repertoire; but it is only half an explanation. In setting out to produce, not just to study, these plays, the Society showed quite plainly that its interest in them was not confined to their social or political themes; the essence of the enterprise was in seeing how far the disturbing power of those themes could be realized in a theatrical performance — the context intended for them by their authors. 'Dramatic force' was as important a criterion in the selection of plays as 'high morality'.[83]

There was also a good deal of sheer pleasure to be derived from putting on or attending these performances. They were arranged to take place once a month on Sundays for nine months of the year, with a break over the summer. The choice of day was significant, for up until the Stage Society's opening production in 1899, there had not been a theatrical performance on the sabbath since the days of Charles I.[84] This fact would have added to the *frisson* of belonging to an *avant-garde* group: not only was it making artistic breakthroughs with its exotic and provocative repertoire, but a political one as well. Fabians had been long associated with anti-sabbatarianism, and it must have been pleasing to them that an organization so closely affiliated with their own had scored a major advance for that cause. But the pleasure of making a political point would have soon worn off; a more enduring and more delicious pleasure would have been the prospect of all those inclement English Sundays being brightened up with a stimulating entertainment. The conscience-catching plays were not the only thing to attract members; there was also the camaraderie which naturally sprang from the regular meeting of people with a particular shared interest; and these joys of social intimacy must have been even greater among the casts, backstage staff and administrative committees involved in mounting the various productions. Though there were some tensions and disputes[85] — an inevitability, perhaps, in any form of collaborative creative work — they were certainly not of the fratricidal, or matricidal, kind that served to weaken the Fabian Arts Group. The great resilience of the Stage Society is clear testimony to this.

A more positive factor in its staying power was that it focussed on the kinds of art which its Fabian members at least had always found especially alluring. Why Fabians in general should have had such a strong personal interest in the performing arts will be examined later. It's a phenomenon that can be observed straightaway in the activities of another kind of 'club' associated with the Fabian Society: the Fabian Summer Schools. This enterprise was started some eight years after the foundation of the Stage Society but it lasted even longer, surviving not only the First World War, as the Stage Society managed to do, but also the Second. The Schools by no means focussed their attention exclusively on the theatre or any other kinds of art; nevertheless, those concerns had a key place in their programme. The approaches adopted towards the arts were not as rigorously academic as the word 'School' might suggest; but this made them all the more popular, perhaps, in their summer setting and a considerable factor in the Schools' enduring appeal over many years. The early demise of the Arts Group, the Summer Schools' contemporary by birth, certainly showed the perils of an over-academic approach.

The choice of season for the Schools was as important as the choice of day for the Stage Society's programmes. There was, admittedly, none of the 'political' resonance about summer activities as there was about Sunday ones. They fulfilled a similar social function, however, in providing Fabians with some stimulating and pleasurable activities at rather slack points in their ordinary routines. Summer was the Fabian Society's traditional period of rest, when its committee meetings and lecture-sessions were wound up for the year. It was an obvious time for Fabians to take a holiday from the jobs which many of them had as teachers, civil servants, doctors, lawyers, clerks and so on; and there was no point in the Society's carrying on in its usual way when it could not depend on fairly regular attendance. On the other hand, probably none of the Fabians working for a salary would have been able to go away for the whole three months, so that there must have been some rather barren-seeming periods when individual members came back to their jobs yet had none of the stimulations of their 'club' to look forward to in their spare time. Even the Stage Society, which helped fill up some blank Sundays in the year, did not operate in the summer. The sense of a whole blank season could only have been relieved by something like the Summer

Schools which were timed to run for about five or six weeks in the middle of the season.

The log-books kept by the Schools indicate that members were not expected to enrol for the whole period; however, the fairly remote locations chosen each year would have discouraged any mere popping in and out for the odd weekend. Country houses, or private schools, in various parts of England and Wales were the favoured spots for holding the annual sessions, though the 1911 School was held as far afield as Saas Grund in Switzerland. Because of a guarantee of expenses from more affluent Fabians — notably Shaw's millionairess wife — tariffs were able to be kept fairly low for those on a middle-class income. (The first Summer School, for instance, charged thirty-five shillings a week, board and residence included.)[86]

Obviously, the attractive locations and reasonable rates made it tempting for certain members — those, for instance, who might not have been able to afford separate breaks from their work — to treat the Schools as an actual part of their summer holiday, and to combine education with recreation. This was not averse to the spirit in which the Schools had been founded, though from the start there were differences among members over the proportion of time that should be devoted, respectively, to curricular and extra-curricular activities, and a quite understandable — even inevitable — confusion over the dividing lines between education and recreation, purpose and pleasure. Where and how were these lines to be drawn?

One of the originators of the scheme, F. Lawson Dodd, had not initially wanted an 'educational side' at all; his idea had been that the Fabians should simply run a 'Holiday Home' for members. The idea of the School, as such, had come from another member, Mabel Atkinson, who, as she acknowledged in later years, had not been in very close touch with the Society until returning from a visit to Germany in 1906, where she had attended a summer school at Jena. Recalling the experience of that school 'on a country walk one winter afternoon', she suddenly saw its adaptability to Fabian purposes and wrote to Edward Pease on the matter. Demonstrating once again that the Fabians were not automatically resistant to foreign ideas, but shrewdly accommodating, a committee was quickly set up to investigate Miss Atkinson's proposals, and a viable compromise reached between these and Dr Dodd's scheme. 'It is proposed to have a considerable amount of holiday-making together with the work', Miss Atkinson wrote, without hint of complaint, early in 1907.[87] Other members continued to argue about the precise amount of recreation time that should or could be allowed, but such disputes did not prevent the School from getting off to a good start, nor did they weaken their general attraction for Fabians in later years.

One party to the dispute remained 'very doubtful about the educational side. They were of the opinion that people who come on a holiday would not want to be bothered with lectures.'[88] Another party was represented by Beatrice Webb, who suspected in like fashion that the recreational side might take over from the educational side, but for that reason desired a more intensive and vigilant regimen of 'teaching, learning and discussion', albeit with 'some off days, and off hours, for recreation and social intercourse'. She sought a 'compromise between studiousness and a certain amount of *carefully devised* entertainment'.[89]

The rather more impulsive cavortings of the 'young folk' attending the Summer Schools were obviously perplexing to her; but while she displayed a predictable puritanism in her desire to bring more discipline into this 'unconventional life', she betrayed no wish to stamp it out. In fact, she was as much amused as bemused by it, and took a wry pleasure in finding herself less shocked by the 'open' conversation and 'startling' clothes of the younger set than either 'the quaker-like Lawson Dodd' or the 'methodist' villagers nearby.[90]

She and Sidney helped direct the 1910 school, and clearly came into some kind of conflict with the regular directors (Mabel Atkinson and Mary Hankinson) on the question of what kind of balance should be struck between educational and recreational pursuits. It might not have arisen if the Webbs — and particularly Beatrice — had not been so bound up at the time in their campaign for the 'Break-up of the Poor Law'; Beatrice, having recently completed her Minority Report on the question for the Royal Commission of 1905-9, was so obsessed with airing her views and having them discussed that she probably would have regarded any other concern — however 'educational' — as a diversion. But it was particularly galling to her at this stage to have precious time taken up with sporting and dramatic activities. She stated: 'I am rather against having professional gymnastic instructors' (a direct dig at Miss Hankinson, who was one) 'or letting any lively man or woman absorb a large part of the company in a play or pageant.' The reason she gave was that 'highly organised games, the learning of parts in plays, and the preparation of dresses and scenery, become an occupation in themselves and turn the mind away for good and all from listening to lectures and quiet fireside discussion'.

If the peculiar pressures of 1910 made her more austere than ever, she did not become a remorseless killjoy even then. Those same pressures made her sympathetic to the longing for 'escape' from the 'whirl of constant talk and discussion', and she emphasized that it was '*not* desirable to exclude games, exercise, music'. Interestingly, it was the high-powered organization of such activities, not the activities themselves, which galled her — Miss Hankinson, she declared, was 'too much of the expert'. In the fields of sport and the arts, the approach which Beatrice wanted to adopt was if anything more casual, more relaxed; paradoxically enough, the careful devising of summer-school entertainment which she recommended meant ensuring that it was less, not more, highly-planned. What was necessary 'to plan out' more vigorously was the intellectual bill of fare: 'a far more *technical* and *specialised* kind of discussion which will attract a better type'. Testifying to her current obsession she even recommended that the discussion groups be organized into 'specialised sections — like the Minority Report'.[91]

In subsequent years, however, she made no attempt to impose such rigid practices on the Summer Schools, and they went on their studiously merry or merrily studious way regardless. For such a heterogeneous bunch as the Fabians, there could obviously be no ideal compromise — that's almost a contradiction in terms — between educational and recreational activities. Beatrice's special preoccupations of the time had tended to blind her to the fact that compromises reached from year to year were about as good as they could be in the sense that they helped secure the wide popularity which kept the institution flourishing. With some disdain, but also a measure of genuine awe, she herself commented on the 'miscellaneous crowd' and 'extraordinarily mixed assembly' which the Schools managed to attract, and this is borne out by other, later reports.[92]

Those fatalists who thought there could be no effective compromise at all in a holiday atmosphere, and that any attempt at an educational programme might as well be scrapped before it was shunned, were shown to be just as shortsighted. Mabel Atkinson recalls in her memoir of the Schools how groundless such prognostications proved: 'When we started, quite the reverse turned out to be the case. People were keen on the lectures, and those that I had arranged were very well attended and provoked a great deal of discussion.' This is also an implicit answer to Beatrice Webb's charge that the regular organizers of the school were only interested in organizing games and entertainments. Miss Atkinson goes on to say expressly: 'I was always very keen on the educational side of the work of the school, and am sorry that Mrs Webb did not appreciate that.'[93]

The log-books of the Summer Schools tend to bear out these self-justifications. No definite pattern can be discerned in the programmes recorded — partly because there are some gaps in the record, and partly because a set pattern or strict agenda seems to have been against the spirit of the whole enterprise. This lack of a formal syllabus enabled Beatrice Webb to dismiss the educational side of things as a mere matter of 'a few lectures and discussions thrown in to give subjects for conversation';[94] but this is vague caricature at best. Even in the leanest years, during the First

World War, when suitably distinguished lecturers were harder to get hold of, there was an average of five to six lectures per week (usually one a day) on as wide a range of topics as the London branch of the Society offered.[95] (Several of these were on topics relating specifically to the arts, particularly drama: precise figures are given in the next chapter.) The organization of lectures was not so loose as to exclude the possibility of various series being arranged round a broad, general theme or subject. At the first school in 1907, for example, there were courses on 'Socialists: their Lives and Ideals'; 'Present Problems of Social Reconstruction'; 'Elementary Economic History'; and 'Modern Dramatists'. Debates and discussion-groups were sometimes co-ordinated to fit in with such themes, though on the whole they appear to have been rather more off-the-cuff affairs initiated by someone with a particular enthusiasm for a subject. On average, such sessions took place at least once a day, and lasted, as with the more formal lecture sessions, for about an hour and a half — perhaps longer when the discussion became particularly intense. The log-books expressly remark on occasions how 'animated' the participants became in these sessions;[96] and this should make us wary of accepting too readily Beatrice Webb's impression that they were merely the pretext for a dilettantish chat.

If Beatrice underestimated the seriousness and sense of purpose of the Schools' educational programme, she also exaggerated the degree of attention given to recreational pursuits and the extent to which these became the focus of any systematic organization. 'Quite a good deal of time was given up to recreation', as Mabel Atkinson herself acknowledged, and some of the activities concerned became an habitual feature of the Schools' routines, with something of the air of military manoeuvres about them: 'long excursions twice a week when the more energetic members turned out for the whole day'; and a class in Swedish drill, 'every morning, immediately after breakfast', in which the redoubtable Mary Hankinson could be seen putting 'a number of athletic young ladies' through their paces.[97] These pursuits may have become compulsive for some — particularly their leaders — but they were not compulsory; those enrolled in the Schools were left pretty much to their own devices outside the three or four hours of the day devoted to classes, and they could take their pleasures as and how they wished from the great variety on offer. Many of these were wholly extempore, and free of any kind of scheduling or direction, apart from the natural kinds imposed by time, weather and place.

Actually, the locations chosen — countryside retreats, readily accessible to mountains, woods and pasture-land, and often the seaside as well, or at least a river or spring — gave fairly unrestricted scope for all manner of leisured outdoor pursuits: climbing, walking, cycling, bathing, boating, fishing. The printed prospectuses[98] always stressed the idyllic setting of the Schools, often including a photograph to enhance the appeal. Here was a rich opportunity for members of the Society to test out, however briefly, those romantic fantasies about the superiority of rural living which had fed the early Fabians' repugnance for industrial capitalism and helped turn them towards socialism in the first place. All the comfort and facilities of a fully-serviced country-house no doubt made it easier to sustain these fantasies, though some of the more intrepid participants made an effort to eschew such cosseting by living in tents on the outskirts and surviving on fruit and nuts.[99]

Curtailments on outdoor activities, imposed by fluctuations in the weather or by the amount of daylight hours available, were always greater than any restrictions of local terrain; though the choice of high summer as the season for holding the Schools kept these curtailments to a minimum. We know that exceptionally bad weather afflicted the 1910 School for a few weeks; but even in these conditions there were plenty of indoor diversions, mainly of a dramatic or musical kind, to punctuate the lectures and discussions; and these were the staple after-dinner fare when it became too dark for most other forms of recreation.

Some of these indoor pursuits were quite informal and impromptu: 'sing-songs', dances, recitations, playreadings and charades — little more, in fact, than an extension into the group of activities which occurred naturally for such people at home, though all the more enjoyable perhaps because of the larger range of participants. Other activities, however, needed to be more carefully organized and prepared for: concerts, fancy-dress balls, revues, mock-trials, and full-scale dramatic performances. Though professional artists, such as Shaw and the Charringtons, were actively involved in these pursuits, they were not as dominant in them as in the Stage Society; there was more opportunity here for the amateur to be at the forefront, and the dividing line between performers and spectators was thinner. Moreover, the particular form taken by some of the musical and dramatic activities blurred the lines between extra-curricular and curricular pursuits at the Schools. Not only were traditional ballads and light romantic airs from various European countries included in the concert programmes, there was also an assortment of folk songs and songs of labour (Welsh numbers, sung by local village choirs; sea shanties; spirituals from the American plantations).[100] And members joined together in renditions of 'ethical hymns' and 'socialist songs' — probably culled from Edith Nesbit's collection of 1908, and later from the *Songs for Socialists* which the Publishing Committee of the Fabian Society spent some two years in compiling and arranging.[101] The immediate appeal of such songs may well have owed more to their melody than to their particular sentiment, whether political or religious, but members can't have been entirely oblivious of the social applications and polemical value of the music they chose to sing and hear. Prior to one sing-song, a debate was held on 'Music as an Educational Force', and on another occasion there was an evening lecture in the shape of 'A Plea for National and Popular Music ... with illustrative playing and singing.'[102]

The constant and frenetic round of theatrical activities at the Schools, which so disturbed Beatrice Webb, had some connection with the Stage Society's work in terms of personnel and programmes; there were readings, for example, from the plays of Ibsen and Shaw, given by Charrington and Shaw himself, among others.[103] In 1909 a full production of a Shavian trifle entitled 'Press Cuttings' was mounted in tandem with a political play on the theme of 'How the Vote was Won'. Both pieces, it was noted, were 'well done' and 'well received' by a 'crowded house'. There was, however, more of an improvisational streak in these proceedings than in Stage Society productions, as was shown when the second play was repeated a couple of weeks later with a substantially changed cast (probably drawing on the most-recently-arrived visitors to the Schools for that year) and with 'a new character and dialogue' written in by one of the replacements.[104]

Even the lightest flummery whipped up by the Fabian thespians tended to have a political base or some spicy topical ingredient which made it all the more appetizing to the assembled audience and which induced in all concerned — audience as much as players — a quite euphoric spirit of community. This is brought out vividly in the report of 'an almost impromptu Revue' staged at the 1916 School:

All the School and a few visitors attended ... and the hilarity ... engendered cannot often have been surpassed ... Among the scenes were 'The Fabian Summer School after the Millennium' and 'The Socialist State of the Future as portrayed by its opponents'. There was a full beauty chorus, with all the usual accessories and inanities. The Revue was followed by dancing and all were extremely happy.[105]

The conviviality of the Schools was testimony to their club-like nature and function. Even Edward Pease, who was anxious to stress their political and propaganda value, movingly acknowledged their social significance as well: 'Apart from the direct interests of the Society, a School of this character is valued by many solitary people, solitary both socially, such as teachers and civil servants, and solitary intellectually because they live in remote places where people of their way of thinking are scarce.'[106] At the outset one of Mabel Atkinson's chief aims in launching the Schools had been to 'help forward the Fabian movement in the provinces'.[107] What better opportunity could there be for members of the far-flung provincial branches to confer on their mutual problems, and in addition meet some of the stars and big-wigs of the central London branch? The atmosphere of a collective working-holiday, relaxing as well as stimulating, not only broke down regional barriers; it also nurtured an ease of social intercourse between the disparate sensibilities attracted to the Fabian Society, and thereby served as a genuinely consolidating force at a time when other forces were contriving to disrupt and divide the movement. For all her reservations about the Schools, Beatrice Webb's 'dominant impression' on witnessing them at first hand was of the harmonious 'well-bredness' among their motley crew of participants:

I.L.P. organisers, M.O.H.s, teachers, minor officials of all sorts, social workers, literary men, journalists and even such out-of-the-way recruits as auctioneers and unregistered dentists — all living in extremely close quarters, and yet not getting on each other's nerves through a too great disparity of speech and behaviour. It is a wonderful instance of the civilising effect of a common purpose and common faith.[108]

In effect, if not by intention, the Fabian Summer Schools were more than a club-within-a-club: they became a kind of super-club.

'Personal relationships' among members were valued by some Fabians almost to the same degree as they were by the Bloomsbury Group, though not so much for their own sake perhaps. Pease, for example, claimed that 'People can only work together efficiently when they know each other. Therefore in practice political and many other organisations find it necessary to arrange garden parties, fetes, picnics, teas, and functions of all sorts in order to bring together their numbers under such conditions as enable them to become personally acquainted with each other.'[109] The Summer Schools, as he acknowledged, proved to be one of the most effective agencies in bringing Fabians (and their sympathizers) together in this way; and the artistic pursuits of the Schools were particularly helpful in cementing relationships because of the communal efforts they called forth. Regular branch activities, however, were themselves quite capable of encouraging a gregarious spirit among members — albeit on a more fragmented geographical basis — and artistic pursuits, again, were a potent instrument in this process.

There was a strong element of continuity in the social rituals of the Fabian Society, for all of its fluctuating fortunes and changing patterns of membership in the years 1884-1918. Venues for meetings, if not specifically 'aristocratic' in the way Shaw suggested in his report of 1892, tended always to have a self-consciously aesthetic quality about them, whether highly refined or slightly bohemian in nature. When the Society was in its infancy, the private drawing-rooms of members were the favoured location. A visitor to one of these observed the 'air of well-to-do taste and comfort', manifested in 'plush-cushioned' seats and an 'ebony and gold grand piano'.[110] Later, as the Society expanded, suites of public rooms in stylish localities were hired. If these were unavailable, or appeared too small for the numbers expected, a hall would be used (in which, according to one report at least, the 'drawing-room' mood prevailed[111]) or a gallery was hired, such as the Sussex Street Galleries in the heart of London's clubland.[112] About the time of the First World War, the Society officially established an 'inexpensive club' of its own in Tothill Street, Westminister, complete with smoking-room, games room, and a 'considerable library' and reading-room providing 'fiction and the drama' as well as 'Socialist and Labour journals of the whole world'.[113]

There was, then, an air of comfort, refinement and charm about Fabian Society gatherings which a body like the Socialist League could never match. It was not a matter of indifference to surroundings on the part of the League; William Morris, at least, was exasperated at having to lecture in dingy and poky rooms in the further reaches of the East End.[114] The League was probably unable to afford the choice locations which the Fabian Society, with its predominantly middle-class subscribers, managed to provide. There may also have been a conscious avoidance, by some of the League's organizers, of any pretensions to grandeur; but such a policy may only have done that body a disservice by discouraging those who already missed out enough on comfort in their working lives and everyday surroundings. The Fabian Society, on the other hand, was shrewd enough to pamper its members. In their group activities, as much as in their personal lives, asceticism was never made a rule, and was indeed deliberately eschewed.

In view of the kind of venues chosen for its everyday activities in London, it is hardly surprising that the Fabian Society's holiday-education programmes should have been conducted mainly in large country-houses. They were the obvious rural equivalent of salon and clubroom. The indoor entertainments provided at the Summer Schools were also an equivalent of those provided in the metropolis — more uninhibited in tone but reflecting the same basic tension between bohemianism and gentility which was inevitable, perhaps, in any gathering of middle-class socialists.

'Entertainments with mingled songs and socialism' were among the 'forms of work' that the Group Secretaries of Fabian Society branches tabled reports on when meeting with the Executive Committee in 1891.[115] There was quite a long tradition behind this work. Organizing musical activities — especially hymn-singing — had been a task of one of the earliest Fabians, Percival Chubb, in a proto-Fabian group known as the Progressive Association.[116] Various other kinds of music continued to form a part of those Fabian meetings which were open to the general public. For instance, a meeting addressed by Shaw in 1908 was prefaced by a half-hour organ recital, including pieces by Sibelius, Schumann, Bach and Elgar.[117] Arrangements were made for a 'vocal union' to perform a selection of choral music at a lecture Shaw delivered to the Sheffield branch of the Society in the same year.[118] In general, however, Fabian 'Entertainments', 'At Homes' and 'Soirées' offered rather lighter musical fare. A visitor at one such gathering — held in 1889 — commented that 'there was nothing of a Revolutionary tone about the entertainment'; all of the songs were 'of the ordinary drawing-room sort'.[119] In later years, the inclusion of a few folk songs and Morris dances, as well as 'one or two Socialist songs', lent a more robust note.[120]

Dramatic activities at branch meetings and at the soirées seem to have been rather more adventurous; conventional farce and costume drama were eschewed, and the programmes were more along the lines of the Stage Society's, concentrating on plays with socially or morally challenging themes. In addition to Ibsen, plays by Strindberg, Tolstoy, Galsworthy, Shaw and Robert Blatchford were mounted by various branches in London and the provinces.[121]

Edward Pease gives the impression that the soirées were deliberately aimed at enhancing the appeal of the Society for its younger recruits,[122] though older members were not discouraged from attending. Indeed, a soirée offering 'music, dancing and light refreshments' was organized specifically in honour of the Webbs on their return from a world tour in 1912.[123] Such events were probably rather restrained compared to the after-dinner activities of the Summer Schools; the 'evening dress' mentioned on the invitation cards, though 'optional',[124] would in itself have lent a more formal note.

If it was only at the Summer Schools that the Fabians felt free to let their hair down, and give full play to their artistic instincts, this does not mean that their other gatherings were devoid of artistic pleasure or of a measure of sheer fun.

At provincial branches, evening meetings sometimes took the form just of moonlight rambles, picnics, or whist drives.[125] Whether that concièrge of the Fabian conscience, Beatrice Webb, would have approved of such frolics in the meetings of the London branch is arguable; though even here, in the regular lecture-meetings, there was fun, as well as stimulation, to be gained on occasions. One meeting in particular stood out in this respect. In 1907, the Reverend Charles Marson was invited to give a lecture on Folk Song. After some introductory comments, his exposition was punctuated by sung performances of a dozen or so of the pieces he was discussing. The accompanist on this occasion was the foremost English folk-song authority, Cecil Sharp, with whom Marson had recently collaborated in collecting and publishing a volume of traditional folk-songs from Somerset. The Fabian audience was encouraged to participate in the singing of the choruses, and according to the report of the meeting in the *Fabian News*, a 'singularly instructive and enjoyable evening' was spent by all involved.[126]

As R.C.K. Ensor noted, in another context, a Fabian meeting was not able to make the same kind of 'human and emotional appeal' as a body such as the Independent Labour Party. At the meetings of this 'predominantly working-class' organization, he intimated, one found a combination of 'sincere rhetoric . . . songs . . . [and] personal warmth' that was unmatched by any Fabian gathering. At the same time, Ensor suggested, it would have taken a complete 'conversion' of outlook for a middle-class man to 'find his feet in the I.L.P.' — a conversion 'more fundamental than is needed for him to join and appreciate the Fabian Society'.[127] And those elements and activities which Ensor praised in the I.L.P. were not, in fact, absent in the Fabian Society; the difference was more one of tone than of substance. The provision of a congenial social atmosphere through group activities — whether in the shape of lectures, sing-songs, theatricals or whatever — was a crucial function of the Fabian Society. If it only gave its members 'something to do in the evenings',[128] that was not a trivial achievement. However debatable its wider influence on public affairs may have been, there can be no debating its value as a focus for the extraordinary energies and enthusiasms of an alienated section of the late-Victorian and Edwardian middle classes, nor its effectiveness as an agency of pleasure and recreation for the same group. The club-like comforts and securities it offered no doubt encouraged a good measure of self-indulgence among its members, as some of them (notably Beatrice Webb) were only too keenly aware. As will be shown in Part III, however, the Society did not insulate its members to the extent of making them oblivious of — or entirely unsympathetic to — forms of pleasure and recreation outside the refinements of its own ambience.

8

Platform or playhouse? : Fabian lecturing on the arts and the arts of Fabian lecturing

A knees-up of the kind occasioned by C.W. Marson's lecture on folk song was not a common occurrence in ordinary meetings of the Fabian Society; the subject matter of most lectures was hardly encouraging to such high jinks. This did not mean that lectures were, as a rule, dull, perfunctory affairs on dryasdust topics. From the outset, there was an intention to make lectures enjoyable in themselves — enjoyable just to listen to — as well as instructive on a wide range of topics. As one Fabian observer recalled: 'Throughout the Victorian age political oratory was relished, like pulpit eloquence, alike as education, edification and *entertainment*. The agencies of *public enjoyment for respectable folk* were of a narrowness unimaginable ... [T]he socialist revival was for a short time without a compelling speaker. Here then, in the England of the late 1880s, was a wide opening for the Fabians'.[1]

It was an opening which they continued to exploit for the next three decades at least, after which the growth of new technological media such as the wireless and the cinema began to compete heavily with the lecture as forms both of education and entertainment. In 1894 William Clarke could write of the Society: 'It is in lectures that its work has largely consisted.'[2] And a report on Fabian lectures prepared by a special committee of the Executive some seventeen years later[3] maintained that this activity was still the most effective form of political education practised by the Society, providing lessons on 'important public questions, or on matters relating to Socialist opinion', not only for the members themselves but also for more general audiences among the nation at large.

Because of the manifold importance it attached to lecturing, it is necessary in any examination of the Society's artistic concerns to see how far, and in what ways, these were reflected in the lecturing programmes. Clues to the relationship are provided by what we know of the substance of Fabian lectures to various kinds of audience in various places, the nature of the audiences' response, and the lecturing styles which were adopted both to instruct and entertain these audiences. Close examination of these things brings out an unsuspected 'artistic side' to the Fabians'

192

personalities which many of them may have suppressed or have failed to develop were it not for the opportunities and pretexts provided by their membership of the Society.

For a group which is normally depicted as having no real concern with the arts, at least on a collective level, the Fabian Society spent a remarkable amount of time talking about them and their creators. The fullest details we have on the topics of the Fabian lectures come from the minute-books and press reports of the main London branch. It is extremely difficult to fit many of these topics into discrete subject categories ('political', 'economic', 'social' and so on) but any attempt to isolate those lectures which, by virtue of their title and reported substance, can be said to have dealt with a predominantly artistic theme or to have drawn mainly on literary and artistic material should yield roughly the following results. The total number of lectures on all subjects delivered before the London branch in the period 1884-1918 was 493; and of these, 42 (or about 8.5%) could be categorized as 'artistic' in their subject-matter, according to the criteria just mentioned. This overall figure, however, conceals enormous variations in the trend from year to year (see Table 1).

Table 1 *Percentages of lectures relating to literary or artistic material, delivered to central London branch of the Fabian Society 1884-1918*

Years	Per cent	Years	Per cent	Years	Per cent
1884-85	0	1899	30.00	1908	7.7
1886	6.3	1900	9.8	1909-10	0
1887	0	1901	35.7	1911	13.3
1888	5.6	1902	21.4	1912-13	0
1889	5.3	1903	0	1914	20.00
1890	28.00	1904	9.1	1915	0
1891-96	0	1905	14.3	1916	12.5
1897	6.3	1906	28.6	1917	0
1898	35.8	1907	6.7	1918	0

Possible reasons for the fluctuations in these figures are discussed below. It needs to be said straightaway that the criteria adopted in arriving at them are probably as arbitrary as those which would have to be used in defining other, 'non-artistic' categories of Fabian lecture-subjects. If, however, they provide only a very crude index of the degree of attention given to the arts by Fabians in their group activities, they err largely on the conservative side. For one thing, they exclude any lectures which dealt primarily with subject-matter beyond the confines of art yet which touched on artistic themes implicitly or incidentally. It would be impossible to calculate the exact number of these; but from what information is available in the brief reports of lectures given in the *Fabian News* and elsewhere, we know there were several such examples over the whole period in question.[4] What these particular lectures demonstrate — through their very lack of direct concentration on artistic themes — are the intimate relationship which Fabians tended to see between aesthetic or literary questions and all the other kinds of questions (educational, religious and moral, as well as social, economic and political) that were bound up with their socialist beliefs.

Yet if it is clear that Fabians talked more about the arts in their meetings than we might have expected from the Society's philistine reputation, does the kind of talk they engaged in effectively dispel that reputation? Some of the statements made by leading members of the Society regarding the Fabians' attitudes to art in their lectures could be seen in one light as supporting the charge of philistinism. The reasons given by Hubert Bland, for example, when he withdrew his offer to prepare a lecture on the writings of Maxim Gorky, might easily suggest that the Fabians' conception of art and of its relationship with other questions of the day was, if anything, *too* inclusive, precluding any appreciation of literature or the other arts on their own terms and from an aesthetic viewpoint. One would have thought that the anti-establishment stance and polemical force of the Russian novelist would have made his work a particularly appropriate subject for Fabian audiences. It was all the stranger, then, that after some reflection Bland should have found Gorky to be quite inappropriate, precisely on the grounds that the latter was 'mainly, if not entirely, an impressionist', with no 'substratum of philosophy' which Bland could 'hitch on to the Fabian Society'. It was 'no use whatever,' he explained to Edward Pease, 'giving a lecture of art and literary criticism'.[5]

This does not necessarily reflect the view of all members of the Society. Bland's reasoning, in fact, could in itself have become a subject of dispute over the role of the Society and its lectures, though Pease seems to have let the matter drop. Pease's own motivation, however — or, in this instance, lack of motivation — hardly helps to redeem the Society's philistine reputation. While he busied himself, both before and afterwards, with arranging various other lectures on artistic and literary subjects, his attitude towards them and their relationship to the Society's other interests appears to have been far less serious-minded than Bland's. Their significance for him lay precisely in the fact that they could be disconnected from the Fabians' primary concerns and provide the needs of certain members for a pleasant confection in their otherwise fairly heavy lecturing diet. When organizing a series in 1905 on 'Prophets of the

Nineteenth Century', he explained to R.C.K. Ensor that he wanted 'somewhat lighter lectures to mix in with the more serious matters dealt with ... [W]e find it desirable to have occasionally literary lectures in order to keep up the interest of our less scientific members.'[6]

Many years earlier, following the first major series of literary lectures in 1890, Bernard Shaw dismissed them as just a hastily arranged expedient designed to fill out the summer meetings of the Society. The Fabian Essayists were among those pressed to contribute 'something or other' to the series, but they proved rather reluctant to do so, by Shaw's account, and there was an air of perfunctoriness and fecklessness about the whole proceedings: 'The Society tided over the summer without having to close its doors; but also without having added anything to the general stock of information on "Socialism in Contemporary Literature".'[7]

From this scatter of opinions on the aims and actual functioning of Fabian lectures on artistic subjects, it would appear that they amounted to no more than a form of light relief for less rigorous members of the Society, and that if the more rigorous members envisaged any greater importance for the arts as a focus of Fabian discussion, it lay in areas beyond the realm of aesthetic appreciation. Both of these attitudes could be used to explain the rather erratic incidence of Fabian lectures devoted specifically to artistic subjects.

There is, however, a good deal of evidence elsewhere to suggest that the Fabian Society as a whole (including some of the leading spokesmen just quoted) were able to regard and to treat artistic themes in lectures with a seriousness that did not rule out a genuine sensitivity to aesthetic qualities and pleasures.

To begin with, there are considerable grounds for doubting the accuracy of Shaw's rather derisive account of the Society's first series of 'literary lectures'. Judging from the audience's response, at least, they seem to have been far from the lacklustre occasions which Shaw depicted. The minute-books of the Society's meetings reveal that at least two of the seven lectures (Sergei Stepniak's on Tolstoy and the Russian school, and Shaw's on Ibsen) attracted a very large crowd,[8] and that sufficient interest was generated on each of the seven occasions to provoke a number of luminaries in the Society — including the allegedly reluctant Fabian Essayists — to contribute to the discussion afterwards. Two of the Essayists besides Shaw delivered lectures in the series: Olivier on Zola and Bland on 'The Protest of Literature and Sentiment'. And of all their number, only William Clarke is not listed as having made any comments on the points raised. Sidney Webb spoke up after five of the lectures (Dryhurst's on 'Bax, Kirkup, Gronlund and Bellamy' and Morris's on 'Gothic Architecture', as well as Stepniak's, Shaw's and Bland's, mentioned above).[9] This is quite an impressive record — surpassing that of all his colleagues in fact — for a man usually characterized as having no interest in art and literature. Pease still had sufficient interest at this stage to contribute to the discussion of two of the lectures (William Boulting's on 'Karl Pearson and Edward Carpenter' and Dryhurst's);[10] and his very silence on the occasion of Shaw's lecture was a testimony to its enormously powerful impact on himself and the rest of the audience. In 1916, when his own interest in the arts had long since waned, Pease could still account Shaw's discourse on Ibsen as 'perhaps . . . the high water-mark in Fabian lectures . . . [T]he effect on the packed audience was overwhelming. It was ''briefly discussed'' by a number of speakers, but they seemed as out of place as a debate after an oratorio.'[11] There were controversial aspects of Shaw's lecture which Pease does not mention. For instance, Annie Besant, who was in the chair, 'protested strongly' against some of Shaw's more provocative statements, though his replies to her were 'applauded far more than her protestation'.[12] At any rate, the very hostility which the lecture provoked in this and other quarters[13] is as weighty a testimony to its impact as the enthusiasm accorded it.

When devising lecture-programmes, the Executive Committee of the Society appears to have been guided to some extent by considerations of topicality, but another important consideration was the availability of appropriate lecturers for the subjects concerned, especially when a whole series had to be arranged. This evidently proved to be a problem when attempts were made to extend the second literary series of 1898-9 and to organize a further literary series in 1900.[14] The same problem might help account for the longish gap between the first and second series.

It was a sign of the seriousness with which the Executive came to regard literary topics that in the report on Fabian lectures which it issued in 1911, it should have given a top ('A') classification to all 'Literary questions bearing on Socialism'. Lectures in this category — which also included those on colonial and military questions, municipal administration, the 'Relation of Philosophy and Religion to Socialism' and 'Socialist Theory and Methods' — were to be 'given by distinguished persons whether Socialists or not with the object of educating ourselves and the public on questions of general public interest'. The usual number of lectures in this class was put at 'four to six per year', and, the Report re-emphasized, 'only the best-known and accredited persons should be asked to give them'.[15] This sort of demand must have added to the normal difficulties of finding willing and suitable speakers. 'B' class lectures had to be fitted into the repertoire, too — about the 'same number' as Class A ones. These concentrated on the practical application of socialist theory to a wide range of financial, commercial, industrial and municipal activities; and did not require as distinguished a group of speakers. (Any willing member of the Society was considered fit to handle them.) They nonetheless took up a good deal of the Fabians' time, so that it was inevitable perhaps that a whole series devoted to one of the more exalted subjects — literary or otherwise — should only crop up every now and then.

The systematic division into 'A' and 'B' class lectures prescribed in the 1911 Report only formalized a traditional Fabian practice of offering as varied a range of subjects and speakers as the socialist 'Basis' of the Society would accommodate. And that 'Basis' was broad and flexible enough to be very accommodating — perhaps too accommodating at times for the word 'socialist' to retain much precision in a Fabian context. There was a persistent, underlying pressure on the Executive to devise a lecture programme sufficiently wide and balanced to attract the motley range of socialists, or potential converts to socialism, who came within the Fabian Society's orbit. The erratic incidence of lectures devoted to artistic subjects was not the reflection of a merely half-hearted interest in those particular subjects so much as a result of the general pressures and problems involved in administering any extensive programme.

It says little for the doctrinal rigour of the Fabians, but perhaps rather more for their responsiveness to the arts, that socialism was far from being an exclusive focus for their discussions in lectures on artistic subjects. In a literal sense, Shaw was not exaggerating when he said that the first series of literary lectures added nothing to the store of knowledge on 'Socialism in Contemporary Literature': William Morris disregarded this title altogether in choosing to contribute a talk on 'Gothic Architecture'; and Shaw himself, while at least sticking to a prominent representative of 'Contemporary Literature', made no attempt to isolate even broad strands of socialism in the writings of Ibsen but on the contrary placed all his emphasis on the divergences between present-day socialists and the Norwegian dramatist.[16] Although the series for which Shaw's lecture provided such a stunning climax may have failed to live up to its tendentious title, it did not thereby fail to be of general interest to those who called themselves socialists.

The second series did not have a title at all; it was referred to simply as a 'literary course'.[17] Its subjects did not even have the controversial value which Ibsen had provided in the early 1890s, when his plays had opened to morally outraged reviews from the bulk of London critics. Zola, the subject of lectures by Sydney Olivier both in the 1890 series and the 1898 series, had by the second occasion lost much of the notoriety attaching to his name through the obscenity trial of his English publisher at the end of the eighties;[18] though he still had some topical value owing to his recent denunciation of the French military authorities for their handling of the Dreyfus case. Olivier, in his second lecture, made clear from his title that he would be dealing with the French novelist not only as a 'Doctrinaire' but also as an 'Artist'. Zola's books, we have seen, were a favourite with

Olivier from his youth. This did not make him uncritical, particularly of what he saw as the novelist's artistic deficiencies. In lesser works, Olivier claimed, Zola had failed to find 'a method for effective artistic expression of his motive purpose'. *Dr. Pascal* was a case in point. Here, Olivier maintained, Zola 'dogmatically asserts, without any attempt to suggest the assertion by dominating the feeling of the reader'. These strictures were not to be applied to major works such as *Germinal*, where the author's accusations against the established order 'from the point of view of Utopian Socialism' had been made through 'powerful artistic methods'.[19] At bottom, artistic power was a more important criterion for Olivier than socialist commitment in judging the overall achievement of an author. In lecturing, in the same series, on George Meredith, another of his youthful favourites, Olivier spoke of the 'refractory and unedifying result' of attempting 'to focus Socialist doctrine in Mr Meredith's novels'.[20]

'Tolstoy and Socialism' was the specific subject of a lecture by G.H. Perris in the second series; though there is little information on the type of relationship he discerned between artist and doctrine. In dealing, in the same series, with Dostoevsky, J.M. Robertson praised his novels for their 'complete subordination of doctrine to art'. Their 'artistic power of sensation and reproduction', Robertson claimed, had never been 'surpassed in the literature of the world'. This only made the 'indictment of society' to be found in Dostoevsky's novels 'all the more decisive'. His 'would-be propagandist books were, as such, failures'.[21]

Robertson was a guest lecturer, and not a member of the Fabian Society, though he had had unofficial links with it in the early days through his associations with Annie Besant, for whose journal, *Our Corner*, he had written several articles on literature. It is not surprising that a professional literary critic such as himself should have placed the weight of his emphasis on aesthetic values. There is no doubt that most Fabians who lectured the Society on artistic subjects, and several of the guest lecturers too, placed greater weight on the 'social teaching' of artists. This provided the specific subject and title for a lecture on Thomas Hardy in the second series, and for a whole series on 'Modern Drama' in 1901-2. Some of the lectures in the drama series drew very large audiences indeed, bearing out predictions that it would be 'one of the most interesting and fruitful that the Society has arranged of late years'.[22]

What, precisely, Fabian audiences found interesting in such lectures is not at all clear from the available résumés and reports; what is clear is that very few of the lecturers concerned, wherever they placed their particular emphasis, contrived to divorce the social teaching of their subject from its qualities and development as an art form. H.W. Macrosty's lecture on George Gissing, in the second literary series, was the exception rather than the rule in the way it set up a quite arbitrary distinction, from the outset, between the writer's 'literary merits' and his 'work as a sociologist', and nowhere hinted at any connection between them.

The same example shows, however, that the Fabians were not so tendentious in their concentration on the social teaching of artists as to consider only socialist teaching. Gissing was further from being a socialist than Ibsen; Macrosty freely admitted that his chosen author could not even be considered a democrat or a believer in progress. Yet, 'since Dickens, no writer has shown so intimate a knowledge of the lower and middle class',[23] and this was what made his work of particular sociological interest to the Fabians.

Dickens himself was one of the most commonly-discussed subjects in Fabian lectures on artistic subjects, ranking in popularity with many artists who had rather more direct connections with socialist movements or ideas (Shelley, Kingsley, Ruskin, Morris, Wagner, Tolstoy, Whitman, Bellamy). Aside from Dickens and Gissing, there were innumerable other non-socialist (even anti-socialist) artists who cropped up at least once or twice as subjects for Fabian lectures, either in London or in the provincial branches. Dostoevsky, Eliot, Conrad, Browning, Tennyson, Meredith and Hardy were only the most notable of these; and they were not confined solely to contemporaries or near-contemporaries. This was shown even in the series on 'Modern Drama', which contrived to include Euripides in its brief — partly owing perhaps to the availability of a particularly distinguished classics lecturer, Gilbert Murray.

Whatever the reasons in this case, Fabian lecture programmes as a whole did not include artistic subjects solely because of their direct application to socialism or even their general sociological significance. Another reason lay in the peculiar kinds of pleasure, at once elevating and entertaining, which certain artists and certain art forms were seen to provide for Fabian audiences. The nature of an artist's ideological bent was not an irrelevant consideration here, but not a crucial one either. No such 'objective' or dogmatic standards were applied by the Society and its speakers. This is shown no more vividly than in the strange case of Hubert Bland, who, we have seen, could reject Gorky as an inappropriate topic for a Fabian lecture yet who was able, only two years earlier, to deliver an extremely enthusiastic lecture on Rudyard Kipling. The enthusiasm which he tried to convey to his fellow-Fabians had much less to do with any specific philosophy of Kipling's that could be harnessed to the Society's concerns than with the sheer exhilaration to be found in reading the Anglo-Indian's poems and short stories.

Kipling, certainly, had no socialist pretensions, and Bland could sum up his thematic relevance for the Fabian Society only in the most vague, general terms: the resolute 'modernism' of Kipling's beliefs coupled with his 'reaction against sentimental humanitarianism'. It would have been indelicate, if not dangerous, to go into some of the precise manifestations of this, such as Kipling's jingoist inclinations; for while some of the Fabians themselves shared these in a muted or covert form, and managed to accommodate them within their socialism, there were others who could not endorse or condone their country's more aggressively imperialist ventures. Only a few years before, some of the anti-imperialist faction had actually resigned from the Society because of its failure to condemn the Boer War.[24] Bland, wisely, did not spell out any of these issues but passed quickly on to a consideration of Kipling's skills as a writer. If his lecture never quite lapsed into 'mere literary criticism', such as he said would happen in dealing with an 'impressionist' like Gorky, it remained very largely in the mould of a belletristic appreciation, lavishly praising here, mildly chiding there, mainly with reference to such conventional literary-critical preoccupations as form, style and content.

Kipling's first work, *Departmental Ditties*, while full of humour, high spirits and an 'extraordinary facility of phrase', was 'largely jingle', Bland wrote. On the other hand, the *Barrack-Room Ballads*, published in 1892, 'proclaimed a new poet, who accepts the modern world, Tramways, Trade Unions and all'. As far as Kipling's prose-works were concerned, one could find 'nearly every fault but dullness', but when these had all been admitted, there still remained 'a stoutish volume of the best short stories ever told in the English language'. According to the syllabus of this lecture, Bland went on to give an excursus on 'the short-story as an art-form'. He discussed, in particular, Kipling's stories of Indian life, and claimed that the author had been the first man to bring that country's 'arid regions of knowledge into the fertile and stimulating kingdom of the imagination'.[25]

Bland, as noted above, considered the degree of emotional 'thrill' given by a work of art to be the essential factor in determining one's response to it; he obviously got a strong, personal thrill from Kipling's writings, and it was this unashamedly subjective feeling of pleasure which provided the chief animating impulse behind Bland's choice of topic and his whole presentation of that topic. As in his theories, so in his practice, Bland may have represented an extreme in Fabian approaches to the arts, rather than the norm, but it is an extreme worth dwelling on because of the way in which it forces us to re-examine the norm, and leads us to question whether any such thing existed. An examination of various other Fabian lectures on the arts shows that Bland's choice of a non-socialist author, and his attention to the aesthetic pleasures (and deficiencies) of that author's work, did not reflect any fundamental difference of approach; yet, among all the lectures concerned, there were so many differences in degree in working out this approach that it would be impossible to fix on any of the Society's treatments of artistic topics as being 'normal' or 'the most characteristic'. Even in the various literary series, as distinct from individual lectures, conformity of treatment was not encouraged, certainly not enjoined; and the resultant inconsistencies were perhaps the best guarantee of sensitivity to the very different kinds of literature being discussed.

If anything was consistently characteristic about Fabian approaches to art, as represented in their lectures, it was the attention given to literature in particular. Literary subjects, including all topics on drama and the theatre, accounted for two thirds of the total number of art lectures given by the central branch of the Fabian Society. Table 2 gives a fuller picture.

Table 2 *Classification of arts lectures delivered to main branch of Fabian Society*

| Date | A | | | | B | C | D | E | F |
	Aa	Ab	Ac	Ad					
1886									1
1888									1
1889				1					
1890	1	3		2			1		
1897	1								
1898		4			1				
1899	1	2							
1900									1
1901	3	1						1	
1902	2								1
1904					1				
1905			1	1					
1906			2						2
1907						1			
1908								1	
1911	1	1							1
1914	1								1
1916									1
Totals	10	11	3	4	2	1	1	2	9
		28							

Key: A — Literature
Aa — Drama and/or theatre;
Ab — Fiction and fiction writers;
Ac — Poetry and poets;
Ad — General literary subjects or subjects associated with more than one literary genre.
B — Music and composers.

C — Domestic arts and crafts.
D — Architecture.
E — Town planning/Garden cities.
F — General or miscellaneous subjects relating to art.

Apart from the preponderance of literary topics, two things are striking about this table: the complete absence of any lectures devoted specifically to painting or sculpture, and the dearth of lectures on those more functional arts (categories C-E) in which the so-called 'utilitarian' Fabians might have been expected to show most interest. More than incidental coverage of these genres could have been given in some of the lectures on art in general (category F); but however great that coverage might have been, it would not alter, significantly, the imbalance in the figures between literary lectures and the rest. It cannot be concluded from these figures alone — such are the perils of mere quantification — that the Fabians were in fact much less interested in the non-literary and non-dramatic arts. To begin with, their preoccupations in lectures — either as speakers or part of an audience — did not necessarily reflect their more general interests outside the confines of the lecture programme, nor their private tastes as individuals. And there were other compelling reasons, apart from the members' basic interest in the subject-matter concerned, why literary topics in particular should have predominated.

The chief function of Fabian lectures, as summed up in the report on them which the Society issued in 1911, was to act as a medium of education, propaganda and discussion on socialist and other issues, for the benefit not only of members but also of the public at large. Of all the arts, imaginative literature was perhaps the best equipped to fulfil this function. As a means of public communication, it was undoubtedly the most pervasive: through printed texts, able to be reproduced on a mass scale, the works of a particular writer were much more generally accessible than those of a painter, sculptor or composer. The appreciation of a play could no doubt be heightened by seeing that play performed (and many Fabians, as we have seen, were actively involved in staging drama); but the appreciation of music has always been much more dependent on performance, and in the days before the mass-production of gramophones and records the opportunities for hearing performances were restricted mainly to concerts or private recitals. The opportunities for appreciating fully a particular painting or piece of sculpture would have been restricted by the need to view those works where they happened to be exhibited; an adequate, second-hand appreciation through photographs is now possible, but the Fabians' heyday preceded the advent of the inexpensive 'coffee-table book' and commercial slide-pack. It also preceded the paperback revolution, but members of the Society (especially of the London branch) would easily have been able to find copies of the major works of drama, fiction and poetry in their local libraries, and there were always editions cheap enough for interested individuals — especially those on middle-class incomes — to own privately. Finally, as Sidney Webb pointed out in one of his earliest lectures, literature in general was a branch of art which required 'less technical knowledge for its appreciation than others'.[26]

For these reasons, it provided the Fabians with a particularly wide and convenient focus for informed discussion. Much more easily than in the case of music or the visual arts, lecture audiences were able to acquire some authoritative foreknowledge of a literary subject, and also to go away afterwards and study the subject for themselves, so that concentration on this branch of the arts would have been particularly effective in facilitating the self-education of members and the interested public.

For propagandist purposes, posters and cartoons might be considered more effective than imaginative literature — in the short run at least — because of their simple message and punchy immediacy. These same qualities, however, made such media rather less suitable as whole subjects for lectures (unless the treatment was to be historical or iconographical[27]) and less congenial to the sensibilities of those middle-class professionals at whom the Fabian Society directed most of its propaganda. Something with more subtlety and outward refinement, as well as greater intellectual substance, was required to stimulate the minds and flatter the vanities of an average Fabian audience, though they were not above finding 'exceptional pleasure', of an almost entirely aesthetic kind it would seem, in posters on display.[28]

The lack of sustained or specific attention to architecture and the domestic crafts is less easy to explain, because William Morris had shown, through his own lectures, how effectively a concern for these arts could be made a part of socialist propaganda. But a continual consciousness of these connections perhaps required the living example of his all-embracing genius; and Morris was dead by 1896. He was not without influential followers in the Fabian Society, from the Essayists of 1889 to Arthur Clutton Brock, author of the Fabian tract on the 'Arts of Use' in 1915;[29] but none of them was a dedicated, practising craftsman in the way Morris had been. For all their interest in other arts, they were essentially literary men, who, except through their writing, could not yoke together their artistic and political concerns as Morris had done. 'Language,' the future Mrs Webb observed in 1883 (before the Fabian Society had even got off the ground), 'is the ordinary medium for influence in practical life';[30] and in this respect, as in so many others, Morris had operated on a level that was quite *extra*ordinary.

By being centred in such a large metropolis, London Fabians were lucky at least in having ready access to the brightest talents among those who specialized in 'the ordinary medium'. Some of these talents were right in their midst. Not only well-known speakers, but also a number of the best-known writers (including Shaw, Wells, Granville Barker and Arnold Bennett) were themselves members at one time or other of the main London branch of the Fabian Society. Yet even this branch, we have seen,

experienced difficulties at various times in getting hold of sufficiently
distinguished speakers for its prospective lectures on literary subjects.
These difficulties must have been considerably greater for provincial
branches, especially for those outside the major university towns.[31] The
factor of distance would have compounded all the normal administrative
problems.

Any records of the lectures delivered at provincial branches are, in fact,
extremely hard to come by, and not nearly as complete as those for
London — a testimony in itself to the relative fragility of these branches.
Minute-books are extant for Fabian Society meetings of various years at
Edinburgh, Sheffield and the universities of Oxford and Cambridge;
though it is impossible to deduce from these alone any pattern of regional
variations in the number and type of lectures delivered on artistic subjects.
Looking for a pattern in these branches' own lecturing habits is fruitless
enough; they seem to have been devoid of any real organizing principle.
Even the idea of a series around a central theme, which became a favoured
method of organization with the main branch, was rarely tried in other
branches, so that a subject relating specifically to the arts would simply
crop up every now and then, as incidentally as subjects relating to
educational or scientific or religious or historical or social and political
issues.

It was not unusual, for example, when the Edinburgh branch in its
winter programme for 1911-12 slipped in a lecture on 'The Social
Significance of Art' between ones on 'The Influence of Heredity and
Environment on the Formation of Human Character' and 'The Salvation
Army'. Prior to this, there had not been any on a subject relating to the
arts for over a year and a half (one on 'The Garden City Movement',
delivered in May 1910, had been the last), but this did not prevent
another from being undertaken (on 'Some Aspects of Robert Burns') only
a month or so afterwards.[32]

The arrangement of lectures at the Sheffield branch (which started up
in 1908) appears to have been just as haphazard. There were talks on and
by Bernard Shaw; the Webbs visited; and a local celebrity in both artistic
and socialist circles, Edward Carpenter, gave a lecture a few months after
being elected a member of the branch. There are no detailed résumés of
the subject matter of these lectures, though from any titles given
(Carpenter's 'Socialism and State Inheritance', for instance) few of them
seem to have been specifically related to the arts even when the speaker
was a practising artist. In 1913, however, sessions on 'Municipal Theatre'
and 'Democracy and Art' were held within the space of a fortnight; and
from early on there were several lectures which probably had some
general application to the arts — for example, Holbrook Jackson's course
of three talks in 1908, which 'to very many listeners . . . assuredly placed

Socialism on a much higher plane than they had been in the habit of thinking of it'.[33]

Owing no doubt to the prestige of the institution which accommodated it, the Oxford University Fabian Society (established in 1895) was able to attract a more impressive range of speakers than ordinary provincial branches. They included not only prominent Fabians: Shaw, the Webbs and Carpenter again; Wallas, Olivier and Bland; Ramsay MacDonald, Charles Charrington, Granville Barker, Stewart Headlam, H.G. Wells. In addition, a large variety of celebrities appeared who had only slender links with the Society or none at all (Keir Hardie, J.A. Hobson, Hilaire Belloc, G.K. Chesterton, and Bertrand Russell, for example). Lectures on artistic subjects were more frequent than at Edinburgh or Sheffield, though not as frequent as at the main branch, and there were none of the literary 'series' to which London Fabians were treated. It was usually the Fabian visitors (or the local branch members) rather than the non-Fabian speakers who treated subjects relating to the arts; and these subjects were a happy-go-lucky miscellany, covering such topics as 'Municipal Theatre' (one of Charrington's hobby-horses); 'Socialism and Literature' (a review of socialist writers from Langland onwards, and including Oscar Wilde who, the speaker acknowledged, 'sometimes savoured of socialism'); and 'Beauty in Civic Life' (Carpenter's subject for the occasion).[34]

There was one series of lectures organized by the Cambridge University branch in 1909, the year after its foundation; but though it included a topic on the arts ('The Aesthetic Ideal'), it was not an artistic or literary series as such, being strung around the very loose theme of 'Ideals' in general. Over the next few years, before the branch outgrew its Fabian origins in 1915 and became known as the Cambridge University Socialist Society, there were a few lectures on a variety of artistic subjects, but nothing very frequent or regular about them.[35]

As with the Oxford branch, the special prestige of the University, and its network of distinguished alumni, enabled the Cambridge branch to attract an extraordinarily distinguished bunch of speakers, Fabian, ex-Fabian and non-Fabian. Many of the same names appear in the records of both university branches. Less fortunately-placed branches could at best hope, in the words of a Fabian organizer at Goldalming, to attract 'a taking name like Wells or Shaw'[36] from within the Society itself; though the timing of a promised visit would still have depended very much on a lecturer's London commitments.

In fact, Shaw and Wells were unable to accept invitations to the Cambridge branch itself, which indicates perhaps that even a venue particularly privileged in other ways could suffer the disadvantages of distance from the capital. There were several other luminaries in the literary and artistic worlds (including Arnold Bennett, G.K. Chesterton,

A.R. Orage, Miles Malleson), who felt constrained at various times to turn down lecture invitations from the Cambridge branch.[37]

The simplest deduction which could be made from the lecture programmes examined above is that the Society's concern with the arts, as manifested in one of its most important agencies of propaganda, was much less intensive outside the confines of the main London branch than inside. It would, however, be very misleading to explain the sparer, and altogether more spasmodic, incidence of Fabian arts lecturing in the provinces solely in these terms. The smallness of the available sample is an obvious difficulty here, though it would be surprising if any further figures that came to light significantly changed the picture.

Administrative and logistic problems in recruiting sufficiently distinguished lecturers for artistic subjects were acute enough anywhere, and were bound to be even more difficult away from the bigger towns such as Edinburgh and Sheffield. Such problems must figure largely in explaining the very uneven 'patterns' of Fabian lecturing in all subjects and in all places (London included). As far as arts lectures in particular are concerned, if the Fabians can be blamed for anything, it is not for a basic lack of concern with the subject-matter but for a certain snobbishness in wanting only big names or experts to treat the range of subjects involved, and a failure to make do with amateur enthusiasts. Indeed, this policy — which became an official one of the central London branch — seems to accord with the group's reputation for élitism. Whether that reputation is wholly justified is a larger question which will be examined in detail in the next part; it needs to be said straightaway, however, that this particular attitude of the Fabians regarding their arts lectures was not just snobbishness; it reflected another quality: their pragmatism and opportunism as socialist permeators. In intention or effect, lectures in general were part propaganda, part education and part pleasure or entertainment; and lectures on the arts, we have seen, were particularly well-equipped for fulfilling each of these functions at one and the same time. They were of special value to the Society, therefore, in attracting converts to socialism who might not be so attracted by some of the Fabians' more mundane preoccupations; even the lecturers involved who came from outside the Society might feel more attracted to it having been given *carte blanche* to air their views within its portals. Particularly distinguished lecturers were not only a potentially good catch in themselves, but could have helped entice otherwise hesitant members of the general public into the Fabian net by providing the promise, if not a guarantee, of a stimulating and enjoyable evening. For provincial branches as much as the central one, it became tactically important perhaps to preserve the aura of promise by exalting arts lectures to the level of a special treat. Geography just made it so much more difficult for provincial branches to supply such a treat as frequently as London.

If there was still, at bottom, less interest in the arts among provincial members than among London ones, that could just as easily reflect a characteristic of national life generally as a distinctively Fabian one. As the nation's capital, cultural as well as political, London undoubtedly offered a more varied array of stimulations to artistic interest, whether professional or dilettantish, creative or critical. In a section of his *History of the Fabian Society*, in which he compared London and the provinces, Edward Pease talked of the superior attractions of the metropolis for 'the young men who aspire to be the next generation of leaders' and dubbed the city 'the brain of the Empire, where reside the leaders in politics and commerce, in literature, in journalism and in art'.[38] However much they might have protested against the squalor and soullessness of London, the most celebrated artists had always tended to gravitate there for at least a part of their working lives; William Morris was perhaps the most notable contemporary example. Part of the stimulation which they found in the metropolis was simply the presence of fellow-artists; the provinces could just not provide congenial company of this kind in such concentration. Obviously the provinces were not devoid of cultural interest, nor in any sense inherently barren; the forerunner of the Fabian Arts Group, after all, was based in Leeds, and must have come to life in the first place because it answered to some need in the area for a particular kind of organized cultural activity. It was, however, soon abandoned by two of its most dynamic members, Jackson and Orage. Frustrated, perhaps, by the limitations of an area remote from the nation's cultural pulse, they decided to try out their organizational skills in London. Simply because of its bigness and greater complexity, London was more challenging and stimulating. Challenge is in itself a part of stimulation, and one of the secrets of London's awful voracity.

The Fabian Arts Group mainly operated through a series of lectures given by distinguished speakers — far more distinguished than the ones which its provincial prototype could have hoped to offer. Yet it survived for only four years. The reasons for its rapid decline are reflected in the very nature of the lecture programme. All that the existent records tell us are the titles of the lectures given and the names of the speakers — and these only for the period February 1907 to June 1908. Yet even in that limited period, the programme gradually moved away not only from any specific relationship to Fabian socialism but also from a direct relationship to the arts. In the months February to December 1907, there were fifteen sessions in all (thirteen lectures, two discussions), of which about eight were related directly to a form of art or a particular artist. (These included a lecture on Tolstoy, given by Aylmer Maude, a Fabian and one of the foremost English translators of Russian novels; lectures on Ibsen by Holbrook Jackson and G.K. Chesterton; lectures on 'The Use of Colour in Architecture' and 'The Philosophy of the Novel'; and lectures by practising artists such as Will Rothenstein — who spoke on 'Some Parallels between Art and Religion' — and W.R. Lethaby of the Arts and Crafts Movement.) In the following year, philosophy, religion and subjects relating to the crafts and Guild Socialism became the main focus of concern, almost to the exclusion of the arts as such. The discussion opened by A.R. Orage on 'Modernism and Romance' was perhaps the only exception.[39] It was one of the ironies of the Arts Group's existence that, after an initial enthusiastic response from the Fabians — according to Pease, its early sessions attracted 'audiences scarcely less numerous than the Society itself'[40] — members soon began to find a more satisfying outlet for their artistic instincts and interests in other quarters of the Society. There is no definite evidence for this, save the fact that other quarters, including the main branch of the Society, kept on providing arts lectures in the traditional ways during the Arts Group's heyday, and that such lectures managed to retain a popular following long after the Group's demise.

The sessions of the Fabian Summer Schools in particular point up the failure of the Arts Group, in that both enterprises were initiated at the same time yet the former survived and flourished for many years after the decline of the latter. True, as the first of the tables below indicate, subjects devoted specifically to the arts never dominated the Schools' lecture-programmes; but they nonetheless formed a substantial part of those pro-grammes, before, during and after the First World War, and some of them proved to be among the most enticing and exciting sessions offered. This is clear from the Schools' carefully kept log-books.

Whenever attendance at these sessions was noted in the log-books, it was said to have been 'large' or 'very large'. Several of them managed to provoke an intense discussion, which would suggest that they were appreciated not simply on the level of a holiday indulgence.[41] As in the case of Shaw's lecture on Ibsen to the main branch of the Society in 1890, audience enthusiasm and involvement could be registered by complete silence as well. Following a lecture delivered by Mrs Despard at the 1909 session on the subject of Shelley's *Prometheus Unbound*, the compiler of the log-book claimed: 'it is difficult to convey any adequate impression of the dramatic intensity of this lecture. One can but say that Mrs Despard held her audience completely for upward of an hour — and at the close her hearers evidently felt that questions would be out of place.'[42]

Having in part a recreational purpose, as well as the obvious educational one, the Schools actually benefited from having a provincial rather than a metropolitan location: it added to the holiday atmosphere. They still had the benefit of all the prestige and planning facilities of the London branch behind them, as it was from that branch that all the preliminary arrangements were made. The Schools were able, therefore, to attract prominent lecturers and guests much more readily than any ordinary provincial branch. Among these were several figures from the artistic, literary and theatrical worlds, including Shaw, William Archer, St John Ervine, Charles Charrington and Janet Achurch, Aylmer Maude, Rupert Brooke, Roger Fry and Rebecca West. The presence of such luminaries in close concentration would occasionally allow a series of lectures to be organized around a common theme — for example, the 'Modern Drama' series at the launching session of the Summer School in 1907.

Subjects relating to drama or the theatre continued to figure largely in the lecture programmes. Tables 3 and 4 show the incidence of lectures devoted specifically to the arts at the Summer Schools, in the period under consideration here, and the numbers of lectures devoted to each of the major artistic and literary genres.

Table 3 *Proportion of lectures devoted to the arts at Fabian Summer Schools 1907-18*[43]

1907	17.1%
1908	4.4%
1909	3.8%
1910	0
1911	0
1912	7.7%
1913	18.5%
1914	17.7%
1915	0
1916	10.3%
1917	21.2%
1918	30.4%

As with the figures for lectures on the arts delivered to the main branch, the fluctuating proportions of such lectures at the annual Summer Schools cannot be taken to represent the actual levels of interest in the subject-matter concerned. These fluctuations were due, again, to a range of mainly contingent factors: first, the need felt by the organizers to offer wide and varying programmes; second, the urgent claims of highly topical issues over those of more general and abiding significance (in 1910, for example, at the height of the Webbs' campaign to abolish the Poor Law, the Schools' sessions were held in association with the National Committee for the Prevention of Destitution, and so tended to concentrate on rather specialist matters of immediate concern to that body); third, the availability of lecturers (the proportion of arts lectures in 1916, for instance, would have been much higher if a number of lecturers

Art, austerity and pleasure

Table 4 *Classification of arts lectures delivered at Fabian Summer Schools 1907-18 — same key as in Table 2*

Date	A				B	C	D	E	F
	Aa	Ab	Ac	Ad					
1907	8	1						1	1
1908									1
1909			2						
1912		1							2
1913	3	1							1
1914		1	1						4
1916	3								
1917	2		1	2	1				1
1918	2	3	1	1					
Totals	18	7	5	3	1	0	0	1	10
		33							

originally invited — Dr Ethel Smythe on 'Tendencies of Modern Music', W.L. George on 'Tendencies of the Modern Novel', and various littérateurs of the calibre of Gilbert Murray, John Galsworthy and Arthur Clutton Brock — had not for one reason or another declared themselves unavailable).[44] Furthermore, there were a number of general series and particular lectures — the sessions on 'The Non-Material Basis of Socialism' in 1915, for instance, or C.H. Norman's 'criticism of Shavianism and of Collectivism generally from the point of view of an anarchist' in 1910 — which were not specifically focussed on art but probably incorporated some broad cultural themes or drew on some artistic or literary sources. There were also many informal discussions on art without a prior lecture;[45] and in the years when there were no discussions or lectures on the arts, the Summer Schools continued to lay on a programme of active artistic pursuits for the visiting Fabians to engage in: singing, dancing, concerts, recitations and play-readings.

It is difficult to know if there were any conscious reasons for the persistent inclusion of drama in the Summer Schools' programmes — whether as an active pursuit or as a subject for lectures and discussions. As people interested in the arts of influencing others, Fabians must have felt a natural attraction to theatre. Its popularity with them also seems to have reflected a highly-developed, if only semi-conscious, histrionic impulse in many of the Society's adherents — and one which they felt relaxed enough about venting to the full in the holiday atmosphere of the Summer Schools. The pure fun of some of the dramatic activities was quite justifiable in this atmosphere, and all the more so because the Schools were not entirely a holiday and members could be recalled to a seriousness of purpose — about drama itself or more mundane topics — in the lecture and discussion sessions.

Ambivalent feelings about drama or the theatre formed an important part of Fabian attitudes to lecturing in general, on whatever subject. For attention to style was as important in its way as the choice of subject-matter in lending potency and plausibility to the Fabians' lectures — and not just verbal style but a vocal and performing style as well, akin to though not the same as the art of dramatic acting.

There is considerable evidence to show that the leading Fabians at least were quite conscious of these artistic components in the lecture-form, and strove conscientiously to master the techniques involved in perfecting the art. From their earliest days they had some splendid models in their midst. Annie Besant was celebrated as an orator long before she became a convert to Fabian socialism in the 1880s. Throughout the previous decade she had preached the doctrines of secularism with a truly religious fervour, worthy of her evangelical education. During the eighties Shaw was quickly acquiring a comparable reputation. His performance as a 'platform artist' — not only at the Fabian Society but at a whole range of venues in and near London — met with considerably greater success than his other artistic enterprise of that decade, novel-writing.[46] By the end of the eighties, he was outdoing Annie Besant herself in courting the favour of lecture audiences. Perhaps (as will be argued below) her elaborate rhetorical style was simply becoming outdated and its effects worn out. Whatever the reasons, her gravely censorious response to Shaw's lecture on Ibsen at the Fabian Society in 1890 met with far less applause than the lecture itself or his subsequent rejoinder to her.[47]

It had required a long and concerted effort on Shaw's part to bring his speaking powers up to the level of a high art; his early years as a public speaker had brought him much more pain than pleasure. Beneath his 'air of impudence', he confessed, he had been 'nervous and self-conscious to a heart-breaking degree'. Only an irrepressible volubility enabled him to open his mouth in the first place, but that did nothing to conquer the 'hidden terror' which remained. A torturing routine of forcing himself to speak whenever the opportunity offered, in whatever unlikely circumstance or place, eventually succeeded in giving him the scintillating self-confidence which became his trademark.[48] The memory of that routine no doubt lay behind the words of a character in Shaw's late play, *Geneva*: 'Public oratory,' Bardo Bombardone declares, 'is a fine art. Like other fine arts, it cannot be practised effectively without a laboriously acquired technique', covering 'style', 'gestures' and 'modulations of . . . voice'.[49]

In some senses, it was a more subtle and demanding technique than stage acting, or at least the kind of stage acting to which the early Fabians would have been most accustomed to seeing in their youth. Passionate declamation of another's words and thoughts was not sufficient to impress the audience in a lecture-hall. When William Clarke, in his introduction to a book of famous political speeches, described oratory as 'the art of persuasion through a human voice', he could just as easily have been describing the highly rhetorical mode of Victorian acting, of which Sir Henry Irving had been the great exponent; but Clarke also stressed the additional — and, in some cases, antithetical — qualities required: 'practical wisdom', 'simplicity' and 'moral feeling'.[50] Shaw explicitly warned aspiring public speakers to avoid the model of 'the old actor who professes to teach acting, and knows nothing of phonetic speech training', for 'art must conceal its artificiality'.[51]

In 1912 Shaw's views were reiterated, with some qualifications, by another of the original Fabian Essayists, Graham Wallas. He had long since quit the Society but was invited back to lecture its 'Speakers Class' on the subject of 'The Psychology of Propaganda'. This, no doubt, was not only because of his expertise as a political psychologist but also because of his own reputation as a lecturer 'with no affectation of either don or cleric, and with an athletic enunciation'.[52] In his talk to the Fabian Speakers' Class, Wallas referred to the 'laws of beauty in rhetoric', but claimed that 'English audiences distrust oratory as a fine art'. A subtle simplicity of approach, as suggested both by Clarke and Shaw in their different ways, was the solution to this problem, but it was in itself partly an artistic strategy. 'Rhetoric,' Wallas advised, 'should be kept just below the point where they [the audiences] are likely to recognize it as rhetoric'; and he went on to quote Shaw regarding the importance of 'artistic sincerity' as much as of 'intellectual' and 'emotional' sincerity: 'one should toil at one's speeches . . . as a good actor toils at his part'.[53]

It is important to consider more closely the relationship between lecturing and acting as demonstrated by the Fabians' experiences and attitudes. There is a sense in which the art of platform oratory — not simply from the speaker's point of view but from the audience's as well — was a surrogate form of theatre, just as writing an 'artistic' sociological report became a surrogate form of novel-writing for Beatrice Webb. Outside observers of Fabian gatherings sometimes felt as if they were watching an actual play. Attending one of the Society's Friday-evening lecture-meetings in 1895, a reporter from the *Sunday Times* described it as

a new and highly original after-dinner entertainment . . . — one compared with which all that a music hall or Oscar Wilde can offer . . . is tame and dull . . . You may reckon, if not always on a good play, at least on an excellent performance. There are unrehearsed Fabian plays as brilliant as 'Arms and the Man' that never get beyond the Fabian footlights.[54]

Another journalist, attending a lecture of Stewart Headlam's nearly ten years later, explicitly compared its final moments, including the rousing cheers it received from the audience, to 'the "curtain" on one of Mr Bernard Shaw's plays'.[55] When the comic novelist, Jerome K. Jerome, joined the Society in 1907, he was immediately (though not very favourably) struck by the theatrical atmosphere of a Fabian meeting, which Shaw's presence in particular, he claimed, did much to engender.[56]

From at least the time of Shakespeare, theatrical metaphors have been applied to all kinds of human and social interaction, however quotidian; and the notion of political activity as a form of theatre has been particularly popular. These metaphors have been given almost scientific legitimacy through the findings of various social anthropologists, psychologists and political theorists.[57] On the surface, the behaviour of the Fabians in their group activities provides an extraordinary example of the practical realization of these metaphors. But Fabian lectures and meetings were not just theatrical occasions, and the art of lecturing was not solely derived from the theatre. There is evidence to show, in fact, that the Fabians, in the years of the Society's prime, tried consciously to make that art a more independent one.

In the first decade of the Society's existence, there was a mock-parliament organized, in which the leading members (including Shaw, Webb, Annie Besant, Bland and Headlam) practised their oratorical skills by assuming the roles of various cabinet-ministers debating crucial issues of the day.[58] Not only were debates and discussions on political issues held — that is, mock-debates, though the issues were real enough — but mock-parties were organized as well, in order to provide a structure for the debates; mock-governments were installed (a Socialist government, with its Fabian cabinet, defeating and replacing a Liberal administration); mock-bills, 'of a decidedly heroic character', were introduced by the new government as a focus for fresh debate; and there was an imitation 'Queen's Speech' to launch the whole proceedings.[59] A column in Annie Besant's journal, *Our Corner*, reported the proceedings *à la* Hansard.

It is tempting, and not implausible, to explain this faithful recreation of Westminster in the jargon of popular psychology: as a form of wish-fulfilment through role-playing. Owing in part to their relative anonymity in the early days of the Society, the Fabians who participated in the Charing Cross Parliament were denied direct access to the real thing. As preparatory exercises for the day when some of its own members might be elected to Westminster, the Fabian cabinet's activities may well have served a useful, long-range purpose. Compared to its Westminster model, however, it remained (in the words of one outside observer) 'a body from which no practical results are expected'.[60] All of the legislative successes in the Charing Cross Parliament were, as another observer put it, simply 'make-believe'.[61] The sessions were less an occasion for political action than for acting politics; they represented a form of amateur theatricals as well as an amateur parliament. This is not to deny their significance for the Fabians, but that significance lay as much in the artistic pleasures they represented as in any political purposes they might have served.

As is always the case with the Fabians, it is hard to draw a hard and fast line between such things; but in the recollections of one, very active participant, the sessions of the Charing Cross Parliament were more memorable as a performance of a make-believe situation than as a rehearsal for a real one. Annie Besant, who assumed the role of Home Secretary in the Fabian Cabinet, and who was apparently the initiator and guiding spirit of the whole enterprise,[62] recounted with affectionate relish the crusades and battles fought within the Charing Cross Parliament, but summed it up simply as a source of 'some amusement'.[63] For her, at least, the sheer fun of role-playing which the mock-parliament provided would seem to have exceeded any serious sense of fulfilment which the roles might have given in realizing the players' own fantasies of political power.

Her recollections could still be misleading as a guide to other participants' motives and feelings and even as a complete account of her own impulses of the time when the Charing Cross Parliament was in full flight. By the time her recollections appeared — the early 1890s — she had already given up any conventional political ambitions, having decided to devote her life to the theosophical religion. And even before the Charing Cross Parliament had been established, she of all the Fabians was the least in need of the political training and oratorical experience it could offer participants. It was easy enough, then, for her to play down its significance in these respects. But in depicting the passionate performances which animated this amateur parliament as no more than an amusement, she managed to play down its full artistic significance as well. This might have been a symptom of her covert puritanism, discussed above. Histrionics as fun were innocent enough, but they were not to be taken too seriously on their own account. Such reservations about the theatrical arts, even in the act of enjoying them, is not directly discernible in Annie Besant, though, as we shall see, they clearly bothered several of her fellow-Fabians. Much of the significance of the Charing Cross Parliament lay precisely in the way it satisfied the dramatic instincts of the participants while assuaging (temporarily at least) their guilt about these. The fulfilment of these instincts could be explained away as simple fun or as serving an ulterior political purpose, such as a training in real parliamentary procedure.

Though the records are vague as to when it came to an end, the Charing Cross Parliament does not seem to have survived into the 1890s. It is difficult to account for this in view of the pleasures it gave and the wider purposes it appeared to serve. One reason may simply have been the loss, with Mrs Besant's apostasy, of its original guiding spirit. Mary Forster, the observer who remarked on its 'make-believe' successes, offered a more general reason. Herself a member of the Fabian Society in the 1890s, she claimed that it had 'more serious work' to attend to in that decade which left members 'no leisure' for make-believe.[64] Certainly, as this statement demonstrates, the Society's sense of self-importance in the world of politics was increasing in the 1890s. (It is much more questionable whether its actual importance, as judged by its influence on political parties and municipal authorities, was increasing at the same rate.)[65] It may be that the experience of the Charing Cross Parliament served to boost the Society's confidence in its capacity for political manoeuvering, but having gained that confidence of maturity, its members came to look on the games and fantasies of their greener days as serving no further purpose. Guilt about their weakness for the pleasures associated with such activities was no longer so easily assuaged. None of the Fabians was as puritanical as, say, the Claphamites had been. (The Sect's sabbatarianism was a religious and social tradition against which, as we have seen, some of the most prominent Fabians, including Annie Besant, launched a vigorous campaign.) A suspicion of the stage and its performers was nonetheless evident in the case of several Fabians, reflecting (and in turn feeding) a certain distaste for their own, or their fellow-members', histrionic impulses.

Beatrice Webb had a gaunt, aristocratic *hauteur* combined with an exotic handsomeness which might have given her considerable stage presence. If she had ever entertained any theatrical ambitions (while taking part in the amateur dramatics of her youth, for instance), they had been effectively suppressed by her mother's ascetic scruples and her own adolescent bout of puritanism. A desire to become a novelist lingered on, but there is no evidence of any hankering to become an actress. When, however, the occasion demanded, Beatrice could easily play the *grande dame*, and was only to be outmatched in the role by the true professional. In a meeting with Mrs Patrick Campbell — hilariously recounted in the diaries of C.R. Ashbee[66] — Beatrice at first could do nothing but sit quietly and seethe within at the actress's grandly trivial social performance; but even when she could stand no more of it and attempted, in retaliation, to put on her own 'most Webby manner', it proved to be of no avail against the flamboyance of a practised upstager. There was too much dignified reserve, too much self-restraint, about Beatrice's performance to counter effectively the power and dazzle of high vulgarity, and she was still disarmed perhaps by a vestigial feeling that 'it is not womanly to thrust yourself before the world'. These words she had committed to her diary as far back as 1887 in reaction against another woman performer — none other than Annie Besant. Beatrice admitted that there were some 'fine' and 'genuine' qualities to be found in Mrs Besant, but there was also something off-puttingly 'artificial' about the outward manner she adopted — an impression, indeed, of 'acting a part'. She was 'the only real orator' of her sex possessing an undoubted 'gift of public persuasion', but 'to *see* her speaking,' Beatrice confessed, 'made me shudder'.[67]

This was at the time when the Charing Cross Parliament was in full swing and a few years before Beatrice's own initiation into the Fabian Society. Time did not abate her suspicion of the histrionic style, especially as adopted by those involved in politics, nor was the sex of the performer concerned a crucial consideration in her judgment. With scarcely-veiled irony — though also with an element of genuine awe and wonder — she observed of Ramsay MacDonald in 1924: 'as a political performer he is showing himself a consummate artist. We never realized he had genius in that direction.' In a more exasperated mood, she dismissed the former Fabian who had come to lead the first Labour Government as 'an egoist, a poseur, and snob' whose very socialism was no more than a carefully cultivated act.[68]

It is more surprising to find an avowed anti-puritan like Hubert Bland displaying a deep distrust of the theatrical arts. He had played the role of Foreign Secretary in the Charing Cross Parliament, and — belying his name — affected an elaborate manner both of speaking and dressing. H.G. Wells recalls him in 'the costume of a city swell, top-hat, tail-coat, greys and blacks, white slips, spatter dashes and . . . black-ribboned monocle . . . debating, really debating, Sir, in a rococo variation of the front bench parliamentary manner'.[69] This same man sneered suspiciously at the professional stage performer, and warned young women against the 'glamour of the footlights' and the attractions of 'the mummer'. The latter, he claimed, was 'no longer a man who does something, but only a man who pretends to do something, who postures and poses and plays at doing something'. The art of the actor, Bland went on, only evoked 'the malign qualities of personal vanity, petty jealousy and peacockiness . . . And then, it is so quite awfully an affair of clothes.'[70]

An ostentatious dresser himself, Bland had an even greater reputation as an undresser of 'advanced' young women. Wells was equally notorious in this respect, but in a less furtive and contrived way: according to him, the elements of intrigue in Bland's amorous affairs had all the stuff of 'drama' about them, and constituted 'a world of roles and not of realities'.[71] However much truth there is in this, there does seem something peculiarly unctuous (if not hypocritical) in Bland's warning to young women about the charms of the professional actor, and these sentiments could be seen simply as betraying his own 'petty jealousy' of a sexual and sartorial competitor. Yet it needs to be kept in mind that his slurs on the actor do not come directly from the mouth of the author but are pronounced by one of his fictional *personae*. They are not automatically identifiable with Bland's own views, and some allowance should be made for intentional irony on his part.

No such allowance can be made in the case of Graham Wallas. His criticism of the theatre, presented in his treatise, *Human Nature in Politics*, was offered almost as a matter of scientific fact, and though it was in a much more sober and less personal vein than Bland's (as befitted an altogether more modest and self-effacing man) it revealed something of the same scepticism about the sincerity or profundity of the emotions that the stage provoked. However affecting, these emotions were also affected ('second-hand', to use Wallas's word), and therefore 'facile' and 'transitory'.[72]

Yet it would be quite wrong to dismiss Fabian reservations about the theatrical arts as representing nothing more than guilt-ridden self-suppression, jealousy, or poker-faced literal-mindedness; they were in some cases the obverse of a discriminating enthusiasm. It was Wallas, we have seen, who, in his lecture on propaganda, reiterated Shaw's belief that a 'good actor' could serve as a model of 'artistic sincerity' to the aspiring lecturer. That this was not a contradiction of his statement on theatrical emotion in *Human Nature in Politics* becomes clear if we read that statement in its full context. He indicated, a few pages earlier, that at least a part of the shallowness he discerned in that emotion stemmed from 'indifferent acting' associated with 'theatrical conventions' and 'mid-Victorian sentiment'; and it was a sort of shallowness, moreover, which was not confined to the theatre alone but was also to be found in other activities such as religious preaching and journalism. What roused his 'critical feelings' about theatre was not its basic form so much as the tendency of its run-of-the-mill practitioners to resort to a stock routine — glibly impressive but requiring no taxing work on their part, nor any fundamental challenge to the prejudices and pieties of their audiences.[73]

Several Fabians may have come to feel that the rather self-consciously staged debates of the Charing Cross Parliament, held mainly before an audience of the converted, represented a fairly futile, if not indifferent, mode of acting *and* preaching. It was the overt 'stageyness' of Mrs Besant on such occasions which repelled the young Beatrice Potter as much as the stageyness of Mrs Pat on social occasions was to repel her — and Sidney — in later years.[74] Bland's jibes at theatre were directed specifically at the posturing of matinée idols; he could still enjoy and admire, as could the Webbs, the sort of theatre represented by Shaw and Ibsen which attempted to undermine Victorian dramatic conventions. In Bland's eyes, Shaw did this with greater subtlety and discretion than Ibsen and was therefore to be prized all the more highly. If there was anything to be criticized in Shaw's plays it was an inclination to moralize about conduct which found an 'outlet in preaching'.[75] Bland, one might say, knew all about this weakness, being a habitual — and rather more self-righteous — moralizer himself.

Some awareness of their own propensity for a declamatory style made the Fabians all the more sensitive to its excesses and all the more vigilant in criticizing these, whether manifested in the theatre, in the pulpit, or on the platform. Certainly, Shaw's career as a theatre critic and director of plays — if not as an actual playwright — served to free the Edwardian stage of much of the artificial posturing and rhetorical ornamentation of previous acting traditions.[76] Shaw's fellow-dramatist and fellow-Fabian, Harley Granville Barker, carried this work even further, but Shaw had initiated the whole crusade on behalf of stage realism as far back as the 1880s, with his championship of Ibsen.

The Fabian lecture with which Shaw began his Ibsen campaign in earnest might well have derived its peculiar power from the practice — which he later recommended to all public speakers — of carefully eschewing the conventions and mannerisms of the 'old actor'. It is impossible to tell from the text alone whether he managed, in delivering this lecture, to make a complete break with traditional histrionic styles, and whether he started, then and there, to apply the most recent techniques of enunciation and voice projection. But over the next few years he made various efforts to encourage his fellow-Fabians to adopt a new approach to lecturing which relied less on an inherited style (whether theatrical, ecclesiastical or parliamentary) and concentrated more on the development of fresh styles, appropriate to public speaking in its own right and cultivated through a close attention to elocutionary techniques. It was not a case of less art and more matter, but of the subtle blending of an art with a science to give new vigour to the matter concerned. Some twenty years before the establishment of the Speakers' Class of 1912,[77] at which Graham Wallas addressed the younger generation of Fabians on 'The Psychology of Propaganda', elocution lessons were being organized by the Society — on a fairly informal basis, though employing professional teachers. The Executive Committee put Shaw in charge of making the arrangements.[78] The new rhetorical exercises would not have been as much fun as the old play-acting methods of the Charing Cross Parliament, and the regular disciplines entailed were hardly calculated to attract widespread enthusiasm or support among the rank and file of Fabians. The very idea, however, of arranging such classes signified a felt need among the vanguard of Fabians for cultivating a new and independent art of speaking, free from any traces of theatrical ornamentation or religious ceremonial.

The classes themselves evidently petered out fairly soon, but that did not prevent the more conscientious from subjecting themselves to the kind of self-discipline which Shaw had already put himself through in the 1880s. The Fabian Society's reputation for lecturing rested not only on its obvious oratorical stars, such as Shaw himself and Wallas. Even those members, such as Webb and Pease, who have laboured most heavily under the dryasdust image of the Society, were accounted 'graphic' and 'lucid' speakers in their day; and their effectiveness was seen to lie precisely in their austerity and simplicity.[79]

The example of William Morris — who, as we have seen, spoke at least three times before the Society in the 1880s — may have been an important influence here. He himself had carefully eschewed the full-dress 'grand manner' of Victorian oratory, partly out of a desire to make his speeches more amenable to working-class audiences.[80] An additional influence, on Sidney Webb at least, may have been the advice of Beatrice, addressed to him shortly before his marriage to her: 'What an immense amount of real *art* goes to make a great speaker — practice, plenty to say, a passionate feeling do not by themselves suffice. You must have the technique of the real artist, with the study of the Art for its own sake apart from its use as an instrument'.[81] There is no more succinct a summing-up of the Fabians' general approach to lecturing in the Society's heyday. Fabian lecturing and art were clearly connected not just in terms of subject-matter but, even more pervasively, in terms of style and technique.

PART III

Fabianism, élitism and popular culture

9

Fabian attitudes to working-class culture

Beatrice Webb's statement, quoted above, that her and Sidney's aim as socialists was to collectivize 'the kitchen of life' so that 'all may have freedom for the drawing-room of life'[1] cannot be taken literally; at the same time, it cannot be dismissed as just a handy and insignificant metaphor. It does seem to assume (however unconsciously) that the ambience of the drawing-room, which permeated so many of the activities of the Fabian Society, represented a standard of well-being and enjoyment to which all sections of society must want to aspire. Referring in later years to the ideal of the 'good life' which they saw enshrined in the social aims of the Bolshevik leaders in the U.S.S.R., the Webbs identified its attributes more precisely with those enjoyed 'by the professional classes of London or Paris' — with 'the conditions of a cultivated existence' among 'men of considerable education who had been trained as lawyers, doctors, professors, scientists and writers of books'.[2] This represented a quite specific linking in the Webbs' minds between the mode of life to which they and most of the Fabians had long been accustomed and the one which they thought best for everyone else.

In affirming the importance of pleasure, particularly artistic pleasure, as part of the 'good life' for all, how far were Fabians in general affected by the tastes and values of their own middle-class upbringings? And how far divorced were their conceptions of pleasure from contemporary working-class ones? The obvious answer to both these questions is: a great deal — certainly enough to accord with the Fabians' reputations for being socialists of a peculiarly élitist stamp.

The word 'élitism' has been used in a multiplicity of senses and applied (often indiscriminately) to a variety of spheres. In the sphere of politics, it has been associated with fundamentally authoritarian or illiberal practices and the perpetuation of at least covert oligarchic structures.[3] Its theoretical exponents adhere to a belief — albeit with less enthusiasm on the whole than its alleged practitioners — in the persistence of political rule 'from above', regardless of the outward form of government. That rule is seen to be conducted by a variety of non-democratic, anti-democratic or (at best) pseudo-democratic minorities: aristocracies of merit or intellect, if not of birth; 'clerisies', if not plutocracies.[4] Some concession to liberalism — a democratic 'tendency' — might be permitted in the shape of mass participation in electing the governing arm of the élite, but once its power has been legitimized in this way, the procedures of governing consist in imposition or manipulation, and the effective exclusion of substantial popular involvement.[5] According to some of the classical theorists of élitism, even a revolution 'from below', arising from 'the discontent of the masses' and leading to a collectivist or communist state, still involves, in the end, domination by another organized minority, from within the ranks of the masses themselves.[6]

In the sphere of education, élitism has been associated with meritocratic principles and practices in particular: a preoccupation with high intellectual ability, reflected in the imposition of standards for which that sort of ability provides the chief or only criterion, and leading to the distribution of the highest opportunities and the greatest privileges in almost exclusive accordance with these standards.[7]

The term élitism has also been used to sum up a variety of specifically cultural (in the sense of artistic) attitudes and tendencies. These are related in some instances, though by no means in all. In one of these senses, élitism has been identified with the continued pursuit and promotion of excellence in art as defined by the highest standards and the most refined forms which civilization has so far produced — by the 'best that has been known and said', in Matthew Arnold's famous phrase. Arnold himself did not describe the pursuit of excellence, and its standards of judgment, as 'élitist' traits. The word 'élite', signifying 'the choicest part' or 'the best', was certainly part of English usage by the time he was writing; but its derivatives 'élitist' and 'élitism' do not seem to have been part of Victorian parlance.[8] That he would have accepted such labels to describe his own cultural outlook cannot be taken for granted. One great difficulty in applying these terms, or in assessing their appropriateness in various contexts, is to make due discriminations between their prescriptive and descriptive uses and between their favourable and derogatory connotations. These are not — and perhaps never can be — very clear-cut things, as is shown vividly in a recent debate on the policy of the Arts Council in Britain. Noel Annan, well-known for his writings on the thought of two so-called élitist coteries, the Positivists and the Bloomsbury Group, declared himself 'a passionate élitist' in the debate, voicing his belief that 'the highest standards in the arts are those you should support'. His position differs from the Arnoldian variety of cultural élitism, as described above, only in its self-consciousness and its more ruthless-sounding tone and plan of procedure. Annan is reported to have opposed 'anything not of lasting value': this was why, he claimed, one had to be 'extremely sceptical of movements like fringe theatre and some aspects of community art'. Fringe theatre was a 'worthless form of art' which did not deserve support.

A devastatingly clear and committed statement, it would appear; though Annan's views — and, moreover, his avowed premises — were challenged by the Secretary General of the Arts Council, Sir Roy Shaw, who claimed that 'Annan's definition of élitism did not mean supporting the highest standards but suggested that the arts should be preserved for a minority.'[9] The ambiguities of the term élitism highlighted here are in themselves compounded by the uncertainty of knowing, from the report of the debate, whether Sir Roy himself subscribed in some degree to the variety of élitism which Annan openly avowed, or whether he considered it to be as reprehensible as the less obvious variety he discerned behind Annan's rhetoric.

This less obvious variety — the preoccupation with a culture that can only be appreciated, or at least only created, by a specially gifted minority — is as much a focus of semantic as of moral and aesthetic controversy. In actively fostering such a preoccupation, another critic working in the Arnoldian tradition, F.R. Leavis, has often been claimed for the élitist camp.[10] Yet he himself condemned the word 'élitism' as a stupid and pernicious misnomer for the belief in the desirability and inevitability of élites.[11]

T.S. Eliot, a fervent believer in social as well as cultural élites, did not feel a like need apparently to dismiss the word 'élitism', though in the book where his cultural views were most systematically expounded he never actually used the word in any sense, favourable or unfavourable. His form of cultural élitism, as it has been called by others, was not quite the same as Leavis's, in that it concerned itself more singlemindedly with the preservation and transmission, as distinct from the creation and appreciation, of culture. These former tasks he saw as lying invariably in the hands of the 'dominant class' of any society, particularly where the higher varieties of culture, or what he called the 'more conscious' or specialized varieties, were concerned.[12]

Where the term 'élitism' has been associated in any way with species of popular culture, it has been used to describe the process (or alleged process) by which the dominant groups within any society contrive to superintend the production of that culture, thereby excluding its main consumers — the mass audience — from any active role in determining its form or its content.[13]

Broad links can be found between some of these varieties of cultural élitism and the other main spheres of élitist principle or practice. For example, there are links with educational élitism in terms of shared procedures: imposition or manipulation or exploitation by a dominant minority. Such links, however, are too broad to permit the assumption that the élitist tendencies of an individual or group will be of even measure in all spheres. The danger in applying the unqualified label, 'élitism', to any or all of these various tendencies is that it obscures the variety of types and levels involved and the existence of counter-tendencies. The person whose views are labelled in this manner becomes associated with an image which — whether considered a good or a bad one — tends to remain fixed, discouraging deeper inquiry and retarding a fuller understanding. All blanket labels carry this danger, of course; but élitism is one of those particularly emotive ones in which the risks of distortion and oversimplification are all the greater because of the passionate allegiance or repugnance that the word itself tends to arouse.

Fabianism has laboured under such an image for many years now. Various observers have marshalled considerable evidence to show that the leading lights of the Fabian Society, Sidney and Beatrice Webb, were élitists in both the political and educational spheres; and, in the former sphere at least, this label has been applied by extension to the Fabians as a whole.[14] They have not, it is true, been expressly called cultural élitists; but this is probably because they have laboured for so long under the philistine image.

On investigating their opinions about culture, it is possible to find various bits of evidence that would help reinforce the élitist label to their general outlook. Certain symptoms of élitism in Beatrice Webb's attitude to art have been noted previously — for example, her special concern for the artistic genius — such as Rabindranath Tagore, Virginia Woolf or Shaw — and her unusual feelings of indulgence towards such figures springing out of deference to their great talents. Other symptoms can be found in the pages of the *Fabian Essays*. When Sydney Olivier and Graham Wallas described here the sorts of art and entertainment which would be provided to all citizens by a socialist state, they placed explicit emphasis on the high art forms, largely associated in their day with the spectator enjoyments of the upper classes. Of all the genres of music and song, for example, they singled out opera. Such forms allowed for the direct participation only of those who had the appropriate talent or genius for executing them. As for the appreciation of such art forms, the impression was given that this depended on their audience's having been educated or refined in a like manner to their traditional upper-class sponsors and brought up in the image of this privileged minority.

The processes involved were depicted as a definite movement away from any forms of present-day proletarian culture — which, in Olivier's eyes at least, suffered from an almost inherent 'coarseness' — towards an ideal in which 'every child should be brought up as a nobleman' (Wallas). 'Even the workers of the employed proletariat,' Olivier noted, '... are generally coarse in their habits. They lack intelligence in their amusements and refinement in their tastes.' Wallas was aware that the 'pleasures chosen by the will of the majority are often not recognized as pleasures at all' and he looked on that tendency with concern because he felt that as long as it continued 'private property and even private industry must exist along with public property and public production'. But for all his stress, explicit and implicit, on the need for the wealthy minority in contemporary society to simplify their lives and renounce their private interests and pleasures, he did not make any real demands on them to change or modify their basic notions of pleasure, least of all in the arts. He implied, by the procedures he advocated, that it was in the pleasures of the majority that all the changes would have to take place if those pleasures were to receive the universal recognition they required. The changes he had in mind were related to a course of education and refinement which went beyond, but took its fundamental direction from, the practices and standards of the wealthy minority in contemporary society. All schools, he felt, should be filled with 'the means not only of comfort, but even of the higher luxury'; and 'associated meals' should be served on 'tables spread with flowers in halls surrounded with beautiful pictures, or even, as John Milton proposed, filled with the sound of music'. Such measures were a part of the process in which the development of all children as noblemen was the projected end-product. Wallas took this ideal of the nobleman straight from the words of the central character in Ibsen's play, *Rosmersholm* (John Rosmer). Both Rosmer and Wallas were rather vague about the particular attributes of the nobleman they had in mind. Wallas, however, says enough about the way of life in question to make clear that this figure was much closer to the model of an upper-class gentleman than any other models of nobility (the Rousseauesque savage, for example, untouched by the sophistications and the hierarchical values of civilized society). Reiterating the expected outcome of the process by which the minority's pleasures at present would become the basis of the majority's pleasure in the future, Wallas claimed: 'at last such a life will be possible for all as not even the richest and most powerful can live to-day'.[15]

To be sure, Olivier and Wallas wished to extend to all the privileges implicit in these art forms — to provide everyone with the education and refinement necessary to appreciate them. But that very wish could be interpreted as a symptom of an élitist frame of mind, in that its fulfilment clearly entailed an imposition from above rather than any initiative from below, or any encouragement to such initiatives.

A form of this élitism can be detected at various points in the writings of another contributor to the *Fabian Essays*, Annie Besant. In a survey of popular amusements in London which she published some three years before the appearance of the Essays, she argued that the 'gates of art' were effectively barred against the poor of London, shutting them out from 'the nobler and higher enjoyments': 'amusements there are', in the shape of the music hall, for example; 'but art there is not'. 'Where,' she pleaded, 'are the music, the painting, the drama that delight, that elevate, that refine?' Again, opera seems to have epitomized these sorts of art. In a contribution to a debate on the soundness of socialism, held in 1887, Mrs Besant evoked the pleasures of the workman's life under that system of government in terms of the easy access he would have to the 'enjoyment of a Patti and of higher art'. (Adelina Patti was then at the height of her fame as an operatic soprano.) Making opera, or any of the other 'higher arts' generally accessible, did not in itself constitute a form of 'imposition' from above, but the way in which Mrs Besant conceived the purpose and effect of an enterprise such as this — and the terminology she used describing some of the associated processes involved — suggested strongly that she felt an imposition of this kind to be a necessary, desirable and even inevitable concomitant. She concluded her survey of popular amusements with the exhortation to 'throw open all treasures of art to the workers; educate the children; train their capacities; polish their tastes' and to let art 'bring them under its gracious sway, softening manners, purifying thought and gladdening life'.[16]

The music hall provided a continuous reference-point for the Fabians in their discussions about working-class culture. This was not inappropriate nor insensitive. They were careful, on the whole, not to speak of either phenomenon — the general or the particular — in monolithic terms that took no account of regional or chronological variations. And in implying, nonetheless, that the kinds of pleasure associated with music hall were of central importance to working-class culture, they were in line both with other professional observers of the time (notably Charles Booth) and also with more recent investigators.[17]

It is clear, however, that recognition of the music halls' social place and significance did not necessarily involve a sympathy with their practices. Indeed, their programmes were sometimes a precise object of Fabian distaste for working-class culture. On the whole, that distaste slipped out quite incidentally, almost unwittingly. It was quite clear, nonetheless. It can be felt vividly, for instance, behind Beatrice Webb's recollections of the work of the middle-class philanthropist, Emma Cons, with whom she was acquainted in the 1880s. Beatrice related in highly admiring tones how this woman, rebelling against the 'self-complacent harshness of doctrine of the C.O.S.' [Charity Organization Society], had come to realize that 'what was needed even more than sanitary but dismal homes was the organization of the pleasures of the poor'. The subsequent account of Miss Cons's schemes of 'organization' suggests that they had a definite 'sanitary' intention in themselves, and a strong purgative effect which Beatrice, in retrospect, could not help registering as a change for the better: 'She . . . took over the management of the Victoria music hall, at that time a disreputable centre for all that was bad — Charles Kingsley's "licensed pit of darkness" — and ran it as a place of popular musical entertainment, free from vice, and unsubsidized by the sale of drink.' Beatrice showed as much admiration for Miss Cons's niece, Lilian Baylis, whose 'genius', she asserted, 'transformed the old music hall into a theatre, presenting excellent operas' and 'admirable productions of nearly all Shakespeare's plays, appreciated by a wide circle of enthusiastic wage-earning patrons'.[18]

Opera, again, we see, provided one of the standards of worth in judging cultural phenomena, even though Beatrice was not a notable enthusiast for that genre. The tendency to judge Victorian working-class culture by the standard of high culture was not a peculiarly Fabian one;[19] and for contemporary observers, whose early social and educational background had afforded them little exposure to anything but the products of high culture, it would have been one that was almost impossible to avoid. While the Fabians' ingrained prejudices are readily understandable, it is less easy to justify the attempts of some of them to make these prejudices, in the name of socialism, a basis of their general social and political — as well as cultural — policies. If this characterization of Fabian policies tends to overstate the degree of conscious self-centredness behind them, it could then be objected that their advocates should have been more conscious of the inherent dangers involved — complacency and presumptuousness, as well as self-centredness — in idealizing and institutionalizing their own prejudices, and more conscientious about avoiding such dangers.

The evidence which prompts and supports such criticism is, however, far too selective to provide grounds for a blanket condemnation of the Fabians' cultural attitudes or even to sustain an unequivocal charge of élitism. The similar charge brought against the Fabians' political views and schemes has also been based on over-selective evidence. The distortions involved in emphasizing the élitist elements of Fabian political thought, without any acknowledgement of other, counter-balancing elements, are now beginning to be recognized.[20] These modifying elements — discernible, for example, in the Webbs' eagerness to augment popular participation in a wide array of voluntary organizations, or in their enthusiasm for apparent signs of such participation in the political system of the Soviet Union — hardly allow them to be labelled straight-out 'democrats'; but they do cast substantial doubt on the appropriateness of the élitist label. Ironically, recognition of these counter-élitist tendencies in the Webbs' political thought has come at a time when the partnership's long assumed indifference to culture in general, and particular distaste for popular or working-class culture, have become the objects of explicit criticism.[21]

The deficiencies of the Webbs should not be taken, automatically, to represent the deficiencies of the Fabian Society as a whole; though this consideration in itself cannot hope to redeem Fabianism from any charge of cultural élitism. Some redeeming features, however, can be found in the very nature of those élitist tendencies noted above in the Fabian Essayists. While their cultural programmes for a socialist state entailed little more than the wider proliferation of their own kind of culture, their motivation in recommending those programmes was nothing if not benevolent. The quality of popular culture was an issue of genuine concern to them, and their object in attempting to imbue it with the riches of high culture was to facilitate, not hinder, complete social levelling. In applying the word 'élitist' to their views — especially by way of criticism or reproach — one must be careful to distinguish it from the type or types of élitism which have no egalitarian ramifications or a resolutely anti-egalitarian aim. If they wished to prescribe or superintend the culture of the majority, their intention was not to keep traditional, 'high art' preserved for a minority audience, nor in any other way to reinforce the current cultural and social divisions between the mass of the population and its ruling élites. The complete opposite was the case.

Much more so even than their political motives and schemes, the Fabians' cultural attitudes constitute an amalgam of élitist and egalitarian elements. Criticisms which label the Fabians flatly as élitists, without discriminating between various types and levels of élitism, or clearly acknowledging the elements in their thought which qualified or ran counter to this tendency, can serve only to compound the distortions in the received image of the Society. A detailed investigation of the Fabians' assumptions and aspirations reveals a whole host of contradictions and self-contradictions regarding the desirability or possibility of élite manipulation on the one hand, and of popular participation on the other. This deep-seated ambivalence in the Fabians' attitudes undoubtedly springs from their own position as a middle-class socialist élite, and represents anything but a cohesive or coherent cultural policy on the part of the Society. But it at least conveys their general sensitivity to the importance of artistic issues in relation to political and educational ones, and shows their capacity for transcending on occasion the assumptions and instincts of their class position. Several of them can be found attempting to confront their élitist tendencies, even pushing these in anti-élitist directions, rather than giving in to them altogether or erecting them into a passionate and unashamed philosophy in the manner of Noel Annan.

As we shall see, the very conception of what might be included in the category 'popular culture' was a contradictory, or at least very variable, one in Fabian thought. Few Fabians, in fact, attempted to define its boundaries expressly, but even those who came close to doing so were not in accord over the matter, and sometimes confused within themselves.

This is hardly surprising, nor particularly blameworthy. Professional sociologists and historians of popular culture continue to present an array of competing or conflicting 'approaches' to the phenomenon, which only condemn it to remaining, on the conceptual level, 'an indistinct term whose edges blur into imprecision'.[22] Certainly very little has been achieved in the way of clarifying the nature and extent of its connections with other kinds of culture — whether in the sense of specific 'class' cultures ('working-class', 'middle-class', 'aristocratic'), or grades of culture ('high', 'middlebrow', 'lowbrow'), or the various undifferentiated, though hardly value-free, categories ('folk culture', 'mass culture' and the like).

It would, admittedly, be very arbitrary to draw any rigid distinctions between popular culture and these other categories;[23] and it would be ahistorical to assume that such categories in themselves have ever conformed to a completely homogeneous type.[24] There is no doubt some value, therefore, in the diversity of interpretations relating to popular culture; and rather than trying to track down an ever-elusive, and perhaps illusory, general meaning, it is perhaps best to make do with a series of limited or 'local' definitions for specific purposes.

It is possible to be more certain about what popular culture isn't. It could never be associated in any way with the determinedly exclusive 'minority culture' which Noel Annan has been criticized for supporting. Another variety, completely antithetical to popular culture, was the butt of William Morris's criticisms, nearer to the time of the Fabian Society's heyday. Morris referred scornfully to 'the art which professes to be founded on the special education or refinement of a limited body or class', claiming that any such form must of necessity be unreal and short-lived. He was not including all of the 'high' or traditional fine arts in this category; he clearly envisaged a continuing role for the 'highest intellectual art' alongside those more popular forms which he chose to encourage — weaving, pottery, domestic furnishings, decorative implement-making and the other domestic handicrafts. High art in his eyes only became artificial and moribund when it deliberately isolated itself from the 'mass of mankind' and became the preserve of a coterie. The idealized landscapes and 'ridiculous figure subjects' dominating the exhibitions at the Royal Academy typified for Morris the barrenness of an artistic genre that had cut itself off from 'the longings of simple people' and surrendered to the values of 'commercialism' and 'the present bourgeois barbarism'.[25]

Of course, if Morris's own pronouncements on handicrafts are any indication, this branch of the arts would appear to have undergone such a serious decline in England that their pleasures were even more remote from the general experience of his so-called 'simple people' than the pleasures afforded by the fine arts. Considering, however, that they could be more readily practised in a domestic or non-institutional environment — and were even envisaged as forming a part of men's everyday work — these 'useful arts' allowed for a much broader, and a more direct, participation by the members of a society. In a literal sense, then, they were more 'popular', or potentially more popular: Morris entertained no hope that they could make any real contribution while capitalism still held sway, and spoke only of their role in the socialist future, as judged by their putative role in the pre-capitalist past. Following Marx, Morris envisaged that the future society would eventually shed any distinctive class character; and, among English socialists of the time, he came the closest to providing a blueprint for a classless art to match. While it involved making radical changes in the current nature of working-class culture, the popular art of the future would be integrally related to common forms of daily work, and so necessitated changes at least as radical in the current forms and conceptions of bourgeois and aristocratic culture. While his notion of the refining power of art proceeded in part from a conventional upper-class assumption concerning the current degradation of the masses, his ideal of a man refined by that power was relatively free of any class tinge.

It must be admitted straightaway that none of the Fabians — though more indebted to Morris than is generally recognized for the nurturing of their youthful socialist instincts — ever came close to working out a comparable blueprint for popular culture in a socialist society. In the case of Olivier, Wallas and Mrs Besant, indeed, we have noted a singular failure to depict the art of the future and the nature of its popularity throughout society as anything more than an extension and redistribution of the most refined artistic enjoyments currently available to members of their own and higher classes. If they had any coherent conception of 'popular culture', it betrays the marks of élitism in two clear ways: in its assumptions about the degraded condition of any current forms of working-class culture, and its plan for improving this condition simply by opening up to the majority of the population a form of naturally 'superior' culture which was then only accessible to a limited class. Such a conception approximates less to a kind of 'ideal' popular culture, growing naturally out of the daily lives of a whole populace, than to a type of popularized class culture, artificially transfused from the smaller bodies in the populace to the larger.

There were other Fabians, however, who, while never ridding themselves or their policies of these élitist assumptions and procedures, saw beyond their limits in the direction in which Morris pointed. The particularly intricate interplay of élitist and egalitarian tendencies in their cultural attitudes deserves a full discussion, not only for the purpose of checking any oversimplifications in the conventional image of Fabian socialism, but also because it brings into focus some of the general problems (social, economic, political and administrative, as well as aesthetic) which must face any participants in the formation of cultural policies for a whole society. By observing the ways in which a group such as the Fabians dealt with, or failed to deal with, the complexities of these general problems, aspiring participants may even gain some lessons in procedure themselves.

One persistent problem appears to be the inevitable intrusiveness of class preconceptions and predilections in any ideas for a cultural policy. The example of the Fabians shows clearly that this problem was not just manifested, or caused, by an inflexible bias against the cultural habits of other classes. The Fabians' attitudes to working-class culture, for instance, were far more complicated than their occasional displays of outright distaste might indicate; and that distaste in itself evolved from a set of complex and ambiguous feelings which cannot be characterized as mere class prejudice. After all, it was through a reaction on the Fabians' part against many of the conventional values and institutions of their own class — as well as of the class above them — that socialism came to root itself in their minds. The artistic values and institutions of the middle and upper classes were by no means immune to that reaction; though the particular artistic genres which these classes enjoyed continued to form the basis of the Fabians' own tastes and — in some cases — of their conception of what art, essentially, was. A sympathetic concern for the classes below them — prime victims, in the Fabians' eyes, of the values and institutions they found so offensive in contemporary society — served to consolidate their socialist inclinations by providing an external and positive focus for their grievances.

A rather exaggerated reflection of these processes and feelings — and an extraordinary testimony to their complexity and ambiguity — can be found in an article which William Clarke wrote on the Fabian Society in 1894. In this he quoted the statement of a famous (but unnamed) English politician who had told him that 'labour men' were 'no use as leaders' and that if the labour movement was to be successful, 'it must be led by educated men'. Clarke affected to endorse this unashamedly élitist viewpoint, but undercut it at the same time by adding a crucial qualification. The politician's verdict, he intimated, rightly pointed in the direction of a union of culture with labour. Only, be it observed, it must be union on equal terms. There must be no lofty condescension on the part of culture any more than base truckling on the part of labour. It must be an equal copartnership, where each partner recognizes that the other has something which he needs. And let me say, as one who knows workmen, that in a certain and very real way, culture has as much to learn from labour as labour from culture. Let the cultured man approach the labouring man on perfectly equal terms, in a cordial and open way; and let both deliver a groaning world from the bondage of riches . . . This idea is to a very great degree the *idée mère* of the Fabian Society, whose members have no higher ambition than to mingle freely with the workmen and share in the common life.[26]

There is a strong element of sentimental hyperbole here which appears all the stronger when judged in the light of Clarke's later disenchantment with the working class. In fact, that disenchantment — marked as it was by an extreme repugnance for working-class tastes and pleasures — may well have had its origins in Clarke's assumption, already apparent in the passage cited, that the life of 'labour' was clearly distinct from the life of 'culture' and bereft of any of the latter's most valuable features. Nevertheless, the above passage, written while Clarke was still a Fabian, did insist that the converse was also true, and suggested that the dissociation between 'labour' and 'culture' could and should be halted so that each side could benefit from the other's attributes. There was no overt prejudice here in favour of the attributes of 'culture' or of the classes that Clarke saw as possessing these; though a type of prejudice — concerning the actual meaning of culture — was still discernible in the implication that the activities and sensibilities of 'labour' had nothing to offer in a cultural sense themselves — nothing about them which could even be called cultural — because the 'labouring man' had not been sufficiently or properly 'educated'.

Clarke himself did not present a good example of that driving impulse which he perceived among Fabians to 'approach the labouring man on perfectly equal terms'. This was a highly idealized image of the Fabians' aims and methods in any case; though there were several prominent members of the Society who came nearer than Clarke to the ideal he depicted. Significant signs of their tendencies in that direction can be found in their attitudes to working-class culture itself: in their tacit recognition that such a thing existed and was not, as Clarke implied, a contradiction in terms; in their general avoidance of a disdainful or condemnatory tone in discussing the tastes and pleasures of working-men, even those which they found particularly crude or debased; in their sympathetic (and by no means condescending) explanations of these alleged crudities; and, most strikingly, in their acknowledgment every now and then that there were certain aspects of working-class culture, even some of the cruder aspects, which had a definite merit in themselves, and were sometimes of greater merit — and greater interest — than their middle- or upper-class versions.

These facets of the Fabians' attitudes were often revealed at the same time as their distaste for working-class culture, and served to modify the strength of that distaste there and then. Ambivalent feelings towards the culture of all classes can be discerned in the writings and pronouncements of several Fabians; and such feelings should alert us to the over-simplification involved in any account of the Fabians' cultural policies which sums up their aims and methods merely in terms of the imposition on all of art from above and the eradication or discouragement of art from below.

Fabian attitudes to the music hall and associated entertainments provide some pertinent evidence in this respect. The unmitigated distaste which Beatrice Webb voiced in her memoirs for the unreformed 'Victoria' hall was by no means characteristic of these attitudes. Indeed, the strength of her distaste in this instance — compounded by her unequivocal praise for the work of Emma Cons and Lilian Baylis in transforming the tone and nature of 'the Vic's' entertainments — cannot be assumed to be completely characteristic of Beatrice's own attitudes. An earlier view of hers, recorded just after her attendance at one of the performances arranged by Miss Cons in the 1880s, expressed some dismay at the insipid refinements which 'that grand woman' had introduced, and evinced a nostalgic relish for the vitality of the older and cruder fare: 'To me it was a dreary performance, sinking to the level of the audience, while omitting the dash of coarseness, irreverence and low humour which give the spice and reality to such entertainments. To my mind the devil is preferable, and in every way more wholesome, than a shapeless mediocrity.'[27]

This view was enunciated five years or so before Beatrice became a Fabian, but it expressed a familiar tension in the minds of those who had already joined the Society and who had started attending similar sorts of entertainment. On the one hand, there was a quite ingrained belief about the debased level of working-class taste; but, on the other, an awareness of the genuine value to be found in some of the manifestations of that taste, despite — or precisely because of — its baseness. The degree of awareness varied from Fabian to Fabian, as did the nature of their valuation, and its effect on their ideas for a cultural policy.

It is significant that an awareness of this kind can be found even in the writings of Fabians who recognized no artistic qualities at all in the manifestations of working-class culture which they witnessed. In the conclusion to her survey of popular amusements in London, Annie Besant conceded that the music-hall entertainments of the poorer classes, though devoid of anything which could be called art, were 'better, far better than nothing', and the detailed sketches she drew comparing the range of fare available at the cheaper and at the more expensive halls, suggested strongly that she felt working-class amusements of this kind to be considerably better than their middle-class counterparts. She did recognize a phenomenon which could be called middle-class 'art', but she was very sceptical of its pretensions to that status. In its very restraints on fun, gaiety and natural bodily delights, it seemed to her to be 'vulgar, crude and superficial to the last degree': it reflected a prurience which was all the worse for being coy and repressed. She found serious shortcomings even in those places of 'higher class' entertainment where the fare offered was free of anything which could be construed as 'coarse or indecent'. The plusher, more expensively priced music hall, patronized by the 'middle-class enfranchised youth', was an example she gave of this type of institution. Her main criticism of the entertainment offered here was that 'it was so profoundly, so preternaturally dull. Melody, wit, grace or downright fun, were conspicuously absent, and there was no enthusiasm in the audience to stimulate the performers.' The standards by which she gauged these shortcomings were set, at least in part, by the kinds of entertainment and audience-response that could be found in the 'cheaper Music Halls', where the patrons were largely working-class. Such establishments, she indicated, had 'a real value' both in terms of the unabashed fun they provided for the 'wearied-out workers' and the general enthusiasm which they elicited as a result. Though she made clear that none of them set any comparable standards in 'melody', 'wit' or 'grace', she did not depict them as incapable of attaining such standards, nor was she content with the notion that their audiences could remain enthusiastic only as long as the fun remained at an unsophisticated and uncomplicated level:

The question remains whether something called music might not be introduced instead of the mere jingle . . . which represents it. It may be that the entertainment is as good as the taste of the majority will permit; but I should like to see the effect of, say, an Irish or Scotch melody, melodiously sung. There are plenty of really good songs, apart from those compositions which only musicians can appreciate, which could, I believe, be successful, if tried.[28]

Her overall preference for the cheaper halls, even with the crude and limited repertoire they offered at present, showed that she felt there were some qualities in working-class culture which could usefully be drawn upon by the culture of the higher classes. The fact, however, that the redeeming qualities which she discerned in the working-class music hall were not primarily 'artistic' — all the fun of its entertainments and the enthusiasm these engendered did nothing to make it an art-form in her eyes — effectively undercut the significance of these contributions in fostering the culture of her ideal socialist world. The limitations, for her, of these contributions were defined by the limitations of her own conception of art, which she could not get away from viewing in terms of the highest, most refined forms; and her ideal of a socialist culture was based simply on the widest possible proliferation of those forms. So strong was the relationship between her own personal ideals in art and the ends of her cultural policies that it is doubtful if the music hall, for all the good points which she saw in it, would have been provided with any incentives to survive in her socialist world or that she would have lamented its passing.

A very different approach to the question of popular culture is represented in Stewart Headlam's attitude to the music hall, notwith-standing the broad similarities which existed between his and Mrs Besant's tastes and distastes. Headlam's personal taste in art was at least as refined as hers. Details we have of the décor and furnishings with which both of them chose to surround themselves at home suggest a fastidiousness and sense of style which could match that of any *fin-de-siècle* aesthete.[29] And Headlam made quite clear at times his feelings about the inferiority of the 'standard of taste of the multitude'. That phrase can be found in some digressionary comments he made on English drama in 1907 while lecturing to the Fabians on the subject of land values. Its derogatory implications are made clear by the explicit distinction he went on to make between 'good plays' and those which he felt were 'playing down to popular taste'. The words 'multitude' and 'popular' here were not necessarily synonymous with 'working-class' but were meant to apply to higher classes as well. In fact, Headlam's special butts seem to have been the hat-wearing matinée lady whose theatrical diet consisted of little else but operetta and melodrama, and the large commercial managements who continually indulged her appetite for this facile fare.[30]

Reflecting the confusions produced, then as now, by the term 'popular',[31] Headlam associated it specifically on another occasion with the cultural and recreational activities of the working class. It is significant that when he did so much of his distaste for 'popular' fare was displaced by, or mixed in with, a good deal of sympathy. For instance, in a lecture he delivered on theatrical and associated entertainments towards the end of the 1880s, he defended melodrama, linking it with tragedy as a form of 'pleasurable education' by which the audiences of a 'popular playhouse' were 'instinctively for the moment, at any rate, loving what is good and hating what is evil'. It was in the course of this defence that he coined the maxim: 'a work of art has failed of its object if it does not give pleasure'; and it was partly on the basis of the relationship he perceived between art and pleasure that he included not only melodrama but also 'the music hall stage or the theatre of varieties' as a definite art-form. In his eyes, the qualifications of the music hall for this status were all the more impressive precisely because it was 'more popular with many people, especially with those whom, with strange inaccuracy, we call the lower classes, than the theatres are'. It represented a type of 'art' which was not for 'the select few' but 'by the people and for the people'.[32]

Here was the crucial difference in Headlam's views from those of

Annie Besant, who, despite her affection for the working-class music hall
and her recognition of its 'real value', was unable to think of it as art in
any sense. The difference was crucial, because Headlam's belief in the
artistic value of this genre, founded as it was on the evident pleasure that
it brought the mass of the people, prompted him to regard it as more than
a trivial and transient cultural form to be replaced by higher things, and
thereby evoked in him a much greater concern for its future fate. The
highly refined tastes and ideals in art which some of his writings and
pronouncements show him to have possessed did not impose on the
cultural policies which he advocated to nearly the same degree as in Mrs
Besant's case.

Like her, Headlam pointed to deficiencies in the current fare offered by
the music halls, much of which he felt represented a 'somewhat spurious
article . . . to the detriment of art and the prejudicing of the public taste'.
But he managed to show, in a much clearer and more substantial way
than Mrs Besant, that such deficiencies were not inherent and not simply
the reflection of public taste. His use of the word 'spurious' pointed to his
belief in the existence of more genuine forms of working-class entertainment, the authenticity of which was being eroded in his view by the
pressures of the law (in particular, 'the ridiculous legal distinction
between theatres and music halls') and was also, he hinted, under threat
from commercial pressures associated with 'the plutocratic evil — the
power which money had in comparison with worth and talent'. These
pressures — from outside or above the working class — were among the
fundamental causes of any debasement which could be witnessed in that
class's tastes, and he wanted to create (or restore) a situation in which no
such pressures were operative. Under the present law, he explained, a
theatre was decreed to be 'a place licensed by the Lord Chamberlain
where you may act stage plays, and where you may dance, and where you
may not smoke', whereas a music hall was 'a place licensed by the County
Council, where you may not act stage plays, where you may only dance if
you have permission to do so, and where you may smoke'. There were
both obvious and subtle ways in which these arbitrary distinctions
contrived to debase the standard of the music hall. For a start, they
empowered the County Council to refuse dancing-licences; and dancing,
in Headlam's view, had been 'the most artistic work' of all the music
hall's attractions. In the 1870s 'a music and a dancing licence always went
together'. The fact that a dancing licence had now become so difficult to
obtain had adverse effects even on the artistic forms which were more
freely sanctioned, notably the music itself. In some instances, the managements were forced to fill the gap left by the forbidden dancer with 'the
comic and serio-comic singer, and superior persons say how vulgar these
places are, forgetful that they through the restrictive laws . . . their

delegates make ... are responsible for that vulgarity'. In other instances, where managements had attempted to slip in, under the music licence, 'any dancing which was incidental to a song', their policy had had a disastrous effect, in that 'a young lady who could not sing but could dance, was forced to try to sing in order to be able to bring in her dance at the end'. Managements which had actually secured a dancing licence had to guard carefully against making their ballets too obviously a form of stage play, with the consequence that 'the written plot or story on which the ballet is founded' could seldom be given to the audience.

Though Headlam frankly acknowledged a need for refinements and improvements in the present state of working-class culture, he by no means viewed the direction these might take solely in terms of a growing approximation to the highest forms of art. If his attitudes to the music hall show him to have been in danger of idealizing any form of culture, it was not those 'high' varieties traditionally associated with the upper classes, but a pristine form of working-class culture supposedly in existence before the imposition of restrictions devised or sanctioned by the upper classes. Perhaps the image he presented of this particular form was too good to be true. It nonetheless highlighted an area of his cultural policies which concerned itself not with changing the basic nature of working-class taste by acts of imposition from outside and above, but, on the contrary, with facilitating the growth of the purest and most authentic elements in that taste by removing what impositions now existed and encouraging some measure of self-direction. In campaigning for the abolition of legal distinctions between theatres and music halls, Headlam's aim was to allow the managements of both these types of institution much more freedom and flexibility 'to cater for the tastes of their audiences'. In fact, the only restriction would come in the shape of 'popular control' — a check, presumably, against any tendency of the managements themselves to dictate, rather than simply cater for, the public's tastes. He was most keen to 'let the public have plays, songs, dances, with or without smoking or drinking, *just as they like*'.[33]

In effect, this was the basis of Shaw's cultural policies as well, though he personally had much less time for popular entertainments of the music-hall variety and resisted on practical grounds the exercise of any control by audiences over the day-to-day management of theatres. Derogatory comments on the fare offered by the music halls were scattered throughout his writings as a professional music critic in the years 1888-94.[34] These did not, however, amount to an indiscriminate attack; and he suggested, at least as strongly as Headlam or Annie Besant, that certain higher-class entertainments, like the commercial theatre, suffered from more general and deep-seated deficiencies. In an article he wrote in 1893, he depicted English theatre-management as largely a version of speculative 'sport', into which 'artistic aims enter about as deeply as the improvement of natural horse-breeding enters into the ambition of our gentlemen of the Turf'. As a consequence, he observed, the public went more and more to the music hall, because that was 'the only place of entertainment where you can be quite sure of not having your evening and your money entirely wasted'. London opera, he felt, was plainly inferior to the music hall in terms of 'real stage art' — by which he meant such things as the costuming, lighting and scenic effects.[35] And some ten years earlier we find him suggesting that higher-class entertainments were unable to match the potential of the music halls as artistic agencies in society. Confronted with a completely indiscriminate attack on the halls by Francis Hueffer, editor of the *Musical Review*, Shaw was roused to defend these against the charges of 'evil' laid at their door, and said he was 'convinced' that once they had been 'freed from the censorship of Middlesex magistrates and the like', they would

do more to educate the people artistically than all the nimminy-pimminy concerts in the world. I have been at these concerts and I have been at music halls and not enjoyed any of them; but I gained the knowledge on which I base my opinion ... Highly cultivated people like to be infantile in their enthusiasms occasionally; hence the esteem in which they hold old ballads ... But there are old ballads which are quite inferior — words and music — to some music-hall songs. On this subject, I am an advocate for music halls absolutely free from restrictions.[36]

This pronouncement was made about a year before the Fabian Society was founded, and nearly two years before Shaw joined. Though he was never as passionate again in his advocacy of the music hall, the general assumptions behind his advocacy here remained with him as a Fabian, and were even seen by him as a part or reflection of the spirit of Fabianism.[37] It was a task for Fabians, in particular, he suggested in 1898, to put the 'wants of the community' first — even where these were completely at odds with their own wants. To operate policies for the benefit of the whole community which involved a conscious frustration of the community's general wants smacked of 'impossibilism' to Shaw; and 'the object of Fabianism,' he averred, 'is to destroy Impossibilism'. Despite his own convictions, therefore, that 'horse tractions, tall hats, furs and feathers, and 99/100ths of what people call art are damnable', he could not have 'refused to help in any of the steps to improve the conditions under which the industries involved in these things are carried on'.[38] He remained an active supporter of amateur artistic activities in the community, and intimated that for various reasons (aesthetic as well as economic and social) these represented a more viable or vital form than much professional or institutional art. For example, he poured scorn on those 'persons with very high ideals in music' who felt they could elevate 'the culture of the neighbourhood' by securing a grant from the municipality, building 'a handsome concert room or opera house' and obtaining the services of 'the best artists from every part of the world'. Such schemes were not only impracticable in his eyes; they also failed to offer any of the 'pleasure', 'interest', 'fun' or 'social atmosphere' which were produced by tapping musical talents from within the neighbourhood itself and organizing artistic activities on the basis of these.[39]

Attempts to serve the community while maintaining a stubborn resistance to its wants and attempts to make one's own wants or likes the foundation of a general policy for the community's welfare did not differ much in effect, as far as Shaw was concerned. The element of futile utopianism which he found in the former enterprise also beset the latter: this was one of the implications of his lecture on 'The Climate and Soil for Labour Culture', delivered to the Fabian Society in 1918. The constituents of that climate and soil, he suggested, could not be dictated by the Fabians' own middle-class cultural or artistic standards, however good these may have been for the Fabians themselves — and they were good enough, by his account of them here, to contradict his usual allegations, reiterated just a few sentences before, concerning the Society's complete disregard for art. Criticism of his fellow-Fabians, in fact, suddenly turned into a justification: 'Which of us,' he asked, with specific reference to the early Fabians,

could seriously believe that the melancholy beauty of such really fine art as our middle class could produce would appeal to the working classes or be of much use to them? . . . I really do not think that . . . the Fabians with their middle-class art culture . . . can put the joy of life into the Labor movement. It cannot be done by a gospel of art . . . or any other gospel of a class or sect. I suggest that what we have to promise to all classes alike is freedom.[40]

Attempting as it does both to criticize and to justify the Fabians, this whole section of Shaw's lecture is a confusing one with regard to his fellow-members' attitudes to the problems of developing a 'labor culture'. It is shot through not only with contradictions, but also with oversimplifications — of the Fabians' attitude to joy, for example — and with evasions. Shaw never fully or clearly answered the question that he asked at the beginning of the passage cited; or, rather, he left it rhetorical and dangling, only answering it with any certainty on his own behalf. In a sense, however, the confusions are significant evidence in themselves of the difficulties involved in making generalizations about the extent to which the Fabians transcended their own wants and likes in mapping out their cultural and social policies, or the extent to which they recognized a need for doing so. It may have been a part of the object of Fabianism to destroy 'Impossibilism'. How far, in fact, individual Fabians managed to escape or contain the excessively utopian notions which Shaw singled out for censure is a matter fraught with ambiguity. Enough evidence has been adduced to show that the avoidance of such notions was by no means complete — that there were, for example, several prominent Fabians who did 'seriously believe' in the potential attractions and uses of 'really fine art' for the working class. Whether, on the other hand, this belief really made them impossibilists or utopians is a matter which may well have been disputed by them — especially by those who also recognized the worth and viability of less 'fine' artistic forms, springing from working-class roots.

There were some Fabians — notably Charles Charrington — who sought a judicious blending of high and popular culture as the basis for a 'communal' policy in the future. Charrington spoke of the necessity of 'higher recreation' to the development of a 'higher civilization', and he specifically recommended such things as the organization of concerts by municipalities and 'giving opportunities for games to the mass of the people which were formerly possessed only by the middle classes'. 'Higher' in his eyes, however, did not mean 'the very high', which Shaw warned against in planning a cultural policy for the mass of the population. The concerts he had in mind were not chamber affairs, with imported celebrities, but open-air ones, given by local bands, or the town-hall variety already on offer in progressive working-class districts such as Battersea.[41]

Active support for certain working-class forms of art can be found even in the writings of Fabians who were 'impossibilist' enough to endorse the official suppression or discouragement of many non-artistic aspects of mass taste. The Webbs themselves were a case in point here. In a Fabian tract published in 1919, Sidney Webb went so far as to endorse 'any plan by which any working-class luxuries, which yield little in subsistence or refinement, could be made the vehicle of any necessary taxation'. Among the prime examples of the 'luxuries' he had in mind was alcoholic drink. This fitted into his category of those articles for which 'there is good reason for preventing consumption in excess, and even also for restricting the consumption in moderation'.[42] (Here was a clear divergence from Shaw, who, although a teetotaller himself, was prepared to recognize that for others alcohol could be a necessary, even indispensable, 'anaesthetic'.[43]) Aside from drinking, there were several other popular pursuits, such as gambling and the more brutal sports, which were inimical to the kinds of refinement aimed at by the Webbs and which, therefore, justified strict controls, in their view, rather than toleration.[44] They were not so blinkered or self-righteous, however, as to suggest that such 'coarse and disorderly amusements' were exclusively a working-class phenomenon or an inherent fault of that class. They showed how attempts in the eighteenth century to control pursuits of this kind were extremely selective, having been directed wholly against 'the humbler classes', and not at the 'licentiousness of the rich', who were allowed a 'practical freedom . . . to be as idle and vicious as they pleased'.[45]

The more refined pursuits of the richer classes did not escape Sidney's censure, when he felt they were being indulged in to an excessive degree. Opera itself — the art form which provided a standard of genuine artistic worth for several other Fabians — was a case in point. We have seen how in the 1880s Sidney had made clear his disapproval, not of the form itself, but of its luxury status and trappings. Even more offensive — to Beatrice as well as Sidney — was the combination which they observed in the previous century of 'luxurious living' on the part of the wealthy and 'the wholesale prescription for the lower orders of an abstinence from all sensual indulgences'. The Webbs were particularly disturbed by the 'vicarious puritanism' on the part of those who ordered and administered the restrictions on working-class pastimes, and the concomitant failure of these officials to provide the people — or even think of providing them — with 'superior forms of recreation' or at least 'the alternative of education'. Late eighteenth-century magistrates, according to the Webbs and the contemporary commentators which they quoted, seemed intent 'merely . . . to deprive the lower orders of their margin of leisure and opportunities for amusement'.[46]

The Webbs' own brand of 'puritanism' was certainly never as deep-dyed as this. Nearly all of their works touched on the problems of organizing and refining the recreational facilities of the 'lower orders', and some — especially Sidney's — were directly and pre-eminently concerned with how a socialist state would tackle those problems, together with the related educational and cultural ones. Their very compulsion to organize and refine was a symptom perhaps of that élitism which other commentators have discerned in their schemes and ideas. If that is so, however, it needs to be pointed out not only that this sort of élitism was, by its very nature, of a non-exclusivist variety; but also that the Webbs' models of organization and refinement were sometimes based on existing working-class forms, or at least on forms that were more easily and more immediately assimilable to patterns of working-class life than 'fine' art.

Summing up in later life the general social and cultural attitudes of the Webb partnership, Beatrice carefully dissociated these from any coterie-type élitism, such as was apparent in the attitudes of the Bloomsbury group and its fringe. In a letter she wrote to E.M. Forster in 1934, she commented on the 'conception of the good' subscribed to by his Cambridge colleague and fellow-writer, Goldsworthy Lowes Dickinson, and noted its divergence from the Webbs' own conception: Lowes Dickinson's, she suggested, was related to his 'exquisite sense of beauty', whereas 'ours . . . I am afraid is always based on the social value of an institution or law — that is, the way in which it will raise or lower the culture and development of what are called the common people'.[47] A few years earlier, she portrayed one of the most prominent members of the Bloomsbury set, John Maynard Keynes, as 'a man of science with a remarkable literary gift' but without the 'make-up of a political leader'. This distinguished economist, she claimed, was 'contemptuous of common men especially when gathered together in herds . . . Hence his antipathy to . . . proletarian culture . . . He dislikes all the common or garden thoughts and emotions that bind men together in bundles.'[48] The Webbs' differences with this kind of outlook were only implied here; though, as seen above, Beatrice spelt out other differences with Bloomsbury, on related grounds, in her scattered observations on Leonard and Virginia Woolf. These differences were not fundamental, as Beatrice herself was aware, and as the Woolfs' decision to become Fabians themselves seems to bear out. The record of the Webbs' artistic attitudes shows, moreover, that neither Sidney nor Beatrice were completely resistant to the claims and charms of the most 'exquisite' forms of beauty, and that the partnership was not free in itself of a certain antipathy to 'proletarian culture'. One substantial token, however, of the Webbs' capacity for sympathy with the 'culture of the common people' can be seen in their abiding admiration for the 'Consumers' Co-operative Movement' in Britain and their transparent wish that its ideals and activities could be more fully developed. This movement was, in their own words, 'genuinely of working-class origin'. Though based partly on the co-operative ideals of Robert Owen, it was initiated in practice, according to the Webbs' account, by the group of flannel-weavers from Rochdale — the so-called 'Rochdale Pioneers' — who in 1844 chose to pool their financial resources and divide amongst themselves the commodities which they needed. Stemming from this 'unselfconscious act' by a small band of workers in a particular locality of Lancashire, the movement had gradually spread itself far beyond the confines of that county. From the outset, Sidney and Beatrice noted, its 'ultimate purpose' was the 'emancipation' of workers 'from wage-slavery by such a reorganization of industry as would enable them to provide themselves with employment' and to secure an arrangement of the 'powers of production, distribution, education and government' such as would 'create a self-supporting home colony'.[49] Providing the members of these colonies with facilities for all kinds of artistic and recreational pursuits — including 'concerts and entertainments' and 'popular lectures' or 'evening classes in literature, science and art' — had been an associated purpose of considerable importance in the early days of the Co-operative Movement. 'Regrettably', Sidney and Beatrice reported, the number and range of such activities being organized at present fell short of 'the hopes and aspirations with which the Movement began'; this shortcoming, in fact, was the most serious one which the Webbs could find in the current policy of the Co-operators.[50]

It would appear from the Webbs' account that other middle-class commentators on the Co-operative Movement had directed their criticisms of it against rather different — and in some sense more central — aspects of its artistic achievement: the quality of the wares it produced and of the packaging and display of these wares; and the level of 'taste' thereby indicated in the co-operative workers' sensibilities. One critic quoted by Sidney and Beatrice went so far as to state that the 'main failure' of these workers was 'psychological', and he located the symptoms of this failure precisely in the fact that the co-operators were 'devoid of artistic taste'; lacking in 'intellectual distinction'; 'keen on a certain rough genuineness of quality, but ... blind to the supreme importance of excellence'. The Webbs questioned both the substance and the relevance of this 'fact'. They conceded the unsatisfactoriness of certain elements in the workmanship of co-operative products (the 'ugliness of Co-operative furniture', the 'banal conventionality of Co-operative clothing', the 'hideous diversity of the founts of type' used in printing Co-operative literature and the labels on Co-operative goods), but they were more prepared to find extenuating circumstances for these deficiencies, and counterbalancing features, than they were when discussing the movement's deficiencies in organizing artistic activities outside working hours. As we have already seen in looking at her general study of the movement published in 1891, Beatrice had been impressed from early on with the overall 'standard of taste' shown by the co-operative communities in the goods they produced and consumed, especially in comparison with the shoddy standards perceived in the produce of capitalist manufacturing concerns. Her later analysis of the Consumers' Co-operative Movement, written in conjunction with her husband after the First World War, reveals an even greater respect for the Co-operators' artistic capacities. Drawing their readers' attention to certain specific achievements of the movement in architecture and interior design, as well as to some of the everyday products on display at Co-operative shops, the Webbs insisted that after seeing such specimens no one could justifiably accuse Co-operators of 'being always oblivious to those qualities of dignity, simplicity, genuineness and appropriateness which are ... the basis of excellence of style'. In acknowledging the 'artistic and intellectual shortcomings' which could still be found in the workmanship of the Co-operators, Sidney and Beatrice felt bound to point out that critics had tended to 'overstate the universality' of these 'shortcomings' and were 'unaware of the many instances in which Co-operators are manifesting, alike in the products and in their administration, an excellence, and even a distinction of quality, which is nothing short of remarkable'.

The Webbs were not able to resist suggesting, at one point, that the Co-operative Movement could achieve yet higher 'standards of quality' and even 'greater appreciation of artistic excellence' by seeking the 'advice and assistance of the trained professional specialist . . . in design and artistic taste'. This could well be seen as a testimony to the persistence of their élitist tendencies; but it in no sense undermined the strength of their belief in the intrinsic artistic merits of much of the Co-operative Movement's work. It was a confirmation of their faith in the value and viability of these specimens of working-class culture that they regarded the defects which they found there as anything but intrinsic. The ugliness and banality of various Co-operative wares were not, the Webbs contended, the result of a basic 'want of sympathy or lack of imagination' on the part of their producers and distributors. Rather, such defects stemmed from the general social and economic climate in which the Co-operators were still forced to work. This was the climate of 'industrialism', dominated by capitalist modes of production and distribution. In describing its effects, the Webbs made clear first of all that it acted as adversely — in fact, more so — on the quality of the wares produced by the orthodox, non-co-operative modes:

The small shopkeeper whom the Co-operative Movement displaces, like the little printing establishment or the mammoth clothing contractor, exhibits at least an equal deficiency in artistic taste. The Co-operative Movement can claim to have made a substantial advance in quality, and even . . . in distinction of style, on the very inferior output of the profit-making organisation of industry catering for customers of like incomes.

The incomes of the majority of customers under the capitalist system of wealth-distribution presented one of the most serious impediments to the attainment of yet higher standards by Co-operative products. Sidney and Beatrice spoke of the sheer 'inability of the mass of the wage-earners to pay for supreme excellence in quality, which can seldom be got without cost'. Critics of Co-operative wares, they claimed, failed 'to make allowance for the proletarian character of the custom which the Movement has to secure'. The Movement's 'proletarian' customers had suffered not only financial deprivation at the hands of industrial capitalism, but severe cultural deprivation as well. 'Generations of industrialism' had subjected the bulk of the workforce to a 'hideous environment' which had 'degraded' their tastes or left them 'very imperfectly educated'. The nature and scope of public demand for manufactured goods was restricted as much by this form of deprivation as by more material forms, with the result that any pursuit of 'supreme excellence' on the part of Co-operative manufacturers was discouraged even further. The fact, however, that a largely 'proletarian organisation' such as the Co-operative Movement had itself managed to secure many advances in the 'elevation of taste', despite the impediments of industrialism, showed the possibility for greater advances — 'slow and gradual' though these would be — as the practices and principles of the present industrial system were swept away and replaced by a more thoroughgoing socialist system.[51]

The 'elevation' in taste which the Webbs talked about here had nothing to do with those processes of refinement fondly envisaged by several other Fabians, whereby the working class of the future would come to appreciate the highest forms of literary, visual and musical art. Sidney and Beatrice showed no overt scepticism, as Shaw did in his later years, about the possibility or desirability of such processes; but in touching on the topic of a 'labour culture' or the aesthetic education of the mass of the working class, they placed the weight of their emphasis on processes which had already been initiated by, or from within, sections of the working-class itself, and which were intimately related — potentially at least — to the very work which that class performed.

The growth and consolidation of this relationship between art and everyday work came to form one of the chief aims or guiding principles of the Webbs' cultural policies for a socialist state in the future. In their draft 'Constitution' for this state, issued by them about a year or so before their work on the Consumers' Co-operative Movement appeared, they even went so far as to suggest that, 'with the elimination of the capitalist profit-making and the competitive wage-system' such activities as coal mining or sewing-machine manufacture or 'for that matter, the shifting of logs of wood from ship to wharf', could become 'truly an art' as distinct from an 'endless repetition of a purely mechanical task'. They looked forward to the time when 'trade unions of manual workers', freed from the struggle to defend the economic position of their members against capitalist encroachment, would have time to develop 'Subject Associations' specifically devoted to the study and advancement of 'the art and science of their occupation'.[52]

Sidney, at least, did not stop at writing in abstract terms about the desirability of bringing art and everyday work into a closer relationship. He employed the Fabians' traditional 'wirepulling' tactics to get influential politicians to help him implement his schemes. This is evident from a letter he wrote in 1924 to the Prime Minister of the first Labour Government, Ramsay MacDonald. He stated here that he had been 'greatly interested' to see MacDonald's public reference to 'the duty of the State to give more encouragement to art'. In this connection, he trusted that the Prime Minister remembered 'the industrial arts as well as what is sometimes called fine art'. He then went on to describe the work of The British Institute of Industrial Art, 'a semi-public organisation . . . constituted by the Board of Trade and Board of Education, with the express aim of raising the standard of decorative and industrial art in this country'. As

President of the Board of Trade, under the new Labour Government, Webb had come into closer contact with the Institute, and he told MacDonald how 'impressed' he was with the 'value and importance' of the activities it was carrying out. The effectiveness of those activities, however, was now being threatened by the decision of the Treasury to discontinue its grants to the Institute, and so Webb was 'approaching the Chancellor of the Exchequer with a view to their revival'. By giving MacDonald some idea of the Institute's aims and methods, he hoped to enlist the Prime Minister's sympathies for this 'attempt on the Chancellor'. He enclosed an official pamphlet on the activities of the Institute since its establishment in 1902; and in a gloss of his own, he explained the wider ramifications of its avowed intention to secure a 'more intimate co-operation between British Art and Industry': 'Comparatively few people can afford to buy pictures and statues, but all of them must have things of common use into which design enters, and it seems to me of great social importance therefore that the art of common things (at least as much as the so called fine arts) should receive State encouragement.'[53]

Webb's interest in bringing about a closer relationship between art and work, and the particular value he placed on the 'art of common things' as a way of consolidating that relationship and its bearing on everyone's daily life, suggest a broad sympathy with the ideals of William Morris. Though it is important to stress these aspects of Webb's thought as a corrective to the view that he and Morris represented polar opposites within the British Socialist movement, it would be misguided to depict the affinities between them as precise parallels. Leaving aside the obvious fact that Morris devoted much more of his time than Webb to explaining the relationships between art and work, there were some differences in their view of the types of art and types of work which they hoped to bring closer together.

Morris's chief and abiding concern was with 'the crafts of house-building, painting, joinery and carpentry, smiths' work, pottery and glass-making, weaving and many others': a 'body of art', he claimed, which was 'most important to the public'; and though in itself constituting a 'lesser' species compared to such 'great arts' as architecture, sculpture and painting, one which he could not 'sever' in his own mind from the latter variety. Throughout his writings he seems to have accepted the kind of distinction which Webb, in his letter to Ramsay MacDonald, firmly made between the 'art of common things' and the 'fine arts'; but he was unwilling to view that distinction in such 'hard and fast' generic terms, contending that it was a recent, and most unfortunate, historical development, which had only facilitated a decline in 'the Arts altogether'. Because of it, he claimed, 'the lesser ones become trivial, mechanical, unintelligent, incapable of resisting the changes pressed upon them by fashion or dishonesty; while the greater ... unhelped by the lesser ... are sure to lose their dignity of popular arts, and become nothing but dull adjuncts to unmeaning pomp, or ingenious toys for a few rich and idle men'.[54] Webb, in his early writings discussed above, had observed with dismay, a process of decline in 'the Fine Arts' as well as in 'the hand-worker's craft'. He attributed the decline of each to the same root cause that Morris always stressed — the commercial pressures of industrial capitalism — but he never suggested that the two species of art and their respective conditions were related to the extent of being mutually dependent. And in all of his joint works with Beatrice, whenever the question of artistic quality under industrial capitalism was touched on, the focus of his — or their — criticisms was concentrated exclusively on the non-'fine' species.

What Webb was willing to include under that particular species signified a more far-reaching departure from Morris. The latter's reaction against the rapid mechanization of industry encouraged by capitalism had not led him to anathematize machinery *per se*; but the adverse effects which the pace and competitive pressures of mechanization had wrought on the status and work of handicraftsmen may well have influenced his belief — held even more passionately by his mentor, Ruskin — that machinery was incapable of being creative in any artistic sense. In a lecture of 1884, he suggested that machines might help extinguish 'all irksome or unintelligent labour' but that 'only the hand of man guided by his soul' could produce 'loveliness and order'.[55] Webb, on the other hand, while certainly viewing handicrafts or the commodities produced by 'manual workers' as forms of art, and lamenting the effects which undiscriminating mechanization had exercised upon manufacture, did not categorically exclude machine-produced commodities from the realm of art — nor from the realm of his personal concern. We have seen how, in one of their earliest joint works, he and Beatrice had suggested that 'the machine-made product' was itself a victim of the artistic impoverishment associated with the 'deterioration of the handicraft' under industrial capitalism. This suggestion was put forward in the late 1890s; and the assumption on which it was based — the potential capacity for artistic perfection in machine-made products as well as handicrafts, under a more equable social and economic climate — may have provided the basis for the Webbs' later views that even the machines which made such products (the sewing-machine, for example) could represent a 'truly' artistic form or process.

That assumption was not articulated early enough nor with sufficient explicitness and conviction to allow one to rank the Webbs among the heralds of a 'machine aesthetic' in England. (Within the Fabian Society

Shaw has much greater claim to this rank.[56]) They were still relatively precocious, however, in their implicit adaptation of Morris-type ideals of the relationship between art, work and everyday life to the realities of the machine age. Close disciples of Morris from the 'arts and crafts movement' — men like C.R. Ashbee and W.R. Lethaby — eventually made that adaptation themselves, but not until the second decade of the new century, when they came under the influence of American and German evangelists for a machine aesthetic (notably Frank Lloyd Wright and Hermann Muthesius), and when the increasing pressure of competition from German and American goods drove home the practical limitations of any aesthetic based exclusively on craft ideals.[57]

The official Fabian tract on 'The Arts of Use', issued in 1915, echoed the Webbs' plea for the spread of art to the commodities of everyday life. It went to even greater lengths to show the potential artistic status of machine-made products, and to explain how a future socialist community would help realize that potential far more than capitalism had done. The author of the tract was Arthur Clutton Brock, an architect and the current art critic of *The Times*, who had achieved considerable popularity and prominence in the Fabian Society in the years immediately preceding the First World War. The lecture on which the tract was based — entitled 'Art and Socialism', and delivered at the beginning of 1914 — attracted a predictably 'large audience'.[58] From the outset, Clutton Brock recognized the existence and value of branches of art besides the 'arts of use', and indicated that, despite popular opinion to the contrary, a socialist regime would actively foster rather than retard the development of all branches. It would attempt to do this by making an interest in them a 'normal' part of everyday life — by wresting art in general from the 'patronage of superior persons' and 'giving it a fair chance with the ordinary man'.

The sense of full communal possession which a socialist regime would help bring about in relation to various objects of public use — trams and railway stations were two specific examples Clutton Brock had in mind — would induce a kind of civic pride in these objects and a general pleasure in their design and workmanship. Because a socialist regime would also bring about the elimination of the capitalist instinct of gain — purely private gain — the natural artistic instinct in designers would no longer be inhibited by the concern of employers to cut down expenses to a minimum in order to ensure maximum profits for themselves. 'Competition of cheapness' in the design and manufacture of useful objects would be replaced by a more healthy and inspired kind — 'competition of excellence'.[59]

It was a testimony to the long-standing interest of Fabians in this higher form of competition, conducive to artistic achievement, that, over twenty years before the publication of Clutton Brock's lecture as an official tract of the Society, Sidney Webb had warned of the non-material costs that were entailed when 'the pressure of competition' in the 'handicraft trades' was 'shifted from the plane of quality to the plane of cheapness'. That shift, he pointed out, was reflected in the general method of employing labour under the present economic system. Webb suggested that at least the London County Council, of which he had recently become a member, was attempting to reverse these trends and to resist the general shift in work-values from 'quality' to 'cheapness': 'representing the people of London', the Council 'declines to take advantage of any cheapness that is got by merely beating down the standard of life of particular sections of the wage-earners'.[60]

The competition of 'quality' or 'excellence' which Fabians like Webb and Clutton Brock endorsed with respect to 'useful' arts and crafts was characteristically ambiguous in its implications. It necessarily entailed a system of merit-grading by which the award of commissions or tenders to the artists and craftsmen concerned would be decided; and such a system could certainly be associated with the kind of 'élitist' assumptions that have been seen behind the Webbs' policies on scholarship-awards for secondary and higher education. At the same time, it was a mode of competition which had — or which was meant to have — a definite egalitarian tendency and effect, in that it was aimed at bringing everyday commodities of a high standard within the reach of a far greater number of consumers than could currently afford them or enjoy them. Any concomitant refinements in the taste of working-class consumers did not represent the imposition of standards from outside and above that class, for the commodities in question would have been produced — in contrast to many specimens of 'fine art' — by members of the working-class themselves in the course of their ordinary working day.

The bulk of commodities produced at present, and in the immediate past, may not boast any real quality or excellence; but this was not an inherent deficiency of theirs but one that was brought about by the very nature of the pressures put upon them by the economic system. Socialism would change that system and readjust the basis of those pressures; and one of the results would be that all commodities of everyday use, whether produced by the individual efforts of the handicraftsman or by the collective effort of designers and machine-workers, would have a chance of becoming truly artistic objects for the delight and refinement of the populace as a whole. Competition 'of excellence', Clutton Brock claimed, was the sort which had helped produce the great French Gothic cathedrals — specimens of a decidedly non-socialist era and environment, but nonetheless conceived and built without regard for how much they might pay. A socialist society would establish this non-materialist attitude to objects of use on a general level; and the realm of art as it appeared to the 'mass of men' would be extended to cover these objects. No longer would it be confined to purely ornamental forms and to creative expressions of 'the highest and most passionate emotions'; a 'prose in art' as well as 'a poetry' would at last be discerned and its own beauties acknowledged and appreciated:

Our notion about art now is ... that it can only be kept alive by the efforts of the cultured few. And there is truth in that so long as the cultured few impose their own conception of art upon a puzzled and indifferent world. Art will only begin to fight a winning battle when the mass of men rediscover it for themselves.[61]

'Our notion' here did not necessarily refer to the Fabians alone; though there were many members of the Society who subscribed, consciously or unconsciously, to the élitist view of art that Clutton Brock was describing. Some of the same people, however — as well as others in the Society — would have endorsed the anti-élitist rider in the last sentence, and looked on socialism as a way of actively facilitating the mass's 'rediscovery' of art. In their very divergences from William Morris's guidelines in the matter, as much as in their affinities with him, these Fabians showed how keen they were to give practical implementation to his ideal of a type of art which had a direct relationship with the everyday working lives of the bulk of the population.

10

Fabians, art and democracy

Despite the various kinds and degrees of élitism which may be found in the pronouncements of most Fabians on subjects relating to culture and the arts, there were no members of the Society who denied the importance of a mass democratic base for art in the future — whether it be the 'arts of use' or the fine arts. The particular form and function of that base were viewed from different angles and explained in different ways by those members of the Society who commented on the matter; but in their debates with themselves, or with anti-democratic and non-socialist critics on questions concerning the compatibility of art with democracy, the Fabians' general line of argument was that democratic advances (especially in the direction of full social democracy) were by no means inimical to the development of art, and were in some ways actually conducive, even imperative, to that development.

Conversely, several Fabians made clear that they considered the development of the arts in society, in the sense of their wider proliferation in any form, could not but correct some of the social and educational imbalances of a capitalist world and thereby actively foster the evolution of social democracy. Though they were not all so explicit on this point, there were (once again) none who denied the basic proposition, whatever riders or qualifications they might have added.

Such a notion as T.S. Eliot's, that there was in fact an inherent conflict between 'culture' and 'equalitarianism',[1] would certainly have been alien to all Fabians. They were not so simple-minded, however, nor so insensitive, as to be oblivious of the tensions, actual and potential, between these two forces. Their responses to the question of art's relationship with democracy were, accordingly, various and complex, and an examination of their range of responses illuminates further the tensions in their own sensibilities between élitist and egalitarian impulses.

Perhaps the most negative comments from a Fabian source on the relationship between art and democracy came from the pen of 'Fabian Bland' — the joint pseudonym of Hubert Bland and his wife, Edith Nesbit — in an article published in 1887. Trying to account for the enormous popularity of Rider Haggard, whose fictional works they felt were largely mediocre, the authors of this article referred to the 'rapid trend of all things towards democracy', and concluded that

however powerful the democracy may be ... there is one thing which, as yet, it cannot do — decide the claims of authors to greatness. Sometimes, indeed, 'the people', the elect, the cultivated, and the uncultivated, shout with one voice their acclamation of a spendid genius. It was so with Burns, with Scott, with Dickens. But when they differ, posterity will ... confirm the verdict of the elect.

Even in this passage, however, there is one phrase ('as yet') which tends to suggest that the crudity of popular judgment in art is not a flaw inherent in democratic societies and may eventually be eliminated. Earlier in the article, the Blands had alluded to the general problems of 'the period of transition from the old to the new' which 'must needs be marked by deterioration in many departments of life', but claimed that this did nothing to alter their faith that the 'democratic tendency will in the long run make for what men call happiness, and raise the standard of attainment to as yet undreamed-of heights'.[2]

As shown in an article written by Hubert Bland, alone, more than twenty years later, his own particular preference was for those writers who could win both 'the noisy applause of the mob and the high approval of the elect'. He argued that Rudyard Kipling was one of the few recent writers who fitted this category; though, in the course of analysing Kipling's *Barrack-Room Ballads* he found himself having to defend that collection against the charges of 'superfine critics' that such 'soldier songs' were 'rude, brutal, vulgar, and ... illiterate'. Bland's defence rested partly on what he identified as 'new' and 'innovatory' approaches to art in Kipling's work, to which new critical canons had to be applied, and partly on the social base of Kipling's audience: 'Wordsworth too,' Bland stated, 'was an innovator; but Wordsworth had not, as Kipling had, the faculty of appealing to the market-place as well as to the study, and in so far as he had it not he was a lesser man than Kipling.'[3]

As seen in a preceding chapter, Bland's whole concept of 'beauty', artistic or otherwise, was equated simply with the physical or emotional thrill which an object gave its beholder — any beholder whether 'cultivated' or 'uncultivated'. In accordance with that highly subjective concept he tried to check those of his readers who might

think scornfully of the humble housewife who decorates her sitting-room with ridiculous china ornaments ... If they give to her the Thrill then they are beautiful in the only sense in which beauty can be predicated of anything ... Do not, in a mad impulse to improve her taste, present her with a statuette of Rodin's ... Besides ... it is important to remember ... that seen by the glimmer of the firelight, amidst the swift play of shadow, cheap china might give you the Thrill of Beauty.[4]

Even though Bland could be charged with appalling condescension here, in his very attempt to eradicate 'the arrogance of our aestheticism', his willingness to recognize a positive aesthetic value in humbler forms of art, appealing to relatively 'uncultivated' tastes, cannot be impugned. It reflects a principle which may have been inculcated in him by his mentor, Thomas Davidson. In his lecture on 'The Significance of Art', this father-figure of the Fabians had asserted that it was a good thing for artists to create both for 'the great, high souls' and 'for "the weak and friendless sons of man" '; and by way of example he said that 'Leonardo and Titian are good; but so also are those humbler sculptors and painters who show beauty and lovableness in the small and common things of nature and events of life'.[5] Sidney Webb, laying down his aesthetic criteria in a lecture he delivered before ever coming into touch with Davidson or Bland or any of the Fabians, felt that the greatest art itself must appeal to a wide range of tastes: while 'the test of what is artistic' remained in general 'subjective and individual', an artist could not 'be said to be a great artist until he had succeeded in touching the hearts ... of the crowd'. By 'crowd' he meant 'not necessarily the whole world', for environmental factors — differences in the kinds and degrees of education received, for example — would prevent even certain classes of Englishman from being able to appreciate the subtleties of an author like George Eliot, whose greatness as an artist was the main theme of Webb's lecture. Agricultural labourers, he maintained, would have difficulty enough finding any appeal in such comparatively simple fare as 'a comic opera or the pathos of Dickens'. In view of these current educational barriers preventing an artist from attaining universal appeal, it was a 'sufficient token' of his greatness if he 'succeeded in touching the chords of many hearts, not merely one or two'.[6]

Despite the scepticism which Bland revealed early on concerning the ability of 'the democracy' to judge artistic greatness, his later comments relating to this subject carefully retreated from any notion that critical dis-abilities or insensitivities with regard to art were particularly a working-class phenomenon. Writing in 1906 on the novelist, Marie Corelli, for whose popularity he was able to find even less artistic justification than in the case of Rider Haggard, Bland observed that her readership was not confined to any specific social classes or occupational groups, but to certain types in nearly all classes. Working-class readers, he contended, actually avoided her works more than middle-class ones: 'They have little time, and I fancy good natural taste, and when they read fiction at all, they read ... Dickens, Thackeray, Scott, and, to some extent George Eliot.'[7] Bland's impressions here — whatever their degree of accuracy — suggest his basic alignment with the tendency of several other prominent Fabians to locate the most mediocre aspects of popular culture in the tastes and leisure activities of their own class rather than in those of the mass of workers.

That tendency cannot automatically be seen as 'typical' of the Fabians;

but the fact that it was shared at various times by Shaw, Besant, Headlam and Bland — regardless of differences in their respective estimates of the artistic status and stature of working-class culture — serves to emphasize that a special animus against the working-class and its pleasures, such as William Clarke developed in his later years, represented an extreme and quite atypical position for a Fabian to adopt. Even Clarke's views were not always so extreme or one-sided. While still an active Fabian, he made a point of stressing the ill-judgment which was to be found in the tastes of higher classes; and he also ascribed a far more positive role to democracy in the advancement of art than Bland was ever wont to do. An article he published in 1893, dealing with what he saw as the limits of 'democratic collectivism', spoke of an 'intense and growing vulgarity of life' as 'the real danger of democracy': 'it is not anarchy but vulgarity, the sway of the commonplace, which has to be feared'. In this instance, however, he did not specifically identify the dangerous forces he perceived with the working class; and in another section of the article discussing the fate of philosophy, religion and art in particular, he argued that the 'greatest minds' in these fields would be 'ignored, despised, persecuted, perhaps detested, I do not say merely by the majority, but by the clever, cultivated, essentially superficial people one meets in drawing-rooms or clubs'. For that reason he felt that the arts — in their 'higher forms' at any rate — could 'never be organized by the collectivity' in the manner of 'railways, docks or food supply'.

This did not mean, however, that the existence of a democratic state was completely without advantages to the artist; he may have to put up with jeering or neglect from 'the mass and the clever critics'; but more severe forms of persecution, such as 'poisoning and crucifying . . . imprisonment or exile', would 'not be established methods of dealing with genius under the *régime* of democracy'. On the contrary, democratic collectivism would give the artist 'completely free scope'. Clarke did not explain why or how in so many words; though other parts of his argument suggested that it would be by the material security which such a system would guarantee to all those who lived under it, and from which an artist in particular would benefit by being released from any financial dependence on private patrons or audiences. However vulgar or 'commonplace' their demands might be, then, the artist would be liberated from their influence. And there would be a greater chance for a greater number of people with artistic impulses or talents to develop them. The seeds of artistic liberation and growth, Clarke suggested, were to be found in the very limits of the collectivist system. That system in itself, he declared, was

no more a Utopia than is commercialism: it is merely . . . a better way of doing business. It embraces the machinery of life, and so gives the higher self, the real individual, a freedom for self-development and artistic expression which individualism can never furnish. It does this because it releases the mass of men from the pressing yoke of mere physical needs. It is not itself the artistic or spiritual expression, but it gives opportunity for that expression to manifest itself. Here then is the real limit of collectivism; it is co-extensive with the machinery and the lower part of life; it furnishes in a right way the physical basis on which the spiritual structure is to be reared. For the first time in the history of the human race there would be freedom for all.[8]

The role of democratic collectivism in nurturing the growth of individual freedom and thereby stimulating the artistic instincts of the whole community was a theme which several other Fabians touched on and which the Webbs in particular developed at length in successive works. Most members of the Society who remarked on the fruitful connections between art and democracy went beyond Clarke's conception of a purely mechanistic relationship, and tended to see it in organic terms as well. (The Webbs themselves provide no exception to this tendency.) In these discussions, words like 'democracy', 'collectivism' and 'socialism' were often interchanged, consciously or unconsciously, and their implied meanings always overlapped. Some degree of resistance to the merely 'commercial' interests of a capitalist-dominated economic and political system provided a central point of definition for the various combinations in which these terms were used; and though commercialism itself was not defined with much precision, one of its inherent features in Fabian eyes (including Clarke's) was an indifference or opposition to the proliferation of beauty and artistic 'taste' throughout the community. The full converse of this view was not simply that anti-commercial forces would help, incidentally, to facilitate the spread of art and beauty — this was as much as Clarke was prepared to concede — but that there was something in the inherent nature of these forces which was expressive of an all-embracing aesthetic impulse.

One of the most explicit and detailed demonstrations of this proposition can be found in a lecture given in 1896 by Ramsay MacDonald — a colleague of Clarke's from the early days of the New Life Fellowship and the Fabian Society, and currently associated with him in the 'Rainbow Circle', a discussion group of dedicated collectivists (both socialist and Radical). Taking as his subject 'Some Common Fallacies in the Attack against Socialism', MacDonald devoted one section of his arguments to dealing with the question: 'Will art and culture survive under Socialism?' — an issue of 'extreme importance', he declared. Under mere 'political democracy', he conceded, there might be some reason to fear for the fate of art, as writers like Alexis de Tocqueville and J.S. Mill had done. MacDonald implied that such a system did not necessarily root out those materialist ambitions and social inequities — 'the pursuit of worldly goods', for example, or 'the drudgery of a large amount of manual labour'

— with which a truly 'artistic age would have nothing to do'. He suggested, on the other hand, that the principles of full 'social democracy' had no such 'aesthetic limitations', and that it was with the realization of these principles that the socialist cause was to be identified. Contemporary society was already advanced some way along the path of social democracy (in a classically Fabian way, he saw socialism as a 'natural stage in social evolution', not as the product of a 'sudden advent'), and 'one of the most hopeful signs of the present day' was a 'revival of taste which seeks for its satisfaction some individuality in everything from a dress-suit to a candlestick'. This development confirmed the fallacy of thinking that socialism would squash all individuality and spontaneity in artistic and other matters: 'What our aesthetic critics have to remember . . . is that this very taste upon which they set so high a value is a revolt against commercialist standards of beauty and decoration, & that it . . . has been associated with the work of a certain wing of the Socialist movement.'

The gist of MacDonald's argument regarding the future of art was that it was bound up closely with the kinds of 'leisure', 'freedom', 'imaginative play' and, above all, 'hope . . . for the mass of the people' which full social democracy was best qualified to provide. In showing, he said, that the changes brought about by such a system would 'not only release man from the cares of this earth, but vitalise him with some new human faith', socialists would provide themselves with the grounds for claiming that a 'new birth for art' was an intrinsic part of their programme. For, ideally, art was a quality pervading 'all life as does an atmosphere': it was not just 'put upon canvas by paint, nor printed in a book with Gothic type . . . nor sung in sweet songs or majestic epic' but permeated the most mundane-seeming aspects of a man's existence. Democracy best realized that ideal because the art expressed by it 'beautifies, opens up & makes appropriate his whole life, his platters, his chairs, his hobnails'.[9]

There were circularities and confusions in this argument which the above summary may have oversimplified. These features of MacDonald's lecture are in themselves an indication of the inextricable links forged in his mind between the development of art and the development of socialism — and, more particularly, between the art of 'common things' and the gradualist, non-revolutionary brand of socialism which the Fabians made their trademark.

Suggestions that some kind of organic relationship exists between art and the presence of democratic, anti-commercial forces within society can be found in the writings of less prominent — and less rebellious — Fabians as well. Towards the end of 1890, at just about the time that he became a member of the Fabian Society,[10] the Rev. Percy Dearmer wrote an article entitled 'Will Democracy Destroy Manners?', in which (anticipating MacDonald) he gave some consideration to the question of art's capacity for survival under a fully democratic organization of society. He suggested first that 'the Conservative side' itself had increasingly less power to keep art alive as the 'snobbery and the lust for gold' in many of its adherents robbed it of 'refinement' and replaced 'the old reverent attachment for the much that was good in the times that are past'. He then made clear his belief that there would be no such dangers to art 'as the masses gain complete power': the 'inspired hand' of pioneering 'Socialist artists' constituted a sufficiently good token for him of what could be expected in the future. In any case, he concluded, 'culture can only be sincere and strong — can only escape the blight of pedantry — when it lives in the people of a country. Otherwise it is dry and seedless.'[11]

Dearmer was a Christian Socialist, and a close colleague of Stewart Headlam, to whose newspaper (the *Church Reformer*) he contributed the article on Democracy and Manners, as well as a regular column of dramatic criticism. Like Headlam, he remained a fairly active Fabian for many years, delivering the odd lecture and contributing to the Society's literature with a tract on *Socialism and Christianity*, published in 1907.[12] Three years before that tract appeared, another colleague of Headlam's from the Christian Socialist movement, the Rev. Charles Marson, delivered his lecture on folk song to the Fabian Society; and this provided a particular illustration of Dearmer's notion that the vitality of culture depended on its connections with genuinely popular roots, uninfluenced by the pressures of 'respectability' or of commercialism. From the Platonic premise that 'popular music expressed the inner life of the people more truly than anything else', he argued that nothing indicated 'more terribly the state to which the capitalist system has brought us than the contemptible, puerile and wearisome trash of our modern music-hall productions'. His standard of judgment here was not (as in Headlam's case) the versions of music-hall entertainment supposedly available in the past, but, rather, the traditional folk culture of rural England, as expressed particularly in the 'peasant' songs of 'crime', 'work', 'war', 'sport', and 'love' which survived in the villages of the south. These 'rich, abundant and magnificent' specimens formed the main subject of his lecture.[13]

It was no ordinary lecture, for, as we have seen, it was illustrated by actual songs, in which the audience participated under the guidance of Cecil Sharp. Sharp himself was a member of the Fabian Society, having joined it in 1900 as a 'profession of faith' in democratic collectivism.[14] From what scraps of information we possess about the occasion, it would seem that it was not just a genteel bourgeois diversion, in the way that so many other manifestations of the contemporary folk-song movement could be characterized.[15]

To begin with, Marson had been commissioned to lecture within the broad field of 'rural problems' — perhaps as a break from the Fabian Society's usual preoccupation with municipal affairs. The specific topic which he chose to discuss implied no disregard for the terms of his commission, nor any degree of trivialization; for, as he explained it, the folk-song phenomenon entailed a very serious rural problem — the problem of how to preserve its authenticity as a form of popular culture from the corrupting forces which had afflicted urban forms of culture after the advent of industrial capitalism. He associated such forces precisely with the attempts of middle-class do-gooders to exorcize the spirit of the 'taproom' from popular musical forms, and to purge those forms of the 'poaching, heathenish, Aspasian, Bohemian element' which was still to be found among their practitioners in the villages of southern England. It was thanks to the persistence of that element in comparatively remote areas that folk song had so far managed to elude 'the massed armies of respectability'; and it was thanks to the 'care' and 'elaborate pains' of the people in such localities that a tradition had managed to survive, 'accurately' and 'unbroken'. Elsewhere the riches of the tradition had been allowed to 'go to waste'; and now even its principal custodians, the peasantry, were 'ceasing to exist' and would 'never be revived by any nostrum with "Back" in it, whether it be to the land or to the Middle Ages'.[16]

Marson's implied objective — to save and collect the extant specimens of this old form of popular culture, so as to make them the basis of new forms, or at least a viable alternative to the bastardized new forms which had already sprung up — could easily be dismissed, in Shavian parlance, as 'Impossibilism'. Was there any real hope of a rural tradition, the most tenacious upholders of which were now a rarity on the rural scene itself, ever becoming a substantial and self-sustaining tradition in non-rural areas? Even if the problems of logistics could be overcome in transferring a culture from its native base to an alien environment, could that culture, in its transplanted form, have anything more than a nostalgic or antiquarian interest for its participants? This seems doubtful, especially in the light of Marson's unwillingness to countenance any adulteration of the cultural forms involved, and his own scepticism — quite realistic in the event — about the effectiveness of any retrogressive social movements, even in areas which had not been subjected to widespread industrialization. His whole conception of folk music seems to have been of that purist variety (subscribed to by Sharp as well[17]) which equated 'folk' with 'rural', and which failed to recognize the existence or value of the newer 'industrial songs' composed by urban workers and adapted more to the latter's particular environment and patterns of work.[18]

Marson's conceptions, in fact, were a curious admixture of realism and utopian idealism. While tending to idealize the capacities of folk-song as a form of genuinely popular culture in contemporary England, he refused to idealize the songs themselves, insisting on their unrefined, and resolutely unrespectable, origins and nature. That he considered their value for the nation at large to lie precisely in these qualities indicates the sincerity of his concern — however futile it may have been — to establish a base for a popular culture that was resistant to the conventions and values of his own particular class. The modes of cultural transference or imposition which his ideas entailed were not élitist in any of the senses used above.

Most other popularizers of rural folk-songs in the late-Victorian and Edwardian periods would seem to have been quite happy about modifying the words, if not the tunes, of the materials they collected and published. The temptation to pander to outsiders' idyllic notions of the countryside — or at least to avoid offending genteel tastes with the cruder elements of the genre — must have been quite strong. Even Cecil Sharp was resigned to the necessity of softening the sentiments of a few of the songs he published, so as to accommodate the demands of the 'more dishonest time' in which he found himself working.[19] In presenting the songs used as illustrative material in Marson's lecture to the Fabian Society, Sharp would appear to have made some concessions to more refined musical ears by harmonizing the pieces 'for concert purposes'; but the fact that all the versions given on that occasion were not in a published form[20] may have meant that the Fabian audience was at least exposed to the original words. The folly of evading or suppressing the unrespectable elements in these songs was part of Marson's theme, so that it is unlikely that he would have deferred to any squeamishness or complacency on the part of the Fabians themselves. Over ten years earlier, speaking in another context, he had warned his fellow 'middle-class Socialists' that 'We are only half-washed from bourgeois slush, and if we do not keep quite clear of the whole mud bath, we soon end by wallowing again in dirty contentment.'[21]

As far as Fabians outside the London branch are concerned, there is little evidence regarding their attitudes to the bases of popular culture on either a national level or in relation to their own particular locality. A pointer to the pockets of interest which might have existed is given in a résumé of a lecture on 'The Social Significance of Art', delivered to the Edinburgh branch of the Fabian Society in 1911 by its first vice-chairman, Peter White. According to the account which appears in the minute-books of that branch, White proceeded to divide contemporary art-forms into two categories: 'popular' and 'intellectual'. The former, he claimed, included those arts which were 'mainly the outcome of habit and custom': 'dancing, national ballads, and primitive music'. The latter was 'more creative and self-conscious in character, although drawing its chief inspiration from the ideas and customs of the common people': at least that was what it should be doing. White stressed the need there was 'for the blending of intellectual and popular art, by greater sympathy on the one side, and by more democratic freedom and opportunity on the other'. In the tradition of William Morris, he suggested that 'the decay of handi-craft' was a reflection of the unfortunate dichotomy which had developed in artistic activities.[22]

Fabians continued to use, and at times misuse, Morris's ideas as a focus for discussing the relationship between the arts, politics and society. The weight of his authority in these matters can be clearly felt in the views expressed by the second generation of Fabians, even when they affected to resist that authority in certain ways. Younger artists in the Society were particularly influenced, as is shown in different ways by the examples of Granville Barker and Rupert Brooke.

Barker's particular commitments were to forms of art in which Morris took least interest perhaps and Fabians the most — drama and theatre. Morris did at one time write a whimsical socialist allegory in the form of a play (*Nupkins Awakened*), but his appreciation of contemporary drama, even of Ibsen and Shaw, was perfunctory at best.[23] It is difficult to account for this apparent blind-spot; though some indirect clues are given in a lecture that Barker delivered to the Fabian Society in 1911 on 'The Necessary Theatre'. His explanation of why the dramatic arts were, or should be, of such burning importance to socialists tended to run counter to Morris's particular conceptions both of socialism and art.

Barker maintained, unexceptionably enough, that 'The drama is the art of the future for many reasons. It is a social art'; but in elaborating the reasons, he tended to endorse, or resign himself to, a vision of future society which would have been repugnant to Morris. It appeared to have no place in it at all for those simple, patiently-practised domestic arts of the past that Morris hoped would enjoy a full-scale revival in a socialist world: 'the movement of the last hundred years has been getting people away from their own fireside, that is "breaking up the home . . ." It [the drama] is economical of time . . . and now that life is getting like the Encyclopaedia Britannica (11th edition), the art of life, like the art of drama is the art of selection.' The drama's organizational requirements as a social art might also have put Morris off; certainly, in the way Barker outlined these requirements, they would have struck Morris as far too 'mechanistic' to bother with or countenance: 'the theatre,' Barker claimed, 'is a social service of some importance and . . . should be somehow publicly organized. It is the art most ripe for public organization . . . The drama can only exist with an elaborate organization, and in buildings over which public authorities already exercise control in the interests of physical safety.'

Yet Barker did not — as Morris had criticized earlier Fabians for doing

— stress the bureaucratic mechanisms of socialism to the extent of ignoring the ends. On the contrary, at the conclusion of his lecture, Barker broadened out its theme to consider the general role of art in a socialist society, explicitly invoking Morris's name in support, and even echoing the latter's criticisms of the Fabians' limitations:

Socialists must consider the place of art in the body politic ... Art is worth having, and we don't recognize this nearly enough, because, after all, the ultimate question is, what sort of human being will Socialism give us? ... The Webbs propose to have no more sickness. That is excellent, for ... art comes from abundance of vitality. But is this all, with a few tram cars thrown in? ... William Morris bequeathed us vision enough to let us see to the end of a century. He asked how the world could be a decent place until men could find joy in their work. We have found no answer to that question. Tramways won't do it. The touchstone for the doctrines of Socialism is this: are they tending to produce the sort of human being we want? What sort that is we don't know yet, but art will teach us ... The problem of the future is made up of the smaller problems of ... personal human relation[s] ... and it can only be solved if we cultivate in ourselves the power of expressing human nature, and the vision of the ideal, seen through the real, for which art strives.[24]

It remains unclear, and Barker himself was patently uncertain, whether he had more of an affinity in the final analysis with a William Morris-type socialism or with that of his fellow-Fabians. This problem is partly a reflection of the eclectic nature of Fabian socialism and the ambiguities in the relationship between its adherents and William Morris. Any notion of a dichotomy between their respective approaches to socialism was bound to cause confusion, as the boundaries between them were not as rigid as supposed, even on the questions of the importance of art to socialism and of socialism to art. The confusion is increased in Barker's case by the fact that his views on the actual organization of art in a socialist society — or, rather, the assumptions underlying those views — diverged from traditional Fabian assumptions at a crucial point as much as from Morris's. Ultimately, he does not seem to have had an especial affinity with either type of socialism, and was more of a 'loner' in the style of H.G. Wells, though not as opportunist or as aggressive perhaps. His passage through the Fabian Society was brief — about nine years — but it was not as brief as Wells's, nor deliberately disruptive. His idiosyncratic views on the arts and socialism, voiced at the time he was serving on the Society's Executive, are worth considering as a kind of control test of general Fabian attitudes and of their élitist or democratic underpinnings.

In speaking of the theatre as a social service that needed to be publicly organized in the manner of all social services, he seemed to be speaking with a characteristic Fabian voice; though in envisaging such an 'elaborate' form of organization, whereby not only the physical safety but also the 'artistic safety' of theatregoers would be looked after by the government, he already seemed to be going beyond the ideas of most

Fabians. He did not define what he meant by artistic safety, though it implied a degree of supervision over the actual material presented to the public which smacked of just the sort of élitism that Shaw branded 'impossibilist'.

There was even a kind of personal arrogance in Barker's élitism such as we find in no other Fabian. This trait comes out strongly in a lecture he delivered to another Fabian group on the subject of the theatre. While implicitly acknowledging the need and desirability of a mass audience for this art form all over England — it should, he insisted, be both a 'national and in a sense a local institution'; 'a local conscience with regard to the theatre ... would be a really healthy thing' — he made clear that the bulk of those who made up the audience were not fit, in his view, to decide on the content of the repertoire, and that he personally would not defer to the dictates of their 'conscience' where they conflicted with his own, more exalted tastes. 'They were sometimes told that the theatre was only to be an amusement', in which case he would have 'nothing to do with it' as he 'would not give up his life to the caprice of the unintelligent public'.[25]

Part of his detailed plan for state support of the dramatic arts certainly fitted in with the recommendations of most other Fabians who addressed themselves to the matter: in order to help a theatre pay its own way, a municipal authority would provide it 'with light, water and so on' and exempt it from rates, thereby freeing it of basic material cares. 'It might be run by a small committee of the council with a liberal proportion of co-opted members' — a typically Fabian procedure, it would appear, and one that was adopted, broadly speaking, in running that quasi-Fabian dramatic club, the Stage Society. But Barker, again, went beyond — and against — Fabian traditions in suggesting that the committee would only have control over financial and administrative affairs, and that even in these it would be responsible not to its constituents so much as to a solitary, and virtually omnipotent, artistic director. The committee, he asserted,

would not, of course, engage the company and select the plays: that is the work of the manager. His business would be to manage the committee as well as the theatre. Even if every member of a local authority were, ipso facto, a blockhead in matters artistic, the problem had better be faced. Bumble has got to be converted. Or the theatre might be given over to an approved manager, bound to provide the required class of plays at agreed prices.[26]

The kind of administrative élitism manifested here was much less temperate than that which underlay the Webbs' ideal of government administration: they expressly rejected the role of 'big personages' in any such enterprise, and claimed to have held 'by the common people, served by an élite of unassuming experts, who would appear to be no different in status from the common man.'[27] There may be an air of romantic self-delusion in this, but it still contrasts with Barker's conceptions and schemes, about which there was nothing 'unassuming' at all, even in intention. It may have been his own intention to become a 'big personage' which led to his drift away both from the Stage Society and the Fabian Society, neither of which could help in realizing such pretensions. When Barker was drawing up his plans for a National Theatre with William Archer, Shaw warned him against any attempt 'to make the Director supreme'. Such a patently anti-democratic manoeuvre, he suggested, was not only unrealistic, politically speaking, but also destructive, in the long run, from the point of view of art:

It would be impossible to go to the country and ask them for half a million of money, not to give the nation a theatre, but to give some private and perfectly irresponsible person a theatre ... There is only one condition on which you can establish an autocracy, and that is, by providing such a minute and elaborate constitution and Articles of War that the Director, like the Captain of a battleship, has no more freedom than his subordinates. If you want elasticity and humanity — in other words, if you want Art — you must have democracy.[28]

Nothing demonstrated Barker's extreme position in the Fabian Society more plainly than his apparent failing, in Shaw's eyes, to abide by this last dictum. For Shaw did not usually feel impelled to defend democratic practices in such an impassioned manner and himself remained very sceptical about any sort of democracy which involved direct government by the people: this was just a crude and impracticable form of it in his eyes; to be effective in any way 'it can only be government by consent of the governed'.[29] If this more refined notion was, in fact, a rationalization of deep-seated élitist instincts, it was not just that. Though the degree of democracy involved in the provision for popular consent was much more limited than it would be in any exercise of popular control, the notion of consent as the abiding basis for government was in itself a limitation on the élitist procedures of imposition and manipulation. Such procedures were 'impossibilist' in Shaw's eyes when they came to involve any positive resistance to the majority's wants and needs, especially in the field of the arts and entertainments.

There were others in the Society who would have endorsed, and gone beyond, Shaw's pleas for democracy in the arts — not only Stewart Headlam, whose views on theatre and the music hall discussed above verged on a kind of laissez-faire populism that was the opposite extreme to Barker's mandarin authoritarianism, but also Barker's fellow actor and director, Charles Charrington, who showed great admiration for the 'extremely modern and democratic' arrangements made for municipal theatre in Germany and recommended them as a model for English theatrical administration.[30]

A short·while after Shaw penned his warning to Barker about the dangers and follies of an anti-democratic policy in the arts, there was a Fabian lecture delivered at Cambridge which directed itself specifically to the relationship between 'Democracy and the Arts'. It has managed to come down to us in a complete, and published, form, because of the later fame of its author, Rupert Brooke. Speaking to the University's Fabian branch (of which he was an active committee member and former president[31]), the future war-poet dealt with his subject exclusively in terms of his own chosen field of artistic endeavour and of other 'high' or 'fine' arts. He expressly dissociated his approach from that of William Morris, 'or at least the Morrisites' — a category which, by Brooke's definition, would have included several of the Fabians whose views are recorded above, particularly the author of the later Fabian tract on the arts, Arthur Clutton Brock. In some ways, his position in the socialist movement is more confusing even than Barker's. For a while, he had resisted becoming a fully-fledged member of the Fabian Society — he started out as just an 'Associate' — precisely on the grounds that he felt himself to be more of 'a William Morris sort of Socialist'.[32] Gradually he was won over to full membership, and by the time he delivered his lecture on 'Democracy and the Arts', he had clearly convinced himself that he had been converted from a Morrisite position. In fact, there were sections of that same lecture which showed a vestigial allegiance to Morris, especially on the question of the social bases of art. At the same time, these sections were not incompatible with what many other Fabians were arguing. Brooke showed signs, too, of going beyond the usual Fabian (and 'Morrisite') position on such questions — but in the opposite direction to Barker. The idiosyncrasies of Brooke's position are remarkable more for their anti-élitist than their élitist colouring.

He started out his lecture by arguing that 'Art' and 'Crafts' were to be clearly separated because it was 'so tempting to slide from the keen edge of Art into the byways, the pursuits that don't disturb'. He did not decry attempts to revive the handicrafts, but insisted that 'Art is a different matter.' Caricaturing the 'Morrisite' position in a rather facile way, he attempted to counter it with reference both to the 'great communal arts' (such as cathedral-building and folk songs) and the finest individual works of art (works of literature such as *King Lear*, for example, or paintings like Rembrandt's 'The Polish Rider'). As far as the latter were concerned, he suggested that people wanted them for what they could 'get out of them' as spectators and not for the pleasure they gave their creators in making them. With regard to the communal arts, he believed that not only was it 'no good going back to the Middle Ages' for models on which to base a revival, but that any form of revival in these arts would be 'a small thing': 'Individuals have made tunes and poems as good as those we are told come from the people. Burns, perhaps, has done so. And you won't find any band of mediaeval rustics in an inn inspired to troll out *Paradise Lost* or a Beethoven Concerto between the bouts of mead.'

Brooke went on to accuse Morris himself of perpetuating the 'infamous heresy' that 'art is an easy thing' which could be performed either in tandem with men's 'ordinary work' or during their 'leisure time'. This critique of so-called Morrisite views — they are presented in such a highly simplified form that Morris himself would probably have disowned paternity for most of them — emphasizes a strong élitist strain in Brooke's own particular view of art. His lecture on 'Democracy and the Arts' contains perhaps the most explicit statements we have from any Fabian of that kind of élitism which identified the creative process in art with the activities of a few highly gifted individuals, engaged in a highly specialized, full-time profession. Where does 'Democracy' come into the argument then?

Midst the much-paraded disagreements with the Morrisite position, there are signs of partial agreement with certain points. The higher varieties of art (literature, music, painting) exercised by individual artists of great talent may have been the only varieties which Brooke thought worthy of the name 'Art' in post-mediaeval times; but he insisted, with as much vigour as any other Fabian, on the necessity of art's appeal to a 'large and varied' audience. An echo of Morris's warning, in 'Art Under Plutocracy', against any art 'founded on the special education or refinement of a limited body or class' can perhaps be discerned in Brooke's assertion that 'A culture sustained by an infinitesimal group of the infinitely elect will not be possible or desirable.' Brooke also referred to the potential effects of 'dark multitudes' on the arts, but specifically identified the threat which these forces presented with 'the blind amoral profit-hunger of the commercial'. Conforming with a familiar Fabian tendency, he suggested that such threats to good art came more from members of the higher, than of the lower, classes. It was 'only natural', in view of their relative deprivation in educational terms, that 'the taste of the lower classes should be at present infinitely worse than ours. The amazing thing is that it is probably better.' Taking into account 'the best of each' (as exemplified in the fields of contemporary journalism, theatre and literature) Brooke found that working-class tastes displayed much more vitality, enthusiasm, and responsiveness to fresh artistic developments than 'middle- and upper-class' ones.

In referring to various kinds of art produced for or by the working class — the repertory theatre in Manchester with its largely 'working-class support'; the literary material in newspapers such as the *Labour Leader* and the *Clarion*; the writings of a group of Cockney poets with whom he had become acquainted in London — he noted the comparative lack of 'primness' to be found in them, marked in certain cases by a conscious colloquial crudity. These were positive qualities in his eyes — qualities which, in terms of health, hope and fulfilment, were to be prized above 'the old-world passion and mellifluous despair of any gentleman's or lady's poetry'. Without modifying the initial limitations he placed on what could legitimately be termed 'Art', he clearly indicated here that an important artistic contribution could be made — indeed was being made — 'from below'.

Though his conception of the boundaries of art, the position of the artist, and the workings of the creative process in art had a decided élitist colouring, he managed to resist the more subtly élitist tendencies which sometimes crept into the writings of earlier Fabians such as Sidney Olivier, Graham Wallas and Annie Besant. Brooke's preoccupation with the higher and finer art-forms — his refusal to consider the 'lesser' or more 'useful' varieties as art at all — never involved him in looking on traditional upper-class versions of these forms as the sole model of fineness, nor in depicting the development of artistic fineness in the community as a whole simply in terms of an increasing capacity on the part of the masses to appreciate these traditional versions. He warned that

Those who have determined to make the State we live in, and are forming for the future, as fine as possible, must be very careful to oppose the force of primness . . . Unnecessarily to divide the traditions we have got from the new life of the time, to assist in divorcing good taste from popular literature, is to rob and weaken both . . . 'Vulgarity!' and 'Bad Grammar' . . . are the epithets corpses fling at the quick, dead languages at living [languages]. They do not matter. More, they are praise.[33]

It would be wrong to suggest that Olivier or Wallas or Besant or any of the Fabians ever endorsed the prim gentility which Brooke attacked here. Even William Clarke, for whom the vulgarity of the masses was to become almost an obsession in his later years, showed some distrust of 'the emasculating effect of over-culture', and praised 'the most representative Bard of Democracy', Walt Whitman, for injecting a 'healthy dash of barbarism in our . . . civilization'. At the same time, Clarke complained of the excessive disharmonies, vulgarisms and uglinesses to be found in Whitman's poetry when judged by the standard of 'the solemn organ music of Milton, the rhythmical perfection of Coleridge, the lyric beauty of Shelley, or the sweet cadence of Tennyson'.[34] Though admired for the radical and rebellious elements in their thought, as well as for their artistic achievement, the writers mentioned by Clarke here were among the favourites of many other leading Fabians as well, and had helped provide the standards of fineness by which that group judged the higher forms of art and assessed their capacity to refine the mass of the working class. On the whole, Fabians did not look to any writers from within the working class itself to provide standards of this kind; they did not even entertain the possibility of doing so. Brooke did not discard their standards (his reference to *Paradise Lost*, cited above, makes it clear that he regarded Milton's work as one of the peaks of high art); but he went beyond most of his colleagues in asserting the relevance of other standards of fineness, drawn from working-class literature and based on the very crudities of its argot.

'The influence of Democracy on the Arts,' Brooke insisted,

need not be bad. To show that it is good, and to make it better, it is most importantly our duty to welcome and aid all the new and wider movements that come with the growth of Democracy . . . to accept where we cannot understand, to endure the boots and accents of the unrefined in the sanctuary for the sake of the new Gods that follow.

He indicated that the gradualist, non-revolutionary methods by which the Fabians hoped to encourage the growth of full social democracy were the most effective ones for ensuring the survival and development of art. When Morris contemplated the possibility of art's temporary demise during the transition to social democracy, Brooke claimed to 'feel deeply' with him. Brooke even confessed to sympathizing with those who 'hold it a waste of time to consider anything for the moment but material social reform'. If a choice needed to be made between art and social reform, they had their priorities right, as far as Brooke was concerned. But he doubted that such a choice needed to be made at all: 'things don't happen that way. We have forsworn Revolution for a jog-trot along Social Reform, and there is plenty of time to take things with us in the way — Art above all'.

This last statement is more in the realm of airy assertion than of solid argument, and Brooke could justifiably be criticized for its compound of vagueness, complacency and naivete. In a later section of his lecture, however, he goes some way to remedying these defects by putting forward a number of detailed suggestions about how English society, 'as we grow more democratic', might set about making appropriate arrangements for the endowment of art and the artist through a wide array of agencies — national and local, governmental and voluntary. As a check against bureaucratic oversystematization and the dangers of fostering 'dead official art', it was a firm principle of Brooke's that 'endowment should be of as various kinds as possible'. A form of élitism, akin to that which has been seen at the basis of the Webbs' educational policies, was implicit in the mechanics of at least one of the schemes which Brooke proposed: a grant by the State of a thousand scholarships 'for life' to aspiring young artists. The abiding aim, however, of all his schemes — including this one — was not to support a meritorious few for whatever benefit they might return to the state in terms of their talent. Rather, he hoped for a situation where as many artistically-inclined people as financial resources allowed would be given complete freedom from material pressures to explore their particular field of interest and to develop their personal talent up to whatever level satisfied them. The endowment of mediocre artists — failures even — was 'an integral part of the scheme'. (This was something of a modification — if not a contradiction — of Brooke's tendency, earlier in the lecture, to identify 'true Art' only with the products of the very highly gifted.) Under his schemes, genius would out — though high talent of this kind would have as much chance of emerging from a youth 'discovered in the back streets' as from any 'upper class rival' of his.[35]

The particularly complex interplay of élitist, anti-élitist and anti-exclusivist impulses in Brooke's lecture to the Cambridge University Fabian Society is possibly another reflection of the personal confusions and naivetes of its 'sentimental and immature' author;[36] but it is not simply that. In varying degrees, a tension between impulses of this kind characterized the response of most Fabians — whatever their temperament or age — to the question of art's relationship with a democratic society or with full social democracy. That tension, indeed, is probably inherent in the mind of any middle-class person who concerns himself with such questions, and a study of its manifestations among members of the Fabian Society should be of abiding interest to those attempting to cope with it in their own minds or in their own political, social and cultural activities.

Conclusion

Fabianism has never been famous for its human qualities; there is an impression, indeed, that it had none. Most historians have followed the example of its opponents (or of embittered ex-Fabians) in painting it as a narrowly utilitarian programme of social and administrative reform, more concerned with the mechanisms of politics than with any of the moral or cultural ramifications of socialism. Its adherents have not come off much better. The traditional association of the Webbs in particular with the Fabian sensibility and approach has given them an assured place in British political mythology, but hardly a flattering one. As a mythological pair, continually invoked by their joint name, they seem to have lost their separate identities and any humanizing traits which those identities might impart. It is the same with all of the Fabians when they, or their ideas, are spoken of collectively. If Fabianism has given the Webbs a bleak reputation, by their connections with it, the reverse is at least as true; and, certainly, it is very difficult to disentangle the individuals involved from the 'group ethos' ascribed to the Society. The resultant stereotyping, not to say dehumanizing, of Fabian socialism and its adherents is particularly misguided, as it would be hard to find any other kind of socialism as happily eclectic and as studiously undoctrinal.

With respect to the Fabians, the whole notion of a single and cohesive group ethos is something of a myth. If there was anything that can be called the quintessence of Fabianism, it lay in its lack of — indeed, very resistance to — any such distillation. That in itself did lead to some frustration and unhappiness in certain quarters of the Society and could even seem like an inverse dogmatism. Charges of dogmatism, however, look rather thin and suspect when they come from members — such as A.R. Orage[1] — who themselves subscribed to more overtly dogmatic forms of socialism and made patent attempts to insinuate these into the Society's programmes. There was a measure, perhaps, of 'repressive tolerance' in the Old Gang's responses to dissident forces within the Society, and one can readily sympathize with the exasperations of the dissidents in their abortive attempts to challenge this conservative (even

271

complacent) strain, but it would be stretching and twisting the term too far to call that strain dogmatic; the dissidents, on the whole, were much more prone to prescribing or pontificating than the 'Old Gang' of Fabians were.

The protean and relatively undogmatic nature of Fabianism can be seen both as its strength, institutionally — one of the secrets of the Society's resilience — and as its weakness, ideologically. The group managed to accommodate such a diverse range of views and personalities that even the label 'socialist' does not convincingly fit them all, and appears incongruous with the Society's general stance — or lack of stance — on certain issues, such as Britain's imperial ventures in South Africa. (Dissidents or apostates, such as Walter Crane, explicitly drew attention to the incongruity.[2]) The labels, however, that are usually applied to the socialism which the Society professed — 'philistine', 'ascetic', 'élitist' — are more than just ill-fitting in certain places; they facilitate a general prejudice which retards historical understanding. Their largely pejorative implications tend to confirm the impression — fostered by the effective and well-justified debunking of the Fabians' political claims — that nothing of past value or current relevance is to be found in Fabian approaches to socialism, and that further study of these is a waste of time: individual Fabians may be interesting for the eccentricities of their private lives, but the interest and significance of their ideas — if they ever counted for much — has now been quite exhausted.[3]

One of the chief aims of this book has been to point up the vitality of Fabian ideas in precisely the area where they are considered to be most impoverished — the sphere of culture, in the sense of the arts and their relationship with work and leisure, morality and religion, politics and social class. Close analysis of the Fabians' artistic attitudes and activities exposes clearly the unfair prejudices involved in stereotyping these people, and their beliefs, as philistine, ascetic and élitist. This is not to suggest, on the other hand, that they were all sophisticated connoisseurs, inspired hedonists, and resolute champions of any and every form of popular culture, for this would be to apply yet more undiscriminating and inappropriate labels to the group. In its ranks, there was an abundant variety of responses to the arts and their relationship to society; and it is in this variety — and the very conflicts and self-conflicts which it engendered — that the unexpected, and far from exhausted, riches of Fabianism may be found, whatever we think of it as a political ideology.

One of the pioneer investigators of twentieth-century cultural developments in English society, Richard Hoggart, has located the dilemma of modern democracy in its need to reconcile the 'free and "open" society' with ever-increasing technological competence and centralization: 'the problem,' he states, 'is acute and pressing — how that freedom may be kept as in any sense a meaningful thing whilst the processes of centraliza-tion and technological development continue'.[4] The Fabians from early on were not unaware of this problem: the very origins of the Society may be seen as a response to it, and an engagement with various aspects of it can be traced in the subsequent pronouncements of all the Society's more articulate and active members — not least the Webbs. They never produced an actual solution — it is difficult and perhaps undesirable to think of the problem involved as ever permanently solvable; but they did suggest many positive and illuminating lines of approach to that problem — approaches which should not be ignored by anyone intent on meeting its constant challenges.

The Society provided a framework in which these approaches could be worked out and defined, at least tentatively; without prescribing a group ethos, it had a group structure which enabled and encouraged its members to explore their own interests in socio-cultural questions, whether as lecturers, tract-writers or simply spectators at the regularly-organized gatherings. Some of their specific views on these matters may be as outdated now as some of the institutions and genres to which they paid particular attention — the music hall, for example. But the central issues on which they were divided among themselves (and at times within themselves, as individuals) have still not been resolved today. The under-lying dilemma for anyone concerned with the organization of the arts in modern society was recently summed up by the President of the Royal Academy in terms of a choice between 'the democratization of culture' and the pursuit of full-scale 'cultural democracy'.[5] The choice is perhaps not as clear-cut as that; part of the dilemma lies precisely in the difficulty of defining any distinctions between these two procedures or goals and of working out the theoretical and practical implications of the relationship between them.[6] The Fabians did not exercise their minds expressly or exclusively on these problems, but they did not ignore them either. Their confusions as much as their basic concerns over such matters reveal them as remarkable harbingers of modern cultural debate, to whom considered attention as such — whether respectful or critical — is long overdue.

Notes

NOTES TO INTRODUCTION

1 'The Socialist Ideal — I. Art', *New Review*, IV (Jan. 1891), 1.
2 See Myra S. Wilkins, 'The Influence of Socialist Ideas on English Prose Writing and Political Thinking 1880-1895', unpublished Ph.D. thesis, University of Cambridge (1957).
3 S.B. Saul, *The Myth of the Great Depression 1873-1896* (1969).
4 *M.A.*, pp. 191-3.
5 Stanley Pierson, *Marxism and the Origins of British Socialism* (Ithaca, 1973) and *British Socialists. The Journey from Fantasy to Politics* (Cambridge, Mass., 1979); Willard Wolfe, *From Radicalism to Socialism. Men and Ideas in the Formation of Fabian Socialist Doctrines, 1881-1889* (New Haven, 1975); Stephen Yeo, 'A New Life: The Religion of Socialism in Britain, 1883-1896', *History Workshop*, 4 (1977), 5-56.
6 *F.E.S.*, p. 46.
7 Pierson, *Marxism and the Origins of British Socialism*, p. 275.
8 E.P. Thompson, *William Morris. Romantic to Revolutionary* (2nd ed., 1977).
9 Robert Parker, *A Family of Friends* (London, 1960), p. 83.
10 Donald Drew Egbert, *Social Radicalism and the Arts* (Princeton, 1970), pp. 440, 476; James W. Hulse, *Revolutionists in London. A Study of Five Unorthodox Socialists* (Oxford, 1970), p. 131.
11 See below, pp. 143, 263.
12 Notably in his *Culture and Anarchy* (1869), reprinted in R.W. Super, ed., *Complete Prose Works of Matthew Arnold*, V (Ann Arbor, 1965), and *Philistinism in England and America, Complete Prose Works*, VII (Ann Arbor, 1974).
13 E.g. S. Webb, 'The Need of Capital', unpublished lecture (1886), fol. 8, P.P., VI. 28; *The Works Manager Today* (London, 1917), pp. 11-12; letters to Beatrice Webb, 13 Sept., 7 Nov. 1891, *L.S.B.W.*, I, 295, 324; letter to May Morris, 7 April 1910, *L.S.B.W.*, II. Cf. B. Webb, 'East London Labour', *Nineteenth Century*, 24 (Aug. 1888), 163; letter to Mary Playne, ?10 June 1898, *L.S.B.W.*, II, 71; B.W.D., 19 Feb. 1906; *O.P.*, p. 15. See also Edward Pease, 'Ethics and Socialism', *Practical Socialist*, 1 (Jan. 1886), p. 18; S. Olivier, 'An Examination of Some Criticisms of Democracy', *To-Day*, 9 (1888), 170; William Clarke, 'The Limits of Collectivism', *W.C.W.*, pp. 28, 37; Hubert Bland, 'The Faith I Hold', *E.B.H.*, pp. 213-16; G.B. Shaw, *Our Theatres in the Nineties*, 1 (1932), 124-5.
14 B.W.D., 12 April 1924.

15 For details of its early social composition, based on these records, see Eric Hobsbawm, 'The Fabians Reconsidered' in his *Labouring Men* (London, 1964), pp. 255-9.

16 Chushichi Tsuzuki, *H.M. Hyndman and British Socialism* (Oxford, 1961), pp. 40, 274, and his introduction to Hyndman's *England For All* (Brighton, 1973), p. xix; E.P. Thompson, *William Morris*, pp. 390-1, 414-15.

17 See his 'Memoranda' in *H.F.S.*, pp. 263-4; his comments quoted in F.G. Bettany, *Stewart Headlam* (London, 1926), p. 139; 'Morris as I Knew Him' in *W.M.A.W.S.*, II, xviii; 'Sixty Years of Fabianism', postscript to *F.E.S.* (5th ed., 1948), p. 213.

18 Cited in S. Winsten, *Jesting Apostle* (1956), p. 78.

19 The difficulties of classifying the Fabians according to occupation are made plain in the one attempt which has been made to do so — Hobsbawm's appendix to his article, 'The Fabians Reconsidered', pp. 268-9. According to his table, only a small proportion of members would appear to have been directly engaged in the 'Arts' in the first twenty years or so of the Society's existence (approximately 4.5% in 1890; 2.5% in 1892; 3% in 1904; 3.7% in 1906); though the smallness of his sample, and his acknowledgement that it is 'not, of course, representative' (there are many Fabians mentioned in the membership lists of the Society about whom we have no biographical information) should warn us against taking these figures as the full measure even of professional interest in the arts. The necessary arbitrariness involved in his classifications, and the fact that few 'overlaps' can really be accommodated, underline the tentativeness of any conclusions which can be drawn from his tables. The 'Arts' figures, for instance, would no doubt have been more substantial if he had not decided to limit that category to practitioners of 'painting, crafts, theatre, music' and to place 'writers' in a separate category (with 'journalists').

20 Margaret Cole in *The Story of Fabian Socialism* (1961), p. 61, claims that such activities (including 'pure' literature) were ignored in this column; but the evidence does not bear her out — see *F.N.* 1894: March, p. 3, May p. 11, June, p. 15; 1895: June, p. 14, Sept., p. 26; 1896: Nov., p. 37; 1897: April, p. 7; 1898: Jan., p. 42; 1899: Sept., p. 26; 1903: March, p. 10, Nov., p. 43; and numerous similar entries.

21 *F.N.*, Aug. 1891, p. 22.

22 Mrs Townshend, *William Morris and the Communist Ideal*, Tract no. 167 (1912); Edith Morley, *John Ruskin and Social Ethics*, Tract no. 179 (1917).

23 2 July 1886 ('The Aims of Art'); 1 March 1889 ('How Shall We Live Then'); 2 May 1890 ('Gothic Architecture'), recorded in the minutes of the Society's meetings for these dates, C/8/A/10-11. For details of other occasions on which Morris may have lectured the Society, see 'A Calendar of William Morris's Platform Career' in Eugene D. Le Mire, ed., *The Unpublished Lectures of William Morris* (Detroit, 1969), pp. 241, 260.

24 See, e.g., lecture list of 1912, pp. 5-7, F.S.C., Box 17; cf. A. Clutton Brock, 'William Morris and his Socialism', lecture delivered to the Fabian Summer School, 23 Aug. 1914, recorded in the School's log-book for that date, F.S.C., C/8/D/13. Much earlier, Ernest Radford was billed to give a lecture on Morris in the series organized by the main branch on 'Socialism in Contemporary Literature' (1890), but was too ill to deliver it. Morris was invited to fill the gap by lecturing on himself, but modestly opted for 'Gothic Architecture' instead. See minutes of meeting for 2 May 1890, F.S.C., C/8/A/11; minutes of the Fabian Society Executive Committee for 22 & 29 April, F.S.C., C/8/B/2.

25. See, e.g., lecture lists of 1890, p. 4; 1891, pp. 3, 8, 12, 13; 1895, p. 6; 1898, p. 9;

1907, p. 8; 1912, pp. 5, 6: F.S.C., Box 17.

26 Minutes 23 Feb. 1906, F.S.C., C/8/A/14.

27 Fabian Society, 'Report of the Special Committee' (1906) — typewritten draft, p. 30, F.S.C., Box 11, sec. 3. Wells's paper is printed in full as Appendix C to Samuel Hynes, *The Edwardian Turn of Mind* (Princeton, 1968), pp. 390-409.

28 'The Soul of Man Under Socialism', *Fortnightly Review*, XLIX (1891), 292-313.

29 Jackson to Pease, 11 Dec. 1906, F.S.C., Box 5, C/9/A, part (b), fol. 33b-c.

30 The phrase is Shaw's in his preface to *F.E.S.* (4th ed., 1931), p. ix.

31 Jackson to Wells, 25 Feb. 1907, W.P.

32 See *H.F.S.*, ch. IX; Hynes, *The Edwardian Turn of Mind*, ch. IV; Lovat Dickson, *H.G. Wells* (1972), ch. 9; Norman and Jeanne MacKenzie, *The Time Traveller* (1973), chs. 12-14; Margaret Cole, 'H.G. Wells and the Fabian Society', in A.J.A. Morris, ed., *Edwardian Radicalism* (1974), pp. 97-113; editorial notes in *L.S.B.W.*, II, 253-7.

33 See below, pp. 129-30, 132.

34 Olivier had joined the Society in 1885, was a long-standing member of its Executive Committee, and had been one of the seven contributors to the *Fabian Essays in Socialism*. For his support of Wells, see N. and J. MacKenzie, *The First Fabians* (1977), pp. 326, 329-30.

35 *The Story of Fabian Socialism*, pp. 147-8.

36 Treatments of the Guild Socialists' ideas may be found in Niles Carpenter, *Guild Socialism* (1922); G.D.H. Cole, *History of Socialist Thought*, III. 1 (1956), ch. 4; Walter Kendall, *The Revolutionary Movement in Great Britain 1900-21* (1969), ch. 16; Margaret Cole, *The Life of G.D.H. Cole* (London, 1971), chs. 1-3; L.P. Carpenter, *G.D.H. Cole* (1973), chs. 1-3; J.M. Winter, *Socialism and the Challenge of War* (1974), pp. 50-7 and chs. 4-5; Frank Matthews, 'The Ladder of Becoming: A.R. Orage, A.J. Penty and the Origins of Guild Socialism in England' in David E. Martin and David Rubinstein, *Ideology and the Labour Movement* (1979).

37 *The Restoration of the Gild System* (1906).

38 Orage to Wells, 23 July 1906; cf. 9 June 1907, W.P. (My emphasis.) Also see his 'Politics for Craftsmen', *Contemporary Review*, XCI (1907), 789-90; though cf. 785-6 for his admission that certain Fabians (including Shaw and Webb) recognized that 'Socialism is something more than a doctrine of State Collectivism designed as a medicine for wage labourers alone.'

39 I have traced it as far back as 1922 in Niles Carpenter's *History of Guild Socialism*, pp. 82-3

40 Philip Mairet, *A.R. Orage. A Memoir* (London, 1936), p. 35.

41 Anne Fremantle, *This Little Band of Prophets* (1960), pp. 123-4; Egbert, p. 480.

42 Gill to the *New English Weekly*, 15 Nov. 1934, reprinted in Walter Shrewing, ed., *Letters of Eric Gill* (1947), p. 311: cited by Egbert, p. 476.

43 Tom Gibbons, *Rooms in the Darwin Hotel* (Nedlands, Western Australia, 1973), p. 99. Cf. John Gross, *The Rise and Fall of the Man of Letters* (Penguin edn, Harmondsworth, 1973), p. 250.

44 *The New Machiavelli* (1910-11; Penguin edn, Harmondsworth, 1970), pp. 164-5; cf. Wells's direct comments on the 'narrow way' of Webbian Socialism in his *Experiment in Autobiography*, I (Cape paperback edition, 1969), 262-3.

45 E.g. Malcolm Warner, 'The Webbs: A Study of the influence of intellectuals in politics', unpublished Ph.D. thesis, University of Cambridge (1967), pp. 75-6, 130-3; Hynes, *The Edwardian Turn of Mind*, ch. IV. Hynes later exonerates Beatrice in a sensitive and illuminating essay, 'The Art of Beatrice Webb',

published in his *Edwardian Occasions* (1972). The charge against Sidney, however, is compounded, in that Hynes suggests that the youthful artistic impulses to be found in Beatrice were suppressed after the formation of her socialist 'partnership' with Sidney, partly owing to her knowledge of his distaste for creative pursuits. See also Hynes's review of the Webbs' letters, 'A Marriage of Minds', *New York Times Book Review*, 30 July 1978, p. 8.

46 A later colleague of theirs, Leonard Woolf, is interesting on this trait: see his *Beginning Again* (1964), p. 115; cf. Sidney's own acquiescent reference to a 'Webb myth' in 'Reminiscences', Part IV, *St Martin's Review*, Jan. 1929, p. 24.

47 B.W.D., 5 Nov. 1910.

48 A demonstration of their diverse views on moral issues, for example, can be found in my article, 'Bernard Shaw, Ibsen and the Ethics of English Socialism', *Victorian Studies*, XXI (1978), 381-401.

49 S. Webb to Wells, *L.S.B.W.*, II, 263.

50 *Experiment in Autobiography*, II, 609-10.

51 See Cole, *History of Socialist Thought*, III. 1, 209-10, & my article, 'Two of the Nicest People if ever there was one: the correspondence of Sidney and Beatrice Webb', *Historical Studies*, 19 (Oct. 1980), 286-92. Cf. Marjorie Pease to J. R. MacDonald, 21 May 1896, MacDonald Papers, sec. 30/69, 5/5, Public Record Office, London; & to Mrs H.G. Wells, 24 March 1906, W.P. Also see Charlotte Shaw to B. Webb, 6 Nov. 1898, & to H.G. Wells, 18 Feb. 1906, W.P.

52 See the full list of tracts (1884-1915) in *H.F.S.*, pp. 273-80.

53 Editorial note in *L.S.B.W.*, III, 3. Cf. M.A. Hamilton, *Sidney and Beatrice Webb* (1933), p. 213; Margaret Cole, ed., *The Webbs and their Work* (1949), pp. 151-2.

54 No. 67: 'Women and the Factory Acts' (1896).

55 *F.E.S.*, p. IV.

56 A text of the Basis is provided in *H.F.S.*, Appendix II.

57 A.M. McBriar, *Fabian Socialism and English Politics* (Cambridge, 1962) p. 112; editorial note in *L.S.B.W.*, I, 105.

58 Wolfe, pp. 251-61.

59 See his *The Socialist Movement* (1911), pp. 103-5; and for an account of his views in later life, see David Marquand, *Ramsay MacDonald* (1977), esp. pp. 458-9.

60 Preface to *New Fabian Essays*, ed. R.H.S. Crossman (1952), p. vii.

61 'The Labour Party on the Threshold', Fabian Tract 207 (1923), p. 11. Cf. editorial note in *L.S.B.W.*, III, 174-5.

62 B. Webb to Friends of Seaham, 22 Jan. 1924, *L.S.B.W.*, III, 197.

63 Barbara Drake, 'The Webbs and Soviet Communism' in *W.W.*, p. 224. Cf. S. Webb, *What Happened in 1931*, Fabian Tract no. 237 (1932).

64 *F.E.S.* (4th edn, 1931), pp. ix-x. As early as his Fabian Society lecture on Ibsen in 1889, Shaw was acknowledging that on the issue of a revolutionary versus a 'parliamentarist' strategy for socialism, Morris may have had the clearer view: see 'Discards from the Fabian lectures on Ibsen and Darwin when publishing them as The Quintessence of Ibsenism & the Methuselah Preface' [hereafter Fabian Lecture on Ibsen], fol. 29, S.P., MS.50661.

65 *F.E.S.* (5th edn, 1948), p. 215.

66 *Soviet Communism* (2nd edn, 1937), pp. 571-2. Cf. S. Webb to J. Walton Newbold, 10 Feb. 1937, and B. Webb to Shaw, 19 Nov. 1939, *L.S.B.W.*, III, 419, 437.

67 Cf. Martin Meisel, 'Shaw and Revolution: the Politics of the Plays', in Norman Rosenblood, ed., *Shaw: Seven Critical Essays* (Toronto, 1971), pp. 106-34; Paul A. Hummert, *Bernard Shaw's Marxian Romance* (Lincoln, Nebraska, 1973), chs, 3,9.

68 *F.E.S.*, pp. 200-1.
69 Cf. *H.F.S.*, p. 237.
70 Cited in Cole, *Story of Fabian Socialism*, p. 32; cf. pp. 326-7.
71 Peter Townsend and Nicholas Bosanquet, eds., *Labour and Inequality. Sixteen Fabian Essays* (1973), p. 3.
72 Fabian Tract no. 70 (London, 1895), pp. 3, 6.
73 Cf. Stefan Collini, *Liberalism and Sociology* (Cambridge, 1979), ch. 1.
74 Annie Besant, *The Evolution of Society* (1886), pp. 19-22; Sydney Olivier in *F.E.S.*, p. 125, and in his lecture on 'Socialist Individualism', reported in *F.N.*, Nov. 1891, p. 33; Touzeau Parris's lecture to the Society on 'Socialism and Individual Liberty', *F.N.* May 1893, p. 9; Grant Allen, 'Individualism and Socialism', *Contemporary Review*, LV (1889), 730-6.
75 *F.E.S.* (6th edn, 1948), p. 213.
76 Winsten, *Jesting Apostle*, p. 75; cf. Jack C. Squire, *Socialism and Art* (1908), p. 5; Asa Briggs' introduction to *F.E.S.* (6th edn, 1962), p. 20.
77 The phrase is used by one of the original Essayists, Hubert Bland, in his 'The Faith I Hold', *E.B.H.*, p. 228.
78 This tendency is exemplified (with particular reference to the Society's artistic views) in M. Cole's *The Story of Fabian Socialism*, pp. 61, 126, 311, and more generally in R.D. Howland, 'Fabian Thought and Social Change in England, 1884-1914', unpublished Ph.D. thesis, L.S.E. (1942), pp. 12-13.
79 Wells to miscellaneous correspondents in the Fabian Society, 16 May 1906, W.P.
80 By H.W. Massingham, 'The Method of Fabianism', *F.N.*, March 1892, p. 1.
81 Cf. Paul Thompson, *Socialists, Liberals and Labour. The Struggle for London 1885-1914* (1967), pp. 212-21.
82 Socialist League Archives, International Institute of Social History, Amsterdam, especially sections 391/1, 3448/2, 3449/1, 3452/1, 2, 4, 3455/1-4, 3456/1-6, 3457, 3458.
83 See below, pp. 45-7.
84 Socialist League Archives, 3456/3-4.
85 Fabian Tract no. 41 (1895), p. 24.

NOTES TO CHAPTER 1

1 Compare the accounts in Wolfe, pp. 153-63; N. & J. MacKenzie, *The First Fabians*, ch. 1; Norman MacKenzie, 'Percival Chubb and the Founding of the Fabian Society', *Victorian Studies*, XXIII (Autumn 1979), 29-55.
2 Chubb to Davidson, 25 Oct. 1884, D.P., Box. 9.
3 Wolfe, p. 158.
4 Cited in Chubb to Davidson, 17 Nov. 1883, D.P.; taken from Emerson's 'Lecture on the Times', republished in Chubb's edition of *Selected Writings from Emerson* (1888), p. 253.
5 Chubb to Davidson, 21 Dec. 1883; 10 Jan., 4 Feb., 21 April, 22 Aug. 1884, D.P., Box 9.
6 *Ibid.*, 10 Jan. 1884.
7 William Knight, ed., *Memorials of Thomas Davidson* (1907), p. 18.
8 Minutes of Fabian Society meeting for 4 Jan. 1884, F.S.C., C/8/A/10.
9 Podmore to Davidson, 16 Dec. 1884, D.P., Box 34.
10 Wolfe, pp. 159-61; cf. McBriar, pp. 2-3.
11 Davidson to Henry Demarest Lloyd, 17 Oct. 1891, L.P., Reel 4.
12 *Seed-time*, 2 (Oct. 1889), 10.

13 *Sower*, 1 (July 1889), 2, 11.
14 *The Education of Wage Earners* (New York, 1904), p. 194.
15 Chubb to Davidson, 18 March 1891; cf. 13 Feb., 24 & 30 March, 1890; 24 March 1891, D.P., Box 9; Knight, ch. V.
16 Clarke to Davidson, 12 May 1883, D.P., Box 10.
17 For accounts of Clarke's early career and thought, see *W.C.W.*, pp. xi-xxix; entry in *D.L.B.*, II (1974), 94-8 (by Alan J. Lee); Eric Hobsbawm, 'The Lesser Fabians' in Lionel N. Munby, ed., *The Luddites and Other Essays* (1971), pp. 235-8.
18 Clarke to Davidson, 13 Jan. 1884, D.P., Box 10.
19 Clarke to Davidson, 13 Jan. 1884.
20 Peter Weiler, 'William Clarke: The Making and Unmaking of a Fabian Socialist', *Journal of British Studies*, XIV (Nov. 1974), 102-8.
21 'The Faith I Hold', *E.B.H.*, p. 225.
22 E.g. in his *The Philosophy of Goethe's Faust* (1906), p. 104.
23 Despite a distaste for Hegel, Davidson admitted that Hegel was 'entirely right in placing art alongside philosophy and religion, as having a most serious and all-embracing content'.
24 'The Significance of Art', undated typescript lecture, fol. 1, D.P.
25 Knight, p. 8.
26 Knight, p. 110.
27 Chubb to Davidson, 18 June 1882, D.P., Box 9.
28 Davidson, 'Art and Fact', offprint from *The Western* (no date), pp. 2, 4-5, D.P.
29 Chubb to Davidson, 2 July 1891, D.P., Box 9.
30 'Art and Fact', p. 2.
31 *The Evolution of Sculpture* (London, 1891), p. 355.
32 *The Evolution of Sculpture*, pp. 346-55.
33 See Thomas Carlyle's translation, *Wilhelm Meister's Apprenticeship and Travels*, II (Centenary edition of Carlyle's works, 1899), 324.
34 'Imitation and Expression in Art' in his *The Claims of Decorative Art* (1892), p. 160. For a comprehensive study of Crane's ideas and activities including his socialism, see Isobel Spencer, *Walter Crane* (1975).
35 At least one member of the New Life Fellowship — J.H. Muirhead — seems to have had a prior acquaintance with Goethe through the influence of his German teacher at school who took him on an extended tour of Germany: see Muirhead, *Reflections by a Journeyman in Philosophy* (1942), p. 21.
36 Chubb to Davidson, 18 June 1882; 7 Feb., 11 March, 5 April 1883; 8 Jan. 1885, D.P., Box 9.
37 Chubb to Davidson, 8 Jan. 1885.
38 *Wilhelm Meister's Apprenticeship and Travels*, II, 371, 408, 414-15.
39 'Rome: A Sermon in Sociology', Part 2, *O.C.*, 12 (Aug. 1888), 89.
40 *Faust*, Part I. Sc. 4 (Everyman edition, 1954), pp. 51-2.
41 Webb to Davidson, 6 Oct. 1894, D.P., Box 34; cf. Chubb to Davidson, 4 Sept. 1888, D.P., Box 9.
42 Chubb to Davidson, 12 Jan. 1882, D.P.
43 'Art and Fact', p. 17.
44 'A Modern Wandering Scholar', *W.C.W.*, p. 313.
45 See, e.g., the anti-Goethean critics dealt with by Henry Hatfield in his *Goethe A Critical Introduction* (New York, 1963), pp. 2-3. On the ambivalent attitudes of Goethe — and other 'romanticists' — to the label romanticism, see Jacques Barzun, *Classic, Romantic, and Modern* (Chicago, 1961), p. 7.
46 'Art and Fact', p. 17.

47 Barzun's phrase in *Classic, Romantic, and Modern*, p. 8. See also W. Jackson Bate, *From Classic to Romantic* (Cambridge, Mass., 1946), pp. 127-8. Cf. *Faust*, Part I, pp. 19, 129. On the relationship between feeling and experience in romanticism, see Lilian Furst, *Romanticism in Perspective* (London, 1969), pp. 214-27.

48 *The Philosophy of Goethe's Faust*, pp. 39, 69-70, 102-4.

49 'Art and Fact', pp. 16-17, 26-9.

50 *Sartor Resartus* (1831), ch. IX (Centenary edition, 1896), p. 153. Webb quoted the first of Carlyle's pleas in a letter he wrote to his future wife (16 June 1890), commenting: 'I long ago closed my Byron: now I will open my Goethe' — P.P., II, 3(i). For the Webbs' views on Goethe, see below, pp. 60, 62-3, 115. On the ideal of renunciation in Goethe, and its uses — or misuses — by some of his English disciples, including Carlyle, see Rosemary Ashton, *The German Idea. Four English Writers and the Reception of German Thought 1800-1860* (Cambridge, 1980), pp. 89-90, 172-3.

51 Good accounts of these can be found in Lilian R. Furst, *Romanticism* (2nd edn, 1976), pp. 1-11; Hugh Honour, *Romanticism* (1979), pp. 11-26; Charles Rosen and Henri Zerner, 'The Permanent Revolution', *New York Review of Books*, 22 Nov. 1979, pp. 23-4.

52 See H.G. Schenk, *The Mind of the European Romantics* (Oxford, 1979), ch. 1.

53 For discussions of the complexities of romanticist ideas on reason, see Harold Bloom, ' "To Reason with a Later Reason": Romanticism and the Rational' in his *The Ringers in the Tower* (Chicago, 1971), pp. 323-37; David Newsome, *Two Classes of Men. Platonism and English Romantic Thought* (London, 1974), pp. 91-4. For a succinct account of romanticism's roots in Enlightenment rationalism and of the continuing interplay between the two currents of thought, see Trygve Tholfsen, *Working Class Radicalism in Mid-Victorian England* (1976), pp. 74-7.

54 Cf. Bate, pp. 21-6; David Irwin, ed., *. Winckelmann. Writings on Art* (1972), pp. 30-1.

55 *The Philosophy of Goethe's Faust*, pp. 41, 74, 102; *Prolegomena to Tennyson's In Memoriam* (Boston, 1889); Davidson to Lloyd, 11 March 1890, L.P., reel 3; Havelock Ellis's reminiscences in Knight, p. 45.

56 *Rousseau and Education According to Nature* (1898), pp. V, 103-4, 141, 214.

57 Cf. C.R. Sanders on the ambiguities in Carlyle's attitudes to Byron and Goethe in *Carlyle's Friendships and other Studies* (Durham, Northern California, 1977), pp. 61-93.

58 See, Ruskin, *Unto this last*, W.J.R., XVII, 112; *Time and Tide*, W.J.R., 424; *Fors Clavigera*, W.J.R., XXVIII, 21-2, 432 & XXIX, 157, 244-5. The general influence of American writers on socialists in England — including the Fabians — is discussed in Henry Pelling, *America and the British Left* (1956), though he gives rather short shrift to the impact of Emerson, Thoreau and Whitman: see especially pp. 57-67, 155-6.

59 René Wellek, 'The Concept of "Romanticism" in Literary History', Part II, *Comparative Literature*, I (Spring 1949), 159, 161.

60 'The Significance of Art', fol. 16.

61 'The Educational Problems which the Nineteenth Century hand over to the Twentieth', undated draft, fols. 35-7, D.P., Box 49. A published version of this forms a chapter of Davidson's *The Education of Wage Earners*.

62 Chubb to Davidson, 7 Oct. 1882, 11 March 1883, D.P., Box 9.

63 Howland, pp. 259-60, 270; E.P. Thompson, *William Morris*, pp. 501, 776, 802-3; Raymond Williams, *Culture and Society* (Harmondsworth, 1961), pp. 160, 183-4; Sheila Rowbotham and Jeffrey Weeks, *Socialism and the New Life* (1977),

pp. 74-5. See also Tom Nairn, 'The English Literary Intelligentsia', in Emma Tennant (ed.), *Bananas* (1977), pp. 69-70.

64 Most persuasively by E.P. Thompson, *William Morris*, pp. 777-9.

65 'The Two Alternatives', *To-Day*, 8 (Sept. 1887), 76.

66 See, e.g., Robert Blatchford, 'The New Party in the North', in Andrew Reid, ed., *The New Party* (1894), pp. 17-19; Rodney Barker, *Education and Politics 1900-1951* (Oxford, 1972), p. 5.

67 *H.F.S.*, p. 27; cf. above p. 7.

68 Fremantle, *This Little Band of Prophets*, pp. 50-1; Bernard Barker, ed., *Ramsay MacDonald's Political Writings* (1972), pp. 21-2; Paul Meier, *William Morris. The Marxist Dreamer*, trans. Frank Gubb (1978), pp. 148-9. A few studies have at least acknowledged the general 'inspiration' or 'solace' which the early Fabians found in the works of certain nineteenth-century creative writers and artists, though they have not tried to assess the relative importance of these sources in any detail. See Gordon K. Lewis, 'Fabian Socialism: Some Aspects of Theory and Practice', *Journal of Politics*, 14 (Aug. 1952), 444; Pierson, *Marxism and the Origins of British Socialism*, pp. 110, 117; Wolfe, pp. 172-6.

69 *The Socialist Movement*, pp. 86-8.

70 'The Faith I Hold', *E.B.H.*, p. 222.

71 E.P. Thompson, *William Morris*, p. 269.

72 'The Faith I Hold, *E.B.H.*, p. 224.

73 'The Fabian Society', *New England Magazine*, X (March 1894), 95-6.

74 'Carlyle and Ruskin and their Influence on English Social Thought', *New England Magazine*, IX (Dec. 1893), 485.

75 'The Fabian Society', pp. 95-6.

76 E.g. Linda Nochlin, *Realism* (Harmondsworth, 1971), ch. 1 (*passim*), pp. 104-5, though cf. p. 226; Barzun, pp. 101-8. For less schematic accounts of the relationship between realism and romanticism, see Marcel Brion, *Art of the Romantic Era. Romanticism. Classicism. Realism* (1966), pp. 8-11; Honour, pp. 319-23.

77 See, e.g., Chubb to Davidson on Comte and the Positivists, 25 May 1882, 3 Jan., 7 Feb. 1883, D.P., Box 10; Clarke to Davidson on Hegelianism, 4 Jan. 1883, & on Positivism, 29 March 1884, D.P., Box 10.

78 Maurice Adams (later the editor of *Seed-time*, journal of the New Life Fellowship) to Davidson, 5 Dec. 1883, D.P., Box 1.

79 Chubb to Davidson, 18 June, 4 July, 7 Dec. 1882; 4 & 7 Feb., 5 April 1883, D.P., Box 9.

80 Chubb to Davidson, 7 Oct. 1882, D.P., Box 9.

81 Clarke to Davidson, 4 Jan. 1883, D.P., Box 10.

82 E.g., Chubb to Davidson, 18 June & 4 July 1882; 7 Feb., 11 March, 5 April, 2 May, 6 & 17 Nov. 1883; 10 Jan., 4 Feb., 25 March, 11 May 1884; 8 Jan. & 24 Feb. 1885, 5 March & 10 Oct. 1886; 27 Sept. 1888; 12 Jan. 1889; 4 June, 2 July, 27 Aug. 1891, D.P., Box 9. Clarke to Davidson, 12 June 1882; 12 May 1883; 13 Jan., 29 March, 12 Dec. 1884, D.P., Box 10; Chubb later went on to edit a selection of Emerson's essays with a critical introduction (see above, note 4). Clarke appears to have met Emerson (see Clarke's essay on 'William Dean Howells' *W.C.W.*, p. 268) and wrote an appreciative tribute, 'Ralph Waldo Emerson', *W.C.W.*, pp. 191-208. Clarke also wrote a substantial monograph on *Walt Whitman* (1892), and appreciations of Ruskin in *W.C.W.*, pp. 401-4 and 'Carlyle and Ruskin'.

83 See reports of the Fellowship's meetings in Chubb to Davidson, 6 Nov. 1883; 10 Jan., 4 Feb., 11 May, 24 Oct., 20 Nov., 1884; May 1885, D.P., Box 9. For recent

discussions of the Fellowship's early meetings, see W.H.G. Armytage, *Heavens Below* (1961), pp. 327-41; George Hendrick, *Henry Salt* (Urbana, 1977), pp. 47-9; Dennis Hardy, *Alternative Communities in Nineteenth Century England* (1979), pp. 176-7.

84 Chubb to Davidson, 21 July 1883, D.P., Box 9.
85 Chubb to Davidson, 2 & 24 May, 27 June 1883, D.P., Box 9.
86 *Commonweal*, 10 Dec. 1887.
87 Ellis, *My Life* (2nd edn, 1967), p. 158.
88 As Chubb suggests in letters to Davidson of 24 Oct., 20 Nov. 1884, D.P., Box 9.
89 For an analysis of the dominance of this stratum in the Society, see Hobsbawm, 'The Fabians Reconsidered', pp. 255f.
90 Chubb to Davidson, 1 April 1882, 24 May 1883, D.P., Box 9.
91 Clarke to Davidson, 22 Jan. 1883, D.P., Box 10.
92 See biographical sketch of Bland in the series 'On Modern Socialism', III, in *Sunday Chronicle* (Manchester), 30 Nov. 1890, p. 2. Cf. N. & J. MacKenzie, *The First Fabians*, pp. 67-8; Doris Langley Moore, *E. Nesbit* (1967), pp. 88, 92, 100.
93 Pease, 'Ethics and Socialism' & 'A Lost Knapsack', *Practical Socialist*, 1 (Jan. & April 1886), 17, 70. For the most detailed account of Pease's early career, based on his autobiographical sketches in the possession of the Pease family, see N. & J. MacKenzie, *The First Fabians*, pp. 15-18. Cf. entry in *D.L.B.*, II, 293-6 (by Margaret Cole); Noël Annan, 'The Intellectual Aristocracy', in J.H. Plumb (ed.), *Studies in Social History* (1955), pp. 265-6.
94 *H.F.S.*, p. 188.
95 See Introduction to his *Mediums of the Nineteenth Century* (New York, 1963), I, v.
96 See Henry Pelling, 'H.H. Champion: Pioneer of Labour Representation', *Cambridge Journal*, VI (1953), 222-3.
97 See Emerson's formulation of these recurrent romanticist ideals in his essay on 'Nature' in *Selected Writings*, p. 14.
98 See, e.g., *Literature and Dogma* (1873) in *Prose Works of Arnold*, VI (Ann Arbor, 1968), 151, 153, 162. Cf. Chubb's criticisms (based partly on Emerson's) of the application of Goethe's methods of culture: letters to Davidson, 4 Feb. & 2 May 1883; cf. 18 June 1882, D.P., Box 9.
99 On Arnold's ambiguous relationship with romanticism, see D.G. James, *Matthew Arnold and the Decline of English Romanticism* (Oxford, 1961), chs. 2, 3, and *The Romantic Comedy* (Oxford, 1963), pp. 273-5; Leon Gottfried, *Matthew Arnold and the Romantics* (1963), pp. 200-18; Warren D. Anderson, *Matthew Arnold and the Classical Tradition* (Ann Arbor, 1965), pp. 20, 29, 195; A. Dwight Culler, *Imaginative Reason. The Poetry of Matthew Arnold* (New Haven, 1966), pp. 19-42.
100 The debates at the Club began in 1885 and continued for several years. See Shaw's account of these in 'Bluffing the Value Theory', *To-Day*, 11 (May 1889), 129; and a recent analysis in McBriar, pp. 30-5.
101 Clarke to Davidson, 12 Dec. 1884, D.P., Box 10. Cf. Chubb to Davidson, 25 March 1884, who told his mentor that he hoped 'to draw impulse and nourishment mainly from Plato, Goethe, the Bible and Emerson', D.P., Box 9.
102 On the origins of this 'undying love for the country and all country things', see Muirhead's *Reflections*, pp. 18-19.
103 Cf. letter to Davidson, 30 Aug. 1882, recounting Chubb's visit to the Louvre, D.P. Box 9.
104 Chubb to Davidson, 25 March 1884; cf. 21 April, 17 July, 22 Aug. 1884.
105 Chubb to Davidson, 25 March 1884.

106 Chubb to Davidson, 25 May 1882.
107 Chubb to Davidson, 4 & 6 July 1883; cf. 27 Sept. 1888.
108 *W.C.W.*, pp. xi-xii, 249.
109 Clarke to Davidson, 8 June 1883; cf. 29 March, 12 Aug. 1883, D.P., Box 10, & Clarke to Lloyd, 16 July 1891, 8 May 1896, 19 Feb. & 7 May 1897, 29 July 1899, 19 Dec. 1900, L.P. reels 4, 7-8, 10, 12.
110 See his detailed recommendations for sightseeing in letter to Lloyd, 24 July 1891, L.P., reel 4.
111 'The Tidiness of Rural England'; 'England's Debt to Wordsworth', *W.C.W.*, pp. 342-3, 393-6.
112 *W.C.W.*, p. xii; cf. 'Art in our Towns', pp. 362-5.
113 'Carlyle and Ruskin', p. 486; cf. *Unto this last*, *W.J.R.*, XVII, 53-4.
114 Clarke to William S. Salter, 3 Nov. 1887, L.P., reel 2.
115 'Carlyle and Ruskin' pp. 487-8; 'The Limits of Collectivism', *W.C.W.*, p. 25.

NOTES TO CHAPTER 2

1 Pierson, *Marxism and the Origins of British Socialism*. p. 123.
2 'Need of Capital', P.P., VI. 28, fol. 8.
3 'What Socialism Means. A Call to the Unconverted' — printed as a pamphlet (1888), p. 6.
4 Clipping in P.P., VI. 95, fol. XIV.
5 'The Economic Function of the Middle Class', P.P., VI. 20, fols. 19, 28-9, 60.
6 See Wolfe, p. 211.
7 'The Difficulties of Individualism', *Economic Journal*, I (June 1891), 377. Republished as Fabian Tract 69 (1896).
8 *Industrial Democracy*, I (1897), 414-17.
9 'The War and the Workers', Fabian Tract no. 176 (1914), 18; *C.C.M.*, pp. 380-1; *E.L.G.*, IV (1922), 482.
10 *The Decay of Capitalist Civilisation* (1923), pp. 92-3; cf. pp. 9-10, 52.
11 Webb to B. Potter, 13 Aug. 1890, *L.S.B.W.*, I, 171.
12 'Rome', II, *O.C.*, 12 (1888), 89; *The London Programme* (1891), pp. 54-6; Webb to Herbert Samuel, 14 Oct. 1892, *L.S.B.W.*, II, 10.
13 Pierson, *Marxism and the Origins of British Socialism*, p. 115.
14 Webb to B. Potter, 21 Aug. 1890, P.P., II, 3 (i).
15 'The Future of London', clipping of press report in P.P. VI. 54.
16 B.W.D., 27 July 1890; Webb to R.C.K. Ensor, 29 May 1912, Ensor Papers, Corpus Christi College, Oxford; advertisement for their planned home after retiring in *New Statesman*, 28 July 1923, p. 483.
17 For details of Webb's early life, see B. Potter to Laurencina Holt, late Dec. 1891, *L.S.B.W.*, I, 382-3; S. Webb, 'Reminiscences', III, *St. Martin's Review*, Dec. 1928, pp. 621-2; *O.P.*, pp. 1-4; Royden Harrison, 'The Young Webb: 1859-1892', S.S.L.H., 17 (Autumn 1968), 15-16; entry in *D.L.B.*, II, 378 (by Margaret Cole); N. & J. MacKenzie, *The First Fabians*, pp. 56-8.
18 *M.A.*, pp. 31-2.
19 *M.A.*, pp. 184-5.
20 *M.A.*, p. 32.
21 *M.A.*, pp. 346-7, 388-9; cf. B.W.D., 1 Feb. 1890.
22 *M.A.*, pp. 348, 401.
23 Editorial note in *L.S.B.W.*, I, 375; B. Potter to S. Webb, 2 May 1890; ?1 & 13 Jan. 1891, *L.S.B.W.*, I, 133, 246-8; S. Webb to B. Potter, 14 Dec. 1890, 19 Jan. 1891, *L.S.B.W.*, I, 241-2, 248; B. Webb to E. Pease, 29 Dec. 1915, *L.S.B.W.*, III, 65.

24 *The Co-operative Movement in Great Britain* (1891), pp. 8, 13-24, 59, 118-20, 190-1, 208-9.

25 Printed in *O.P.*, pp. 210-11; cf. McBriar, *Fabian Socialism and English Politics*, pp. 149-50, for a penetrating analysis on this passage and the light it throws on the Webbs' attitudes to utilitarianism. See also *M.A.*, pp. 61-2; *L.S.B.W.*, I, 12; Mary Peter Mack, 'The Fabians and Utilitarianism', *Journal of the History of Ideas*, 16 (Jan. 1955), 76-9.

26 B.W.D., 1 Feb. 1890.

27 B.W.D., 29 Oct. 1873, 18 Jan. 1874, 30 March 1879, 14 Dec. 1879, 2 Jan. 1883.

28 B.W.D., 25 Sept. – 1 Nov. 1873 (*passim*), 14 May 1881, 3 & 8 July 1882; & B. Potter to S. Webb, 23 Aug. & ? Sept. 1890, *L.S.B.W.*, I, 179, 184-5.

29 B.W.D., 30 March, 14 Dec. 1879.

30 Beatrice to Richard Potter, 25 Nov., 8 Dec., 19 Dec. 1880, P.P., II, 1 (i); B.W.D., notes following entry of 14 Dec. 1879, & June 1880, 9 Nov. 1880, 30 June & 1 July 1882.

31 See S.R. Letwin, *The Pursuit of Certainty* (Cambridge, 1965), p. 344; though cf. Beatrice's own recollections of her father's entertaining 'intellectuals of all schools of thought, religious, scientific and literary', *M.A.*, p. 64.

32 *M.A.*, p. 35.

33 B. Potter to Webb, ?23 March 1892, *L.S.B.W.*, I, 399.

34 B.W.D., 11 July 1875, 18 Dec. 1887; B. Potter to S. Webb, Nov. 1891, P.P., II, 3 (ii), ?13 Feb. 1892, *L.S.B.W.*, I, 389.

35 B.W.D., 15 June 1878, 2 Feb. 1881, 27 Aug. & 14 Sept. 1882, 22 Jan. & 25 Feb. 1887, 4 & 20 Aug. 1889; *M.A.*, pp. 141, 153, 356.

36 See Ernest Rhys's memoirs of the Davidson circle in *Everyman Remembers* (1931), p. 43.

37 B.W.D., 3 Oct. 1879, 14 May 1881, 6 Oct. 1885, 28 Sept. 1886, 30 Sept. & 13 Dec. 1887; notes following entries of 28 July & 8 Nov. 1879; letters to her parents, 23 Dec. 1880, & Webb, 4 July 1892, P.P., II, 1 (i) & II, 3 (ii).

38 *M.A.*, p. 113.

39 B.W.D., 18 Jan. 1874.

40 *M.A.*, p. 113.

41 *M.A.*, p. 113.

42 *M.A.*, pp. 153, 389, 392; B.W.D., 1 Jan & 13 March 1885, 17 Aug. 1889.

43 B.W.D., 17 Aug. 1889.

44 See. e.g., her letter to S. Webb, 14 June 1907, & to Mary Playne, 21 June 1907, *L.S.B.W.*, II, 260, 267-8; & to H.G. Wells, 5 Jan. 1942, *L.S.B.W.*, III, 453.

45 *M.A.*, pp. 401-2.

46 *O.P.*, p. 3.

47 See Wolfe, pp. 184f.

48 *St. Martin's Review*, Dec. 1928, p. 622.

49 *O.P.*, p. 3. There may also have been personal reasons, associated with a hushed-up domestic crisis in the Webb household, which led to Webb's being sent abroad at this time — see editorial note in *L.S.B.W.*, I, 72.

50 Webb to B. Potter, 29 June, 18 Sept. 1890, *L.S.B.W.*, I, 157-8, 189.

51 Wolfe, p. 214.

52 *F.E.S.*, pp. 45-6; cf. lecture to Fabian Society by Rev. Joseph Wood on 'Municipal Socialism', reported in *F.N.*, Dec. 1891, p. 37; Sarah Howard 'The New Utilitarians? Studies in the origins and early intellectual associations of Fabianism', unpublished Ph.D. thesis, University of Warwick (1976), pp. 26-42, 256-8.

53 *F.E.S.*, pp. 45-6. Cf. Nairn, 'The English Literary Intelligentsia', p. 65.

54 'Stopford A. Brooke', *W.C.W.*, p. 250. See Pierson, *Marxism and the Origins of*

British Socialism, pp. 40-2 & Wolfe, pp. 36-7 on the injections of romanticism in J.S. Mill's utilitarian philosophy; though cf. Pierson, pp. 124-5, for a discussion of Webb's 'Benthamite' utilitarianism which takes no account of the qualifications to such views which the latter made in his letter to Beatrice of 29 June 1890. Cf. also Perry Anderson, 'Components of the National Culture', *New Left Review*, 50 (1968), 56.

55 S. Webb to B. Potter, 16 & 29 June 1890, *L.S.B.W.*, I, 153, 157-9.
56 Barzun, *Classic, Romantic and Modern*, p. 96.
57 S. Webb to B. Potter, 29 June 1890; cf. 19 Jan. 1891, *L.S.B.W.*, I, 248.
58 S. Webb to B. Potter, 12 Oct. 1890, *L.S.B.W.*, I, 212; cf. Jeanne MacKenzie, *A Victorian Courtship. The Story of Beatrice Potter and Sidney Webb* (1979), ch. 8.
59 Cf. John B. Halstead, ed., *Romanticism* (1969), pp. 60-71, including translated extract from Heine's *The Romantic School* (1836); François Fejtö, *Heine, A Biography*, trans. Mervyn Savill (1946), chs. 14, 36; Nigel Reeves, *Heinrich Heine. Poetry and Politics* (Oxford, 1974), pp. 137-77; Max Brod, *Heinrich Heine. The Artist in Revolt*, trans. Joseph Witriol (Westport, Connecticut, 1976), ch. 8.
60 S. Webb to Marjory Davidson (later the wife of Edward Pease), 12 Dec. 1888, *L.S.B.W.*, I, 119. Cf. Webb's lecture, 'The Ethics of Existence' (c.1880-1), where he traced a tradition of 'solemn melancholy' in the poems not only of Heine but also of Shelley, Byron, Lamartine, Leopardi, Tennyson and Browning: P.P., VI, 3, fol. 11.
61 S. Webb to B. Potter, 13 Aug. 1890, *L.S.B.W.*, I, 167-70; cf. 2 Aug. 1890, P.P., II, 3 (i). See also S. Webb to Wallas, 19 Oct. 1885, P.P., II, 2.
62 S. Webb to Wallas, 8 June & 8 Dec. 1885, 17 Aug. 1887, P.P., II, 2; Webb's lectures on 'Heredity as a factor in Psychology and Ethics' (c.1880-1), 'The Reformation' (c.1883), 'The Future of London' (1893), P.P., VI. 5, 12, 54.
63 S. Webb to Wallas, 7 Aug. 1886, *L.S.B.W.*, I, 99.
64 Cf. Wallas's reference at this time to 'the serious works of . . . Zola' in his lecture on 'Tithes', Wallas Papers, B.L.P.E.S., Box 16.
65 *The London Programme*, p. 80.
66 Webb to B. Potter, 21 Sept., 11 Oct., 30 Nov. 1890, 14 March 1891, *L.S.B.W.*, I, 194, 209, 232, 264; & Webb's lectures: 'On Serving God' (undated), P.P., VI. 1, and 'The Factors of National Wealth' (c.1889), P.P., VI. 39, fol. 120; *Socialism in England* (1890), pp. 42, 88; 'The Difficulties of Individualism', pp. 360-2.
67 S. Webb to B. Potter, 11 Oct. 1890, *L.S.B.W.*, I, 209.
68 It would take up too much space to give exact documentation here; but there is at least one reference to each of the following authors in Sidney's writings up to the early 1890s: Chaucer, Shakespeare, Bunyan, Defoe, Swift, Pope, Johnson, Blake, Keats, Shelley, Carlyle, Tennyson, Browning, Thackeray, Dickens, Charles Reade, Trollope, George Eliot, Kingsley, Arnold, Meredith, James Thomson, Hardy, R.L. Stevenson, Olive Schreiner.
69 See Wolfe, pp. 188n, 189.
70 'George Eliot's Works', P.P., VI. 6, fols 1-2.
71 'Socialism and Economics', c.1885, P.P., VI. 22, fol. 5.
72 'On Economic Method', c.1884-5, P.P., VI. 25, fols. 16, 24-6.
73 'Need of Capital', P.P., VI. 28, fol. 24.
74 Pierson, *Marxism and the Origins of British Socialism*, p. 123.
75 Clipping of the London letter of the National Press Agency (15 Feb. 1890), with marginal comment in Webb's hand — P.P., VI. 95.
76 *Socialism in England*, p. 109.

77 *Socialism in England*, pp. 33-4; cf. *The Teacher in Politics*, Fabian Tract 187 (1918), 7.
78 *The Labour Party on the Threshold*, Fabian Tract 207 (1923), 15.
79 See E.P. Thompson, *William Morris*, pp. 270-2; Paul Meier, *William Morris. The Marxist Dreamer*, trans. Frank Gubb (Hassocks, Sussex, 1978), II, 299-301.
80 B.W.D., 7 Sept. 1890.
81 Cited in R.H. Tawney, *The Webbs in Perspective* (1953), p. 7.
82 *Commonweal*, 25 Jan. 1890, p. 28.
83 The impression of a dichotomy is fostered by at least one recent historian, Peter Clarke, in his recurrent distinction between 'mechanical' and 'moral' reformers and revolutionists: *Liberals and Social Democrats* (Cambridge, 1978), pp. 65, 71, 198, 261-3. Morris (despite his derogatory use of the word 'mechanism' in talking of the Fabians' objectives) never insisted on any such rigid distinction, and Clarke himself has to modify or qualify it at certain points in dealing with individual Fabians — see, e.g., pp. 74, 197.
84 'What Socialism Means', *Practical Socialist*, June 1886, p. 89; cf. McBriar, p. 14.
85 *Commonweal*, 25 Jan. 1890, p. 28.
86 Obituaries of Morris in *Daily Chronicle*, 6 Oct. 1896, p. 9; *Clarion*, 10 Oct. 1896, p. 325; 'Morris as I knew him', *W.M.A.W.S.*, xxxviii-ix. Cf. Meier, I, 201-2; Jack Lindsay, *William Morris* (1975), p. 371.
87 Cf. Meier, I, 80, 148-9. Thompson (p. 548) at least acknowledges Morris's 'open, fraternal and responsible' feelings in criticizing the Fabians but suggests (on the basis of one anonymous article in an unofficial Fabian periodical) that the Fabians themselves did not return such feelings.

NOTES TO CHAPTER 3

1 On the conflicts between evangelical dogma and romanticism, see Elisabeth Jay, *The Religion of the Heart. Anglican evangelicalism and the nineteenth-century novel* (Oxford, 1979), pp. 55, 146-7, 166. On the convergences, or potential affinities, of evangelicalism and romanticism, see Jay, p. 7, & Frederick C. Gill, *The Romantic Movement and Methodism* (1937), pp. 159, 166-7.
2 *Commonweal*, 25 Jan. 1890, p. 29.
3 Morris to Wallas, 14 June 1888, Wallas Papers, Box 1, B.L.P.E.S.
4 For detailed accounts of Wallas's early life and its impact on the development of his thought, see Martin Wiener, *Between Two Worlds. The Political Thought of Graham Wallas* (Oxford, 1971), ch. 1; Terence H. Qualter, *Graham Wallas and the Great Society* (1980), pp. 1-3.
5 Wallas's introduction to an edition of Ruskin's *The Two Paths* (1907), p. 13.
6 Muirhead, pp. 51-2.
7 *Ibid.*, pp. 9-10. The quoted extract is from Morris's introduction to 'The Nature of Gothic', printed separately by the Kelmscott Press in 1892.
8 Introduction to *The Two Paths*, pp. 9, 12.
9 Especially in their reverential harking back to certain mediaeval ideals of art and social organization: see Frederic Harrison, *Tennyson, Ruskin, Mill and other Literary Estimates* (1899), pp. 101-2; cf. J.A. Hobson, *John Ruskin Social Reformer* (1898), pp. 194-5. See also correspondence between Ruskin and Harrison in *W.J.R.*, XXVIII, 662-4.
10 *W.J.R.*, XVII, 79-80; cf. Wiener, pp. 8-9.
11 *W.J.R.*, XVII, 79-80.
12 *W.J.R.*, XVII, 105.

13 Cf. John D. Rosenberg, *The Darkening Glass. A portrait of Ruskin's genius* (1963), pp. 142-3, n. 7.

14 For a later discussion by Wallas of Bentham's own applications of the criteria of pleasure and pain, and their relation to the development of the ' "Greatest Happiness Theory" or "Utilitarian Principle" ', see his lecture on 'Jeremy Bentham' (1922), printed in *Men and Ideas* (1940), esp. pp. 22-3. Cf. the discussion of J.S. Mill's revolt against the mere arithmetical calculation of pleasure in Benthamite utilitarian philosophy: Wallas, *Life of Francis Place 1771-1854* (1898), ch. III.

15 Cf. Mary Peter Mack, 'Graham Wallas' New Individualism', *Western Political Quarterly*, XI (March 1958), 15, 18, 22-9.

16 *S.O.L.W.*, pp. 60-1, 64-5.

17 *S.O.L.W.*, pp. 49, 51, 66-7; cf. Wiener, pp. 3-4; Peter Clarke, p. 10.

18 *S.O.L.W.*, pp. 26-7; cf. p. 46.

19 Wiener, pp. 4-6.

20 For details of Ruskin's early and intense Evangelical beliefs, inculcated from childhood by his mother and aunt, see *Fors Clavigera*, *W.J.R.*, XXVII, 70 f. For his later rejection of Evangelicalism, see his biography, *Praeterita*, *W.J.R.*, XXXVI, 492, 495, and scattered comments in *Fors Clavigera*: *W.J.R.*, XXVII,

21 Cf. Olivier's references to Mill and to the doctrine of evolution in relation to the development of his religious outlook: *S.O.L.W.*, pp. 47, 49, 51. For a discussion of Olivier's interest in Samuel Butler's evolutionary theories, see N. & J. MacKenzie, *The First Fabians*, p. 59.

22 See Ian Bradley, *The Call to Seriousness. The Evangelical Impact on the Victorians* (1976), pp. 197-202; though cf. Peter Clarke, pp. 12-13.

23 Cf. editorial notes, *L.S.B.W.*, I, 3, 72-3; B. to S. Webb, ?26 Sept. 1925, *L.S.B.W.*, III, 244.

24 Biographical sketch of Wallas prefacing his article on 'The Motive Power', *Sunday Chronicle*, 7 Dec. 1890, p. 2.

25 'John Stuart Mill on Socialism', *To-Day*, 2 (Nov. 1884), 49f.

26 'How I Became a Socialist', *C.W.W.M.*, XXIII, 278-9.

27 Wallas, *Men and Ideas*, p. 11.

28 'Personal Duty Under the Present System', *Practical Socialist*, 1 (July–Aug. 1886), 119, 125.

29 'The Motive Power', p. 2.

30 'Tithes', Wallas Papers, Box 16.

31 'The Society of the Future', *W.M.A.W.S.*, II, 456. Cf. Morris to Robert Thompson, Jan. 1885, in Philip Henderson, ed., *Letters of William Morris to his Family and Friends* (1950), p. 228.

32 Wiener (p. 27, n. 58) dates it between 1886 and 1888.

33 'Art', Wallas Papers, Box 16.

34 *F.E.S.*, p. 146.

35 Letter printed in *The Book of the Opening of the William Morris Labour Church at Leek* (1897), p. 8.

36 *F.E.S.*, pp. 146-8.

37 *C.W.W.M.*, XXIII, 211-14.

38 *F.E.S.*, pp. 102-3.

39 *Commonweal*, 25 Jan. 1890, p. 29.

40 *F.E.S.*, pp. 102-4; cf. pp. 114-15, 127.

41 'Perverse Socialism', part I, *To-Day*, 6 (Aug. 1886), 48; part II (Sept. 1886), 112-14. Cf. Olivier's articles in *Freedom*, I (1887): 'The Logic of Communism'

(July), 39; 'A Critic of Anarchism' (Oct.), 50-1.

42 'Idols of the Sty', part II, *To-Day*, 10 (Oct. 1888), 98-9.

43 *S.O.L.W.*, pp. 73-4, 76.

44 *F.E.S.*, p. 112 (my emphasis). The only scholar to appreciate the concern with human creativity underlying the utilitarianism of the Fabian Essayists is Adam Ulam in his *Philosophical Foundations of English Socialism* (Cambridge, Mass., 1951), pp. 77-8.

45 *F.E.S.*, pp. 124-6.

46 *S.O.L.W.*, p. 73.

47 *S.O.L.W.*, p. 74.

48 See N. & J. MacKenzie, *The First Fabians*, p. 59, quoting from family papers in the possession of Olivier's descendants.

49 *S.O.L.W.*, p. 63.

50 *S.O.L.W.*, pp. 24-5.

51 For a recent discussion of the 'Romantic-Naturalist' tradition, with references to the 'post-romantic' efforts (on the part of Mill and others) to counter it, see James McIntosh, *Thoreau as Romantic Naturalist* (New York, 1974), esp. pp. 19, 57-60, 79, 90. Cf. Mill's essay, 'Nature' (1853-4), in J.M. Robson, ed., *Collected Works of J.S. Mill*, X (Toronto, 1969), 373-428.

52 See report of a Fabian Society dinner in Olivier's honour in *Daily Chronicle*, 6 Jan. 1900. Cf. C. Tsuzuki, *Edward Carpenter 1844-1929. Prophet of Human Fellowship* (Cambridge, 1980), pp. 12, 60, 80-1.

53 *S.O.L.W.*, pp. 24-5.

54 Norman Kelvin, *A Troubled Eden. Nature and Society in the Works of George Meredith* (Stanford, 1961), p. 10; cf. pp. 127, 201.

55 This phrase is used in *The Adventures of Harry Richmond* (Constable Memorial edition, 1910), II, 350.

56 For a discussion of Meredith's ideas on reason and their proximity to Mill, see Kelvin, ch. 3 & p. 225, n. 10.

57 Meredith's handling of these themes has led one critic to present the novelist's radicalism in quasi-Marxist terms: Jack Lindsay, *George Meredith His Life* and *Work* (1956) — see esp. pp. 105-10, 181-7 for discussions of *Evan Harrington* and *Harry Richmond*, the two novels which Olivier specifies as having influenced him. Cf. Graham Wallas's comments on the impact of Meredith's social criticism — *Human Nature in Politics* (1916), pp. 184-5.

58 *S.O.L.W.*, pp. 23-4, 30.

59 *M.A.*, pp. 192-4.

60 *Sunday Chronicle*, 7 Dec. 1890, p. 2.

61 *S.O.L.W.*, p. 27.

62 *S.O.L.W.*, pp. 25-6, 45.

63 He retained an active interest in both novelists long after his boyhood; they each formed the subject of lectures delivered to the Fabian Society in 1898 — see *F.N.*, June, p. 13, Nov.–Dec., pp. 33, 37.

64 *S.O.L.W.*, p. 62.

65 S. Webb to Wells, 8 Dec. 1901, *L.S.B.W.*, II, 144.

66 *O.C.*, VII (Aug. 1886), 124.

67 *Practical Socialist*, 1 (Aug. 1886), 135.

68 'The Aims of Art', *C.W.W.M.*, XXIII, 89, 95; cf. 'Art Under Plutocracy' (1883), 'How We Live and How We Might Live' (1884), *C.W.W.M.*, XXIII, 10, 164-9.

69 *Modern Socialism*, 2nd edn (1891), p. 50; see also pp. 23, 47-9 (first published as articles in *O.C.*, VI, Feb.–May 1886). Cf. 'The Socialist Movement', *Westminster*

Review, CXXXIX (July 1886), 213, 226; *The Evolution of Society* (1886), pp. 13-14; 'The Law of Population and its relation to Socialism', *O.C.*, VI (June 1886), 13, 113, 116; *Is Socialism Sound?* — debate with G.W. Foote (1887), pp. 24, 100-10, 133, 140-1.
70 *F.E.S.*, p. 168.
71 *F.E.S.*, pp. 154, 159.
72 *Commonweal*, 25 Jan. 1890, p. 29.
73 For the most comprehensive accounts of her career at this stage, see Gertrude M. Williams, *The Passionate Pilgrim* (1931), pp. 47-184; Arthur H. Nethercot, *The First Five Lives of Annie Besant* (1961).
74 *An Autobiography* (1893), pp. 314-15.
75 Besant to Morris, 9 March 1886, Morris Papers, British Library Add. MS.45345, fol. 108.
76 See *S.A.*, I, 135-6; N. & J. MacKenzie, *The First Fabians*, pp. 81-3. Cf. *The Letters of William Morris*, pp. 275, 295, 304; Morris to his daughter, Jenny, 18 Aug. 1888, printed in J.W. Mackail, *The Life of William Morris* (1899), II, 210; Morris to Besant, 9 Feb. 1890, Morris Papers, Brit. Lib. Add. MS.45345, fol. 183.
77 *An Autobiography*, p. 311.
78 Wolfe, pp. 233-8, is especially good on these.
79 A. Besant, *Autobiographical Sketches* (1885), pp. 3-9, 11, 14, 19.
80 A. Besant, *An Autobiography*, pp. 51-2; *Autobiographical Sketches*, p. 22.
81 *Autobiographical Sketches*, pp. 10, 24.
82 *An Autobiography*, p. 104; *Autobiographical Sketches*, pp. 39-60. *Literature and Dogma* is reprinted in *Collected Prose Works of Matthew Arnold*, VI.
83 *An Autobiography*, p. 144.
84 *An Autobiography*, pp. 237-8; cf. p. 154 for quotations from a pamphlet she wrote in 1874 which declared that 'the true basis of morality is utility; that is, the adaptation of our actions to the promotion of the general welfare and happiness'.
85 *An Autobiography*, p. 153.
86 'The Gospel of Atheism', quoted in *An Autobiography*, p. 152.
87 'A World without God', quoted in *An Autobiography*, p. 172.
88 *O.C.*, VIII (Sept. 1886), 159-62.
89 *An Autobiography*, p. 304; *Modern Socialism*, p. 115; *F.E.S.*, p. 151.
90 Cited in Nethercot, p. 411.
91 *Autobiographical Sketches*, pp. 37-8.
92 *An Autobiography*, p. 299; cf. *Modern Socialism*, p. 15.
93 'Socialism, Its Fallacies and Dangers', *O.C.*, IX (March 1887), 132.
94 *S.A.*, I, 140-1.

NOTES TO CHAPTER 4

1 *Commonweal*, 25 Jan. 1890, p. 29.
2 *F.E.S.*, pp. 21-3, 197-200. Cf. 'The Lesser Arts', *C.W.W.M.*, XXII, 34; 'Art and Socialism', *C.W.W.M.*, XXIII, 195-6; 'Communism' *C.W.W.M.*, XXIII, 271-3; *Unto This Last*, *W.J.R.*, XVII, 53-4; *Munera Pulveris*, *W.J.R.*, XVII, 153-7, 278.
3 See Archibald Henderson, *George Bernard Shaw. Man of the Century* (1956), p. 177.
4 Untitled lecture to Bedford Debating Society, 10 Dec. 1885, S.P., MS.50702, fols. 163, 184-5.
5 *Munera Pulveris*, *W.J.R.*, XVII, 156. For a summing-up of the complexities of Ruskin's attitude to the machine, see Hobson, *John Ruskin*, p. 210; Herbert

Sussman, *Victorians and the Machine* (Cambridge, Mass., 1968), pp. 76-103.

6 'The Revival of Handicraft', *C.W.W.M.*, XXII, 335-6; 'How We Live and How We Might Live', 'Useful Work versus Useless Toil', 'Art under Plutocracy': *C.W.W.M.*, XXIII, 19, 24-5, 117-18, 179-80. Cf. *News from Nowhere*, *C.W.W.M.*, XVI, 93-7. The best secondary accounts of the complexities of Morris's attitudes to the machine are in Meier, *William Morris*, II, 332-40, and Sussman, pp. 104-34.

7 S.P., MS.50702, fols. 187-8.

8 *Modern Painters*, *W.J.R.*, VI, 333; *The Seven Lamps of Architecture*, *W.J.R.*, VIII, 60, 81-6; 'The Opening of the Crystal Palace', *W.J.R.*, XII, 418-19; *Aratra Pentilici*, *W.J.R.*, XX, 354.

9 Gillian Naylor's phrase in *The Arts and Crafts Movement* (1971), p. 163; though she does not consider Shaw in her discussion of the advocates of a machine aesthetic.

10 *The Quintessence of Ibsenism* (1891), pp. 61-2. Cf. McBriar, *Fabian Socialism*, p. 151.

11 'The Climate and Soil for Labour Culture' (1918), printed as 'Socialism and Culture' in Louis Crompton, ed., *The Road to Equality. Ten Unpublished Lectures and Essays by Bernard Shaw* (Boston, 1971), p. 284. Cf. William Irvine, 'Shaw, the Fabians and the Utilitarians', *Journal of the History of Ideas*, VIII (April 1947).

12 S.P., MS.50702, fols. 166-72.

13 *Modern Painters*, *W.J.R.*, III, 91.

14 S.P., MS. 50702, fol. 190.

15 Morris to Shaw, 8 & 14 July, 2 Aug. 1884, S.P., MS.50541, fols. 1-3.

16 Shaw: 'William Morris' (1899) and 'William Morris as Actor and Playwright' (1896), reprinted in *Pen Portraits and Reviews* (1932), pp. 201-17; 'Morris As I Knew Him', *W.M.A.W.S.*, II, ix-xl. See also E.E. Stokes Jnr, 'Shaw and William Morris', *Shaw Bulletin*, 4 (Summer 1953), 16-19, and 'Morris and Bernard Shaw', *Journal of the William Morris Society*, I (Winter 1961), 13-18; Hulse, *Revolutionists in London*, pp. 122-30; Elsie B. Adams, *Bernard Shaw and the Aesthetes* (Ohio State University Press, 1971), pp. 3-13. But cf. James Redmond, 'William Morris or Bernard Shaw: Two Faces of Victorian Socialism', in J. Butt & I.F. Clarke, *The Victorians and Social Protest* (1973), pp. 156-76.

17 Engagement diary, 21 Feb. 1880, Shaw Papers, B.L.P.E.S.

18 See Shaw's comparison of the evolution of his and Ruskin's thought in his 'Art Corner' column in *O.C.*, VI (Dec. 1885), 19-22. Cf. his account of Ruskin's devastating influence — much greater than Morris's, he maintained — on 'the educated, cultivated and discontented' class in England: *Ruskin's Politics* (1921), pp. 8-18.

19 'Morris As I Knew Him', *W.M.A.W.S.*, II, x.

20 *S.A.*, I, 114-15.

21 See Charles Archer, *William Archer: Life, Work, Friendships* (1931), p. 119.

22 *An Unsocial Socialist* (Standard edition, 1932), pp. 68-9, 74-6, 134-5, 165, 204-10, 214-15, 259.

23 See especially his *The Sanity of Art* (1908), first published in 1895 in the American anarchist magazine, *Liberty*, as 'A Degenerate's View of Nordau'.

24 *S.S.S.*, pp. 24-5; cf. *London Music in 1888-89* (1937), p. 13.

25 *S.S.S.*, pp. 11-12.

26 *S.S.S.*, p. 45.

27 *Immaturity* (Standard edition, 1931), Preface, p. x.

28 'On Going to Church', *Savoy*, I (Jan. 1896), 23-5; *Immaturity*, Preface, p. xix.
29 *S.S.S..*, p. 72.
30 *London Music in 1888-89*, pp. 15-16.
31 *Immaturity*, Preface, p. xii.
32 *London Music in 1888-89*, p. 16.
33 *S.S.S.*, pp. 70-1.
34 *S.A.*, I, p. 63; cf. *Everybody's Political What's What* (1944), pp. 81, 181-2.
35 For a summing-up of some English romanticists' attitudes to education, see A.S. Byatt, *Wordsworth and Coleridge in their Time* (1970), ch. 3; William Walsh, *The Use of Imagination. Educational Thought and the Literary Mind* (Harmondsworth, Middlesex, 1966), chs. 1, 2, 5. Cf. above, p. 47.
36 *Our Theatres in the Nineties*, III, 170.
37 *S.S.S.*, p. 114; *Our Theatres in the Nineties*, III, 170-3.
38 Cf. discussion of the distinction between 'romantic' and 'romanticist' in Barzun, pp. 7f.
39 Cf. Julian Kaye, *Bernard Shaw and the Nineteenth Century Tradition* (Norman, Oklahoma, 1958).
40 *The Quintessence of Ibsenism*, pp. 25-9.
41 *S.A.*, I, 113; cf. editorial note in *B.S.C.L.*, I, 145. For an analysis of Shelley's influence on Shaw, see Roland A. Duerksen, 'Shelley and Shaw', *Publications of the Modern Language Association*, LXXVIII (March 1963), 114-27.
42 *S.A.*, I, 92.
43 Fabian Tract no. 41, p. 4.
44 *S.A.*, I, 131-2.
45 Cf. Shaw, *Socialism . . . and Fabianism*, Fabian Tract no. 233 (1930), 11-12, 17; *F.E.S.* (1948), p. 229.
46 Shaw to J. Stanley Little, 26 Aug. 1889, *B.S.C.L.*, I, 220.
47 Shaw to Charles Charrington, 28 Jan. 1890, *B.S.C.L.*, I, 240.
48 Shaw to Little, 26 Aug. 1889, *B.S.C.L.*, I, 220.
49 *Love Among the Artists* (1881; Standard edition, 1932), pp. 84-5, 89, 96-7, 299-300. Cf. *An Unsocial Socialist* discussed above.
50 Preface to *Three Plays for Puritans* in Dan H. Laurence, ed., *The Bodley Head Bernard Shaw*, II (1971), 27; cf. Preface to *Misalliance*, IV (1972), 133-4. On the complexities of Shaw's attitude to puritanism, see Norbert F. O'Donnell, 'Shaw, Bunyan and Puritanism', *P.M.L.A.*, LXXII (June 1957), 520-33.
51 Shaw to Morris, 23 Sept. 1891, *B.S.C.L.*, I, 310-12.
52 See, e.g., *Modern Painters*, *W.J.R.*, IV, 49 & VII, 423; 'Inaugural Address at the Cambridge School of Art', (1858), *W.J.R.*, XXII, 36-7; 'The Lesser Arts', *C.W.W.M.*, XXII, 6-7; 'Art and Socialism', *C.W.W.M.*, XXIII, 195-6.
53 *Ruskin's Politics*, pp. 20-1.
54 Reprinted in *London Music in 1888-89*, p. 13.
55 *An Unsocial Socialist*, pp. 160-1.
56 See Janet Minihan, *The Nationalization of Culture* (1977), p. 27.
57 S.P., MS.50685, fols. 56-7.

NOTES TO CHAPTER 5

1 Kitty Muggeridge & Ruth Adam, *Beatrice Webb A Life 1858-1943* (1967), pp. 136-9; Hynes, *Edwardian Occasions*, pp. 152-72.
2 Cf. Paul Thompson, *Socialists, Liberals and Labour* (1967), pp. 143-4.
3 S. Webb to B. Potter, 6 April 1891, *L.S.B.W.*, I, 269.

4 B. Potter to S. Webb, Sept. 1890, P.P., II, 3 (ii).
5 S. Webb to B. Potter, 10 Oct. 1890, *L.S.B.W.* I, 206; 5, 6, 17 Feb. 1892, P.P., 18 June 1892, *L.S.B.W.*, I, 420.
6 S. Webb to B. Potter, 13 Aug., 10-12 Oct., 17-19 Sept. 1890; 22 Dec. 1891, *L.S.B.W.*, I, 168, 190, 359.
7 *O.P.*, pp. 2-4.
8 *M.A.*, pp. 70, 112; B.W.D., Autumn 1872, 3 Aug., Sept. 1874; cf. Muggeridge & Adam, pp. 52, 62-3; Letwin, *The Pursuit of Certainty*, pp. 344-50.
9 B.W.D., 29 Jan. 1885.
10 'George Eliot's Works', P.P., VI. 6, fol. 7.
11 See Howard, 'The New Utilitarians?', pp. 45-53.
12 'Rome', Part 2, *O.C.*, 12 (Aug. 1888), 89. On Sidney's interpretation (or misinterpretation) of the renunciation theme in Goethe, see Wolfe, p. 277, n. 74; Paul M. Haberland, 'A Fabian View of Goethe', *University of South Florida Language Quarterly*, XV (Fall 1976), 14-16.
13 S. Webb to B. Potter, 6 April 1891; cf. 14 March 1891, and B. Potter to S. Webb, 25 Oct. & ?early Dec. 1891: *L.S.B.W.*, I, 264, 268-9, 316, 342.
14 'The Way Out', P.P., VI. 19, fols. 10, 56-8.
15 Lecture printed as *What Socialism Means* (1888), pp. 6-7.
16 Fabian Tract no. 69, pp. 6, 11.
17 Notes for talk on 'Opera in Italian', S.P., MS.50721A, fols. 13-15.
18 Lecture on 'The Factors of National Wealth' (c.1889), P.P., VI. 39, fols. 76-7; Fabian Tract no. 69, pp. 11, 15.
19 Ruskin on occasions singled out for criticism the extravagance of current operatic productions in England: *Modern Painters*, *W.J.R.*, VI, 390-2; *Fors Clavigera*, *W.J.R.*, XXVII, 40.
20 B. Potter to S. Webb, Sept. 1890, P.P., II, 3 (ii); cf. editorial note, *L.S.B.W.*, I, 369.
21 For references to the simplicity and frugality of their domestic and social lives, or for their praise of simple living in general, see: B. Potter to S. Webb, 11 Aug. 1890; B.W.D., 21 June 1893, 20 June 1894, 15 March 1902, 29 April 1903, 22 Aug. 1909, 1 June 1916, 20 Feb. 1930; *O.P.*, p. 12; S. Webb to B. Potter, 21-24 Sept. 1891, *L.S.B.W.*, I, 198; 28 Oct. 1923, *L.S.B.W.*, III, 184; S. Webb, *The War and the Workers*, Fabian Tract no. 176 (1914), 20; draft of article by Webb on 'Conscience and the Conscientious Objector' (c. 1917), P.P., VII. 31, fols. 1-2.
22 B.W.D., 9 Oct. 1894.
23 B.W.D., 7 April 1924; cf. 3 Aug. 1930, 4 Aug. & 28 Oct. 1931.
24 *O.P.*, 33-5. Early interviewers of the Webbs were inclined to find the house more pleasant and attractive than later observers — see interviews in *Young Woman*, (Feb. 1895), 145, & *Woman's Signal*, 21 Feb. 1895, p. 113; cf. M.A. Hamilton, *Sidney and Beatrice Webb* (1933), pp. 71-3; Margaret Cole, *Beatrice Webb* (1945), pp. 60-1; Muggeridge & Adam, p. 15.
25 B.W.D., 11 May & 25 Sept. 1933.
26 B.W.D., 25 Sept. 1933.
27 *O.P.*, p. 14; cf. *M.A.*, pp. 355-6; B. Potter to S. Webb, ?8 Dec. 1891, *L.S.B.W.*, I, 345; B.W.D., 15 June 1906.
28 Lecture on 'Peace on Earth', P.P., VI. 52, fol. 14.
29 *C.S.C.G.B.*, p. 341.
30 *F.E.S.*, pp. 47-52. Cf. synopsis of Webb's lecture on 'Co-operation and Socialism', P.P., VI. 46; 'The Work of the London County Council', *Contemporary Review*, 67 (Jan. 1895), 138, 141-2; S. & B. Webb, 'Can Industry be Organised by the National or Municipal Government?', *New Statesman*, 8 May 1915, Special

Supplement, pp. 7, 15; S. Webb & Arnold Freeman, *Great Britain After the War* (1916), pp. 5-6, 77.

31 *Commonweal*, 25 Jan. 1890, p. 28.

32 *The Case for an Eight Hours' Bill*, Fabian Tract no. 23 (1891), 3.

33 *C.C.M.*, p. 375; cf. p. 380, & *E.L.G.*, I (1906), 357-8.

34 *F.E.S.*, pp. 50-5.

35 'Useful Work versus Useless Toil' (1884), *C.W.W.M.*, XXIII, 116-7; cf. 'At a Picture Show', (1884), *W.M.A.W.S.*, II, 419.

36 *Commonweal*, 18 May 1889, p. 157; cf. Morris to Shaw, 11 Oct. 1894, S.P., MS.50513, fol. 19.

37 *British Weekly*, 29 June 1893, p. 146; cf. B. Potter to S. Webb, ?12 Dec. 1891, *L.S.B.W.*, I, 352.

38 *Industrial Democracy*, II, 848-9; *The Principles of the Labour Party* (1919), sections II & III; *C.C.M.*, pp. 480-1. Cf. Webb & Freeman, *Great Britain After the War*, p. 10; B. Webb, 'Efficiency and Liberty: Russia', *Listener*, 9 Feb. 1938, pp. 1, 5.

39 *New Statesman*, 8 May 1915, Supplement, p. 17; cf. *The Principles of the Labour Party*, sec. II.

40 Webb & Freeman, *Great Britain After the War*, p. 71.

41 *C.S.C.G.B.*, p. 238; cf. B. Webb to William Robson, 26 Oct. 1934, *L.S.B.W.*, III, 403-4.

42 *New Statesman*, 8 May 1915, Supplement, p. 29; cf. *The Principles of the Labour Party*, sec. III; *C.C.M.*, pp. 480-1.

43 *Industrial Democracy*, II, 849.

44 Cf. Winter, p. 286.

45 *The Webbs in Perspective* (1952), p. 8. One of the few historians of Fabianism to give due recognition to this point is A.M. McBriar in his Oxford D. Phil. thesis, 'Fabian Socialist Doctrine and Its Influence in English Politics' (1949), pp. 359-63. Cf. his *Fabian Socialism and English Politics*, pp. 160-2.

46 B. Potter to S. Webb, 22 June 1890, *L.S.B.W.*, I, 155.

47 See Leonard Woolf, *Beginning Again*, p. 117.

48 B. Webb to L. Woolf, 16 March 1915, *L.S.B.W.*, III, 54.

49 B.W.D., 2 Jan. 1914, 9 June 1925.

50 B. Webb to Shaw, 14 Nov. 1939, 2 Aug. 1941, *L.S.B.W.*, III, 436, 451.

51 Woolf, *Beginning Again*, p. 119.

52 B.W.D., 27 Oct. 1939, 1 Aug. 1940, 22 Jan. 1941.

53 B. Potter to S. Webb, ?early April 1891; cf. 25 Feb. 1891, *L.S.B.W.*, I, 255, 266-7.

54 B.W.D., 13 Aug. 1938.

55 B.W.D., 24 Oct. 1939.

56 B. Webb to Palme Dutt, 15 June 1942.

57 B.W.D., 22 Jan. 1941; cf. entry for 27 Oct. 1939.

58 S. Webb to B. Potter, 21-24 Sept. 1890, *L.S.B.W.*, I, 194.

59 *British Weekly*, 29 June 1893, p. 146.

60 B.W.D., 20 July 1920.

61 S. Webb to E.D. Simon, 19 May 1913, *L.S.B.W.*, III, 20.

62 See explanation of their approach to 'documentary' and 'literary' sources in their *Methods of Social Study* (1932); new edition, Cambridge (1975), p. 101.

63 *E.L.G.*, I, 33n., 361, 581.

64 F.R. Leavis, 'Beatrice Webb in Partnership', *Scrutiny*, XVI (June 1949), 176. Cf. quotations from poems by Walt Whitman and Emily Brontë, B.W.D., 24 Aug. 1901, 1 Feb. 1903.

65 S. Webb to B. Potter, 8-9 Oct. 1891, *L.S.B.W.*, I, 203.
66 B.W.D., 18 Jan. 1897; Shaw to S. Webb, 26 July 1901, *B.S.C.L.*, II, 230.
67 4 Feb. 1924, *The Journals of Arnold Bennett*, III (1933), ed. Newman Flower, 28-9.
68 B.W.D., 20 Sept. 1938; John Parker, 'The Fabian Society and Fabian Research Bureau', *W.W.*, p. 249.
69 Malcolm Muggeridge, *Chronicles of Wasted Time*, I (1972), 148; II (1973), 269.
70 B.W.D., 19 March 1932, 6 Aug. 1933, 20 June 1938, 19 Oct. 1940; B. Webb to E.M. Forster, 24 April 1934, *L.S.B.W.*, III, 393.
71 B.W.D., 15 Jan. 1941; cf. 10 July 1924, 5 Dec. 1925, 5 Feb. 1927, 11 May 1933, 27 Dec. 1937, 12 Jan. & 20 June 1938, 27 Oct. 1939, 7 April 1941.
72 B. Webb to Wells, 10 Feb. 1909, *L.S.B.W.*, II, 323; B.W.D., 24 Feb. 1909.
73 B.W.D., March 1909; cf. N. & J. MacKenzie, *The Time Traveller*, pp. 245-6.
74 B.W.D., 30 Oct. 1932; cf. 5 Dec. 1925, 4 Jan. 1932, & letter to S. Webb, ?early Summer 1929, *L.S.B.W.*, III, 314-15.
75 *M.A.*, p. 114.
76 Cf. Michael Timko, 'The Victorianism of Victorian Literature', *New Literary History*, VI (Spring 1975), 607-27.
77 'Inaugural Address at the Cambridge School of Art', *W.J.R.*, XVI, 183, 197. Cf. *Modern Painters*, *W.J.R.*, III, 48-9; 'The Relation of National Ethics to National Arts' (1867), *W.J.R.*, XIX, 176-81.
78 B.W.D., 30 Oct. 1932.
79 B.W.D., 5 Feb. 1927, 15 Jan. & 7 April 1941; B. Webb to L. Woolf, Autumn 1920, *L.S.B.W.*, III, 141 — cf. editorial note, 446.
80 B.W.D., 27 Oct. 1939.
81 B.W.D., 2 Jan. 1883, 30 Sept. 1889. Cf. I.B. Nadel, 'Beatrice Webb's Literary Success', *Studies in Short Fiction*, 13 (Fall 1976), 441-6.
82 B.W.D., 1 Feb. 1895, 18 April 1896.
83 B. to S. Webb, 1 May 1908, *L.S.B.W.*, II, 312.
84 B. Webb to Wells, 24 Feb. 1909, *L.S.B.W.*, II, 325.
85 B. Webb to Forster, 24 April 1934, *L.S.B.W.*, III, 393-4.
86 *E.L.G.*, V, 183n., VI, 12n., VII, 48n., 374.
87 S. Webb to Jane Burdon-Sanderson, 25 Nov. 1887, *L.S.B.W.*, I, 111.
88 *Methods of Social Study*, p. 55.
89 *Soviet Communism*, II, 915-21. There are numerous other references to cultural institutions and facilities of various sorts — e.g. I: 34, 154, 160; II: 663-4, 907-13, 921-34, 941-2, 960-9, 1116, 1127-8, 1210, 1214-16.
90 S. to B. Webb, 28 April 1898, P.P., II, 3 (i); 7 July 1902, 18 Dec. 1910, *L.S.B.W.*, II, 153, 365. Cf. B.W.D., 5 June 1902, 16 Jan. & 24 July 1903; 30 July & 29 Nov. 1905, 27 Dec. 1909, 13 March 1910, 13 Sept. 1916.
91 B.W.D., 13 March 1910; S. to B. Webb, 17 June 1907, *L.S.B.W.*, II, 264, & 5 Sept. 1912, P.P., II, 3(i); B. Webb to Catherine Wells, Sept. 1907, *L.S.B.W.*, II, 273.
92 B.W.D., 4 Sept. 1906.
93 B.W.D., 13 March 1910.
94 B.W.D., 16 Jan. 1903.
95 S. to B. Webb, 7 July 1902, *L.S.B.W.*, II, 153.
96 S. Webb to Shaw, 28 April 1898, *L.S.B.W.*, II, 262.
97 Entry by Sidney in B.W.D., 12 Nov. 1898.
98 B.W.D., 28 May 1932 (Appendix); S. to B. Webb, 25 Sept. 1934, P.P., II, 3(i); Barbara Drake, 'The Webbs and Soviet Communism', *W.W.*, p. 227.

 99 B.W.D., 28 May 1932 (Appendix); S. to B. Webb, 18 & 25 Sept., 1 Oct. 1934, P.P., II, 3(i).
100 *Soviet Communism*, II, 918.
101 S. Webb to B. Potter, 13 Sept. 1891, *L.S.B.W.*, I, 295.
102 B.W.D., 25 Sept. 1932.
103 B.W.D., 25 March 1939.
104 B.W.D., 11 Jan. 1939; cf. 24 May & 8 Dec. 1933, 23 May 1936, 14 Sept. 1938.
105 B.W.D., 11 Jan. 1939.
106 *Scrutiny*, XVI (1949), 175-6; cf. Leavis's appraisal of Beatrice in his introduction to *Mill on Bentham and Coleridge* (1971), pp. 18-29.
107 B.W.D., 27 Oct. 1937.
108 S. to B. Webb, 14, 15, 20 Oct., 3, 14, 27 Nov. 1930, 23 Nov. 1933, P.P., II, 3(i).
109 B.W.D., 5 Dec. 1925.
110 B.W.D., 23 Dec. 1925; cf. 24 July 1926, 20 Sept. 1927, 2 Feb. 1929, 11 May 1933. See also S. to B. Webb, 11, 12 Dec. 1922, *L.S.B.W.*, III, 162, 164.
111 Catalogue of the Webbs' furniture and effects (1948), P.P., III, 3(ii), item 3, p. 9.
112 B. Webb to William Robson, 11 Sept. 1931, *L.S.B.W.*, III, 365.
113 'What I Believe', *Nation*, 3 June 1931, pp. 605-6; B.W.D., 30 Oct. 1932, 19 Sept. 1939.
114 B.W.D., 20 April 1909.
115 See the inventories of the Webbs' household goods and pictures (1911, 1924-5, 1930, 1934), P.P., III, 3(i-ii).
116 B.W.D., 31 March 1898.
117 Webb to Wallas, 7 Aug. 1886, 13 Oct. 1888, *L.S.B.W.*, I, 99, 116; & to B. Webb, 9 April 1900, *L.S.B.W.*, II, 128, 1 Dec. 1920, *L.S.B.W.*, III, 143, 4 March 1925, 20 June 1936, P.P., II, 3 (i); *London Education* (1904), pp. 14, 24; lecture on 'The Future of Soviet Communism' (1936), P.P., VI, 89.
118 *The History of the Foundation of the London School of Economics and Political Science* (1963), pp. 78, 80.
119 A. Clutton Brock, *Socialism and the Arts of Use*, Fabian Tract no. 177 (1915).
120 Caine, p. 80.
121 Webb to May Morris, 7 April 1900, *L.S.B.W.*, II, 127.
122 S. Webb, 'The Work of the London County Council', *Contemporary Review*, 67 (Jan. 1895), 142; *O.P.*, pp. 79-80. Cf. Naylor, p. 179.
123 Gill to H.G. Wells, 24 Sept., 7 Nov. 1905, W.P. Cf. Susan Beattie, *A Revolution in London Housing: L.C.C. housing architects and their work 1893-1914* (1980), and reviews of this book in *Times Literary Supplement*, 27 June 1980, and *New Statesman*, 4 July 1980.
124 Webb to May Morris, 7 April 1900, *L.S.B.W.*, II, 127.
125 Entry by Sidney in B.W.D., 12 Nov. 1898.
126 *Soviet Communism*, pp. 927, 932-4.
127 B. Webb to Kate Courtney, 31 Jan. 1926, P.P., II, 1.
128 See her descriptions of scenic views in various countries (England, Ireland, Canada, Italy, Switzerland): letters to S. Webb, 25 April 1893, early 1901, 9, 11, ?13, ?16 July 1902, April/May 1905, 29 April 1908, 26 Feb. 1910, P.P., II, 3(ii) & *L.S.B.W.*, II, 161, 163, 307-8; B.W.D., 19 July 1911, 15 July 1916, 22 Nov. 1923; 'The Committee on the Control of Industry', *Crusade*, III (Dec. 1912), 223.
129 S. to B. Webb, 30 April 1908, *L.S.B.W.*, II, 308, 30 May 1929, P.P., II, 3(i).
130 See E.M. Forster, 'Webb and Webb', in his *Two Cheers for Democracy* (Abinger edition, 1972), p. 210; cf. editorial note in *L.S.B.W.*, I, 73.
131 S. to B. Webb, 16 July 1907, *L.S.B.W.*, II, 270; cf. editorial note, p. 270.

132 B.W.D., 9 April 1924.
133 B.W.D., 25 Sept. 1900, 2 July 1929.
134 S. Webb to B. Potter, 18 Sept, 1891, P.P., II, 3(i); cf. 24 Sept. 1890 & Webb to Wallas, 2 July 1885, *L.S.B.W.*, I, 87, 198.
135 *C.S.C.G.B.*, p. 351.
136 Gertrude Himmelfarb, 'Process, Purpose and Ego', *Times Literary Supplement*, 25 June 1976, p. 790; cf. Winter, pp. 51-2.
137 B. Webb to Shaw, 13 June 1914, *L.S.B.W.*, III, 31-2; speech by B. Webb reported in *Manchester Guardian*, 18 Oct. 1929, p. 17; 'Efficiency and Liberty: Russia', *Listener*, 9 Feb. 1938, p. 281; B.W.D., 24 Oct. 1939.

NOTES TO CHAPTER 6

1 *The Future of Socialism* (1956), 522-4.
2 'The Society of the Future', *W.M.A.W.S.*, II, 457-9, 462; 'Art and Socialism', *C.W.W.M.*, XXIII, 213.
3 *W.J.R.*, VII, 424, 427; XXVIII, 440, 641.
4 Cf. George Orwell, 'Reflections on Gandhi' in *Collected Essays, Journalism and Letters of George Orwell*, IV (1968), 466-7.
5 B.W.D., 22 Aug. 1909, 5 Nov. 1910.
6 See Webb's obituary of Headlam (c.1924): typescript in P.P., VII. 40.
7 Preface to *Too True to be Good, Bodley Head Bernard Shaw*, VI, 406. Cf. *Everybody's Political What's What*, pp. 187, 326-7.
8 'The Climate and Soil for Labour Culture', printed in *The Road to Equality*, pp. 313, 326-7.
9 'Signs of the Time', MS in MacDonald Papers, Public Record Office, 30/69, 6/178, fol. 19. Cf. Eric Gill's use of the term 'asceticism' in his *Autobiography* (1940), p. 212.
10 Syllabus in supplement to *F.N.* of 1916.
11 'The Significance of Art', fols. 8, 19, 36, D.P. Cf. undated lecture on Aeschylus, D.P., Box 46, fol. 7.
12 Chubb to Davidson, 3 Jan. & 5 April 1883, 2 July 1891, D.P., Box 9.
13 *Walt Whitman*, pp. 67-8.
14 *W.C.W.*, pp. 199, 248-9, 264, 391; *Walt Whitman*, p. 31.
15 See my article, 'Bernard Shaw, Ibsen and the Ethics of English Socialism'.
16 'How London Amuses Itself: West and East', *O.C.*, VIII (July 1886), 13.
17 *Autobiographical Sketches*, p. 292.
18 See Nethercot, *The First Five Lives of Annie Besant*, pp. 155-6.
19 *An Autobiography*, p. 239.
20 'A Midsummer Holiday', *O.C.*, V (Jan. 1885), p. 6.
21 *Is Socialism Sound?*, pp. 104-6, 150-2; 'London', *O.C.*, XI (Jan. 1888), 24; 'The Basis of Socialism', *Sunday Chronicle*, 14 Dec. 1890. p. 2.
22 S. Webb to B. Potter, 14 March, 18 Sept., 5 Dec. 1891; Peter Clarke, pp. 30, 35.
23 See Webb's obituary of Headlam, P.P., VII. 40, fols, 3, 5; Brian Simon, *Education and the Labour Movement* (1965), pp. 207f.
24 Bland to Wells, 24 March 1906, W.P.
25 See Wells's comparison of his and Bland's exploits in *Experiment in Autobiography*, II, 604-7. Cf. my letter on 'Fabian Ethics', *Times Literary Supplement*, 6 June 1980.
26 *With the Eyes of a Man* (1905), pp. 104-5, 109; *Letters to a Daughter* (1906), pp.

84, 87; *The Happy Moralist* (1907), p. 146; *Olivia's Latchkey* (1913), p. 38; *E.B.H.*, p. 172.

27 *Letters to a Daughter*, p. 19.

28 See biographical sketch heading his article, 'On Modern Socialism', *Sunday Chronicle*, 30 Nov. 1890, p. 2.

29 *Letters to a Daughter*, p. 29.

30 'Beauty', in *With the Eyes of a Man*, pp. 55, 57, 63.

31 For recent surveys of the sources and components of this tradition, see R.V. Johnson, *Aestheticism* (1969); Bernard Bergonzi, 'Aspects of the Fin de Siècle' in Arthur Pollard, ed., *The Victorians* (1970), pp. 364-85; Robin Spence, *The Aesthetic Movement* (1972).

32 Preface to *The Renaissance*, Pater's *Works* (Library edition, 1910), I, ix.

33 'Observations on the Art of Life', *With the Eyes of a Man*, p. 119.

34 'Aesthetic Poetry' was the title he chose in publishing a revised version of his review of *The Earthly Paradise* in *Appreciations* (1889), pp. 213-27. In its original form the essay was published in the *Westminister Review*, XC (1868), 300-12. The conclusion to the original essay later formed the conclusion to *The Renaissance* (first published 1873), from which Bland probably took the passage counselling the love of art for its own sake.

35 See E.P. Thompson, *William Morris*, pp. 147-50; though cf. pp. 658, 680.

36 See especially 'Art Under Plutocracy', *C.W.W.M.*, XXIII, 173, cf. 'The Society of the Future', *W.M.A.W.S.*, II, 464-5.

37 'Beauty', *With the Eyes of a Man*, pp. 63-4.

38 *Works*, V, 38.

39 'Beauty', *With the Eyes of a Man*, pp. 62-3, 69, 74-5.

40 *Bodley Head Bernard Shaw*, II, 527.

41 'Mr. Shaw's "Man and Superman"', *With the Eyes of a Man*, pp. 83-4.

42 *Bodley Head Bernard Shaw*, II, 527-8.

43 'From Dickens to Ibsen', S.P., MS.50693, fols. 201ff.

44 Elsie B. Adams, *Bernard Shaw and the Aesthetes* (Columbus, Ohio, 1971). Cf. Sidney P. Albert, 'Bernard Shaw: The Artist as Philosopher', *Journal of Aesthetics and Art Criticism*, XIV (June 1956), 419-38.

45 Bland to Pease, 17 March, 3 April 1903, F.S.C., Box 1.

46 Cf. *E.B.H.*, pp. 14-15, 36-7, 89-91.

47 See, e.g., Headlam's *The Church Catechism and the Emancipation of Labour* (1874); cf. his Fabian Society lecture on 'Maurice and Kingsley', reported in *F.N.*, Nov. 1905, pp. 53-4.

48 For biographical details, see Bettany, *Stewart Headlam*; & *D.L.B.*, II, 172-8 (entry by David Rubinstein).

49 Bettany, pp. 6-8.

50 'The Bishop of London and the Ballet', *C.R.*, IV (Oct. 1885), 234-7; cf. Bettany, pp. 25-8, 43-4, 59, 65-71.

51 Ruskin to Headlam in *C.R.*, III (Feb. 1884), 25; cf. letter to Headlam, 18 July 1879, *W.J.R.*, XXXVII, 292-3.

52 'The Outlook', *C.R.*, III (Jan. 1884), 1; cf. Headlam's gloss on this editorial, cited in Bettany, p. 113.

53 Obituary of Headlam, P.P., VII. 40, fol. 1.

54 Bettany, pp. 70-1.

55 Bettany, p. 134; *D.L.B.*, II, 175.

56 Draft Report on Fabian Policy, c.1910, Ensor Papers, box marked '3 Socialism. Fabian Society'.

57 *The Socialist's Church* (1907), pp. 55-6.

58 *Fabianism and Land Values* (c.1908), pp. 10-12.

59 Cited in Bettany, pp. 139-40.

60 'Applause', *C.R.*, V (May 1886), 111-12; cf. 'Church and Stage', *C.R.*, III (Feb. 1884), 43.

61 *The Function of the Stage* (1889), pp. 9-11, 21-2; cf. his preface to *The Theory of Theatrical Dancing* (1888), p. xiii.

62 'The Danger of Municipal Puritanism', syllabus & report in *F.N.*, Oct. & Nov. 1904, pp. 37, 41-2. For earlier attacks on the Council's puritanism, see 'On the Licensing of Theatres and Music Halls', *C.R.*, IX (Jan. 1890), 18-20.

63 *F.N.*, Nov. 1904, p. 42; & report of the discussion after Headlam's lecture in *Reynold's Newspaper*, 16 Oct. 1904, p. 1.

64 'The Work of the London County Council', *Contemporary Review*, 67 (Jan. 1895), 136-8.

65 *The Ballet* (1894), pp. 9-10, 13.

66 'The Anti-Puritan League', proof copy enclosed in letter from Bland to Wells, 24 March 1906, W.P. For Headlam's connections with the League, see Bettany, p. 128.

67 For Headlam's acknowledgement of the affinities between his ideals and Morris's, see 'The Nonconformist Conscience', *C.R.*, X (Oct. 1891), 221.

68 Lionel Trilling, 'The Fate of Pleasure,' in his *Beyond Culture* (Penguin edn, Harmondsworth, 1967), p. 78.

NOTES TO CHAPTER 7

1 Webb to Ensor, 8 Aug. 1903, Ensor Papers.

2 *F.E.S.*, (3rd ed., 1920), p. i.

3 As we know now from most major studies of the Society, its political influence in any active and direct sense was much less than most of its members claimed in their self-confident rhetoric.

4 Cf. Introduction, p. 19.

5 For an excellent background discussion of some of the ambiguities in these attitudes, see Peter Bailey, '"A Mingled Mass of Perfectly Legitimate Pleasures"': The Victorian Middle Class and the Problem of Leisure', *Victorian Studies*, XXI (Autumn 1977), pp. 7-28.

6 Shaw to Ensor, 22 Feb. 1910, Ensor Papers.

7 Wells to Pease, 16 Sept. 1908, F.S.C., Box 1.

8 Notably in *The New Machiavelli* (1911) but also in *Ann Veronica* (1909), chs. 7-8.

9 Crane to Olivier, 9 Jan. 1889, F.S.C., Box 1.

10 See Gillian Naylor, *The Arts and Crafts Movement* (1971); Isobel Spencer, *Walter Crane* (1975), pp. 141-58; Peter Stansky, 'Art, Industry and the Aspirations of William Martin Conway', *Victorian Studies*, vol. XIX (June 1976), esp. pp. 465-6.

11 *H.F.S.*, p. 188.

12 Crane to Pease, 29 July 1890, F.S.C., Box 1.

13 Fabian Society Executive Committee Minutes, 20 Dec. 1907, F.S.C., Part B, C/8/B/9.

14 See, e.g., Executive Committee Minutes for 10 & 24 June, 7 & 22 Sept. 1898; 24 Sept., 3 March 1899; 14 June, 19 July 1901; 15 July 1904; 26 May, 23 June, 1905; 26 Feb. 1914: F.S.C., C/8/B/6-8, 12.

15 See, e.g., Executive Committee Minutes for 20 Jan., 3 & 17 Feb., 20 & 27 Oct. 1891; 23 April, 17 Oct., 12, 16, 30 Dec. 1892; 29 June 1906; 20 Dec. 1907; 14 Feb. 1908; 12 March, 2 April, 7 & 21 May, 25 June, 9 July, 8 & 29 Oct. 1909; 28 Jan., 25 Feb. 1910; 10 Nov. 1911; 9 Feb., 6 & 21 June, 4 Oct., 22 Nov. 1912; 20 March, 8 May 1914; 23 April, 23 July 1915; 28 July, 15 Dec. 1916; 23 Feb. 1917: F.S.C, C/8/B/2-3, 8-13.
16 Fabian Tract no. 41, pp. 11-12, 18, 27.
17 See below, p. 219. Cf. S. Webb's introduction to *F.E.S.* (3rd edn, 1920), p. ii.
18 B. to S. Webb, 29 April 1908 in *L.S.B.W.*, II, 307; *O.P.*, p. 408.
19 See Introduction, pp. 9-12. Cf. Carswell, p. 31.
20 Mairet, pp. 22-6. Cf. *F.N.*, Dec. 1904, p. 48; *Yorkshire Weekly Post*, 7 Oct. 1905; James Webb, *The Harmonious Circle* (1980), pp. 200-3, 206.
21 Pease to Ensor, 16 Feb. 1907; cf. report of Propaganda Committee of Fabian Society, 4 June 1907, Ensor Papers.
22 *H.F.S.*, p. 188.
23 Executive Committee Minutes, 13 & 17 Dec. 1906; 11 Jan. 1907: F.S.C., C/8/B/9.
24 Report in *F.N.*, Jan. 1907, p. 20 (my emphasis).
25 *F.N.*, pp. 20-1.
26 *F.N.*, p. 20.
27 See below, pp. 207-8.
28 Tom Gibbons, *Rooms in the Darwin Hotel* (Nedlands, Western Australia, 1973), pp. 104-13; Stanley Pierson, *British Socialists* (Cambridge, Mass., 1979), pp. 193-6.
29 *F.N.*, Feb. 1907, p. 20.
30 *F.N.*, June 1902, pp. 21-2.
31 Orage to Wells, 23 July 1906, W.P.
32 Mairet, pp. 36-7; cf. Shaw to Wells, 14 Aug. 1907, W.P.
33 *New Age*, 2 May 1907, p. 3.
34 Webb to Wells, 15 June 1907, W.P.
35 Mairet, pp. 44-5; Wallace Martin, *The New Age under Orage* (1967), p. 26.
36 *New Age*, 14 Jan. 1909, pp. 235-6.
37 Martin, pp. 205-11; Pierson, *British Socialists*, pp. 197-8.
38 *H.F.S.*, p. 188.
39 *F.N.*, 1911: Jan., p. 15; April, p. 37; July, p. 61.
40 Cf. Mairet, p. 45.
41 *H.F.S.*, p. 188.
42 C.B. Purdom, *Harley Granville Barker* (1955), p. 13 & *Bernard Shaw's Letters to Granville Barker* (1956), p. 14. Cf. *F.N.*, Dec. 1899, p. 39.
43 *F.N.*, Nov. 1899, p. 35.
44 Cf. lists of officers in the booklet issued by the Incorporated Stage Society, *Ten Years 1899-1909* (1909), pp. 6, 10-11; and in the privately-printed prospectus, *The Stage Society* (1899) — copy in letter file of Ensor Papers.
45 *Ten Years 1899-1909*, p. 7; *The Stage Society*, n.p.
46 *Bernard Shaw's Letters to Granville Barker*, pp. 3-4.
47 J.T. Grein to *Sunday Times*, printed 17 Feb. 1907 and cited in N.H.G. Schoonderwoerd, *J.T. Grein. Ambassador of the Theatre 1862-1935* (Assen, 1963), p. 179.
48 *F.N.*, Nov. 1904, p. 44; April 1905, pp. 17, 24.
49 Grein to *Sunday Times*, 17 Feb. 1907.
50 *Ten Years 1899-1909*, p. 33.
51 *Ten Years 1899-1909*, pp. 8-9. Cf. Purdom, *Harley Granville Barker*, pp. 9-17.
52 Barker to Pease, 11 ?July 1903, F.S.C., Box. 1.

53 Purdom, *Harley Granville Barker*, p. 122 (citing personal letter from R.C.K. Ensor); cf. letters from Barker to Pease, undated and 7 March 1912, F.S.C., Box 1.
54 For full details of the repertoire, see Desmond MacCarthy, *The Court Theatre 1904-1907. A Commentary and Criticism* (1907).
55 *Ten Years 1899-1909*, pp. 13, 19, 22-3, 32, 43-4, 60.
56 *Augustus Does His Bit* (1917) and *O'Flaherty V.C.* (1920): cf. *Bernard Shaw's Letters to Granville Barker*, pp. 5-16.
57 Barker to Murray, 30 Nov. 1907, cited in Purdom, *Granville Barker*, p. 75.
58 'W.A.' and 'H.G.B.' [Archer and Barker], *Schemes and Estimates* [for a National Theatre] (1904).
59 See *Ten Years 1899-1909*, p. 9.
60 Cited in 'Michael Orme', *J.T. Grein. The Story of a Pioneer, 1862-1935* (1936), p. 149. The author of this book was Grein's wife.
61 Schoonderwoerd, p. 159.
62 Schoonderwoerd, p. 147; cf. p. 165.
63 Grein to *Sunday Times*, printed 3 Dec. 1905 and cited in Schooderwoerd, p. 178.
64 See Shaw to Barker, 7 Dec. 1908, in *Bernard Shaw's Letters to Granville Barker*, p. 144.
65 *Ten Years 1899-1909*, p. 14.
66 Cf. Margery M. Morgan, *A Drama of Political Man. A Study in the Plays of Granville Barker* (1961), pp. 145-6, 157-8. On the tenuousness of Barker's relationship with Fabianism, see below, pp. 262-5.
67 Two of his plays (*Cupid and Compromise* and *What the Public Wants*) were produced by the Stage Society in 1908 and 1909 respectively: see *Ten Years 1899-1909*, pp. 82, 94-5.
68 S. Webb, *F.E.S.* (3rd edn, 1920), p. x.
69 This is exemplified in Sidney Webb's comment on Zola, cited above, p. 65.
70 *Ten Years 1899-1909*, p. 15.
71 Michael Barker, *Gladstone and Radicalism: the reconstruction of liberal policy in Britain, 1885-94* (Brighton, 1975).
72 See next chapter, p. 197.
73 For details of their special attraction to this play, see my article 'A Transplanted Doll's House: Ibsenism, Feminism and Socialism in Late Victorian and Edwardian England', in Ian Donaldson, ed., *Transformations: Studies in Modern European Drama* (forthcoming).
74 Cf. Hobsbawm, 'The Fabians Reconsidered', pp. 250-71.
75 Ibsen to Brandes, 17 Feb., 24 Sept. 1891 in J.W. McFarlane, ed., *Ibsen. A Critical Anthology* (1970), p. 79 & Mary Morison, ed., *The Correspondence of Henrik Ibsen* (1905), p. 218.
76 Shaw, 'What about the Middle Class . . .?', Part II, *Daily Citizen* (Manchester), 19 Oct. 1912.
77 *Daily Chronicle*, 6 Jan. 1900.
78 Shaw, Fabian Tract no. 41, p. 3; Olivier in *F.E.S*, p. 105.
79 Fabian lecture on Ibsen, fol. 22.
80 For details, see my article 'A Transplanted Doll's House'.
81 See 'A Transplanted Doll's House' for details of earlier productions in which Fabians were involved. The Stage Society itself mounted other Ibsen productions: *Pillars of Society* (1901), *The Lady from the Sea* (1902), *When we Dead Awaken* (1903), *Lady Inger of Östråt (1906)* — see *Ten Years 1899-1909*, pp. 28-9, 35, 37, 66-7.
82 'Gray Quill' (pseud.), 'The Liverpool Fabian Society. Some Memories of Strenuous

Days and Personalities that are Gone', press clipping (c.1920s) in F.S.C., Box 8.
83 *Ten Years 1899-1909*, p. 9.
84 Orme, p. 93.
85 Shaw to Charles Charrington, 30 Nov. 1900, 28 June 1901; & to the Stage Society Casting Committee, c.16 March 1903, in *B.S.C.L.*, II, 200-1, 227-9, 317-18.
86 Summer School Prospectus for 1907, F.S.C., Box 9; *H.F.S.*, p. 199. For a general historical survey of the Summer School movement, and of the Fabian contribution to it, see Joseph R. Starr, 'The Summer Schools and Other Educational Activities of British Socialist Groups', *American Political Science Review*, 30 (1936), 956-74.
87 Mabel Atkinson to R.C.K. Ensor, 17 March 1907, Ensor Papers.
88 Mabel Palmer (née Atkinson) to Margaret Cole, 1 July 1955, F.S.C., Box 9.
89 B. Webb, *O.P.*, pp. 457-8: diary entry for 4 Sept. 1910 (my emphasis).
90 *O.P.*, p. 415: diary entry for 15 Sept. 1908.
91 *O.P.*, pp. 456-8: diary entries for 19 Aug. & 4 Sept. 1910.
92 *O.P.*, p. 455: diary entry for 19 Aug. 1910. Cf. W. Faulkner, 'Fabians at Work and at Play. Impressions of the Fabian Summer School', *Southport Visitor*, 31 July 1913, clipping in Fabian Society Collection, Box 9.
93 Palmer to Cole, 1 July 1955, F.S.C., Box 9.
94 *O.P.*, p. 457: diary entry for 19 Aug. 1910.
95 Cf. Pease's figures in *H.F.S.*, p. 200: the log-books indicate that he slightly underestimated the number of lectures.
96 Fabian Summer School log-books, 29 Aug. 1910; 11 Aug. 1912; 25 Aug. 1916; 22 Aug. 1917; 20 Aug. 1918: F.S.C., Part B, C/8/D/12-13. Cf. entries for 18 Aug. 1910, 30 Aug. & 2 Sept. 1915, 20 Aug. 1916, 23 & 24 Aug. 1917.
97 Palmer to Cole, 1 July 1955, F.S.C., Box 9; 'Fabians at Work and at Play'.
98 Prospectuses for the Schools of 1907, 1917, 1920, 1922 & 1924 can be found in F.S.C., Box 9.
99 'Fabians at Work and at Play'.
100 A full concert programme is reproduced in the log-book entry for 20 Aug. 1909; cf. 4 Aug. 1909: F.S.C., C/8/D/12.
101 Log-book, 13 Sept. 1912, 8 Sept. 1916; Pease to Ensor, 17 Aug. 1909, Ensor Papers. Cf. reports of the Song Book/Publishing Committee in the Executive Committee Minutes for 21 Oct. 1910; 16 June 1911; 10 Nov. 1911; 17 May, 21 June, 5 & 12 July, 4 Oct. 1912: F.S.C., part B, C/8/B/10-11.
102 Log-book, 27 Aug. 1915, 5 Sept. 1917: F.S.C., C/8/D/13.
103 Log-book, 23, 25, 30 Aug., 5 & 6 Sept. 1912; 4 & 5 Aug. 1914: 1 & 8 Sept. 1916; 23 Aug., 7 Sept. 1917: F.S.C., C/8/D/12-13.
104 Log-book, 6 & 19 Aug. 1909, F.S.C., C/8/D/12.
105 Log-book, 22 Aug. 1916, F.S.C., C/8/D/13.
106 *H.F.S.*, p. 200.
107 Atkinson to Ensor, 17 March 1907.
108 *O.P.*, p. 456; diary entry for 19 Aug. 1910.
109 *H.F.S.*, p. 200.
110 'A Socialist Drawing Room — Rose-Coloured Revolution', *Morning Post*, 25 March 1886, clipping in F.S.C., Box 14; cf. Wells, 'The Faults of the Fabian' in Hynes, *The Edwardian Turn of Mind*, p. 396.
111 'Fabiana', *To-Day*, XI (May 1889), 152.
112 Ticket for Fabian soirée, 26 June 1907, F.S.C., Box 21.
113 *The Fabian Common Room* — printed circular, F.S.C., Box 17.
114 See E.P. Thompson, *William Morris*, pp. 419-21.

115 Abstract of minutes of meeting of Group Secretaries and the Executive Committee, 24 Sept. 1891, F.S.C., Box 17. Cf. *F.N.*, May 1902, pp. 18-19 ('Business Notes').
116 MacKenzie, 'Percival Chubb and the Founding of the Fabian Society', pp. 34-5.
117 Printed handbill for meeting of 24 March 1908, F.S.C., Box 17.
118 Sheffield Fabian Society, Minutes of the Executive, 3 Feb. 1908, Sheffield City Libraries, MD.3471.
119 'Fabiana', *To-Day*, X (May 1889), 152.
120 See, e.g., programmes of soirées for 26 June 1907, 20 May 1908, F.S.C., Box 21; Executive Committee Minutes, 30 March, 25 May, 9 June 1906, 10 May 1907, 27 Jan. 1911: F.S.C., C/8/B/8-10. Cf. Ada Galsworthy letter, 1907, cited in Catherine Dupré, *John Galsworthy* (London, 1975), p. 130.
121 *F.N.*, March 1909, p. 30, April 1911, p. 38, Dec. 1911, p. 5; Executive Committee Minutes, 27 May 1910, F.S.C., C/8/B/10; soirée programme of main London branch, 10 July 1908, F.S.C., Box 21; programme of Forest Gate branch, 1911, F.S.C., Box 8; Liverpool Fabian Society, *23rd Annual Report* (1915), pp. 4, 7.
122 *H.F.S.*, p. 200.
123 Executive Committee Minutes, 19 April 1912, F.S.C., C/8/B/11; printed announcement of soirée for 20 May 1912, F.S.C., Box 21.
124 Ticket and programme for soirée of 26 June 1907, F.S.C, Box 21.
125 Sheffield Fabian Society: Minutes of the Executive for 25 Sept. 1908; 26 April, 7 June, 20 Sept. 1912; cf. *5th Annual Report* (1911).
126 *F.N.*, June 1904, p. 26. For a further discussion of this lecture, see below, pp. 259-61.
127 Ensor: manuscript notes on socialist societies (for a lecture?), undated, Ensor Papers, Box marked '3 Socialism Fabian Society'; 'Memorandum of the I.L.P.', Sept. 1907, pp. 30-2, F.S.C., Box 11, sec. 1.
128 The phrase is John Vincent's in his witheringly funny account of the Fabians, 'Love Among the Socialists', *New Society*, 14 July 1977, p. 86.

NOTES TO CHAPTER 8

1 S.K. Ratcliffe, 'Shaw as a Young Socialist', in C.E.M. Joad, ed., *Shaw and Society* (London, 1953), p. 57.
2 William Clarke, 'The Fabian Society', *New England Magazine*, X (March 1894), 92.
3 Fabian Society Executive Committee Minutes, 7 & 21 July 1911, F.S.C., Part B, C/8/B/11.
4 Most notably the seven lectures on 'The Basis and Prospects of Socialism' (1888) which were published as the *Fabian Essays in Socialism*; William Morris, 'How We Shall Live Then' (1889); Joseph Wood, 'Municipal Socialism' (1891); Stewart Headlam's lectures on Board Schools in London (1894) and 'The Danger of Municipal Puritanism' (1904); Hubert Bland's lectures on Nietzsche (1898) and 'The Faith I Hold' (1907); H.G. Wells, 'Socialism and the Middle Classes' (1906); Sydney Herbert, 'The New Environment' (1910); Jack Gibson, 'Socialism and Sport' (1913).
5 Bland to Pease, 3 April 1903; cf. 17 March 1903, F.S.C., Box 1, and Executive Committee minutes, 1 May 1903, F.S.C., C/8/B/7.
6 Pease to Ensor, 19 July 1905, Ensor Papers.
7 Shaw, *The Quintessence of Ibsenism* (1st edn, London, 1891), pp. v-vi.
8 Minutes of meetings for 6 June, 18 July 1890, F.S.C., C/8/A/11.
9 Minutes of meetings for 2 & 16 May, 6 June, 4 & 18 July, 1890.

10 Minutes of meetings for 16 May, 20 June 1890.
11 *H.F.S.*, pp. 94-5.
12 *Star*, 19 July 1890, p. 1; Herbert Burrows, 'Socialism of the Sty', *Justice*, 26 July 1890, p. 2.
13 See my article, 'Bernard Shaw, Ibsen and the Ethics of English Socialism', pp. 393-7.
14 Executive Committee minutes, 3 & 24 Feb., 14 & 28 April 1899; 23 Feb., 20 & 27 April 1900: C/8/B/6-7.
15 Executive Committee minutes, 7 July 1911, C/8/B/11.
16 Fabian Society lecture on Ibsen, S.P., Add MS.50661; cf. my discussion of this in 'Bernard Shaw, Ibsen and the Ethics of English Socialism', pp. 384-9.
17 Executive Committee minutes, 11 Feb. 1898, C/8/B/6.
18 Clarence Decker, *The Victorian Conscience* (New York, 1952), pp. 90-100.
19 Olivier, 'Emile Zola as Artist and Doctrinaire', *F.N.*, June & July 1898, pp. 13, 17-18.
20 Olivier, 'George Meredith's Writings: A Side-view on Tendency', *F.N.*, Nov. 1898, p. 33.
21 J.M. Robertson, 'Dostoevsky', *F.N.*, Dec. 1898, Jan. 1899, pp. 37, 41.
22 *F.N.*, Sept. 1901, p. 25.
23 H.W. Macrosty, 'George Gissing', *F.N.*, April 1899, p. 6.
24 Cf. McBriar, *Fabian Socialism and English Politics*, pp. 119-30.
25 Bland, 'The Work of Rudyard Kipling' *F.N.*, July 1901, pp. 17-18; syllabus in minutes of Fabian Society meeting for 14 June 1901, C/8/A/13.
26 S. Webb, 'George Eliot's Works', c.1881, P.P., VI. 6, fol. 1.
27 In the 1913 lecture programme of the Cambridge University branch of the Fabian Society there was one lecture on 'Past Politicians and Pictorial Satire': see Cambridge University Fabian Society Papers, MS. Add. 7452, Business Meetings Minute Book, 21 Nov. 1913.
28 See report of the lecture and exhibition at the 1922 Summer School on 'Character and Utility in the Poster' — Fabian Summer School Log Book, 30 Aug. 1922, F.S.C., C/8/D/12.
29 This tract was itself based on a Fabian lecture delivered in 1914. Despite its concentration on the functional arts it has been included under the 'General or Miscellaneous' category in Table 2 because it also considered the relationship between socialism and the fine arts.
30 B.W.D., 2 Jan. 1883.
31 Cf. *H.F.S.*, p. 192.
32 Edinburgh Fabian Society Archives, National Library of Scotland, Acc. 4977, Book 7: minutes of meetings, *passim*.
33 Sheffield Fabian Society Archives, Sheffield City Libraries: minutes of the Executive (MD 3471) and of General Meetings (MD 3472), 21 Feb. 1908 & 7 Jan. 1913; Annual Reports (MD 3473), 1908, 1909.
34 Oxford University Fabian Society, Bodleian Library, Oxford: minute books 1895-1915, *passim*, esp. 26 May 1899, 21 May 1906, 14 May 1912.
35 There were two such lectures in 1910 (one on 'Town Planning', illustrated with lantern slides; and Rupert Brooke's lecture on 'Democracy and the Arts'); there was one lecture on an artistic subject in 1911 (Granville Barker on 'The Necessary Theatre'); no records exist for the lecture programme of 1912; there was a lecture in 1913 on Pictorial Satire, and then no more artistic subjects before the branch dropped its Fabian name two years later. See details in minute books of the Cambridge University Fabian Society, *passim*.

36 G. Kendall to R.C.K. Ensor, 28 March 1908, Ensor Papers; cf. minutes of the Edinburgh Fabian Society, 4 May 1911.
37 Cambridge University Fabian Society Archives, 1908-15, *passim*.
38 *H.F.S.*, p. 193.
39 See lists in 'London Fabian Calendar', *F.N.*, Feb. 1907 — June 1908, *passim*.
40 *H.F.S.*, p. 188.
41 E.g., entries for 20 Aug. 1907, 13 Aug. 1908, 9 Sept. 1912, 9 Sept. 1913, 23 Aug. 1914, 20, 22-4 Aug. & 4-5 Sept. 1917, 20, 25, 29 Aug. & 3, 5 Sept. 1918, Fabian Summer School log-books, F.S.C., C/8/D/12-13.
42 Log-book: 3 Aug. 1909, F.S.C., C/8/D/12.
43 In the few years after this period, there was no significant drop in the high proportions of the last years of the war until 1922, when the percentage fell to 9.1. In 1919 the peak of 31.9% was reached; in 1920 the figure stood at 20.5% and in 1921 at 25%.
44 Executive Committee minutes, 26 May 1916, C/8/B/13.
45 The log-books list the following: 'Socialism and Art' (16 Aug. 1909), 'The Artist and the Community' (11 Aug. 1912), 'The Work of the National Trust' (26 Aug. 1912), 'Didacticism and the Drama' (4 Sept. 1913), 'Art and War' (4 Sept. 1915), 'The Art of Criticism' (31 Aug. 1917), 'Some Ideals in English Literature' (25 Aug. 1918).
46 Shaw, 'How I Became a Public Speaker', *S.S.S.*, pp. 56-64.
47 See above, note 12.
48 Shaw, *S.S.S.*, pp. 56-8; cf. Fabian Tract no. 41, p. 16.
49 *Bodley Head Bernard Shaw*, VII (1974), 126.
50 William Clarke, ed., *Political Orations from Wentworth to Macaulay* (London, 1889), p. x.
51 Shaw, *S.S.S.*, p. 64.
52 Obituary of Wallas in *Nation*, 14 Sept. 1932, p. 232; cf. report of a lecture by Wallas to Oxford University Fabian Society, minutes for 8 June 1909.
53 Wallas, 'The Psychology of Propaganda', *F.N.*, March 1912, pp. 27-8.
54 *Sunday Times*, 17 Feb. 1895, p. 10.
55 *Reynold's News* (London), 16 Oct. 1904, p. 1.
56 Jerome to Wells, 20 May 1907, W.P.
57 E.g., Conor Cruise O'Brien, 'Politics as Drama as Politics', in O'Brien & W.D. Vanech, eds., *Power and Consciousness* (1969), pp. 215-43; Erving Goffman, *The Presentation of Self in Everyday Life* (1969); Elizabeth Burns, *Theatricality: A study of convention in the theatre and in social life* (1972); Victor Turner, *Dramas, Fields, and Metaphors* (Ithaca, New York, 1974); Ferdinand Mount, *The Theatre of Politics* (1972); Norman Shrapnel, *The Performers. Politics as Theatre* (1978).
58 The first report of this 'new local parliament' appears in *O.C.*, X (July 1887), 60. Details of the 'cabinet' posts and their holders are given in the August issue of the same year, p. 125. Cf. J. Morrison Davidson, 'The Annals of Toil', *Time and Echo* (London), 30 Oct. 1892, p. 6.
59 Annie Besant, *An Autobiography*, p. 319.
60 'A Socialist Drawing Room — Rose-Coloured Revolution', *Morning Post* (London), 25 March 1886, clipping in F.S.C., Box 14.
61 Mary Forster, 'The History and Basis of the Fabian Society', *Commonwealth* (New York), 14 Jan. 1893, p. x.
62 Nethercot, *The First Five Lives of Annie Besant* (1961), pp. 252-3.
63 Besant, *An Autobiography*, p. 319.

64 'The History and Basis of the Fabian Society', p. x.
65 Cf. McBriar, *Fabian Socialism and English Politics*; Paul Thompson, *Socialists, Liberals and Labour*, pp. 138-49.
66 Entry for 19 Jan. 1903, Diaries, Vol. 5, fols. 299-302, Ashbee Papers, King's College, Cambridge.
67 B.W.D., 27 Nov. 1887.
68 Margaret Cole, ed., *Beatrice Webb's Diaries 1924-1932*, entries for 6 March 1924, 22 June 1925; cf. 10 Sept. 1926, 21 Dec. 1929, 28 Oct. 1931.
69 Wells, *Experiment in Autobiography*, II, 603, 661.
70 Bland, *Letters to a Daughter*, pp. 42-3, 45-7.
71 *Experiment in Autobiography*, II, 603, 606.
72 Wallas, *Human Nature in Politics* (1908), pp. 41-2.
73 *Human Nature in Politics*, pp. 38-42.
74 *O.P.*, pp. 9, 273.
75 Bland, 'Mr Shaw's "Man and Superman" ' in *With the Eyes of a Man*, pp. 83-4; cf. his 'Ibsen and Mr Shaw' in *The Happy Moralist*, pp. 191-7, and Introduction to *E.B.H.*, pp. vii-viii.
76 Bernard F. Dukore, *Bernard Shaw, Director* (1971), esp. pp. 21-2, 81-2.
77 For administration details, see Executive Committee minutes, 10 Nov., 15 Dec. 1911; 12 Jan. 1912: C/8/B/11.
78 Executive Committee Minutes, 22 March − 5 Dec. 1892, *passim*, C/8/B/3.
79 *Labour Record and Review* (London), III (May 1907), 50; *Daily Dispatch* (London), 27 March 1908, p. 6.
80 Editorial note in *The Unpublished Lectures of William Morris*, pp. 15-16.
81 B. Potter to S. Webb, 25 Jan. 1892, *L.S.B.W.*, I, 387 (Beatrice's emphasis).

NOTES TO CHAPTER 9

1 Interview in *British Weekly*, 29 June 1893, p. 146; cf. B. Potter to S. Webb, 12 Nov. 1891, *L.S.B.W.*, I, 352.
2 *Soviet Communism*, II, 1053.
3 See Gaetano Mosca, *The Ruling Class*, trans. Hanna D. Kahn (New York, 1939), p. 482 & *passim*; S.E. Finer, ed., *Vilfredo Pareto — Sociological Writings*, trans. Derek Mirfin (1966), pp. 52, 159; Robert Michels, *Political Parties. A sociological study of the oligarchical tendencies of modern democracy*, trans. Eden and Cedar Paul (1962), *passim*, esp. chs. 1-2; James H. Meisel, *The Myth of the Ruling Class* (1962), pp. 348-53.
4 See Pareto, pp. 109-11, 155; Mosca, 'The Final Version of the Theory of the Ruling Class', reprinted in J.H. Meisel, p. 383; Michels, *First Lectures in Political Sociology*, trans. Alfred de Grazia (New York, 1965), pp. 75-6 and ch. VI; C. Wright Mills, *The Power Elite* (New York, 1956), chs. 5-7; Christopher Kent, *Brains and Numbers: Elitism, Comtism and Democracy in Mid-Victorian England* (Toronto, 1978), pp. 148-9.
5 See Mosca, *The Ruling Class*, pp. 52-3, 57, 68, 154-7, 259, 310, 326, 332-5, 413-17, 482 and 'The Final Version', pp. 387-9; Mills, pp. 305, 309-10, 316-17. Cf. J.H. Meisel, pp. 4, 355; Samuel Beer, *Modern British Politics* (1965), p. 108; Reba N. Soffer, *Ethics and Society in England* (Los Angeles, 1978), pp. 250-1; Eva Etzioni-Halévy, *Political Manipulation and Administrative Power* (1979), *passim*; G. Lowell Field & John Higley, *Elitism* (1980), pp. 64-8.
6 Mosca, *The Ruling Class*, pp. 51, 115, 282, 418, 446, 485-6 and 'The Final Version', p. 390; Pareto, pp. 22, 64ff., 77ff., 137-41, 155; Michels, *First Lectures*,

p. 151; T.B. Bottomore, *Elites and Society* (Penguin edn, Harmondsworth, 1966), pp. 136-7.

7 See Geraint Parry, *Political Elites* (1969), p. 86; Harold Entwhistle, *Class, Culture and Education* (1978), pp. 6-11, 18, 75-82; Lesley Johnson, *The Cultural Critics* (1979), pp. 81-3, 124-5, 130, 178, 190-2.

8 Kent, p. 3; cf. Raymond Williams, *Keywords* (1976), pp. 96-8.

9 Reported in *The Times*, 20 July 1978, p. 3.

10 See, e.g., Johnson, *The Cultural Critics*, pp. 98-9; Alan Swingewood, *The Myth of Mass Culture* (1977), p. 10. Cf. Leavis, *Mass Civilisation and Minority Culture* (Cambridge, 1930), pp. 3-5, 18-20, 25-6, 32.

11 *Nor Shall My Sword* (1972), p. 169.

12 *Notes Towards the Definition of Culture* (1948; Faber paperback edition, 1962), pp. 42-8; cf. Clive Bell, *Civilization* (1938), pp. 205-9.

13 Swingewood, pp. 10-18; Dennis Alan Mann, ed., *The Arts in a Democratic Society* (Bowling Green, Ohio, 1977), p. 9. See also Zev Barbu, 'Popular Culture: A Sociological Approach' in C.W.F. Bigsby, ed., *Approaches to Popular Culture* (1976), pp. 54-6; Stephen Yeo, *Religion and Voluntary Organisations in Crisis* (1976), pp. 292, 311. Cf. Williams, *Culture and Society*, pp. 300-2, 307, 322; Richard Hoggart, *The Uses of Literacy* (Penguin edn, Harmondsworth, 1958), pp. 250, 330-46; Denys Thompson, ed., *Discrimination and Popular Culture* (2nd edn, Harmondsworth, 1973), pp. 9, 18: though none of these three critics specifically used the word élitism to sum up the processes they are describing.

14 Gordon K. Lewis, 'Fabian Socialism: Some Aspects of Theory and Practice', *Journal of Politics*, 14 (Aug. 1952), 455, 458, 463; J.D. Young, 'Elitism, Authoritarianism and Western Socialism' S.S.L.H., 25 (Autumn 1972), 70. Cf. Simon, pp. 173-4, 203-4, 232, 237-8; Barker, *Education and Politics 1900-1951*, p. 18; J.M. Winter, p. 285; E.T.J. Brennan, *Education for National Efficiency: the contribution of Sidney and Beatrice Webb* (1975), pp. 28-30.

15 *F.E.S.*, pp. 124, 147-8.

16 'How London Amuses Itself', Part II, *O.C.*, VIII (Aug. 1886), 116; *Is Socialism Sound?*, p. 133; cf. p. 141.

17 Cf. Gareth Stedman-Jones, 'Working-Class Culture and Working-Class Politics in London, 1870-1900 . . .', *Journal of Social History*, 7 (Summer 1974), 479-80, 491-2.

18 *M.A.*, p. 272, n.7.

19 Cf. Martha Vicinus, 'The Study of Victorian Popular Culture', *Victorian Studies*, XVIII (June 1975), 474.

20 See, e.g., Adrian Oldfield, review of *W.W.* in S.S.L.H., 33 (Autumn 1976), 74; Rodney Barker, *Political Ideas in Modern Britain* (1978), p. 106; Peter Clarke, p. 197.

21 Richard Johnson, 'Culture and the Historians', in John Clarke, Chas Critcher & Richard Johnson, eds., *Working Class Culture* (1979), pp. 45-8; cf. Brian Harrison, *Drink and the Victorians* (1971), p. 86.

22 Ray B. Brown, 'Popular Culture: Notes Towards a Definition' in his edition of essays on the subject by various writers: *Popular Culture and the Expanding Consciousness* (New York, 1973), p. 14. Cf. Bigsby, pp. viii, 17-18, 39.

23 Cf. Vicinus, 'The Study of Victorian Popular Culture', pp. 474, 478-81, and *The Industrial Muse. A study of nineteenth-century British working class literature* (1974), pp. 1-6; Mann, pp. 3-4, 71, 121, 133, 138, 149.

24 Cf. Peter Burke, *Popular Culture in Early Modern Europe* (1978), p. 22 & ch. 2; Clarke, Critcher & Johnson, pp. 19-20, 30-1, 62-3, 70, 210-11, 219, 235, 240, 242,

246-7; Henry Pelling, *Popular Politics and Society in Late Victorian Britain* (1968), p. 5.

25 'Art Under Plutocracy', *C.C.W.M.*, XXIII, 173; 'The Exhibition of the Royal Academy', *W.M.A.W.S.*, I, 225-41; 'Individualism at the Royal Academy', *W.M.A.W.S.*, II, 140.

26 'The Fabian Society', *New England Magazine*, X (March 1894), 99.

27 B.W.D., 8 Nov. 1885; extract in *M.A.*, pp. 278-9.

28 'How London Amuses Itself', I, *O.C.*, VIII (July 1886), 13, 17-20; II (Aug. 1886), 116.

29 See Nethercot, *The First Five Lives of Annie Besant*, p. 111; Selwyn Image's recollections of Headlam in Bettany, p. 128.

30 *Fabianism and Land Values*, p. 12.

31 Cf. David Bradby, Louis James & Bernard Sharratt, *Performance and Politics in Popular Drama* (1980), especially James's introduction.

32 *The Function of the Stage*, pp. 10-11, 26; cf. report of Headlam's lecture on 'Church and Stage', *C.R.*, III (1884), 43.

33 *The Function of the Stage*, pp. 27-8; 'On the Licensing of Theatres and Music Halls', *C.R.*, IX (Jan. 1890), 19; report of speech at Newcastle (1884) cited in Bailey, *Leisure and Class in Victorian England* (1978), p. 158.

34 *London Music in 1888-89*, pp. 233-4; *Music in London* (1932), I, 43-4; II, 61-4, 240; III, 137-8, 215-16.

35 *Music in London*, II, 168, 270-1.

36 Shaw to Hueffer, 19 Jan. 1883, *B.S.C.L.*, I, 58.

37 For a more general account of the links between Shaw's socialism and his musical interests, see W.H. Mellers, 'G.B.S. and Music Criticism', *Scrutiny*, VI (1937), 329-33.

38 Shaw to Lady Mary Murray, 1 Sept. 1898, *B.S.C.L.*, II, 61.

39 See, e.g., his lecture, 'The Needs of Music in Britain' (1920), published in Dan H. Laurence, *Platform and Pulpit* (1962), pp. 161-4.

40 Reprinted in *The Road to Equality*, p. 327.

41 Charrington, lecture on 'Communal Recreation', reported in *F.N.*, May 1900, pp. 9-10.

42 'National Finance and a Levy on Capital', Fabian Tract no. 188 (1919), 12. For further details of the Webbs' unfavourable attitudes to alcoholic consumption, see Harrison, *Drink and the Victorians*, pp. 81-6.

43 Shaw to Lady Murray, 1 Sept. 1898, *B.S.C.L.*, II, 60.

44 *E.L.G.*, I, 357; *The History of Liquor Licensing in England* (1903), pp. 24, 85-6, 118-19, 124; *The Story of the Durham Miners* (1921), pp. 17-21.

45 *History of Liquor Licensing*, p. 139.

46 *E.L.G.*, I, 357-8, 586n; *History of Liquor Licensing*, p. 150.

47 B. Webb to Forster, 24 April 1934, *L.S.B.W.*, III, 393-4.

48 B.W.D., 9 Aug. 1926.

49 *C.C.M.*, p. 1; cf. account of 'the origin and growth' of the movement in Beatrice's first major work, *The Co-operative Movement in Great Britain*, pp. 59f.

50 *C.C.M.*, pp. 84-5; cf. pp. 38-9, 298-300.

51 *C.C.M.*, pp. 373-81.

52 *C.S.C.G.B.*, p. 300; cf. pp. 58, 165.

53 Webb to MacDonald, 26 June 1924, MacDonald Papers, P.R.O., 30/69, 1/210. The pamphlet he enclosed was entitled *Some Particulars with Regard to the Aims and Activities of the British Institute of Industrial Art* (H.M.S.O., 1923).

54 'The Lesser Arts', *C.W.W.M.*, XXII, 3-4; cf. 'Art Under Plutocracy',

C.W.W.M., XXIII, 165-6.
55 'Art and Socialism', *C.W.W.M.*, XXIII, 206.
56 See above, p. 98.
57 See Naylor, *The Arts and Crafts Movement*, chs. 6-7; Nikolaus Pevsner, *Pioneers of Modern Design*, (Harmondsworth, 1960), ch. 1.
58 Report in *F.N.*, Feb. 1914, pp. 17-18.
59 *Socialism and the Arts of Use*, Fabian Tract 177 (1915), *passim*. For a fuller discussion of this tract, see my D. Phil. thesis, 'Fabian Socialism and the Arts . . .' (Oxford Univ., 1978), pp. 287-95.
60 'The "Economic Heresies" of the London County Council', *London*, 16 Aug. 1894, pp. 521-2.
61 *Socialism and the Arts of Use*, pp. 8, 12.

NOTES TO CHAPTER 10

1 *Notes Towards the Definition of Culture*, p. 16.
2 'Popular Judgment in Literature. A Note on Mr. Rider Haggard', *O.C.*, X (Dec. 1887), 321-3.
3 *E.B.H.*, pp. 35-40.
4 'Beauty', *With the Eyes of a Man*, p. 32.
5 'The Significance of Art', fol. 32, D.P.
6 'George Eliot's Works', P.P. VI. 6, fols. 1-2.
7 *E.B.H.*, p. 87.
8 'The Limits of Collectivism', *W.C.W.*, pp. 34-9.
9 'Some Common Fallacies in the Attack Against Socialism', fols. 10-17, 31-5, MacDonald Papers, P.R.O., 30/69, 6/176.
10 See Nan Dearmer, *The Life of Percy Dearmer* (1940), p. 47.
11 'Will Democracy Destroy Manners?', *C.R.*, XI (Nov. 1890), p. 253.
12 Tract no. 133; cf. Nan Dearmer, p. 90.
13 Report in *F.N.*, June 1904. Cf. printed syllabus of the lecture in minutes of meetings of the Fabian Society, 24 June 1904, F.S.C., C/8/A/14.
14 See A.H. Fox Strangeways, *Cecil Sharp* (Oxford, 1933), p. 23.
15 See Ronald Pearsall, *Victorian Popular Music* (1973), pp. 206-8.
16 *F.N.*, June 1904, p. 26.
17 See A.L. Lloyd, *Folk Song in England* (1967; Paladin edition, 1975), p. 30.
18 For discussions of the nature and rise of the industrial songs, see Lloyd, ch. 6; Vicinus, *The Industrial Muse*, ch. 1; J.S. Bratton, *The Victorian Popular Ballad* (1975), chs. 2, 4-5.
19 Lloyd, p. 184; Pearsall, pp. 205-8, 210-11.
20 *F.N.*, June 1904, p. 26; & syllabus of the lecture in F.S.C., C/8/A/14.
21 'A Word for Fabians', *C.R.*, XII (Dec. 1893), 286.
22 'The Social Significance of Art', Edinburgh Fabian Society Papers, National Library of Scotland, Acc. 4977, Book 7 — minutes of meeting for 21 Dec. 1911.
23 See Philip Henderson, *William Morris. His life, work and friends* (Penguin edn, Harmondsworth, 1973), p. 405. Cf. Shaw on the reasons for Morris's lack of interest in modern theatre — 'William Morris as Actor and Playwright', *Pen Portraits and Reviews*, pp. 210-17.
24 Barker, 'The Necessary Theatre', reported in *F.N.*, July 1911, pp. 58-9.
25 Barker, 'The Economics of the Theatre', delivered to Oxford University Fabian Society, 3 Nov. 1907; see press reports in O.U.F.S. papers, Bodleian Library, Oxford.

26 'The Necessary Theatre', p. 58.
27 B.W.D., 21 Aug. 1928.
28 Shaw to Barker, 7 Dec. 1908, *Bernard Shaw's Letters to Granville Barker*, p. 144.
29 See, e.g., Preface to *The Apple Cart*, *Bodley Head Bernard Shaw*, VI, 263; 'Democracy as a Delusion', lecture delivered 23 Nov. 1927, draft in F.S.C.; Allan Chappelow, *Shaw — 'The Chucker Out'* (1969), pp. 163-72.
30 'A Municipal Theatre', lecture delivered to Fabian Society on 15 Jan. 1897, reported in *F.N.*, Feb. 1897, p. 47.
31 See lists of meetings, and reports, of the Cambridge Univ. Fabian Society, 1909-13, in Rupert Brooke Papers, King's College Library, Cambridge; and minutes of committee meetings, 21 Nov. 1911, C.U.F.S. Papers, Cambridge Univ. Library, MS. Add. 7451. For further details of Brooke's association with the Fabians, see Geoffrey Keynes, ed., *The Letters of Rupert Brooke* (1968), pp. 70, 79-80, 114, 124, 126, 154; Christopher Hassall, *Rupert Brooke* (1964: Faber paperback edition, 1972), pp. 117-20, 136-7, 145-51, 156-7, 176-7, 193-5, 204, 224, 242-6; John Lehmann, *Rupert Brooke. His life and his legend* (1980), pp. 31-6.
32 Quoted in Edward Marsh, ed., *The Collected Poems of Rupert Brooke: with a memoir* (1918), p. xxx.
33 *Democracy and the Arts* (1946), pp. 5-6, 9, 11-13; delivered as a lecture on 24 Nov. 1910.
34 *Walt Whitman*, pp. 52-6, 94-5.
35 *Democracy and the Arts*, pp. 7-8, 13, 21, 24-5.
36 These epithets are Samuel Hynes's, in his recent study, 'Rupert Brooke', in *Edwardian Occasions*, p. 150.

NOTES TO CONCLUSION

1 Orage to Wells, 9 June 1907, W.P.
2 Crane to MacDonald, 25 Feb. 1900, MacDonald Papers, 5/10.
3 Hobsbawm, 'The Fabians Reconsidered', pp. 250-1; Vincent, 'Love Among the Socialists', p. 85.
4 Hoggart, p. 345.
5 Sir Hugh Casson, 'The Arts and the Academies', Romanes Lecture, University of Oxford, 13 Nov. 1979.
6 This dilemma is implicitly stated by Willis H. Truitt, 'Art for the People', and in the quotation he gives from Lenin's 'On Proletarian Culture' in Mann, pp. 66-9. Truitt's suggestions for resolving the dilemma are every bit as confused and vague as many Fabians' suggestions and subject to rather more hyperbole. Herbert J. Ganz's suggestions in the same book (pp. 115-17) are rather more cogent, though they do not in substance offer much of an advance on Fabian schemes and are rather less hopeful in spirit about the possible alliance of democracy and art. Cf. Mann's conclusions, pp. 140-1.

Bibliography

1. MANUSCRIPT SOURCES

C.R. Ashbee Papers, King's College Library, Cambridge.
Cambridge University Fabian Society Papers, Cambridge University Library.
Thomas Davidson Papers, Yale University Library.
Edinburgh Fabian Society Papers, National Library of Scotland, Edinburgh.
R.C.K. Ensor Papers, Corpus Christi College, Oxford.
Fabian Society Collection, Nuffield College, Oxford.
E.M. Forster Papers, King's College Library, Cambridge.
H.D. Lloyd Papers, State Historical Society of Wisconsin, microfilm edn, Madison, 1970.
J. Ramsay MacDonald Papers, Public Record Office, London.
William Morris Papers, British Library, London.
Oxford University Fabian Society Papers, Bodleian Library, Oxford.
Passfield Papers, B.L.P.E.S.
G.B. Shaw Papers, British Library, London;
  B.L.P.E.S.
Sheffield Fabian Society Papers, Sheffield City Library.
Socialist League Archives, International Institute of Social History, Amsterdam.
Graham Wallas Papers, B.L.P.E.S.
H.G. Wells Papers, University of Illinois.

2. NEWSPAPERS AND PERIODICALS

— from the period, or parts of the period, 1880-1939. All published in London, unless
  specified otherwise. Details of individual items from these are contained in the
  footnotes.

British Weekly
Church Reformer
Clarion (Manchester)
Commonweal
Contemporary Review
Crusade
Daily Chronicle
Daily Dispatch
Economic Journal
Fabian News
Fortnightly Review
Freedom

Justice
Labour Leader
Labour Record and Review
Listener
London
Manchester Guardian
New Age
New England Magazine (Boston)
New English Weekly
New Review
New Statesman
Nineteenth Century
Our Corner
Pall Mall Gazette
Practical Socialist
Reynold's Newspaper
St. Martin's Review
Saturday Review
Savoy
Seed-time (originally the *Sower*)
Spectator
Star
Sunday Chronicle
Time
The Times
Times Literary Supplement
To-Day
Westminster Review
Woman's Signal
Young Woman

3. BOOKS AND PAMPHLETS BY CONTEMPORARIES

(c. 1880-1930) — together with some earlier works of contemporary relevance and some later memoirs. All published in London, unless specified otherwise.

Archer, William and Granville Barker. *Schemes and Estimates for a National Theatre* (1904).

Arnold, Matthew. *Complete Prose Works of Matthew Arnold*, ed. R.H. Super. 11 vols. (Ann Arbor, 1960-77).

Ashbee, C.R. *The Last Records of a Cotswold Community*. Preface by Sidney Webb (Campden, 1904).

Ball, Sidney. *Memories and Impressions*, arranged by Oona H. Ball (1923).

Bax, E. Belfort. *Reminiscences and Reflexions of a Mid and Late Victorian* (1913).

Bennett, Arnold. *Letters of Arnold Bennett*, ed. James Hepburn. 3 vols. (1966-70).
  The Journals of Arnold Bennett, ed. Newman Flower. 3 vols. (1932-3).

Bernstein, Edward. *My Days of Exile: Reminiscences of a Socialist* (1921).

Besant, Annie. *An Autobiography* (1893).
  Autobiographical Sketches (1885).
  The Evolution of Society (1886).
  Modern Socialism. 2nd edn. (1891).

Bibliography

Besant, Annie and Foote, G.W. *Is Socialism Sound?* (1887).
Bland, Hubert. *Essays by Hubert*, ed. Edith Nesbit Bland (1914).
  The Happy Moralist (1907).
  Letters to a Daughter (1906).
  Olivia's Latchkey (1913).
  With the Eyes of a Man (1905).
Blatchford, Robert. *My Eighty Years* (1913).
The Book of the Opening of the William Morris Labour Church [at Leek] (1897).
Booth, Charles. *Charles Booth's London*, ed. Albert Fried and Richard Elman from Booth's *Life and Labour of the People in London* (Penguin edn, Harmondsworth, 1971).
Brooke, Emma. *Transition* (1895).
Brooke, Rupert. *Collected Poems, with a memoir*, ed. Edward Marsh (1918).
  Democracy and the Arts (1946).
  The Letters of Rupert Brooke, ed. Sir Geoffrey Keynes (1968).
Carlyle, Thomas. *The Works of Thomas Carlyle*. 30 vols. (Centenary edn, 1896-9).
Carpenter, Edward. *Angels' Wings. A series of essays on art and its relation to life* (1898).
  My Days and Dreams (1916).
  Towards Democracy (1911).
Carpenter, Niles. *Guild Socialism. An historical and critical analysis* (1922).
Clarke, William. *A Collection of His Writings*, ed. Herbert Burrows and J.A. Hobson (1908).
  Walt Whitman (1892).
Clarke, William, ed., *Political Orations from Wentworth to Macaulay* (1889).
Clodd, Edward. *Grant Allen A Memoir* (1900).
Crane, Walter. *An Artist's Reminiscences* (1907).
  The Claims of Decorative Art (1892).
Davidson, Thomas. *The Education of Wage Earners* (New York, 1904).
  The Evolution of Sculpture (1891).
  The Parthenon Frieze (1882).
  The Philosophy of Goethe's Faust (1906).
  Prolegomena to Tennyson's In Memoriam (Boston, 1889).
  Rousseau and Education According to Nature (1898).
Ellis, Havelock. *My Life*. (2nd edn, 1967).
Emerson, R.W. *Selected Writings from Emerson*, ed. Percival Chubb (1888).
  Selected Writings of Emerson, ed. Brooks Atkinson (New York, 1950).
Fabian Society. *Songs for Socialists* (1912).
Fabian Society Tracts, nos. 1-237 (1884-1932).
Gill, Eric. *Autobiography* (1940).
  Letters of Eric Gill, ed. Walter Shrewing (1947).
Goethe, J.W. von. *Faust*, trans. Theodore Martin. (Revised edn, Everyman's Library, 1954).
  Wilhelm Meister's Apprenticeship and Travels, trans. Thomas Carlyle. (Centenary edn of Carlyle's *Works*, 1899).
Halstead, John B. ed. *Romanticism* (1969).
Harrison, Frederic. *Tennyson, Ruskin, Mill and other Literary Estimates* (1899).
Headlam, Stewart. *The Ballet* (1894).
  The Church Catechism and the Emancipation of Labour (1874).
  The Function of the Stage (1889).
  Fabianism and Land Values (1908).

The Socialist's Church (1907).
Headlam, Stewart, ed. *The Theory of Theatrical Dancing* (1888).
Hobson, J.A. *John Ruskin Social Reformer* (1898).
Hyndman, H.M. *England For All* (1881; new edn, Brighton, 1973).
  Further Reminiscences (1912).
  The Record of an Adventurous Life (1912).
Ibsen, Henrik. *Collected Works*, ed. William Archer. 12 vols. (1906-12).
  The Correspondence of Henrik Ibsen, ed. Mary Morison (1905).
Incorporated Stage Society. *Ten Years 1899-1909* (1909).
Jackson, Holbrook, *Bernard Shaw* (1907).
  The Eighteen Nineties (1927).
Katanka, Michael, ed., Fabian Biographical Series:
  (i) *Radicals, Reformers and Socialists* (1973).
  (ii) *Writers and Rebels* (1976).
Knight, William, ed. *Memorials of Thomas Davidson* (1907).
MacCarthy, Desmond. *The Court Theatre 1904-1907. A Commentary and Criticism*
  (1907).
MacDonald, J.R. *Ramsay MacDonald's Political Writings*, ed. Bernard Barker (1972).
  The Socialist Movement (1911).
McFarlane, J.W., *Ibsen. A Critical Anthology* (1970).
Mackail, J.W. *Life of William Morris*. 2 vols. (1889).
  William Morris and his Circle (Oxford, 1907).
Mann, Tom. *Memoirs* (1923).
Meredith, George. *The Adventures of Harry Richmond* (1871; Memorial edn, 1910).
  Evan Harrington (1860; Memorial edn, 1910).
Mill, J.S. *Collected Works of J.S. Mill*, ed. J.M. Robson, 19 vols. (Toronto, 1963-77).
  Mill on Bentham and Coleridge. Intro. by F.R. Leavis (1950).
Morris, William. *The Collected Works of William Morris*, 24 vols. (1910-15).
  Letters of William Morris to his Family and Friends, ed. Philip Henderson (1950).
  Selected Writings and Designs, ed. Asa Briggs (Harmondsworth, 1962).
  The Unpublished Lectures of William Morris, ed. Eugene D. Le Mire (1969).
  William Morris: Artist, Writer, Socialist, ed. May Morris (Oxford, 1936).
Morris, William and Bax, E.B. *Socialism: Its Growth and Outcome* (2nd edn, 1896).
Muirhead, J.H. *Reflections by a Journeyman in Philosophy* (1942).
Muggeridge, Malcolm. *Chronicles of Wasted Time*, vols. 1 & 2 (1972-3).
Nesbit, Edith. *Ballads and Lyrics of Socialism* (1908).
Olivier, Sydney. *Letters and Selected Writings*, ed. Margaret Olivier (1948).
Orage, Alfred. *Orage as Critic*, ed. Wallace Martin (1974).
Pater, Walter. *Appreciations* (1889).
  The Renaissance (1873).
  Works, 10 vols. (Library edn, 1910).
Pease, Edward. *History of the Fabian Society* (1916).
Penty, A.J. *The Restoration of the Gild System* (1906).
Podmore, Frank. *Mediums of the Nineteenth Century* (New York, 1963).
Reid, Andrew, ed. *The New Party* (1894).
Rhys, Ernest. *Everyman Remembers* (1931).
Ruskin, John. *The Works of John Ruskin*, ed. E.T. Cook and Alexander Wedderburn,
  39 vols. (1903-12).
  The Two Paths. Lectures on Art and Its Application to Decoration, ed. Graham
  Wallas (1907).
Salt, H.S. *Company I Have Kept* (1930).

The Life of Henry David Thoreau (1890).
Seventy Years Among Savages (1921).
Shaw, G.B. *The Bodley Head Bernard Shaw. Complete Plays with their Prefaces*, ed. Dan H. Laurence. 7 vols. (1970-4).
Collected Letters, ed. Dan H. Laurence. 2 vols. to date (1965, 1972).
Everybody's Political What's What (Standard edn, 1944).
The Intelligent Woman's Guide to Socialism, Capitalism, Sovietism and Fascism (1928).
Immaturity (Standard edn, 1932).
Letters to Granville Barker, ed. C.B. Purdom. (1956).
London Music in 1888-89 (Standard edn, 1937).
Love Among the Artists (Standard edn, 1932).
Music in London. 3 vols. (Standard edn, 1932).
Our Theatres in the Nineties. 3 vols. (Standard edn, 1932).
Pen Portraits and Reviews (Standard edn, 1932).
The Quintessence of Ibsenism (1891; 2nd edn, 1913).
Ruskin's Politics (1921).
The Perfect Wagnerite (1898).
Platform and Pulpit, ed. Dan H. Laurence. (1961).
The Road to Equality. Ten Unpublished Lectures and Essays, ed. Louis Crompton. (Boston, 1971).
The Sanity of Art (1908).
Shaw An Autobiography, ed. Stanley Weintraub. 2 vols (1969 and 1971).
Sixteen Self Sketches (Standard edn, 1949).
An Unsocial Socialist (Standard edn, 1932).
Shaw, G.B., ed. *Fabian Essays in Socialism* (1889; 2nd edn, 1908; 3rd edn, 1920; 4th edn, 1931; 5th edn, 1948; 6th edn, 1962).
Some Particulars with Regard to the Aims and Activities of the British Institute of Industrial Art. H.M.S.O. pamphlet, 1923.
Squire, Jack C. *Socialism and Art* (1908).
Thoreau, H.D. *Walden and Other Writings of Henry David Thoreau*, ed. Brooks Atkinson *(New York, 1937).*
Wallas, Graham. *The Art of Thought* (1926).
The Great Society (1914).
Human Nature in Politics (1908).
The Life of Francis Place 1771-1854 (1898).
Men and Ideas, ed. May Wallas (1940).
Webb, Beatrice (née Potter). *Beatrice Webb's Diaries*, ed. Margaret Cole. 2 vols. (1952, 1956).
The Co-operative Movement in Great Britain (1891).
My Apprenticeship (1926; Penguin edn, Harmondsworth, 1971).
Our Partnership, ed. Barbara Drake & Margaret Cole (1948; new edn, Cambridge, 1975).
Webb, Sidney. *The Eight Hours Day* (1891).
London Education (1904).
The London Programme (1891; new edn, 1895).
The Restoration of Trade Union Conditions (1917).
Socialism in England (1890).
The Story of the Durham Miners 1662-1921 (1921).
What Socialism Means: A Call to the Unconverted (1888).
The Works Manager Today (1917).

Bibliography 315

Webb, Sidney and Beatrice. *A Constitution for the Socialist Commonwealth of Great Britain* (1920; new edn, Cambridge, 1975).
The Consumers' Co-operative Movement (1921).
The Decay of Capitalist Civilisation (1923).
English Local Government from the Revolution to the Municipal Corporations Act. 10 vols. (1906-29).
The History of Liquor Licensing in England Principally from 1700-1830 (1903).
The History of Trade Unionism (1894).
The Letters of Sidney and Beatrice Webb, ed. Norman MacKenzie. 3 vols. (Cambridge, 1978).
Industrial Democracy. 2 vols. (1897).
The Prevention of Destitution (1911).
The Principles of the Labour Party (1919).
Soviet Communism: A New Civilisation? (1935; 2nd edn, 1937).
Webb, Sidney and Freeman, A. *Great Britain After the War* (1916).
Wells, H.G. *Ann Veronica* (1909).
Anticipations of the Reaction of Mechanical and Scientific Progress upon Human Life and Thought (1901).
Experiment in Autobiography. 2 vols. (1934; Cape paperback edn, 1969).
The New Machiavelli (1911).
Tono-Bungay (1909).
Whitman, Walt. *The Complete Poems*, ed. Francis Murphy (Penguin edn, Harmondsworth, 1975).
Wilde, Oscar. *The Letters of Oscar Wilde*, ed. Rupert Hart-Davies (1963).
Winckelmann, J.J. *Writings on Art*, ed. David Irwin (1972).
Woolf, Leonard. *Beginning Again. An Autobiography of the Years 1911-1918* (1964).
Woolf, Virginia. *The Diary of Virginia Woolf*, ed. Ann Olivier Bell. 3 vols. to date (1977-80).
The Letters of Virginia Woolf, ed. Nigel Nicolson. 6 vols. (1975-80).
Wordsworth, William. *Selected Poetry and Prose*, ed. J. Butt (Oxford, 1964).
Zola, Emile. *Germinal*, trans. H. Ellis (Everyman edn, 1933).

4. SECONDARY SOURCES — BOOKS AND PARTS OF BOOKS (MAINLY POST-1930).

All published in London, unless specified otherwise.
Adams, Elsie B. *Bernard Shaw and the Aesthetes* (Columbus, Ohio, 1971).
Adelman, Paul. *The Rise of the Labour Party* (1971).
Altick, Richard D. *Victorian People and Ideas* (1974).
Anderson, Warren D. *Matthew Arnold and the Classical Tradition* (Ann Arbor, 1965).
Annan, Noël. 'The Intellectual Aristocracy', in J.H. Plumb, ed., *Studies in Social History* (1955).
Archer, Charles. *William Archer. Life, Work and Friendships* (1931).
Armytage, W.H.G. *Heavens Below: Utopian Experiments in England 1560-1960* (1961).
Arnot, R. Page. *William Morris: The Man and the Myth* (1964).
Arvon, Henri. *Marxist Esthetics*, trans. Helen R. Lane (New York, 1973).
Ashton, Rosemary. *The German Idea. Four Writers and the Reception of German Thought 1800-1860* (Cambridge, 1980).

Bibliography

Barker, Michael. *Gladstone and Radicalism: the reconstruction of a liberal policy in Britain, 1885-94* (Brighton, 1975).
Barker, Rodney. *Education and Politics 1900-1951: a study of the Labour Party* (Oxford, 1972).
Political Ideas in Modern Britain (1978).
Barzun, Jacques. *Classic, Romantic and Modern* (Chicago, 1961).
Bate, W. Jackson. *From Classic to Romantic* (Cambridge, Mass., 1946).
Baxandall, Lee, ed. *Radical Perspectives in the Arts* (1972).
Beattie, Susan. *A Revolution in London Housing: L.C.C. architects and their work 1893-1914* (1980).
Beer, M. *A History of British Socialism*. Vol. II (1920).
Beer, Samuel. *Modern British Politics* (1965).
Bell, Clive. *Civilization* (1938).
Bell, Quentin. *Virginia Woolf. A Biography.* 2 vols. (1972).
Bellamy, Joyce and Saville, John, eds. *Dictionary of Labour Biography.* 5 vols. to date (1972-9).
Bentley, Eric. *Bernard Shaw* (1950; 2nd edn, 1967).
Bergonzi, Bernard. *The Turn of a Century. Essays on Victorian and Modern Literature* (1973).
Berst, Charles A. *Bernard Shaw and the Art of Drama* (Urbana, Illinois, 1973).
Bettany, F.J. *Stewart Headlam. A Biography* (1926).
Bigsby, C.W.F., ed. *Approaches to Popular Culture* (1976).
Bloom, Harold. *The Ringers in the Tower. Studies in Romantic Tradition* (Chicago, 1971).
Bottomore, T.B. *Elites and Society* (Penguin edn, Harmondsworth, 1966).
Bradby, David, Louis James & Bernard Sharratt. *Performance and Politics in Popular Drama* (1980).
Bratton, J.S. *The Victorian Popular Ballad* (1975).
Brennan, E.T.J. *Education for National Efficiency: the Contribution of Sidney and Beatrice Webb* (1975).
Briggs, Asa and Saville, John, eds. *Essays in Labour History 1886-1923* (1971).
Brion, Marcel. *Art of the Romantic Era — Romanticism. Classicism. Realism* (1966).
Britain, I.M. 'A Transplanted Doll's House: Ibsenism, Feminism and Socialism in Late Victorian and Edwardian England', in Ian Donaldson, ed. *Transformations. Studies in Modern European Drama* (forthcoming).
Brod, Max. *Heinrich Heine. The Artist in Revolt* (Westport, Connecticut, 1976).
Brown, Ray B., ed. *Popular Culture and the Expanding Consciousness* (New York, 1973).
Burke, Peter. *Popular Culture in Early Modern Europe* (1978).
Burns, Elizabeth. *Theatricality: a study of convention in the theatre and in social life* (1972).
Burns, Tom and Elizabeth. *Sociology of Literature and Drama* (1973).
Byatt, A.S. *Wordsworth and Coleridge in their Time* (1970).
Caine, Sydney. *The History of the Foundation of the London School of Economics and Political Science* (1963).
Carpenter, Charles A. *Bernard Shaw and the Art of Destroying Ideals* (Madison, Wisconsin, 1969).
Carpenter, L.H. *G.D.H. Cole. An Intellectual Biography* (1973).
Carswell, John. *Lives and Letters . . . 1906-1957* (1978).
Chandler, Alice. *A Dream of Order. The Medieval Ideal in Nineteenth Century English Literature* (1971).
Chappelow, Allan. *Shaw — 'The Chucker Out'* (1970).
Chapple, J.A.V. *Documentary and Imaginative Literature 1880-1920* (1970).

Chesterton, G.K. *George Bernard Shaw* (1910).

Clarke, John, Chas Critcher & Richard Johnson. *Working Class Culture — Studies in History and Theory* (1979).

Clarke, Peter. *Liberals and Social Democrats* (Cambridge, 1978).

Clayre, Alasdair. *Work and Play. Ideas and experience of work and leisure* (1974).

Clayton, J. *The Rise and Decline of Socialism in Great Britain 1884-1924* (1926).

Cole, G.D.H. *A History of Socialist Thought.* Vol. II (1954). Vol. III (1956).

Cole, Margaret. *Beatrice Webb* (1945).

　'H.G. Wells and the Fabian Society', in A.J.A. Morris, ed. *Edwardian Radicalism 1900-1914* (1974).

　The Life of G.D.H. Cole (1971).

　The Story of Fabian Socialism (1961).

　Women of Today (1938).

Cole, Margaret, ed. *The Webbs and their Work* (1949).

Conrad, Peter. *The Victorian Treasure House* (1973).

Crompton, Louis. *Shaw the Dramatist* (1969).

Crosland, C.A.R. *The Future of Socialism* (1956).

Crossman, R.H.S., ed. *New Fabian Essays* (1952).

Dearmer, Nan. *Life of Percy Dearmer* (1940).

Decker, Clarence R. *The Victorian Conscience* (New York, 1952).

Dickson, Lovat. *H.G. Wells: His Turbulent Life and Times* (1970).

Dietrich, R.F. *Portrait of the Artist as a Young Superman. A Study of Shaw's Novels* (Gainesville, Florida, 1971).

Drabble, Margaret. *Arnold Bennett. A Biography* (1974).

Dupré, Catherine. *John Galsworthy* (1975).

Egbert, D.D. *Social Radicalism and the Arts. Western Europe* (New York, 1970).

Eliot, T.S. *Notes Towards the Definition of Culture* (1948; Faber paperback edn, 1962).

Ellehuage, M. *The Position of Bernard Shaw in European Drama and Philosophy* (New York, 1966).

Ellmann, Richard, ed. *Edwardians and Late Victorians* (Oxford, 1960).

Ensor, R.C.K. *England 1870-1914* (Oxford, 1936).

Entwhistle, Harold. *Class, Culture and Education* (1978).

Ervine, St John. *Bernard Shaw: His Life, Work and Friends* (New York, 1956).

Etzioni-Halévy, Eva. *Political Manipulation and Administrative Power* (1979).

Fejtö, François. *Heine. A Biography,* trans. Mervyn Savill (1946).

Field, G. Lowell & Higley, John. *Elitism* (1980).

Fischer, Ernst. *The Necessity of Art. A Marxist Approach,* trans. Anna Bostock (Penguin edn, Harmondsworth, 1963).

Fox Strangeways, A.H. *Cecil Sharp* (Oxford, 1933).

Fremantle, Anne. *This Little Band of Prophets* (1960).

Fromm, Harold. *Bernard Shaw and the Theater of the Nineties* (Laurence, Kansas, 1967).

Furbank, P.N. *E.M. Forster A Life.* Vol. 2 (1978).

Furst, Lilian. *Romanticism* (2nd edn, 1976).

　Romanticism in Perspective (1969).

Gaunt, William. *The Aesthetic Adventure* (1945).

　The Pre-Raphaelite Tragedy (1942).

　Victorian Olympus (1952).

Gibbons, Tom. *Rooms in the Darwin Hotel. Studies in English Literary Criticism and Ideas 1880-1920* (Nedlands, Western Australia, 1973).

Gibbs, A.M. *Shaw* (Edinburgh, 1969).

Gill, Frederick. *The Romantic Movement and Methodism* (1937).

Goffman, Erving. *The Presentation of Self in Everyday Life* (1969).

Gottfried, Leon. *Matthew Arnold and the Romantics* (1963).
Hamilton, M.A. *Sidney and Beatrice Webb* (1933).
Hardy, Dennis. *Alternative Communities in Nineteenth Century England* (1979).
Harris, Frank. *Bernard Shaw* (1931).
Harrison, Brian. *Drink and the Victorians* (1971).
Harrison, Royden. *Before the Socialists* (1965).
Hassall, Christopher. *Rupert Brooke. A Biography* (1964).
Hatfield, Henry. *Goethe. A Critical Introduction* (New York, 1963).
Henderson, Archibald. *Bernard Shaw. Playboy and Prophet* (1932).
   George Bernard Shaw. His Life and Works (1911).
   George Bernard Shaw. Man of the Century (1956).
Henderson, Philip. *William Morris. His Life, Work and Friends* (Penguin edn,
   Harmondsworth, 1973).
Hendrick, George. *Henry Salt. Humanitarian Reformer and Man of Letters* (Urbana,
   1977).
Hewison, Robert. *John Ruskin. The Argument of the Eye* (1976).
Hilton, Timothy. *The Pre-Raphaelites* (1970).
Hobsbawm, Eric. *Labouring Men. Studies in the History of Labour* (1964).
   'The Lesser Fabians', in Lionel N. Munby, ed. *The Luddites and other Essays* (1971).
Hoggart, Richard. *The Uses of Literacy* (1957; Penguin edn, Harmondsworth, 1958).
Holroyd, Michael, ed. *The Genius of Shaw* (1979).
Honour, Hugh. *Romanticism* (1979).
Houghton, Walter E. *The Victorian Frame of Mind* (Clinton, Mass., 1957).
Hugo, Leon. *Bernard Shaw. Playboy and Prophet* (1971).
Hulse, J.W. *Revolutionists in London. A Study of Five Unorthodox Socialists* (Oxford,
   1970).
Hummert, Paul A. *Bernard Shaw's Marxian Romance* (Lincoln, Nebraska, 1973).
Hunt, John Dixon. *The Pre-Raphaelite Imagination: 1848-1900* (1968).
Hynes, Samuel. *Edwardian Occasions* (1972).
   The Edwardian Turn of Mind (1968).
Irvine, William. *The Universe of G.B.S.* (New York, 1949).
James, D.G. *Matthew Arnold and the Decline of English Romanticism* (Oxford, 1961).
   The Romantic Comedy (Oxford, 1963).
Jay, Elisabeth. *The Religion of the Heart. Anglican Evangelicalism and the Novel*
   (Oxford, 1979).
Joad, C.E.M. *Shaw* (1949).
Joad, C.E.M., ed. *Shaw and Society. An Anthology and a Symposium* (1953).
Johnson, R.V. *Aestheticism* (1969).
Johnson, Lesley. *The Cultural Critics* (1979).
Jones, Peter d'A. *The Christian Socialist Revival 1877-1914* (Princeton, 1968).
Kapp, Yvonne. *Eleanor Marx.* 2 vols. (1972, 1976).
Kaufmann, R.J., ed. *G.B. Shaw. A Collection of Critical Essays* (1965).
Kaye, Julian B. *Bernard Shaw and the Nineteenth Century Tradition* (Norman,
   Oklahoma, 1958).
Kelvin, Norman. *A Troubled Eden. Nature and Society in the Works of George
   Meredith* (Stanford, 1961).
Kendall, Walter. *The Revolutionary Movement in Great Britain* (1969).
Kent, Christopher. *Brains and Numbers: Elitism, Comtism and Democracy in Mid-
   Victorian England* (Toronto, 1978).
Klingender, Francis D. *Art and the Industrial Revolution* (1947).
Knopfelmacher, U.C. & Tennyson, G.B., eds. *Nature and the Victorian Imagination*

(Berkeley, 1977).
Landow, George P. *The Aesthetic and Critical Theories of John Ruskin* (Princeton, 1971).
Laurenson, Diana and Swingewood, Alan. *The Sociology of Literature* (1972).
Leavis, F.R. *Mass Civilisation and Minority Culture* (Cambridge, 1930).
   Nor Shall My Sword (1972).
Leavis, F.R. and Thompson, Denys. *Culture and Environment* (1933).
Leavis, Q.D. *Fiction and the Reading Public* (1932).
Lee, H.W. and Archbold, E. *Social Democracy in Britain* (1935).
Lehmann, John, *Rupert Brooke. His Life and Legend* (1980).
Letwin, S.R. *The Pursuit of Certainty: David Hume, Jeremy Bentham, John Stuart Mill, Beatrice Webb* (Cambridge, 1965).
Lichtheim, George. *A Short History of Socialism* (1970).
Lifshitz, Mikhail. *The Philosophy of Art of Karl Marx* (1933; new edn, Bristol, 1973).
Lindsay, Jack. *George Meredith. His Life and Work* (1956).
   William Morris (1975).
Lloyd, A.L. *Folk Song in England* (1967; Paladin edn, 1975).
Lucas, John, ed. *Literature and Politics in the Nineteenth Century* (1971).
Lynd, Helen Merrell. *England in the Eighteen Eighties. Towards A Social Basis for Freedom* (1945).
McBriar, A.M. *Fabian Socialism and English Politics 1884-1918* (Cambridge, 1962).
McCarran, Margaret. *Fabianism in the Political Life of Britain 1919-31* (1957).
MacCarthy, Desmond. *Shaw: the Plays* (1951).
McIntosh, James. *Thoreau as Romantic Naturalist* (New York, 1974).
MacKenzie, Jeanne. *A Victorian Courtship. The Story of Beatrice Potter and Sidney Webb* (1979).
MacKenzie, Norman and Jeanne. *The First Fabians* (1977).
   The Time Traveller. The Life of H.G. Wells (1973).
McKibbin, Ross. *The Evolution of the Labour Party 1910-1924* (Oxford, 1974).
Mairet, Philip. *A.R. Orage. A Memoir* (1936).
Mann, Dennis Alan, ed. *The Arts in a Democratic Society* (Bowling Green, Ohio, 1977).
Marquand, David. *Ramsay MacDonald* (1977).
Martin, David E. & Rubinstein, David, eds. *Ideology and the Labour Movement* (1979).
Martin, Wallace. *The New Age Under Orage* (1967).
Meier, Paul. *William Morris. The Marxist Dreamer*, trans. Frank Gubb. 2 vols. (Hassocks, Sussex, 1978).
Meisel, James. *The Myth of the Ruling Class* (1962).
Meisel, Martin. *Shaw and the Nineteenth Century Theatre* (Princeton, 1963).
Michels, Robert. *First Lectures in Political Sociology*, trans, Alfred de Grazia (New York, 1965).
   Political Parties (1962).
Mills, C. Wright. *The Power Elite* (New York, 1956).
Minihan, Janet. *The Nationalization of Culture* (1977).
Moore, Doris Langley. *E. Nesbit* (Revised edn, 1967).
Morgan, Kenneth. *Keir Hardie* (1975).
Morgan, Margery M. *A Drama of Political Man. A Study in the Plays of Harley Granville Barker* (1961).
   The Shavian Playground (1972).
Mosca, Gaetano. *The Ruling Class*, trans. Hanna D. Kahn (New York, 1939).
Mount, Ferdinand. *The Theatre of Politics* (1972).

Muggeridge, Kitty and Adam, Ruth. *Beatrice Webb: A Life 1858-1943* (1965).
Nairn, Tom. 'The English Literary Intelligentsia', in Emma Tennant, ed., *Bananas* (1977).
Naylor, Gillian. *The Arts and Crafts Movement* (1971).
Nethercot, Arthur H. *The First Five Lives of Annie Besant* (1961).
  Men and Supermen: The Shavian Portrait Gallery (Cambridge, Mass., 1954).
Newsome, David. *Two Classes of Men. Platonism and English Romantic Thought* (1974).
Nochlin, Linda. *Realism* (Penguin edn, Harmondsworth, 1971).
Nowell-Smith, Simon. *Edwardian England 1901-1914* (1964).
O'Brien, Conor Cruise, & Vanech, W.D., eds. *Power and Consciousness* (1969).
Ohmann, Richard M. *Shaw. The Style and the Man* (Middletown, Conn., 1962).
Orme, Michael. *J.T. Grein. The story of a pioneer 1862-1935* (1936).
Orwell, George. *Collected Essays, Journalism and Letters*, ed. Sonya Orwell & Ian Angus (1968).
Pareto, Vilfredo. *Sociological Writings*, trans. Derek Mirfin & ed. S.E. Finer (1966).
Parker, Robert. *A Family of Friends. The Story of the Transatlantic Smiths* (1960).
Parry, Geraint. *Political Elites* (1969).
Pearsall, Ronald. *Victorian Popular Music* (1973).
Pearson, Hesketh. *Bernard Shaw. His Life and Personality* (1942).
Pelling, Henry. *America and the British Left. From Bright to Bevan* (1956).
  Origins of the Labour Party (2nd edn, Oxford, 1965).
  Popular Politics and Society in Late Victorian Britain (1968).
Pevsner, Nikolaus. *Pioneers of Modern Design* (Harmondsworth, 1960).
Pierson, Stanley. *British Socialists. The Journey from Fantasy to Politics* (Cambridge, Mass., 1979).
  Marxism and the Origins of British Socialism (Ithaca, New York, 1973).
Poirier, Philip. *The Advent of the Labour Party* (1958).
Pollard, Arthur, ed. *The Victorians* (1970).
Prawer, S.S. *Karl Marx and World Literature* (Oxford, 1970).
Purdom, C.B. *Harley Granville Barker* (1955).
Qualter, Terence H. *Graham Wallas and the Great Society* (1980).
Quennell, Peter. *John Ruskin. The Portrait of a Prophet* (1949).
Rattray, R.F. *Bernard Shaw: A Chronicle* (Luton, n.d.).
Redmond, James. 'William Morris or Bernard Shaw: Two Faces of Socialism', in J. Butt and I.F. Clarke, eds. *The Victorians and Social Protest A Symposium* (1973).
Reeves, Nigel. *Heinrich Heine. Poetry and Politics* (Oxford, 1974).
Rosenberg, John. *The Darkening Glass: A Portrait of Ruskin's Genius* (New York, 1961).
Rosenblood, Norman, ed. *Shaw: Seven Critical Essays* (Oxford, 1971).
Rowbotham, Sheila, and Weeks, Jeffrey. *Socialism and the New Life: the Personal and Sexual Politics of Edward Carpenter and Havelock Ellis* (1977).
Ryan, Alan. *J.S. Mill* (1974).
Sanders, C.R. *Carlyle's Friendships and other studies* (Durham, Northern California, 1977).
Saul, S.B. *The Myth of the Great Depression 1873-1896* (1969).
Schenk, H.G. *The Mind of the European Romantics* (Oxford, 1979).
Schoonderwoerd, N.H.G. *J.T. Grein. Ambassador of the theatre 1862-1935* (Assen, 1963).
Schücking, L.L. *The Sociology of Literary Taste*, trans. Brian Battershaw (2nd edn, 1966).
Schumpeter, J.A. *Capitalism, Socialism and Democracy* (1943).
Selver, Paul. *Orage and the New Age Circle* (1959).

Sen Gupta, S.C. *The Art of Bernard Shaw* (Oxford, 1936).
Shrapnel, Norman. *The Performers. Politics as Theatre* (1978).
Simon, Brian. *Education and the Labour Movement* (1965).
Smith, J.P. *Unrepentant Pilgrim. A Study of the Development of Bernard Shaw* (1966).
Smith, Warren Sylvester. *The London Heretics* (1967).
Soffer, Reba. *Ethics and Society in England* (Los Angeles, 1978).
Spence, Robin. *Aestheticism* (1969).
Spencer, Isobel. *Walter Crane* (1975).
Strauss, E. *Bernard Shaw. Art and Socialism* (1942).
Sussman, Herbert L. *Victorians and the Machine. The Literary Response to Technology* (Cambridge, Mass., 1968).
Swingewood, Alan. *The Myth of Mass Culture* (1977).
Swinnerton, Frank. *The Georgian Literary Scene 1910-1935* (Revised edn, 1969).
Tawney, R.H. *The Radical Tradition* (Penguin edn, Harmondsworth, 1966).
The Webbs in Perspective (1953).
Tholfsen, Trygve. *Working Class Radicalism in Mid-Victorian England* (1976).
Thompson, Denys, ed. *Discrimination and Popular Culture* (2nd edn, Harmondsworth, 1973).
Thompson, E.P. *William Morris. Romantic to Revolutionary* (1955; new edn, 1977).
Thompson, Laurence. *The Enthusiasts. A Biography of John and Katharine Bruce Glasier* (1971).
Portrait of an Englishman (1951).
Thompson, Paul. *Socialists, Liberals and Labour. The Struggle for London 1885-1914* (1967).
The Work of William Morris (1967).
Toffler, Alvin. *The Culture Consumers* (1964).
Torr, Dona. *Tom Mann and His Times* (1956).
Townsend, Peter and Bosanquet, Nicholas, eds. *Labour and Inequality. Sixteen Fabian Essays* (1973).
Trilling, Lionel. *Beyond Culture* (1965; Peregrine edn, 1973).
Tsuzuki, Chushichi. *Edward Carpenter 1844-1929. Prophet of human fellowship* (Cambridge, 1980).
H.M. Hyndman and British Socialism (Oxford, 1961).
The Life of Eleanor Marx 1855-1898. A Socialist Tragedy (Oxford, 1967).
Turner, Victor. *Dramas, Fields, and Metaphors* (Ithaca, New York, 1974).
Ulam, Adam B. *Philosophical Foundations of British Socialism* (Cambridge, Mass., 1964).
Valency, Maurice. *The Cart and the Trumpet. The Plays of Bernard Shaw* (1972).
Vicinus, Martha. *The Industrial Muse. A study of nineteenth-century British working class literature* (1974).
Wall, Vincent. *Bernard Shaw. Pygmalion to Many Players* (Ann Arbor, 1973).
Walsh, William, *The Use of Imagination. Educational Thought and the Literary Mind* (Harmondsworth, 1966).
Watson, George. *The English Idelogy. Studies in the Language of Victorian Politics* (1973).
Webb, James. *The Harmonious Circle* (1980).
Wiener, Martin J. *Between Two Worlds. The Political Thought of Graham Wallas* (1971).
West, Alick. *A Good Man Fallen Among Fabians* (1950).
Willey, Basil. *Nineteenth Century Studies* (Penguin edn, Harmondsworth, 1964).
Williams, Raymond. *The Country and the City* (1973).
Culture and Society 1780-1950 (1958; Penguin edn, Harmondsworth, 1961).

Keywords (1976).
The Long Revolution (1961).
Williamson, Audrey. *Artists and Writers in Revolt. The Pre-Raphaelites* (1976).
Wilson, Colin. *Bernard Shaw. A Reassessment* (1969).
Winsten, Stephen. *Days with Bernard Shaw* (n.d.).
Jesting Apostle. The Life of Bernard Shaw (1956).
Salt and His Circle (1951).
Winsten, Stephen, ed. *G.B.S. 90 Aspects of Bernard Shaw's Life and Work* (1946).
Winter, J.M. *Socialism and the Challenge of War. Ideas and Politics in Britain 1912-1918* (1974).
Wolfe, Willard. *From Radicalism to Socialism. Men and Ideas in the Formation of Fabian Socialist Doctrines 1881-1889* (New Haven, 1975).
Yeo, Stephen. *Religion and Voluntary Organisations in Crisis* (1976).

5. PERIODICAL ARTICLES (MAINLY POST-1945)

Adams, Elsie B. 'Bernard Shaw's Pre-Raphaelite Drama', *Publications of the Modern Language Association* (hereafter *P.M.L.A.*), LXXXI (Oct. 1966).
Albert, Sidney, F. 'Bernard Shaw: The Artist as Philosopher', *Journal of Aesthetics and Art Criticism*, XIV (June 1956).
Anderson, Perry, 'Components of the National Culture', *New Left Review*, 50 (1968).
Bailey, Peter. ' "A Mingled Mass of Perfectly Legitimate Pleasures": the Victorian middle class and the problem of leisure', *Victorian Studies*, XXI (Autumn 1977).
Britain, I.M. 'Bernard Shaw, Ibsen and the Ethics of English Socialism', *Victorian Studies*, XXI (Spring 1978).
' "Two of the Nicest People if ever there was one": the correspondence of Sidney and Beatrice Webb', *Historical Studies*, 19 (Oct. 1980).
Cherry, D.R. 'The Fabianism of Shaw', *Queens Quarterly*, LXIX (Spring 1962).
Clarkson, J.D. 'Background of Fabian Theory', *Journal of Economic History*, XIII (Fall 1953).
Duerksen, Roland A. 'Shelley and Shaw', *P.M.L.A.*, LXXVIII (March 1963).
Dyson, A.E. 'The Socialist Aesthete', *Listener*, LXVI (Aug. 1961).
Gassner, John. 'Bernard Shaw and the Making of the Modern Mind', *College English*, XXIII (April 1962).
Haberland, Paul. 'A Fabian View of Goethe', *Univ. of South Florida Language Quarterly*, XV (Fall 1976).
Harrison, Royden. 'The Young Webb: 1859-92', S.S.L.H., bulletin 17 (Autumn 1968).
Himmelfarb, Gertrude. 'The Intellectual in Politics: The Case of the Webbs', *Journal of Contemporary History*, 6 (1971).
'Process, Purpose and Ego', *Times Literary Supplement*, 25 June 1976.
Hynes, Samuel. 'A Marriage of Minds', *New York Times Book Review*, 30 July 1978.
Irvine, William. 'Shaw, the Fabians and the Utilitarians', *Journal of the History of Ideas*, VIII (April 1947).
Jones, Howard Mumford. 'Shaw as a Victorian', *Victorian Studies*, I (Winter 1957).
Judges, A.V. 'The Educational Influence of the Webbs', *British Journal of Education Studies*, X (Nov. 1961).
Leavis, F.R. 'Beatrice Webb in Partnership', *Scrutiny*, XVI (June 1949).
Lewis, Gordon K. 'Fabian Socialism: Some Aspects of Theory and Practice', *Journal of Politics*, XIV (Aug. 1952).
Mack, Mary Peter. 'The Fabians and Utilitarianism', *Journal of the History of Ideas*, XVI (Jan. 1955).

'Graham Wallas' New Individualism', *Western Political Quarterly*, XI (March 1958).

MacKenzie, Norman. 'Percival Chubb and the Founding of the Fabian Society', *Victorian Studies*, XXIII (Autumn 1979).

Melitz, J. 'The Trade Unions and Fabian Socialism', *Industrial and Labour Relations Quarterly*, XII (June 1958).

Meller, Helen E. 'Cultural Provisions for the Working Classes in Urban Britain in the second half of the Nineteenth Century', S.S.L.H., bulletin 17 (Autumn 1968).

Mellers, W.H., 'G.B.S. and Music Criticism', *Scrutiny*, VI (1937).

Milburn, J.F. 'The Fabian Society and the British Labour Party', *Western Political Quarterly*, XI (June 1958).

Murphy, Mary E. 'The Role of the Fabian Society in British Affairs', *Southern Economic Journal*, XIV (July 1947).

Nadel, I.B. 'Beatrice Webb's Literary Success', *Studies in Short Fiction*, 13 (Fall 1976).

Nethercot, Arthur H. 'G.B.S. and Annie Besant', *Shaw Bulletin*, I (Sept. 1955).

'The Quintessence of Idealism; or the Slaves of Duty', *P.M.L.A*, LXII (Sept. 1947).

O'Donnell, Norbert, F. 'Shaw, Bunyan and Puritanism', *P.M.L.A.*, LXXII (June 1957).

Oldfield, Adrian. Review of 1974 reprint of *The Webbs and their Work*, S.S.L.H. bulletin 33 (Autumn 1976).

Pelling, Henry. 'H.H. Champion: Pioneer of Labour Representation', *Cambridge Journal*, VI (Jan. 1953).

Pierson, Stanley. 'Ernest Belfort Bax: 1854-1926. The Encounter of Marxism and Late Victorian Culture', *Journal of British Studies*, XII (Nov. 1972).

'Edward Carpenter, Prophet of a Socialist Millennium', *Victorian Studies*, XV (Spring 1970).

Ricci, David M. 'Fabian Socialism: a Theory of Rent as Exploitation', *Journal of British Studies*, IX (Nov. 1969).

Rodenbeck, John von B. 'Bernard Shaw's Revolt against Rationalism', *Victorian Studies*, XV (June 1972).

Rosen, Charles, & Zerner, Henri. 'The Permanent Revolution', *New York Review of Books*, 22 Nov. 1979.

Samuel, Raphael. Editorial introduction to 'Documents and Texts from the Workers' Theatre Movement (1928-1936)', *History Workshop*, 4 (Autumn 1977).

Saville, John. 'Background to the Revival of Socialism in England', S.S.L.H., bulletin 11 (Autumn 1965).

Stansky, Peter. 'Art, Industry and the Aspirations of William Martin Conway', *Victorian Studies*, XIX (June 1976).

Starr, Joseph R., 'The Summer Schools and Other Educational Activities of British Socialist Groups', *American Political Science Review*, 30 (1936).

Stedman-Jones, Gareth. 'Working-Class Culture and Working-Class Politics in London, 1870-1900; notes on the remaking of a working class', *Journal of Social History*, 7 (Summer 1974).

Stigler, George J. 'Bernard Shaw, Sidney Webb and the Theory of Fabian Socialism', *Proceedings of the American Philosophical Society*, CIII (June 1959).

Stokes, E.E. (Jnr). 'Morris and Bernard Shaw', *Journal of the William Morris Society*, I (Winter 1961).

'Shaw and William Morris', *Shaw Bulletin*, 4 (Summer 1953).

Timko, Michael. 'The Victorianism of Victorian Literature', *New Literary History*, VI (Spring 1975).

Vicinus, Martha. 'The Study of Victorian Popular Culture', *Victorian Studies*, XVIII (June 1975).

Vincent, John. 'Love Among the Socialists', *New Society*, 14 July 1977.

Weiler, Peter. 'William Clarke: The Making and Unmaking of a Fabian Socialist', *Journal of British Studies*, XIV (Nov. 1974).

Wellek, René. 'The Concept of "Romanticism" in Literary History', *Comparative Literature*, I (Winter and Spring 1949).

Young, J.B. 'Elitism, Authoritarianism and Western Socialism', S.S.L.H., bulletin 25 (Autumn 1972).

Yeo, Stephen. 'A New Life: The Religion of Socialism in Britain, 1883-1896', *History Workshop*, 4 (Autumn 1977).

6. THESES, CONFERENCE PAPERS, LECTURES

Bailey, Peter. 'Rational Recreation and the Entertainment Industry: the Case of the Victorian Music Halls', paper delivered at 1975 conference of the Society for the Study of Labour History, Sussex University — taken from the author's Ph.D. thesis, British Columbia (1974).

Britain, I.M. 'Fabian Socialism and the Arts, c.1884-1918, with particular reference to the thought and attitudes of Sidney and Beatrice Webb'. Oxford University D.Phil. thesis (1978).

Casson, Sir Hugh. 'The Arts and the Academies'. Romanes Lecture, Oxford University (1979).

Clark, W.R. 'The Literary Aspects of Fabian Socialism'. Columbia University Ph.D. thesis (1952).

Hobsbawm, Eric. 'Fabianism and the Fabians, 1884-1914'. Cambridge University Ph.D. thesis (1950).

Howard, Sarah. 'The New Utilitarians? Studies in the Origins and Early Intellectual Associations of Fabianism'. Warwick University Ph.D. thesis (1976).

Howland, R.D. 'Fabian Thought and Social Change in England, 1884-1914'. London University Ph.D. thesis (1942).

McBriar, A.M. 'Fabian Socialist Doctrine and Its Influence in English Politics'. Oxford University D.Phil. thesis (1949).

Stabler, Ernest. 'London Education 1890-1910, with special reference to the work of Sidney and Beatrice Webb'. Harvard University Ed.D. thesis (1951).

Summerfield, Penny. 'The Effingham Arms and the Empire: Working-Class Culture and the Evolution of the Music Hall'. Paper delivered at 1975 S.S.L.H. conference, Sussex University.

Warner, Malcolm. 'The Webbs — A Study of the Influence of Intellectuals in Politics (largely between 1889-1918)'. Cambridge University Ph.D. thesis (1967).

Wilbur, W.C. 'The Origins and Development of Fabian Socialism to 1890'. Columbia University Ph.D. thesis (1953).

Wilkins, Myra S. 'The Influence of Socialist Ideas on English Prose Writing and Political Thinking, 1880-1895'. Cambridge University Ph.D. thesis (1957).

Index

Achurch, Janet (Mrs Charles Charrington), 174, 186, 209
acting, and Fabian lecturing, 211-12, 217; *see also* histrionic impulses of Fabians, theatrical profession
Adams, Maurice, 281 n.78
Addison, Joseph, 128
Adelaide (South Australia), 135, 140
aesthetic instincts of British socialists, 3-4, 257-8; of Fabians, 27, 42, 49, 51, 53-4, 68, 75, 82, 84, 89-91, 92-3, 100-1, 107, 108, 110, 113, 127, 168, 173, 188, 193-4, 257, 258
aesthetic movement, 155-6
aestheticism, of Thomas Davidson, 30; B. Webb's differences with, 125, 132; Bland and, 153-4, 255
America, *see* U.S.A.
amusements, *see* entertainments
anarchism, in Socialist League, 21; in Fabian Society, 170, 179; in Ibsen, 178
Annan, Noël, 224-5, 230, 231
Anti-Puritan League, 150, 151, 160, 298 n.66
anti-sabbatarianism, 149, 180
Archer, William, 209, 265
architecture, W. Clarke's responses to, 51; Shaw's responses to, 102, 107-8; Webbs' responses to, 119, 138-41, 245; Fabian lectures on, 195, 197, 201, 203, 207-8; Morris on, 197, 248; Co-operative Movement and, 245
aristocratic/upper-class culture, 226-7, 231, 232, 234, 239; *see also* high art(s)/culture, middle-class/bourgeois culture
Aristotle, 36
Arnold, Matthew, versus philistinism, 5, 6; influence on Fabian Society, 43, 44, 50, 63; romanticism and, 47-8, 282 n.99; Webbs' interest in, 60, 61, 114, 285 n.68; *Literature and Dogma*, impact of on A. Besant, 91; cultural elitism and, 224

art/the arts, Fabians' alleged indifference to, 4, 7, 8-9, 17-18, 113, 193, 241, 263; and class, 5, 223-70 *passim*, 272; and education, 5, 85, 104, 159, 230, 231, 240; and work, 5, 147, 153, 165, 247, 250, 272; and leisure, 5, 267, 272; and morality, 5, 31, 61, 72, 77, 98, 100, 146, 152, 153, 154, 159, 272; and politics, 5, 166, 272; and religion, 5, 30, 86, 87, 90, 93, 102, 208, 272; as implicit concern of (Fabian) socialism, 9, 19, 67, 88, 110, 123, 153, 164, 251-2; definitions and conceptions of, 9, 66, 147, 153, 154, 228, 233, 236, 248, 262, 267, 268, 270; lack of definite Fabian attitude to, 17; Davidson circle's interest in, and the origins of Fabianism, 30-2, 37; as source of socialism, 38-43, 83, 84, 86, 93, 101, 106-7; and nature, 32, 37, 82, 83, 141; and science, 61, 66, 125; and economic conditions, 81, 98, 100, 109, 118, 120, 147, 249; and civilization, 82; as a humanizing influence, 88, 100, 110, 120, 122, 159; Fabians' distaste for cult of, 107-8, 110, 117, 145, 149; amateurs in, 109, 240-1; and pleasure, 131-2, 147, 154-5, 159, 165, 199; Fabian lectures on, 192-219; Fabian Summer School discussions of, 210, 304 n.45; and democracy, 253-5, 259, 265, 266, 267, 269; *see also* culture, communal arts, community arts, domestic arts, fine art(s), handicrafts, high art(s)/culture, industrial arts, intellectual arts, popular arts/culture, useful arts, and under individual artistic genres
'art for art's sake', Fabian attitudes to, 77, 98, 130, 152-5, 159, 219; *see also* aestheticism, didacticism in art, form and content, purpose in art, style
art galleries, Fabians' visits to, 59, 62, 282 n.103; public provision of as part of Fabian cultural schemes, 78, 82, 120, 121; as venues for popular culture, 133; A. Besant

Index

329

42; on art and socialism, 97
Credi, Lorenzo di, 138
Cromwell, Oliver, 108
Crosland, Anthony, 143, 146
culture, definitions and conceptions of, 5, 32, 43, 47, 224, 241, 259, 272; Fabians' alleged indifference to, 5, 143, 229-30, 271; versus philistinism, 6; proto-Fabians' concerns with, 32, 43; versus commercialism, 40; various Fabians' concerns with, 45, 81, 82, 93, 94, 113, 143; Webbs' concerns with, 53, 54, 113, 117, 133, 247; Shaw's concerns with, 96-7, 241; élitist notions of, 224-6, 229-30, 253; grades of, 231; and labour, 233-4, 241, 247; and egalitarianism, 253; see also aristocratic/upper-class culture, art/the arts, folk culture, mass culture, middle-class/bourgeois culture, minority culture, popular arts/culture, working-class/proletarian culture
dancing, provision of rooms or schools for as part of Fabian cultural schemes, 120, 160; Ruskin's interest in, 157; Headlam's interest in, 160; at music halls, 238-9; as a popular art, 261; see also ballet, recreation
Dante Alighieri, 31, 32, 35, 90
Darwin, Charles, 61, 63, 73, 99; see also evolution/evolutionary theory
Davidson, Thomas, early life and career of, 25; ideal of brotherhood, 25; divisions among his disciples over the implementation of his vision, 26-7, 48; initial sympathy with socialism, 28; growing aversion to materialist aspects of socialism, 28; as progenitor of the Fabian Society, 28-9, 106; formative influence on proto-Fabians, 29, 30, 31, 32, 33, 38, 41, 43-5, 47, 49-50, 52, 56; tensions with P. Chubb, 29; on the significance of art, 30, 279 n.23; aestheticism of, 30, 37; interests in classical art, 30; avowed bias against romantic art, 31, 32, 36; as transmitter of works of Dante and Goethe, 31, 32; meets S. Webb, 34; on Goethe's Faust, 34-5; unconscious romanticist elements in writings of, 35, 36, 37-8, 44; joint interests in Rosmini and Zola, 60; artistic interests of compared with B. Webb's, 60, 61; as an anti-ascetic, 147-8; as advocate of an art of common things, 255
Dearmer, Rev. Percy, 258-9
decorative arts, see furniture and furnishings, handicrafts
Defoe, Daniel, 285 n.68
democracy, Fabians' concerns with, 14, 17, 176, 272-3; and art, as subject of Fabian lectures, 204, 266, 267-70; concessions to

under elitist regimes, 224; as basis for the development of art, 253-4, 255, 256, 257, 258, 259, 267, 269; as a basis for administering the arts, 265; see also social democracy
De Quincey, Thomas, 50, 99
design schools, as part of Fabian cultural schemes, 120, 121
Despard, Mrs, 208
Dickens, Charles, and the reaction against orthodox political economy, 23, 63; as a source of British socialism, 39, 40, 43; read by various Fabians in their formative years, 60, 86, 103, 285 n.68; as subject of lectures by Fabians, 155, 199; as a popular artist, 254, 255
Dickinson, G. Lowes, 243
didacticism in art, Fabians' reservations about, 135, 155, 197-9; Fabian lecture on, 304 n.45; see also 'art for art's sake', form and content, purpose in art, style
dock strike in London (1889), 61, 107
Dodd, Dr F. Lawson, 182, 183
domestic arts, 201-2, 262; see also handicrafts
Donizetti, Gaetano, 107
Dostoevsky, Feodor, 198, 199
drama, Thomas Davidson and proto-Fabians' interest in, 31, 35; Fabian lectures on, 185, 198, 199, 201, 209, 211, 237, 304 n.45; reasons for Fabian preoccupation with and reservations about, 177-81, 210-11, 212-18; as refiner of human nature, according to A. Besant, 228; Morris's lack of interest in, 262, 308 n.23; see also acting, histrionic impulses of Fabians, literature, plays, theatre, theatrical profession, and under names of dramatists
Dreyfus case, 197
drink, varying Fabian attitudes to, 159, 229, 242, 307, n.42
Drury Lane, theatres and performers of, 156-7
Dryhurst, A.R., 195-6
duty, Davidson circle's concern with, 43; various Fabians' concerns with, 63, 76, 81, 92

economic climate in late-Victorian England, 1, 3, 4; see also Great Depression
economics, place of in Fabian concerns and thought, 7, 17, 26, 66, 76, 93, 99-101, 109, 110, 113, 194; emphasis on criticized by Thomas Davidson, 28; Ruskin's concerns with, 109; of culture, in Fabian schemes, 233, 265, 269
education, and the arts, 5, 85, 104, 159, 187, 230, 231, 240; Fabian disputes over administration of, 15, 151; Goethe's

and achievements of, 139-40; attacks on
cultural and recreational policies of, 139,
151, 159-60, 238, 298 n.62; S. Webb's
defence of, 139-40, 160, 251
London School of Economics, 12, 138, 139
Louvre, the, 282 n.103
love, and its relation to art, 31, 60, 147;
as a social ideal of Fabians, 58, 81, 82
luxury, Morris's criticisms of, 80, 108;
Shaw's criticisms of, 97, 108, 110;
Ruskin's criticisms of, 108, 109; various
Fabians and proto-Fabians' attitudes to,
110, 147, 148, 161, 227; Webbs' criticism
of, 116-19, 120, 141, 143-4, 242, 243

MacDonald, James Ramsay, disputes with the
Webbs, 15, 119, 216; as member of the
New Life Fellowship, 27; as a Fabian, 27,
205; on literary and artistic sources of
British socialism, 40; versus
commercialism, 146; as a political
performer, 216; as Prime Minister, 247-8;
on art under socialism, 257-9
Macrosty, H.W., 198-9
machine aesthetic, Shaw as a herald of, 97-8,
249-50; Webbs' receptiveness to, 249-50;
late conversion of Morris's disciples to,
250; American and German evangelists of,
250; *see also* industrial arts, useful arts
machinery, romanticist reactions against, 47;
Ruskin's attitudes to, 51, 53, 54, 97;
attitudes of Morris and his disciples to, 51,
55, 97, 249, 250; W. Clarke's attitudes to,
51, 97; Webbs' attitudes to, 53, 54-5, 97,
247, 249-50; Shaw's attitudes to, 97-8,
249-50; *see also* industrial arts,
industrialism, useful arts
Malleson, Miles, 206
Manning, Cardinal Henry, 2
Mansfield, Richard, 135
marriage question, and the Fabians, 17, 177
Marshall, Alfred, 67
Marson, Rev. Charles, 190, 192, 259-61
Marx (-Aveling), Eleanor, 20, 21
Marx, Karl, and the reaction against
orthodox political economy, 2; as a source
of Fabian socialism, 38, 39, 41, 48, 76, 94,
99, 100; S. Webb's criticisms of, 67, 68; as
influence on William Morris, 69, 232;
Shaw and, 76, 99, 100, 158; *Capital*, 41,
94, 99, 100
mass culture, 135, 231, 242, 251-2, 258,
259, 268; *see also* popular arts/culture,
working-class/proletarian culture
masses, relationship with ruling elites in
politics and culture, 225, 230, 231;
assumed degradation of under capitalism,

226-7, 232, 247, 257; *see also* working
class, working-class/proletarian culture
match-girls' strike (1888), 88
materialism, Davidson circle's attitudes to,
26, 29; Fabian Society's reputation for, 27;
romanticist reaction against, 47, 48;
concerns with and beyond in Fabians'
schemes, 80-2, 122, 123, 256-8, 269;
secularism and, 91-2, 149
Maude, Aylmer, 207, 209
Maupassant, Guy de, 60
Maurice, F.D., 3, 156, 157
mediaeval art and society, various Fabian
attitudes to, 40, 64, 108, 139, 251, 260,
266; William Morris's attitude to, 40, 41;
Ruskin's attitude to, 108, 286 n.9; Comte's
attitude to, 286 n.9
melodrama, 237
Meredith, George, 40, 85, 86, 198, 199, 285
n.68, 288 notes 56, 57 & 63; *The
Adventures of Harry Richmond*, 85, 288
n.57; *Evan Harrington*, 288 n.57
meritocratic principles and practices, in
education, 224; as part of Fabian schemes,
251, 269
Michelangelo, 99, 138
middle class, pre-Fabian reactions against, 3,
17, 178-9; as dominant element in Fabian
Society, 6, 20, 39, 45, 106, 189, 203, 230;
leadership of in English socialist
organizations, 6, 7; Fabians' alienation from
and criticisms of, 20, 54, 86, 106, 107,
148, 149, 191, 233, 235, 245, 255, 260,
261, 267; members of in New Life
Fellowship, 25, 45; socialists on necessity
for self-sacrifice by, 76, 116, 144; Fabians'
inescapable attachments to, 116, 141, 223,
229, 233, 241, 261
middle-class/bourgeois culture, Fabian Society
activities as an example of, 165; extensions
of as part of Fabian cultural ideas and
schemes, 223, 229, 230, 233-4, 242; as a
concept, 231; Morris and, 231, 232; Fabian
criticisms of, 234-6, 255, 267; *see also*
aristocratic/upper-class culture, popular
arts/culture
Mill, John Stuart, and the reaction against
orthodox political economy, 2, 63; as a
source of British socialism, 38, 48;
influence on Webbs, 61, 62, 67; various
Fabians and, 73, 75, 76, 84, 99, 287 n.21;
on art and democracy, 257; reaction of
against Benthamite utilitarianism, 63, 73-4,
285 n.54, 287 n.14; resistance of to
Romantic-Naturalism, 288 n.51; *Principles
of Political Economy*, 73, 75; *System of
Logic*, 73

Ramsay MacDonald, 15, 119, 216; aesthetic and cultural concerns of as socialists, 55, 56, 57, 58, 119, 120, 121, 122-4, 125-6, 127, 128, 133, 134, 135, 142, 143, 223, 243-7, 249, 250, 257, 273; as influences on each other, 57, 61-2, 64, 113, 114, 118-19, 124, 125, 138, 142, 219, 277 n.45; courtship of, 69, 113, 114, 128; austerity of, 118-20, 124, 125, 126, 128, 141, 142, 146, 150, 292 n.21 & n.24; feelings of inadquacy about artistic matters, 120, 124, 125-6, 127-8; and education, 122, 123, 243, 251, 269; artistic interests, pleasures and tastes, 124, 126, 128, 129, 133-4, 136, 137, 138, 140-1, 142; ascetic reputation of, 142, 143; anti-asceticism of, 143, 144, 145, 147; puritanism of, 145, 150, 152, 243; and Guild Socialism, 150, 171-2; tension between élitist and anti-élitist elements in socialism of, 223, 226, 229-30, 243-4, 251, 264-5; and Co-operative Movement, 244-7; *A Constitution for the Socialist Commonwealth of Great Britain*, 123, 142, 247; *The Consumers' Co-operative Movement*, 244-7; *English Local Government*, 128

Wedekind, Frank, 177

Wells, H.G., as a Fabian, 7, 19, 165-6, 169, 203, 205; campaign to reform Fabian Society, 8, 10, 11, 158, 163, 263; Special Committee of Fabian Society to report on criticisms of, 8-9, 151; as a novelist, 10, 12-13, 124, 129-30, 165-6; relationship with and portrayal of the Webbs, 10, 12-13, 124, 127, 129-30, 172, 276 n.44; relationship with and attitudes to Fabian 'Old Gang', 10, 151, 158, 165-6, 216, 276 n.34; as amorous adventurer, 151, 216; *Anticipations*, 10; *The New Machiavelli*, 12-13, 130, 141; *Tono-Bungay*, 129-30, 132; *The War in the Air*, 129

West, Rebecca, 209

Westminster Abbey, 92

Whelen, Frederick, 174, 175

White, Peter, 261-2

Whitman, Walt, 'simple-life' doctrines of, 36-7; as source of British socialism, 39, 43, 280 n.58; Davidson circle and, 44; Webbs

and, 65, 293 n.64; various Fabians and, 78, 148, 268, 281 n.82; Fabian lectures on, 199

Wilde, Oscar, 205, 212; *Salomé*, 174; 'The Soul of Man Under Socialism', 7, 8

Wilson, Charlotte, 170

wireless, 137, 192; *see also* B.B.C.

Wood, Rev. Joseph, 302 n.4

Woolf, Leonard, 124, 131, 244, 277 n.46

Woolf, Virginia, 7, 124, 125, 129, 131, 226, 244

Wordsworth, William, Thomas Davidson and, 36; as a romanticist, 36, 84; as source of British socialism, 39, 40; Davidson circle and, 44, 48, 49, 50; various Fabians and, 87, 90, 254

work, and art, 5, 147, 165, 232, 247, 248, 250, 251, 252, 267, 272; Ruskin and Morris on pleasure and, 72, 263; S. Webb's ideals and practices of, 115, 116; *see also* labour

working class, in S.D.F. and Socialist League, 7; literary and artistic influences on, 39; Fabian concerns with social conditions, politics and culture of, 57-8, 86-8, 89, 92-3, 94, 96-7, 101, 106, 109-10, 116-17, 120, 121, 122, 123, 149, 223-52 *passim*, 256, 257, 267, 268; Morris's concerns with, 87-8, 89, 96, 219; Ruskin on cultural deprivation of, 99; *see also* labour movement, masses

working-class/proletarian culture, complexity of Fabian attitudes to, 226-7, 233, 234-5, 256; music halls as focus of Fabian concerns with, 228; tendency to use standards of high culture in judging, 229; Webbs' alleged distaste for, 229-30; as a concept, 231; Morris and, 232; as a basis for culture of higher classes, 234, 236; idealization of by Headlam, 239; J.M. Keynes' alleged antipathy to, 244; Co-operative wares as specimens of, 246; *see also* mass culture, popular arts/culture

Wright, Frank Lloyd, 250

Zola, Emile, 43, 60, 86, 177, 195, 197-8, 285 n.64, 288 n.63; *Dr Pascal*, 198; *Germinal*, 65, 198